Welcome Are Lands

a novel by

James Irwin Kruger

ISBN 0-7414-2469-X

Cover design, photograph and sketch by Glen Martin

Published by:

INFIИITY
PUBLISHING.COM

1094 New DeHaven Street, Suite 100
West Conshohocken, PA 19428-2713
Info@buybooksontheweb.com
www.buybooksontheweb.com
Toll-free (877) BUY BOOK
Local Phone (610) 941-9999
Fax (610) 941-9959

Printed in the United States of America

Printed on Recycled Paper

Published March 2005

Welcome are all the earth's lands, each for its kind.
Welcome are lands of pine and oak...
Lands of the make of the axe.

The axe leaps!
The shapes arise!
Shapes ever projecting other shapes.

- Poet Walt Whitman,
Song of the Broadaxe

Expansion westward with its new
opportunities, its continuous touch with
the simplicity of primitive society, furnish
the forces dominating American character.

Historian Frederick Jackson Turner

Other novels by James Irwin Kruger

Stranger in the Mirror

The Secret Files of Moshe Shomeir

Tiger Lily

Beach Street

The Bachelor Portraits

This book is dedicated to my mother, Virginia Irwin Kruger,
who inspired my interest in Minnesota history,
and instilled in me a deep appreciation
of our family's contribution to building that state.

Part I

The Frontier

1850 to 1860

Chapter 1

Hannah shook Stephen awake in the pre-dawn darkness, chucked his clothes onto the bed, and ordered him to get a move on.

"Don't make a sound," she cautioned him in a hoarse whisper. "No use waking the whole house."

She gave him his breakfast alone in the kitchen – a stack of flapjacks slathered with salted butter and dripping with maple syrup, a crisp piece of side meat, chewy in the middle, and a beaker of milk fresh from the cooler.

"In case you get hungry later," she said, stuffing a corn cake into the pocket of his coat that hung on the back of his chair. "Did you bring down your slop jar?"

He paused with his fork in midair. He would never get used to Hannah's direct manner of speaking.

"It's on the back stoop," he said. "I'll empty it in the privy before I go."

"You bet you will," she said gruffly. "And you'll rinse it, too – use the garden pump. Lord knows I have enough to do today, with your pa leaving and all."

He knew very well what day it was. There'd been talk of little else for weeks. That's why he was being hustled out from under foot, sent down into town with Williams to help with the shopping. He knew it was just an excuse. His mother thought there might be some last minute unpleasantness. This was her way of shielding him from the bitterness that had become oppressive since his father announced his determination to "go west."

Gimpy old Williams, who'd been with Grandfather Shevley forever, brought the wagon around back as soon as the sun was up. Hannah bustled out and handed the aging woodsman her shopping list as Stephen climbed aboard.

"Mind you, scatterbrain, keep your eye on the boy and be back here before the afternoon coach comes through or you'll have me to reckon with."

"Yes'm," said Williams wearily as he released the brake and prodded the mare. As the wagon rattled down the drive to the river road Stephen looked back and saw his grandfather framed in his bedroom window, hands folded behind him, an unlit cigar clenched in his teeth. Stephen waved.

"Who you wavin' at?" Williams asked.

"Grandpa."

"He'll be in no wavin' mood."

"He never is."

"Especially not today, with your pa goin' west."

"We'll be back in time, won't we?"

"If the horse don't spook, and the creek don't rise. But it'll be close. I'll split that last minute thin as a shingle, and I'll get you back in time to say good-bye to your pa, and that's all. No time for a lot o' talk, and you be glad of it. Too much talkin' going on 'round here as it is."

Stephen longed for the day his father would keep his promise to build them a home in the west, mostly because they'd never had a home of their own. He was born in Grandpa and Grandma Craft's house in Boston. He grew up there and thought of it as home, but he knew it really wasn't. His mother and father often talked about having a place of their own, but then they came to Maine to live with Grandpa Shevley. They'd been there now for two years, and Stephen hoped Shevley House would never become their home. It had been that way from the start. Ephraim Shevley had greeted the return of his youngest son with smug detach-ment. It was as if he'd won a long and bitter battle and now was lording it over the loser. It was not a warm and loving household as it had been with the Crafts. Maybe it was the size of the place, Stephen thought. It was huge, three stories of granite blocks, and as elegant as a castle. But it was a cold, forbidding place. The whole third floor had been closed off for more than thirty years, and even some of the rooms on the second floor were locked and never opened. Only the dining room was warm and inviting. Grandpa Shevley insisted that elegance be maintained there. That meant dressing for dinner, and that each night a place be set for his late wife. Stephen's father said it always had been that way, ever since he was a boy.

"Some of the house had to be closed off," Vincent explained when they first arrived. "My father wouldn't hire more help after my mother died, and there was only Hannah to run the house. And Hannah — well, Hannah is Hannah. She didn't exactly give the place a woman's touch. It'll be different now we're here. Your mother will see to it."

As it turned out, there was nothing Eleanor could do. Ephraim made it clear that there were limits beyond which she could not go, certain doors that were not to be opened, some passageways that a curious lad must not explore.

"Plenty of space for all of us," the old man grumped. "Tend to your own rooms, and do as you please there. Hannah will take care of the rest."

With the passage of time the boy realized that a deep animosity permeated Shevley House. With a child's sensitivity he felt that somehow it was their fault, and he knew that they should not have come.

The tension didn't seem to bother his uncles, Gideon and Thaddeus. They were cheery, good-natured men who occupied a large suite of rooms in the east wing. From the beginning they both had gone out of their way to try to make their younger brother and his family feel at home. But even they couldn't dispel the chill of Ephraim's black, icy moods. Stephen was perplexed by the old man's orneriness. If he didn't want Vincent to come home and bring his family, why did he insist on it?

"I'm not sure," Eleanor said thoughtfully when Stephen asked. "He's not entirely well, you know. I think he felt he was going to die, and wanted all three of his sons around him. It's not for us to pry. We must do everything we can not to aggravate your grandfather. He's been very generous in sharing his home with us."

"He makes Daddy angry," Stephen pointed out.

"I think that's because they're so much alike — opinionated, headstrong, obstinate. Your father has wanted to go west for years, Stephen. He only came back to Maine because his father said he needed him, that the lumber company needed his business talents. But now it seems that was not the case at all. There's nothing your father can do here that his brothers cannot do, and do well. His presence only seems to make Grandpa Shevley unhappy. That's why he's anxious to leave, to go west, and make a home for us."

"We could go back to Boston," Stephen suggested.

"You and I may do just that," she said, "but not right away. We'll wait until your father summons us. We'll go to Boston to say goodbye before we leave for the west."

"I guess I'd like to go west."

"In time," she said vacantly, fondly brushing his cheek with her fingertips. "All in good time."

Ephraim's three sons had been born in Shevley House. Thaddeus and Gideon were older, and as much alike as twins. From the beginning they were destined to be the heirs to their father's business. They were sent off to college together for a classical education when Vincent was only ten years old. It was said that Thaddeus and Gideon took after their mother in both looks and temperament, while Vincent was cut from his father's cloth. It was this family lore, as well as the difference in their ages, that set the youngest son apart over the years. Vincent had never known his mother. "She died," he said when Stephen asked. It was a simple statement of fact, related without context, without emotion. He rarely spoke of his childhood, but on one occasion he shed a little light on his early days.

"I made my own way," he said, "and more often than not it was the wrong way, as Hannah would be the first to tell you. She was tough, but she was fair," he allowed, "but after my brothers came home from college with their fancy education, I ran off every chance I got. I don't know how many times I headed down the river road, but they always caught up with me before I reached the bay. Then one spring morning Hannah let me go into town with Williams. It was just the break I needed. I slipped a note into the old man's pocket and sneaked away. Got myself a job on a fishing boat, and never looked back."

He was fourteen at the time and big for his age, and at fifteen, after making his way to Boston, he shipped out as a cabin boy aboard a whaler. By the time he was twenty he'd earned his papers and was a second mate aboard a merchant vessel. He traveled everywhere – New York and London, Savannah and New Orleans. He sailed around Cape Horn and throughout the Pacific. He visited Shanghai and crossed the Indian Ocean. He rounded the Dark Continent, and called at many of the ancient and exotic ports of the Mediterranean. He visited Calais and Bremen, and sailed across the wild North Sea. At twenty-six he was ashore in Boston when he read that the Craft Mercantile was outfitting its own small fleet, and he applied for command of one of its vessels. He was on the verge of being hired when he was invited to John Craft's home for dinner, and there met Craft's wife and their beautiful daughter, Eleanor. His dream of being master of his own ship went out with the next tide. He was offered instead a position as Craft's executive assistant at the mercantile. It was an easy decision for him, with Eleanor tipping the scales in favor life ashore.

Over the years, however, Vincent grew restless. It may have begun when Stephen was born; some primal stirring that drives a man to make a proper home for his family. Or maybe it was simply wanderlust, an insatiable curiosity to know what lies around the bend of the river, or the turn in the road, or beyond the far horizon. At one point it was decided that Vincent would leave Eleanor and Stephen in the care of her parents while he headed west to make his fortune. But before he could get away a letter arrived from Maine. His father wrote that he was in failing health, and wanted only to see his three sons together again. He asked if Vincent would consider coming home and applying the skills he'd learned in managing the mercantile to the operation of the Shevley family's lumber business. Would he, old Ephraim asked, give a dying old man the satisfaction of knowing his sons were reunited at last, that he might face the end of his life at peace with the world?

"It's not so much to ask," Eleanor said. "If he is as frail as he claims, this may be but a brief investment of our time in order to bring immense satisfaction to a dying man. You would expect no less from your own son."

"It's too late for me to play the dutiful son," Vincent argued. "I know very well that my brothers are doing an excellent job running Shevley Lumber. They don't need me. It's a ruse. My father simply can't bear to have me running free, living my own life. If he's ill, it's because I got out from under his thumb, and he wants me back. I know him. He is a domineering old tyrant who feels I've made a fool of him, and he won't rest until he breaks my spirit. I refuse to let him."

"What harm could a year do?" she asked. "Would you allow injuries done to you as a boy keep you from your responsibilities as a man? Why doesn't the prodigal return, if only to see how the years might have changed a strained relationship? I'll support you, my dear one, and your son will learn patience and obedience from your example. He will come to know his grandfather and his uncles. It will help him understand his own place in the family whose name he bears. He'll be proud of you, and you of him."

So despite deep misgivings, Vincent deferred his plan to head west and brought his family to Maine, determined to make a final effort to placate the old man, to see if there was a place and a purpose for him in his father's domain. But his best intentions were doomed to failure. Ephraim's health quickly improved once Vincent arrived. The old man managed to shake off the depression that debilitated him, seemed to thrive on the perverse pleasure he found in punishing his wayward son with emotional abuse.

"The very sight of me irritates him," Vincent complained when he could no longer tolerate the situation. "He is whole again, no thanks to me, and so I'm going to go west. I did what I could. I put aside my own dreams of happiness for us all. I worked hard, and did my best. But I failed. There is no satisfying him, and so it's time to move on. It will be just as we originally planned. I will go on ahead and establish myself, and then I'll send for you. It will be only a matter of months. I'll build a home for us, if I have to do so with my own hands, and we'll all be together again."

For weeks after Vincent's announcement there had been talk – quarrelsome talk, hurtful talk. His brothers spoke of the dangers that lay ahead, summoning visions of a perilous wilderness, blood-thirsty savages and raging rivers, images aimed at convincing him that it would be foolhardy to travel alone into such an environment, let alone to bring one's wife and child there. Ephraim, on the other hand, used words as if they were little knives, sharp words calculated to inflict small but painful wounds. Vincent responded with restraint at first, then with exasperation, and finally with anger.

"I'm not a fool," he roared. "I'm not going in search of El Dorado on the far side of the continent. I'm not lured by California gold. I don't believe in easy money or dreams of impossible riches. But I know there are vast forests in the west, and it is there that I'm going to seek my fortune. I know the value of hard work. I am prepared to pay any price to succeed. If it is too much to ask that you look after my wife and son for a few months, then I shall take them back to Boston. They will be welcomed there, loved and appreciated until I can send for them."

And so the conflict raged through the days of packing and planning, arguing and quarreling among the men, while mother and son cowered on the sidelines, tears of helplessness often welling in Eleanor's eyes. It was a period of turmoil that was to reach its climax on the morning of Vincent's departure, when 10-year-old boys were best absent until it was time to say goodbye.

The noon coach was approaching from the north when Williams prodded the mare to a trot in order to reach the drive only moments before it arrived. Stephen caught sight of his mother and father walking slowly across the front lawn toward them. Thaddeus and Gideon were standing on the porch, hands clasped behind their backs, each rocking to and fro as if impatient for the coach to arrive. In the library window Ephraim Shevley could be seen through the glass, his scowling countenance partially obscured by a cloud of cigar smoke. Williams halted the wagon for a moment while Stephen leaped down, then snapped the reins and guided the rig to the back of the house where Hannah waited to check his load against her shopping list. Stephen ran to his father and clung to him.

"Whoa, lad! I'll drop my bag!" Vincent cried with a laugh.

"Let me take it," Stephen said, grasping the handles.

"Be careful, it's heavy," said Eleanor.

The boy half dragged the bag to the road just as the coach groaned to a halt amid billowing dust. The driver climbed down, grabbed the bag and stowed it behind, lashing it securely with heavy leather straps.

"Say goodbye to your father, Stephen," Eleanor said. The boy blushed, hunched his shoulders and shoved his hands deep into his pockets, scuffing the dirt with his foot.

"I'm going to miss you, son," said Vincent, grasping the lad's shoulder with his left hand and extending the right. Stephen laid his hand weakly in his father's and allowed it to be shaken firmly. "You'll be your mother's man for a time. See that you take good care of her."

"Yes, sir."

"It won't be long."

"No, sir."

The horses pranced and the coachman glanced impatiently at Vincent, saying, "I've got a schedule, you know."

"You'd better run up to the house now and give Williams a hand unloading the wagon," Vincent said, leaning down and grasping the boy in a bear hug. Then Stephen pulled away and ran across the yard.

"Good-bye, son!" Vincent called. "Good-bye!"

But the boy kept running until he reached the corner of the house where he paused and looked back to see his mother and father in a close embrace. Then he took off running again, not stopping at the back door, but racing past the pump and the vegetable garden and beyond the cabin where Williams lived, and down past the barn and through the bramble patch to the oak grove, and over the wall at the riverbank where he fell panting in the long grass under the willows and began to cry. It was more than an hour later when Williams came looking for him. The old man laid a gnarly hand on his head and patted it.

"Hannah wants you to dump the potatoes in the bin," he said at last. "You'd better splash some water on your face and run along home. No use getting her riled."

The old fellow lingered a moment, but when Stephen didn't respond, he went quietly away, leaving the boy to his grief. It was growing dark before Stephen finally collected himself and wandered back to the house.

"Good lord!" Hannah exclaimed. "Look at the clock, and look at you. And you're to sit at the dinner table tonight. Take that kettle off the stove and follow me."

He trailed her through the dark and silent house to his room where she stripped him to the waist and gave him a good scrubbing. As she laid out a clean shirt she ordered him to listen for the clock.

"I've got to get back to the kitchen, so when you hear it strike seven, you get your ma and bring her downstairs. Do you understand?"

"Yes'm."

He appeared as ordered, rapped lightly at his mother's door, and led her down to the dining room as his father had done. He noticed her eyes were red.

"Did you have a busy afternoon?" she asked.

"Yes'm."

"Yes, m'am," she corrected him.

"Yes, m'am."

The Shevley men were standing behind their chairs awaiting them. The long mahogany table was laid with china and silver and crystal, all aglitter in the light of a dozen candles. Ephraim stood at the head with his sons to his left. At the far end of the table the usual place was laid for a grandmother Stephen had never known. He led his mother to her chair at his grandfather's right, seated her, and stood nervously waiting for a signal. Then with a nod from the master of the house the men took their seats while Ephraim rang a small silver bell to signal Hannah that they were ready to be served. It was an hour marked by awkward attempts at small talk, as if everyone knew that a wrong word might stir passions best left undisturbed. At last the two brothers found an innocuous subject, the soaring price of lumber, and tried their best to include Eleanor and their father in the conversation. Eleanor appreciated their efforts and tried to join in, but Ephraim's stubborn silence subdued them all. He did not speak until after dessert, when he stood and raised his glass.

"We must put an end to this talk of business matters and try to forget the provocations of the past. We should remember that there is a gentlewoman among us. We must turn our thoughts to her future and that of her son. I propose a toast to you, my dear Eleanor, and to the one commendable thing my youngest son has done since the day he tore himself from his mother's womb and left her to die in her childbed. He married a lady."

"To Eleanor," his sons chorused. Eleanor's cheeks reddened with anger and she lowered her eyes as the men drained their glasses of claret.

"For that good marriage," Ephraim went on, "he owes thanks to Almighty God, for it was an impulsive act performed with neither my counsel nor my blessing – nor even my prior knowledge. But the good Lord watches over fools, and it is He we have to thank for your gracious presence, madam. You will always be welcome in this house, whether the prodigal returns or not. Since Stephen also has been commended to our care, it seems appropriate that I offer some comment on his upbringing, which shall remain in your capable hands. We are pleased with the results you have achieved thus far, results that you have accomplished in the face of great odds, and we look forward to his further development as a gentleman, as a Shevley. I give you his esteemed uncles as examples of the gentility and refinement that their dear departed mother represented so completely, and that she, during her short lifetime, was able to instill in them. We all regret that your son's father failed to receive the benefits of his mother's influence, but we are assured of the benevolence of God in his choice of you as the boy's mother. As for you, Stephen, I charge you to bear your name proudly, for yours is an honored heritage, and with respect to your father, perhaps an awful stigma. If you can learn to live up to the former, you should have no trouble living down the latter. We pledge to you both our loyalty and our devotion."

So saying, Ephraim Shevley excused himself and marched from the dining room to enjoy a snifter of brandy and a cigar alone in his study. Eleanor, who had sat with her head bowed during the old man's oration, raised her eyes and fixed them on the flickering candle directly in front of her. She stared at it motionless for a moment, then sagged as if suddenly drained.

"Eleanor," Gideon said apologetically. He pushed his wine glass aside and leaned across the table toward her. "Eleanor, you must not let father upset you. He has had some trying times lately, as I'm sure you are well aware. He loves you and Stephen dearly, we know that to be a fact, and he meant it when he said you are welcome here. He spoke for all of us."

"If there had been any other way..." she began.

"There, now," said Thaddeus sympathetically, "you mustn't think in terms of what might have been. Vincent will be back sooner than you think. Have no fear, he will not carry you and the boy off to the wilderness, of that I am sure. He'll realize soon enough that it is no place for him, and certainly no life for a woman and a child. But he's stubborn, as you well know. It was that stubbornness more than anything else that so irritated his father. Vincent was always the rebel, ever since he was a little boy. It was his nature to reject sound advice in favor of finding things out for himself. You'll see; he'll be back."

"Don't misinterpret us, dear sister," Gideon interjected. "We have the greatest respect for Vincent's initiative, his pluck and daring. Perhaps if Thaddeus and I were ten years younger..." He let the thought evaporate, as if in the sudden realization that it was absurd.

"Indeed we do respect him," Thaddeus said, picking up Gideon's train of thought. "But trust us, Vincent will be back. Maine is his home, and lumber is in his blood. A third of the company will be his one day, his right and his heritage."

"You are both very kind," Eleanor said, "but you do not know Vincent as I do. He will not be back. These past two years were his final effort, his last attempt to live the kind of life your father feels he ought to live. He failed, and it was not because he didn't try. He tried so very hard. He proved to himself that the life in which you have succeeded so admirably is not the life for him."

She then took Stephen's hand and spoke directly to him.

"Your father must make his own way in this world. He has always been that way, ever since he ran away from home when he was not much older than you are now, Stephen. However indefensible that act might have been, in retrospect it serves to show just what kind of man he is today, a man determined to pursue his dreams. He may be headstrong, but he is a good man and an able one. We must maintain our faith in him."

"My dear Eleanor," Gideon said, "Vincent has had many dreams. But despite all of them, he came back to Shevley House. Somewhere deep inside he must have realized that this is where he belongs."

"He came back out of a sense of duty – duty to his father and to you, his brothers," Eleanor responded. "But there was no real place for him here, no challenge. He felt stifled and useless. I was surprised he stayed as long as he did. But he is gone now in pursuit of his dreams, and he will not come back. When he has prepared a way for us, we will follow him, and I pray to God it will be soon, for we are a burden on you, and more especially on your father. If his health should fail again, we would never forgive ourselves."

"Don't concern yourself with his health," Thaddeus said. "Despite the rancor of the past few weeks, he is as vigorous as ever, as you can see for yourself. Vincent was his burden, but also his blessing. That has been true since Vincent's birth. Oftentimes our father can only remember the hurt of losing his beloved wife. In his anger he inevitably holds Vincent responsible for that tragedy. But he loves his youngest son dearly. Forgive him his blindness in moments of passion; forgive him his selfishness in trying to hold on to his favorite child – yes, his favorite, though he'd never admit it. It is not easy to watch the child of his middle age turn his back and leave. When you pray, pray for the ease of the old man's soul. Pray for Vincent's early return to his rightful place in this family."

"You are both so kind," Eleanor sighed, "and yet so blind to your brother's real self. Vincent is so much like his father, and at the same time so much like you both – a tough exterior protecting a gentle heart. Some of his mother's character does live on in him, believe me, and much, too, of his father's. I believe that's why Grandfather Shevley hated to see him go. It was like losing a part of himself, and also a part of his late, beloved wife. But Vincent has done what he must do. He won't be back."

"The lady will not be convinced, Gideon."

"Alas, it seems she will not."

"Then, madam," said Thaddeus, "we can only pledge to you our loyalty and our devotion, as our father has done already on our behalf."

"It's all the more precious and meaningful, coming from you. Thank you both. I promise that we will try to be worthy of your kindness. And now, Stephen, we should say goodnight and go to our rooms. It has been a trying day."

*　　*　　*

Months passed without word from Vincent. The summer drew to an end. The leaves turned and fell, and the long, dark days of winter descended, bringing on the dull routine of lessons and endless hours of reading that only served to whet Stephen's appetite for excitement and stir his youthful energies with the urge to be free. He longed to race through the snow-laden woods, to skate on the frozen river or romp with the village boys who ventured near on Saturdays – until Hannah caught sight of them, and shooed them away. His uncles were solicitous, but chess was their idea of a fine way to pass a winter's afternoon, and after presenting him with a new pair of skates for Christmas, they were unwilling to join him on the ice.

Grandfather Shevley, apparently unable to maintain a state of high dudgeon, lapsed into a sullen silence that seemed to dare the world to intrude, and no one in Shevley House ever tried. His self-enforced solitude had little impact on his sons, who remained their jovial selves at dinner while the old man sat mute at the head of the table, storms of emotion clouding his face, split by lightning bolts of angry frustration and thundering grunts of disapproval. His presence at table made Stephen so uncomfortable that he was relieved when shortly before Christmas the old man came down with the grippe and took to his bed for several weeks, allowing only Hannah to attend to his needs. His grandfather's absence made the lad's holidays quite a pleasant experience.

Eleanor, although at times doting and affectionate toward Stephen, was all too often lost in thought, and he knew without a doubt that she dwelled upon the fate of her beloved husband in the distant unknown they called "the west." It was most difficult at bedtime when she would hold him closely and mumble vacantly about the future when they all would be together again. If such moments were meant to reassure him, they did not. Each day his father receded farther into the background until he ceased to be a player in the lad's life, but only an apparition, the ghost of hope itself, hope of a reunion that seemed evermore unlikely and unreal.

During that first winter without his father Stephen began tagging after Williams, grateful for the attention the grizzled woodsman showered upon him, eager to do whatever the old man asked. As a result the barn was never so clean, nor the driveway so free of ice and snow. And in the spring he willingly took on the responsibility of cultivating the vegetable garden and keeping it free of weeds.

"You're just like your pa," Williams told him fondly, "and like old man Shevley used to be before Father Time caught up with him. You're not afraid of hard work. It perks you up like a tonic; it wipes your cares away. Your uncles ought to send you into the woods for a season, then you'd see. It'd be good for you, make a man of you, as it never did them. You don't want to grow up like they did, inhaling cigar smoke and reading ledgers and chatting with women-folk like a couple of dandies. You're made for the rough and tumble. You'll want a man's life, just like your pa. You never heard tell of him shying from a day's labor."

The fact was that no one had heard tell anything of Vincent for over a year, until the mare trotted up the driveway late on a warm summer's morning with the week's groceries and a small bundle of mail – and Williams slouched in the driver's seat. Hannah nearly pulled him off the wagon, scolding him for being drunk, before realizing she was nagging a corpse. Then she fainted dead away. In all the excitement, the mail was overlooked for a time while Thaddeus and Gideon debated what to do with Williams. After some confusion they decided to carry the body to the icehouse to keep it fresh, but that brought Hannah around sufficiently to protest. "Not in MY cooler," she fumed. So instead they stretched the old man out in the bed of the wagon and drove it around to his cabin behind the barn, laid him out on the table and opened the windows to catch what little breeze might chance by. Meanwhile Stephen was sent to hail the noon coach and hand the driver a note, asking him to send out the undertaker and gravediggers as soon as he got to town. By that time Eleanor had found Vincent's letter, broken the wax seal, and read it over twice. It was addressed to her at Shevley House, River Road, Penobscot County, Maine. It was dated March 23, 1852, and opened with an apology for the scrawling script. He explained he was composing the letter as he rode a cook raft down a river called the St. Croix, following a flotilla of logs toward the river's junction with the Mississippi. He described his journey from Maine, told how he'd ridden a barge on the Erie Canal from Albany to Buffalo, and caught a sailing vessel across Lake Erie to Ft. Detroit. He'd followed a wagon road westward through some excellent stands of timber to the port of Grand Haven, and thence by a military barge across Lake Michigan to Green Bay. There he made inquiries and eventually invested his stake in a lumbering venture. He'd spent the winter in the woods of northern Wisconsin as superintendent of a timber-cutting operation. He expected to triple his money once the raft reached the town of Stillwater, where agents from Rock Island, Illinois, were paying top dollar for logs to feed an insatiable demand for building materials occasioned by the westward expansion. After cashing out he planned to follow the Mississippi River upstream to a village called St. Anthony. There were falls at St. Anthony, he explained, and his plan was to establish a mill. While it was being built, he would spend the summer cruising an area to the north of the village where the virgin forest was said to be so rich and thick that "a man has to walk sideways through it." He would go to see for himself, the letter said, and if the reports were true he was going to put down roots, build a home for his family and send for them, perhaps within a year. In the meantime, letters could be directed to him at St. Anthony, Territory of Minnesota, and would they please tell his brothers to expect a letter soon concerning certain business matters of great importance.

"Yes, I expected as much," Thaddeus said ruefully on hearing that bit of news.

"Of course," Gideon concluded. "It takes money to build a dream."

Eleanor could only pray that the dream would soon become a reality. To keep her mind occupied she immersed herself in Stephen's schooling. Ephraim Shevley gave her free rein in his magnificent library, and permission to conduct music lessons in the parlor where a grand piano had silently gathered dust since the death of his wife. Eleanor wrote to Bangor for appropriate texts in mathematics and music, and established a rigid schedule of lessons, more in winter than in summer, when Stephen was allowed ample time to work and play outdoors. Since his father's departure and Williams' death, he had felt quite alone in Shevley House, and found that the schooling administered by a doting mother helped to the pass his lonely days. During his off hours Hannah usually scheduled chores for him, although the gardening and barn had become the exclusive province of an Irish couple, the O'Hearns, hired by the Shevley brothers to take over Williams's duties and give Hannah whatever help she might need. The O'Hearns lived in the small cabin that once was home to the aged woodsman, and the structure and its immediate surroundings were now to be avoided out of respect for the privacy of its new occupants. On pleasant afternoons Stephen would wander down by the river to lie in the warm sun, and watch the water flow by toward the bay, wondering what he would see if he launched a raft and set off himself for wherever the current might carry him. In winter he spent his spare time in his room, nestled in an overstuffed chair where he would read for hours in one of the books his grandfather allowed him to take from his library. Oftentimes he found his mind wandering and he would gaze off beyond the yard and the barn and the O'Hearns' cabin to the knoll above the river where a wrought iron fence marked the family burial plot, and outside the fence a snow-covered mound that marked Williams's resting-place. At times like these Stephen could almost hear the old woodsman chiding him, "Look how the crisp, fresh air is wasted when all it can do is rattle your window and you don't even answer its call. Come outside and bend your back to some honest work, a man's work. The breeze is sweet with the smell of new-cut pine. Fill your lungs with it, lad. It'll make a man of you, like your pa, and his pa before him."

But it was warm by the fire, and there were books to read and dreams to dream. He had no desire to be like his father, whose face he could barely remember, or like his grandfather, who lay coughing and wheezing away his mean and miserable life in the downstairs bedroom. Stephen wanted to be his own man, and he needed time to think about a serious matter like maturity. His father's occasional letters never failed to mention how eager he was to have his wife and son join him in the west. But Minnesota Territory sounded wild and frightening to Stephen, with its sweltering summers and bitterly cold winters, thick woods and savage Indians, and not even the rudiments of civilization, nor yet a roof to shelter them. And so the waiting went on. His mother found some solace in the locket she wore on a delicate silver chain about her neck, a locket that held their only picture of her long-absent husband. The image seemed to give her great pleasure, cheering her lonely days. But Stephen knew she had her fears, too. At night he could hear her muffled weeping in the next room, her secret sadness a counterpoint to the howling winds that rustled the branches of the trees and swept through the empty hallways of Shevley House, rattling each locked door as it passed. Sometimes his mother would weep for hours before she finally cried herself to sleep. Only then could he relax into the downy softness of his pillow, exhausted by suspenseful listening, his heart pounding furiously in the darkness. He took comfort in the secret knowledge that she was afraid, too. It made him less ashamed of his own fears, helped him to bear those moments when she would draw him close to her, run her fingers through his hair, and look beyond him with eyes that were full and wide with wonder. He could feel her heart pounding with passions that seemed to well up from deep within her, passions that expressed themselves in whispered ramblings that fell hypnotically upon him and whirled in confusion in his head.

"Yes, Stephen, he has sent for us at last. We're to sail to Boston for the holidays to make our farewells, then take the cars west to join him. What a hard life he has led. Such a brave and courageous man, so tall and noble. You're nearly as tall yourself after all these years. Surely you'll be as tall, as grand, and good. He'll be so proud of you; you've grown so. We'll make a new home, our own home, when we're all together again. It will be soon."

But there was no joy in her words, no excitement. Her tear-clouded eyes looked out upon visions he could not share, visions colored by longings and wishes, hopes and fears. It seemed to him that a terrible dread overwhelmed her, that whatever illusions had sustained her during the lonely years had deserted her now in the moment of her greatest need. He felt totally inadequate. There was nothing he could do to help her. Together they moved like actors through the final scenes of a tragedy, bidding good-bye to Shevley House on a dry, bitterly cold November day, enduring a rough passage to Massachusetts aboard a storm-tossed vessel, and landing in Boston to the warm but worried embrace of the Crafts. His grandparents' words were stolidly encouraging about the impending journey, but their eyes told another story, and their reassurances did little to restrain his mother's secret demons. He could still hear her weeping at night alone in her room, and though she put on a brave face in front of her parents, she was noticeably less courageous when they were alone together. No longer the child he was four years ago, he became impatient with her trepidation, tired of trying in vain to set her mind at ease.

On their long journey he had a lot of time to think about the future. Would his father remember him? After all, it had been four long years. Would he even recognize him? He knew he had changed; everyone said he had grown taller, looked more grown up. Would he still love him as he did when he was a little boy? In the dawning wisdom of youth he suddenly realized that his mother must be thinking similar thoughts: Had she changed, had her husband changed?

Would they go on as before, or would their lives be different now?

That spark of insight came to him most clearly as they endured the jarring discomfort of a railway car rumbling and rattling over the prairie somewhere between Chicago and the Mississippi River. She had been staring out the window at the dwindling drifts of dirty snow when suddenly she grasped his hand and her eyes widened as if she had seen something off in the distance. He could feel a violent shudder pass through her, culminating in a desperate, whispered cry.

"Vincent!"

Chapter 2

The iron rails had only recently reached the Mississippi at Rock Island, and the depot still exuded the sweet aroma of fresh-cut pine. While Eleanor lingered to claim their baggage, Stephen raced through the building to an elevated deck that overlooked the street. The river town was a wildly thriving place, compared to the unhurried villages of the Penobscot Valley. Horse-drawn rigs of every description splashed through the soggy street, while crowds of people elbowed their way along the wooden sidewalks, dodging plumes of mud sent their way by passing vehicles. In open doorways knots of villagers gathered in animated discussion, and the cries of teamsters and the slap of reins joined in the cacophony. There was an air of excitement to it all, such as Stephen had never experienced before. The burly stationmaster dragged a trunk and plunked it at his feet.

"Lady said to keep on eye on this," he announced. "Couple of bags to come."

As the man turned to re-enter the depot a buckboard pulled up where Stephen stood. Its driver tied off the reins and stepped onto the deck.

"Let me know if you need a hand with that trunk," he said with a smile. "I'll just be a minute." He strode across the platform toward the depot entrance, stepping quickly aside as Eleanor suddenly emerged followed by the stationmaster with their smaller bags. In a sweeping gesture the man removed his hat and bowed as she passed.

"Has this rig been taken?" she asked Stephen.

"I don't know, but that man said he'd help us."

"What man?"

"The one you nearly ran into at the door."

"He was rude," Eleanor said.

"What did he do?"

"He spoke to me, and we've never met!"

"What did he say?"

"He asked me to excuse him and made a broad gesture."

"I saw him bow and hold the door for you."

"Never mind. The stationmaster will order a carriage for us."

"But that man..."

"Please, Stephen. We mustn't talk to strangers."

The man reappeared and flung his bags onto the rig.

"Do you want me to help you with that trunk?" he asked Stephen.

"We don't talk to strangers," said the lad.

"That's too bad. This town seems to be full of strangers," he said, looking up and down the street. "Why not let me..."

"I beg your pardon, are you addressing us?" Eleanor asked haughtily. She took Stephen's hand and walked briskly to the end of the platform, looking confidently down the street.

"If you need a lift," the man called after them, "I'm afraid I've got the last rig available at the livery. It's not much, but I'd be happy to share it. After all, this isn't Boston."

"How did you know..." Eleanor sputtered.

"Come along, son," the man said with a smile. "Give me a hand and I'll get you and your mother to the hotel. Unless you're expecting someone," he said to Eleanor.

"Well, I'll be!" Eleanor exclaimed, allowing herself to be helped aboard the vehicle. In a moment the buckboard was splashing through the street.

"Watch your skirts," the man cautioned. "There's been a sudden thaw and no time to dry out."

"Really!" Eleanor gasped in indignation.

"Oh, I'm sorry," the man apologized. "I forgot my manners. My name is Jonathan Wells."

"We're the Shevleys," said the boy leaning forward from his perch atop the trunk. "My name's Stephen."

"How do you do, Stephen. It's a pleasure to meet you both. I didn't mean to be impertinent, Mrs. Shevley, but most folks need a helping hand when they're new in town. You heading down river to St. Louis?"

"We're going upriver," Stephen said.

"Well, now, there's a coincidence," said Wells, pulling the buckboard up in front of the hotel. "And here we are, Rock Island's finest. The proprietor here is also the ticket agent for the riverboats, which you may find helpful."

Eleanor looked forlornly at the hotel, and her chin stiffened, a look of determination came into her eyes.

"We're grateful for your assistance, Mr. Wells. I'm sure we can manage by ourselves now. Stephen, help the gentleman with the trunk and I'll take the bags."

At that moment she looked as Stephen was often to remember her – fragile, lovely, resigned to her fate – a delicate flower uprooted from her native habitat and set down in an alien soil, confronting her fears of the unknown with touching courage. He understood those fears, even shared them, and he envied her bravery. Wells introduced them to the proprietor and politely excused himself – somewhat reluctantly, Stephen thought – with a wish that they fare well on their journey.

They were relieved to learn that arrangements had been made for their stay and for their passage aboard a riverboat, and soon were left alone in a tiny room with a washstand and mirror, a chair, one bed, a cot and a hurricane lamp. Eleanor shivered in the cold draft that came through a broken windowpane. She lifted their traveling bag onto the bed, opened it, and removed a blue dress, holding it up with a shake of her head, deploring its wrinkles.

"Do we have to dress for dinner?" Stephen asked wearily.

"It would be proper," she said absently.

"I'm tired," he said, slumping onto the cot. "Why not have something sent up?"

"What an excellent idea!" she exclaimed with a laugh, sitting down beside him and taking his hand. "It's gratifying to find that your father has taken such good care of us. It makes me feel much closer to him. And it means it won't be long before we're all together again. You've been such a great help, Stephen – so patient for one so young. But we're near the end of our journey now, and it's time we relaxed a bit. I'll ask to have a light supper brought up and then we can get a good night's sleep. We'll both feel better in the morning."

There came a knock at the door and before either of them could respond it swung open and a large, scraggly-haired woman burst through in a cloud of steam. Without a word she went to the commode and filled the bowl with hot water from her bucket.

"For washin'," she said as she left the room. "You'll need it after riding on that filthy train."

"But dinner..." Eleanor began.

"Dinner's on the table in thirty minutes, so you'd better hustle." With that she was out the door and down the hall. Eleanor ran after her.

"Wait, please! Couldn't we have something sent up?"

"Is there someone sick?" the woman asked.

"Not sick," Eleanor said, drooping helplessly, "just terribly, terribly tired."

The woman brushed a wild strand of hair from her brow, looking Eleanor up and down with a skeptical eye.

"I guess I could bring up a tray, but it ain't part of the regular service."

"We'd pay," Eleanor was quick to assure her, "and we'd be ever so grateful."

But before she could finish the woman had vanished down the stairs.

*   *   *

The river town began to stir at first light. The shrill cry of a teamster split the thin shroud of sleep and Stephen lazily uncoiled from his blankets and knuckled the remnants of a dream from his eyes. Hearing the rattling of wagons as they blundered through the stillness of the street below, he arose, pulled on his shoes and went to look out the window.

Night shadows were receding rapidly and wisps of fog swirled in the distance.

"Are you up, Stephen?" his mother asked sleepily.

"Yes," he yawned, pulling his nightshirt closer about him to ward off the chill. The jumble of quilts on the bed stirred and a tousled head appeared.

"Why are you standing by the window?" she asked. "It must be freezing there."

"I'm looking at the river."

"Can you really see it from there?" she asked, slipping into a robe and coming to his side.

"See," he said, pointing. "See the steam rising? That must be the river."

Before she could reply, there came a knock at the door and the woman with the scraggly hair stormed in and filled the washbowl from her bucket. "Better get a move on," she advised. "We quit servin' at nine. Hand me that tray, boy." And as quickly as she had come, she was gone.

"She reminds me of Hannah," Stephen observed.

Eleanor smiled at his innocence and drew him close to her.

"She makes Hannah look like a princess," she said. "They're a very strange sort, these frontier people. I don't mean to be rude or condescending, but they are indeed very strange."

He could feel her shudder.

"Are you cold, mother?"

"No, Stephen. I'm not cold. I was just thinking about your father. Poor Vincent – four years among such people. And this village is quite civilized compared to Vincent's descriptions of St. Anthony. I don't know how he's managed."

Stephen pulled away from her and stretched out a magnificent yawn, unwilling at that early hour to trouble himself about such matters. But later as he dressed he tried to imagine how his father might look after all these years. He could remember the day his father left, could hear again the man's voice calling across the years, "Goodbye, Stephen.

Goodbye!" He finished dressing and sat thoughtfully watching his mother brush her long tresses in front of the mirror. On the bed the contents of her purse lay scattered where they fell during her search for her brush. From among the items he picked out a small oval locket and opened it. Inside was a tiny tintype of his father. The face was stern, handsome, a moustache above the thin line of his lips, his jaw rigid under a neatly trimmed beard. Stephen stared at the eyes, shaded by heavy brows, searching for what might lie behind them. Then he held the locket up to the light, turning it slightly. In a flickering the image vanished.

"Are you ready Stephen?" she asked, collecting the items on the bed and replacing them in her purse.

"Yes'm," he said, handing her the locket.

"Yes, m'am," she corrected him, taking the locket and fastening its chain about her neck. "Do you miss your father?"

"I guess so," the lad replied, opening the door for her. "I remember the day he left," he added with some uncertainty.

She paused and looked at him with a melancholy expression.

"Yes," she said, giving his hand a squeeze. "So do I."

"Good morning," said a cheery voice at the bottom of the stairs.

"Good morning, Mr. Wells," said Stephen.

"I trust you're both rested after your journey."

"We are," Eleanor said pleasantly. "But I'm afraid our journey is far from over."

"Yes!" Wells exclaimed quickly as if to take advantage of a fallen barrier. "I recall you said you were heading upriver, and so am I, and very soon, it seems."

"What do you mean?" she asked.

"The first boat of the season, the Galena, arrived here several days ago and sent a scouting party upriver to see if the ice was breaking up. I've heard that a report came back last night. With any luck we may be on our way before nightfall. I hope you've made arrangements."

"My husband has seen to it," Eleanor said. "The proprietor here found our names on the passenger list. Everything is in order."

"Then we're to be traveling companions, unless your husband is meeting you here."

"He's to meet us at the dock in St. Paul."

"Then if there's anything I can do to be of assistance, just let me know. But first, breakfast. Will you join me? It will give us an opportunity to get better acquainted."

At the table he explained that it had been a bitterly cold winter and that navigation on the Mississippi was still blocked by ice when he arrived more than a week ago. But the spring thaw had begun, and soon the northbound channels would open sufficiently to allow the big passenger boats to pass.

"It still feels like winter, despite the thaw," Eleanor noted, eliciting a broad smile from Wells.

"It's Boston, I'm sure of it," he said. "It's a Boston accent."

"We haven't lived in Boston for years," Eleanor said with a laugh. "We've only just come from Maine."

"No, I'm sure of it. Wintah, thaw'r – only a Bostonian would pronounce those words in that manner."

"I must admit you're right," she said brightly. "I was just having a bit of fun at your expense. We're natives of Boston, Stephen and I, but for the past four years we've lived in Maine with my husband's family."

"I was nearly certain," Wells said, "except for Stephen. His accent wasn't quite Boston."

"How do you talk like Boston?" Stephen asked.

"There are certain patterns of speech peculiar to many sections of the country," Wells explained.

"I've heard of a southern accent," the lad said.

"Exactly. Most settled areas will develop a distinctive way of speaking, influenced by many factors, most predominantly the national origin of the majority of settlers. They might not notice it themselves, but an outsider can readily tell by listening to speech patterns and the pronunciation of certain words."

"Why don't I have a Boston accent?" Stephen asked.

"Most accents result from imitation. We listen to the speech around us, and we imitate the sounds. We do it as children, and we do it as adults. Children are the best imitators, the quickest learners. You were uprooted from Boston at an early age and spent time in Maine – apparently long enough to begin adapting to the new sounds around you. It must have taken the Boston edge off your accent – at least that's my theory."

"If your theory is valid, Mr. Wells, why is it that you seem to have no accent?" Eleanor asked.

"The truth is that my accent was once quite distinctive. I was born and reared in Virginia, in the mountain country to the west. If you're familiar with that area, you'll understand what I mean. But for many years now I've traveled widely and visited many places. Apparently when one is exposed to many accents, the process breaks down and the wanderer is left with the colorless speech you hear from me."

"I think you are quite well-spoken, Mr. Wells. How is it that you have traveled so extensively? Is it your business to travel?"

"No, I'm not a businessman, only a humble soldier, transferred here and there at the whim of my superiors. I am between posts at the moment, and therefore not in uniform."

"A soldier? Really?" Stephen asked excitedly.

"Are we at war, Mr. Wells?" Eleanor asked. "We haven't had a scrap of news for days."

"No, no, nothing of the sort. It amuses me that people are so quick to glamorize what is essentially a very mundane profession – most of the time. The fact is that I'm simply being transferred from one post to another. I've been assigned to Fort Snelling in Minnesota Territory. There I expect the usual monotony, barring an Indian uprising."

"Indian uprising!" cried Stephen. "In Minnesota? That's where we're going. My father didn't tell us about an Indian uprising."

"Easy, lad. I didn't say that either. I merely said..."

"And to think that I had almost accustomed myself to the idea of living on the frontier!" Eleanor exclaimed.

"Wait! Wait! If I've frightened you unnecessarily, I'm sorry. It was just idle chatter. Please, don't be alarmed. There's no Indian uprising in the territory. From what I've been told, the worst you can expect is freezing winters and blisteringly hot summers. But there I go again. I know nothing firsthand about the territory. I expect you both will be quite happy there."

"Let's go down to the landing," Stephen urged when they had finished breakfast. "I want to see the Galena."

"You're a lad after my own heart," said Wells, grasping Stephen's shoulder and shaking him manfully. "There's something about rivers and roads and rails – everything that leads a man on. I don't know if it's a blessing or a curse," he said wistfully. "Pardon my musing, Mrs. Shevley, but I detect in Stephen a touch of the wanderlust that infects many men in the spring. But have no fear, it's typically only a seasonal ailment."

"But apparently a very common one," Eleanor said gently. "We both have been looking forward to this journey for a long time, and now that we're so close, I'm getting excited, too."

A number of people already had turned out to inspect the Galena. Stephen squeezed through the crowd to the point where the boat's gangplank bridged the lapping waters of the Mississippi, there to stand in awe of the vessel's towering majesty. High above him a man in a broad-brimmed hat and billowing white shirt directed the loading operation by shouting through a megaphone.

"Lively, there, step lively," he bellowed at the trudging stevedores, "we're not spending the summer here. Get a move on, or we'll fire up and steam off and leave you to wallow in the mud. Hop to it!"

Then he turned, arms akimbo, and yelled directly at Stephen.

"Look sharply, lad, and mark it well. The Galena is the finest boat on the Mississippi. Keep clear of the gangway, or one of those men may pick you up, pack you aboard like side of beef, and ship you off to the north woods before you can tell 'em different."

Eleanor came quickly to Stephen's side and began to pull him back into the crowd, but Wells stepped forward and called out: "We'll be sailing with you, Captain Hanks. I'll watch the lad; he's never seen anything quite like the Galena."

"So he's your boy, Lieutenant. Well, bring him aboard, and your lady, too. Stomp the mud off your boots and come take a look at the pride of the Mississippi. I've got good news for you!"

The three went aboard and Wells introduced Eleanor and Stephen to the steamboat captain.

"I know that name," said Hanks. "Shevley. Yes, Mrs. Shevley, your husband arranged for your passage to St. Paul. Best cabin available, were his orders, and that's what I've reserved for you and the boy."

"And the news, captain – what is the news?" asked Wells.

"My scouting party sent word back through overland travelers that the breakup was underway as far north as the Wisconsin line."

"Then we'll be sailing soon?" Wells asked.

"As soon as we're loaded. Get your bags packed and stand by. When you hear two short blasts of the Galena's whistle, you come a'runnin. I hope to cast off around noon, so send your luggage down as soon as possible."

As they left the boat landing Stephen noticed a fierce looking man in the crowd who seemed to be staring at him. He was dressed in buckskin and wore a knitted cap topped with tassel. The cap barely covered an unruly mane of red hair that enveloped the man's head and merged into his bushy beard. His eyes were clear and wild, and his cheeks burnished and dark as the leather he wore. As he passed, Stephen could almost feel those wild eyes following him up the street toward the hotel. He did not look back.

*   *   *

Two shrill blasts from the Galena's whistle set a ragamuffin to scampering through the muddy street beneath their window shortly after mid-day, calling out loudly and setting the crowd astir.

"Steamboat!" he cried. "Cap'n Hanks is firin' up! The Galena's building steam! Steamboat! Steamboat!"

The signal prompted a general exodus toward the landing. The townspeople surged into the street from homes and shops along the way to join the procession. Young boys led the parade, while prim little girls tugged at their mothers' skirts to hurry them along. Men laughed with one another and jostled their way through the crowd, some shouting with excitement, all animated as they were swept along with the current of humanity. Stephen, who had hitched a ride aboard the hotel's baggage wagon, watched from his perch atop their trunk, thrilled at the way the whistle had energized the crowd. As the wagon neared the landing he could hear the powerful throb of her engines, their rhythmic beat resounding over the din. He leapt to the ground and ran to the water's edge to behold the sleek, white river goddess in all her glory, tremendous clouds of black smoke billowing from her stacks. Moored for and aft, the vessel lay parallel to the river's flow, affording a magnificent view of her graceful form. A gilded star hung on a line strung between her stacks. From the lacy filigree of the main deck railing brilliant banners flapped in the breeze. Stephen could see Captain Hanks in the window of his wheelhouse, like a high priest in his black hat, scarlet bandana and flowing white shirt. His hands rested on the wheel as he calmly surveyed the supplicants who came to pay homage to his goddess in her moment of grandeur. Stephen drank in all the wonder of the

31

scene and it filled him with an excitement that chilled him to the bone.

Boarding the vessel, he went to the railing where he joined Lieutenant Wells and Eleanor, who were looking down to watch as a hulking stevedore hoisted the Shevleys' trunk to his shoulders and struggled across the gangway. Midway he shifted his grip, lost his balance and dropped the heavy load onto the walkway. He teetered precariously for an instant, then arched gracefully into the icy water. The crowd roared with delight and at the same instant the red-haired frontiersman in buckskin raced forward, lifted the trunk to his shoulder and trooped into the Galena's hold with it.

"We'd better step lively and look after that trunk," Wells said. But the press of the passengers against the railing made it impossible for them to move. In a moment the pulleys squealed, the ropes grew taut, and the gangway rose into the air, and swung gracefully onto the lower deck. The throng on the shore sent up a mighty cheer of farewell as the mooring lines splashed free and the steamboat drifted clear of the dock. Whistles screamed in a rush of steam and the engines struggled to turn the giant paddle wheels.

Ah woo, tat-tat-tat-tat-tat. Ah woo, tat-tat-tat-tat-tat.

The engines idled for a moment amid a loud clanking of gears, and the boat lurched toward midstream, the paddles whipping the water to foam.

Ah woo, tat-tat-tat-tat-tat. Ah woo, tat-tat-tat-tat-tat.

Scarves, caps, flags all waved in a frenzy of farewell as the crowd raced along the river bank to follow the packet boat as she labored into the channel and began her slow, graceful churning upstream against the icy and relentless current. Eleanor watched as a large tree limb floated by amid chunks of ice and her fingers tightened on Stephen's hand. He saw there were tears in her eyes.

"It's curious," Wells mused. "All these people on the move, their hearts filled with the same hopes and fears that you and I feel. They're all heading into the great unknown, searching for a new life, for wealth, for adventure – always searching. Yet in their hearts their greatest longing is for home."

"Do you long for your home, Lieutenant?" she asked.

"Do I?" he asked, pondering her question. "Yes, I think I do. But it's a home of dreams, not a home of memory. I have no real home, no family. But I do long for a home – someplace, someday. Perhaps the life I've chosen is only a means to that end, a way of searching. I've traveled a lot, and I suppose I have a lot of traveling yet to do. I tell myself I'm searching for adventure, excitement. But every so often something happens, such as meeting you and Stephen, that convinces me those are not the real reasons for my search. It's difficult to explain. At first I thought that meeting you might have stirred memories of a home I once knew, memories of myself at Stephen's age, memories of a settled, more tranquil life. But the truth is that my only memories are of a foundling home, and how much I hated it. So what stirred me wasn't a memory at all. It was a dream."

"You may be a soldier, Lieutenant, but you have the soul of a poet," Eleanor said.

"Kind of you to say that, but I find myself more morose than poetic, and incidentally growing colder by the minute. Let me help you find your stateroom so you can get settled in for the trip. Then I'll check on your trunk. I didn't like the looks of that fellow who carried it aboard."

As he was about to leave them at their door, Eleanor impulsively touched his sleeve, as if to hold him a moment longer.

"Thank you, Lieutenant. Thank you for all your kindness. I don't know how we would have managed."

"My motives were selfish, Mrs. Shevley. You and Stephen – well, it's been my pleasure entirely."

His expression was one of sadness and Eleanor, noting it, brought her hand to her lips to hide the smile that brought a sparkle to her eyes.

"Why, here we are saying goodbye!" she exclaimed. "I'm afraid you won't be rid of us yet. We have the whole voyage ahead of us, and soon thereafter we may be neighbors."

"Yes, I'd almost forgotten," he said with a smile. "Why don't we celebrate our new friendship by having dinner together tonight. You'd like that, wouldn't you, Stephen?"

"Sure, I would."

"Then I'll come by for you. And in the meantime, I'll check on your trunk, just to make sure it's safely stowed."

Later Eleanor went to the salon to write a letter to her parents, while Stephen stretched out on his bunk to rest. It took a while to get used to the movement of the vessel, and in the meantime he idled away his time watching the bright specks of dust that danced in the rays of the early afternoon sun that lanced through the shutters. Listening to the throb of the steam engines, he soon fell into a sound sleep. When he opened his eyes again, the door to the cabin was just closing. As the latch fell with snap, he raised himself up on his elbows and looked around the room. He was alone with only a vague recollection of his mother's departure. She must have come back to look in on him, he thought, and finding him asleep, had left again. He fell back on the bunk, obsessed by a strange sense of timelessness. It seemed like only moments before that she had been there at his side, but now he was alone. Had the blink of an eye seemed like passage of hours? He rose up and went to the window and opened the shutters. The sun was low on the western horizon, hanging like a great orange balloon over the birch trees that lined the riverbank. Five o'clock, he thought, maybe six. Grappling with the loose ends of time, he recalled seeing the sunlight filtering through the shutters, the bright specks of dust sparkling before his eyes. The sun was high then; now it was low. He must have slept two hours, maybe three. The hand at the door a moment ago had not been the hand of his mother departing. It was another time and another hand. He looked carefully around the room; nothing had changed. Yes, someone had looked in on him, his mother or maybe the lieutenant.

Fully awake now, he went to the mirror and straight-ened his clothes then went out on deck. His mother, approaching on the arm of the young officer, called to him.

"Stephen! Here we are, dear. We were just coming to awaken you for dinner. It was such a lovely sunset. Did you see it?"

"No. I was asleep."

"I just found your mother in the salon and we've come to get you. It's time for dinner. I'll bet you're hungry."

"Yes," the lad said, still confused, but certain now that it could not have been his mother or the lieutenant at his door.

"Well, then, let's be on our way. Incidentally, I found your trunk earlier, and you'll be happy to know it's quite safe. That fellow who carried it aboard has taken it upon himself to stand guard over it – or sit upon it, really. Strange fellow, but harmless enough."

*   *   *

It grew ever colder as the steamboat beat northward, so cold that Stephen got the trunk key from his mother and went to the lower deck to unpack his heavy winter coat. He was surprised to find that steerage was crowded with passengers bundled in blankets and scarves and huddled together for warmth against the icy winds that swept through the area. In the few minutes it took to locate the trunk the lad heard a half dozen or more languages being spoken by the passengers who found what comfort and protection they could amid the piles of baggage. Just as Wells had said, the wild-looking man in buckskin was seated atop the trunk, staring at Stephen as he approached.

"I want to get out my coat," the lad said, holding out the key to establish his right.

Without a word the man got up and stood clear, never shifting his gaze. Stephen turned the key in the lock, rummaged through their belongings, and withdrew his winter coat. Quickly closing the lid, he turned the key in the lock

35

again and stood back. The man's gaze never wavered. "Much obliged," Stephen said, backing away as he slipped the key into his pocket. He moved as rapidly as he could through the crowd of shivering passengers, glancing back only after he had reached the ladder and begun climbing. The man in buckskin was seated on the trunk again, still staring at him.

Chapter 3

He awakened to an unusual stillness. The mighty pulse of the engines had ceased. The stateroom was bright with sunlight and the vessel rocked gently as the current flowed under it. He yawned, expelling a cloud of vapor, shivered under the quilts for a moment, then bravely cast them aside and sat upright. His mother still slept soundly. Peering through the shutters he found the countryside reposing under a coverlet of new-fallen snow. On the riverbank a sleepy village sent thin columns of silver-blue smoke into the morning air. Birds sang tremulously while steam rose from the earth as the spring sun engaged old man winter in his last desperate battle. He dressed hurriedly, making a clatter at the wash basin that awakened his mother. She quickly sent him to the galley for a pot of tea, and when he returned he brought the news.

"We're at a place called Read's Landing at the foot of Lake Pepin. The lake's still frozen, and we can't go on until Captain Hanks takes a closer look at the ice. We might be here for a while, but it's all right to go ashore, if we want to. Let's do it, mother. Let's go ashore."

"Now then, don't get too excited. We'll have to see if there's time for that. I hope this won't mean a long delay. And just look out there – it's winter again"

"No, it's just a light snow. And the sun's out. It won't last. Let's go ashore and ask how far it is to St. Paul. Maybe we could even hire a wagon and team to take us the rest of the way. Maybe it's only a few miles."

Captain Hanks soon dispelled any thoughts of a speedy overland dash to St. Paul.

"Much too far, no roads, and unpredictable weather. It would be foolhardy. We'd do better to take our chances through Lake Pepin." The lake, he explained, was a lengthy wide spot in the river, and although it was miles long it was still the most direct route to St. Paul. "No need for long faces. The break-up has begun. Another day or two of sun like we have today, and we'll get through."

"Captain, won't the break-up endanger the Galena?" asked a passenger. "Those chunks rushing by seem to be getting bigger."

"Sir, I've waited here for the thaw many a time. I'm usually the first to reach St. Paul, and I've never arrived without my boat – or my passengers. So make yourselves comfortable and don't stray too far from the landing. When we do leave, we will leave in a hurry. Meals will be served on board."

The following morning, amid a blasting of whistles and the shouts of the crowd, the riverboat War Eagle steamed into Read's Landing and moored beside the Galena. Captain Hanks engaged the pilot of the War Eagle in an animated conversation, while the passengers lining the rails of each boat hollered greetings back and forth. Soon Hanks and the captain of the War Eagle crossed their respective gangways, met on the landing, and made their way to the wharfinger's shack. When they emerged a half-hour later the War Eagle's captain climbed aboard a wagon and headed up the river trail to judge the ice pack for himself. When he was safely out of sight, Hanks strode on board and gave the order to fire up the boilers. The Galena's passengers cheered while their counterparts aboard the War Eagle loudly decried the obvious treachery. In less than an hour he'd built a full head of steam and gave a blast of the whistle to summon any stragglers back on board. Soon the lines were cast off and the Galena was steaming northward again to the very edge of the ice-bound lake. There the river, flowing downstream from under the thinning ice, formed an ever-widening patch of navigable water. Chunks of ice as large as barrels banged against the prow of the vessel. As passengers crowded the rail watching anxiously, the Galena crunched its way through the rubbery surface of the lake's winter cover. When the ice grew thicker the paddle wheels strained against the growing resistance, but the Galena continued to slowly advance. To either side jagged tree trunks loomed, trapped in winter's frigid grip. At one point the shattered remains of a smaller vessel, its timbers protruding like so many stiff, frozen fingers, drew gasps of alarm from the Galena's passengers.

"The ice seems to be closing in behind us!" one said.

"We're going to be stranded here!" worried another.

But as the steamboat crunched through heavier and heavier barriers, so did it suddenly turn clear and glassy once again, leading toward open water. Smug in his aerie, the Galena's expert pilot steered her through the channel, ordering more steam until the huge boat broke free and began to glide along as if on the surface of a placid pond.

No sooner had relief come to the wary passengers than a cry arose: "Look! Behind us! It's the War Eagle following in our wake!"

Eager for a race they cheered the Galena on, but instead the engines slowed and the steamboat prepared to land at the village of Red Wing. With smooth, practiced maneuvers, Hanks guided his vessel into the landing, quickly moored her fore and aft, and issued a series of whiplash commands to the roustabouts who hustled cargo from the lower deck, down the gangplank, and onto the landing. On the passenger gangway, a handful of travelers destined for Red Wing scurried ashore with their luggage as the crowd at the landing caught the spirit of the race and cheered them on. In the distance the black smoke of the War Eagle drew nearer. With the cargo off-loaded and passengers safely ashore, Captain Hanks scaled the ladder to his wheelhouse and ordered the crewmen to stand by the mooring lines, while casting a disdainful glance at the War Eagle. It was now only a half mile away, and bearing down fast.

"Pull out, Cap'n!" came the cry. "We can't let the War Eagle get ahead of us!"

"Hold fast!" the captain shouted. "Hold fast!"

"He can't pull out," Jonathan Wells observed. "If he does, the War Eagle will ram us for sure."

The challenger was now nearly abreast of the Galena, its passengers clamoring for a victory over her hapless rival.

"Hold fast!" Hanks called out again as a sigh went up and the War Eagle steamed past. "Now! Cast off!" the captain shouted.

The heavy lines splashed into the roiling water and the huge riverboat floated free of the landing and chugged into the main stream.

"Take them, Hanks! Take them!" cried the passengers.

But the confident river pilot held his pace, maintaining a respectful distance as the Galena's paddle wheels struggled in the War Eagle's wake. A few miles further on the captain, his black hat set at a jaunty angle and his red bandana flowing in the wind, gave orders to build up steam. In minutes the Galena pulled abreast of the War Eagle, and the two vessels churned the river to a froth as they battled the current, their prows tossing large blocks of ice to either side. Then suddenly the huge boats came to a bend in the river, and rounding the turn came upon a small island dead ahead. Hanks held his position, commanding the wide channel, and passengers on both vessels fell into a stunned silence as the War Eagle let loose a piercing blast of its whistle. With no other choice than running aground on the island, the War Eagle's captain first reduced his speed, then threw the paddle wheels into reverse with a loud clanging of gears. Amid cries of fear and dismay, the War Eagle rocked wildly in the Galena's wake, then swung about until the current hit it abeam, threatening to drive it into the riverbank. By then the Galena was a hundred yards ahead, and rapidly increasing her lead. Her passengers raised a cheer that echoed throughout the darkening river valley.

Once the sun had set, only an intrepid few remained on deck to watch Captain Hanks guide the Galena through the mists of evening. In some places the fog became so thick it obscured the riverbanks, and the vessel's running lights illuminated only a ghostly world of gray that severely limited visibility. The captain cut his speed as darkness shrouded the great valley of the Mississippi, but continued on course, maneuvering this way and that to avoid large snags of tangled branches set free by the day's thaw. The steamboat shuddered each time a large block of floating ice slammed against her prow, eliciting a murmur of dismay from the shrinking crowd of observers on deck. On occasion the boat would swing sharply to one side, then right itself again in the channel as the black outline of rocky ledge slipped by the dark.

"That was a close one!" Stephen muttered, squeezing his mother's hand.

"Nearly slammed into that cliff, we did!" said a man nearby.

"The captain must have eyes like a cat!" said another. "I never saw it coming."

Time after time Hanks made similar blind maneuvers as if following the channel by sheer instinct or remarkable memory. Overhead the wheelhouse was but a dim glow while the deck lanterns faded into golden halos of ineffectual light. Still the Galena churned along through a dark world of racing water and shadowy riverbanks, while low-hanging branches brushed the top deck railings. The vessel steamed onward for several hours until at last in the distance a speck of light appeared and steadily grew larger.

"We've made it!" cried out a passenger.

"We're here!" exulted another.

"Three cheers for Captain Hanks!"

Through the wild chorus Hanks' voice boomed loudly through his megaphone:

"Landing ahead! St. Paul! Deck hands stand by the mooring lines. Passengers prepare to disembark." He punctuated his orders with several long blasts from the Galena's whistle, signaling his approach. Soon a cheering crowd on shore appeared on the landing in the glow of dozens of lanterns, while torches were ignited along the edge of the dock to guide the vessel safely into port.

A pounding arose in Stephen's breast as he first caught sight of the sea of faces on shore. His mother's hand squeezed his tightly as she uttered a tremulous, "We're here! Oh, thank God, Stephen, we're here at last!"

Together they pushed their way to the railing and for a long moment looked not at the faces in the welcoming crowd, but into each other's eyes. Stephen was sure he saw in his mother's face the same confusion of fear and happy anticipation that lurked in his own heart. They waited until the initial crush was over, then made their way to the lower deck. There they found the red-haired man in buckskin, smiling broadly, one foot planted firmly on their trunk.

"I'll give you a hand with this," he said.

"We'll tend to that ourselves, thank you," Eleanor said emphatically. "If you don't mind..."

"I don't mind a bit!" said the frontiersman, hoisting the heavy trunk to his shoulder. "You just follow me."

"Wait! Wait!" Eleanor called after him. "You don't seem to understand."

But the man in buckskin crossed the gangway and stepped onto the dock, heading toward the wharfinger's shack. Mother and son quickly snatched up their travel bags and hurried after him, struggling now through a surge of disembarking passengers.

"There he goes, Mother," Stephen said, panting under his load. "He just went into that little building."

In moments they reached the door through which he had entered, but immediately found their way blocked by a tall man with a black beard whose eyes shone fiercely in the blaze of torch lights. Eleanor fell back at the sight of him. Then, with all the fear and despair and loneliness that had accumulated over the years, she exclaimed, "Vincent, it's you!"

Dizzied by the whirl of events, Stephen eased himself down on his travel bag, and rested his head in his hands, trying to collect himself. As his parents embraced, the strangeness of the scene weighed heavily upon him. His impulse was to weep in relief, just to stare at the street with tear-dimmed eyes and weep as the crowd milled around him and laughter and shouting and happy greetings filled the cold night air. In the passing crowd he caught sight of Jonathan Wells, now dressed in his Army uniform. He was about to hail him when the sound of his own name brought him back to the reality of the moment.

"Stephen, my boy! Stand up and let me look at you."

He got up slowly, unbent, rather, in his weariness, and faced the man who held his mother in his arms.

"Look at him, Eleanor, look at him, would you! He's become a man, I swear." He held out his hand and Stephen grasped it firmly. "A man indeed!" Vincent exclaimed. "But let's not stand here in the cold. Come inside. I have some business to attend to."

He guided them into the shack where the red-haired man in buckskin was seated on their trunk. At a small table sat a bespectacled man in an overcoat. The man eyed them impassively.

"Where's the key?" Vincent asked.

"The kid's got it," said the man on the trunk.

"Give Ben the key, Stephen," said Vincent.

"Vincent – what...?"

"In a moment, Eleanor. This is important. Give Ben the key. Stephen."

He fished it out of his pocket and handed it over. Vincent watched intently as Ben unlocked the trunk, lifted the lid, and began pawing through clothing. Eleanor gasped as some of her dresses fell to the floor.

"Is this it?" Ben asked, holding up Eleanor's jewelry box.

"Now, just a minute!" she exclaimed in outrage.

"Open it," Vincent commanded.

"Nothing here but these," Ben said, holding up a handful of rings and necklaces.

"Give me the lid," Vincent ordered. He snatched the lid from Ben's hand and began clawing at the decorative paper that covered it. From beneath the paper he extracted a folded document which he opened and inspected carefully. Then with a smile he handed it to the man at the table, who adjusted his spectacles and glanced over the paper.

"That's a certified list of serial numbers," Vincent explained. "Each number represents a military land warrant legally purchased from its owner by the Shevley Land Company of New York. Take it for safekeeping, and tomorrow I'll come by the land office and we'll tally it up for the exchange. I suppose you've got the deeds drawn up?"

The man at the table nodded affirmatively as he tucked the document into his inside coat pocket.

"It's a pleasure doing business with you, Mr. Shevley," he said. "It'll take a few hours to do the paper work. Why don't you come by the office sometime tomorrow afternoon? The deeds and surveyor's maps will be waiting for you."

Vincent shook the man's hand and led him to the door, signaling Ben to follow him. Eleanor, meanwhile, began picking up the clothing that had been spilled from the trunk. There were tears in her eyes.

"Eleanor..." Vincent began, his arms outstretched. But she ignored him. He then turned to Stephen. "Help your mother, boy," he ordered. "We've got a few miles to travel yet tonight."

*   *   *

It was a cold, jolting ride through a strange dark land. Eleanor sat in stony silence next to her husband, while Stephen rode in the back of the wagon. Vincent's halting speech served as a weird accompaniment to their nightmarish journey.

"I'm sorry for all that commotion at the landing, but it was something that just couldn't wait. That's the reason I couldn't come down river to meet you. We just came out of the woods. We've got a raft of logs tied up above the falls, and a new mill we're trying to get into operation. There was just too much to do, too much I had to look after. I sent Ben McAlpine down to see that you got here safely. He's my right-hand man, and I would trust him with my life. He isn't the most presentable individual, so I ordered him to keep his distance."

"Your Mr. McAlpine seemed more interested in our trunk than in us, I must say," Eleanor commented icily.

"Well, I know – I told him to take particular care to see that the trunk arrived in good order. Our future depended on it, Eleanor. And as for tonight, it was a matter of urgent business that just couldn't wait."

"We barely had time to say hello."

"But that's all over now. You're here, and we're all together again. Everything is going to be fine. You'll see."

There was an awkward silence. The wagon wheels filled the void with their groans and squeals, and the team snorted, their hot breath white in the frigid air. Vincent clucked softly to them, urging them on.

"Say, that must have been quite a trip, all the way from Boston. Gideon wrote that you'd be coming by rail. What'd you think of the train, son?" he asked, looking back to flash Stephen a smile.

"It was fine," Stephen said, his teeth chattering in the cold.

"You did a fine job, watching after your mother and all. And you've turned out to be quite a man. And that riverboat, wasn't that something, Eleanor?"

Embarrassed by his mother's refusal to answer, Stephen spoke up instead. "That riverboat was really something, all right." But his mother's anger had effectively stifled Vincent's efforts to make amends, and the family rode along in silence. Those first few hours in Minnesota Territory would linger long in Stephen's memory – the bitter cold, the seemingly interminable ride through the dark, the only sounds the creaking of the wagon, the horses' hooves clomping on the frozen road, the helpless feeling of being at the mercy of the mighty river as a flat-bottomed ferry pulled them across the rushing water, the roar of St. Anthony Falls upstream. It wasn't until the ferry landed and the team struggled up the rise on the western bank that Vincent again attempted to engage his wife in conversation.

"The place isn't much," he said modestly. "I tried to fix it up – aired the blankets, brought in new straw. Ben's been staying with me. He's a good man, born and raised in the woods. He's the best timber cruiser you could ask for. He's trapped all along the Rum River, where all the adjacent land is about to become ours. I'll have the deeds in hand tomorrow. That document that my brothers hid in your trunk was – well, it's like a letter of credit, certification for military land warrants that Thaddeus and Gideon have been buying up for several years. That piece of paper represents 15,000 acres of the richest pinelands in the territory. It wasn't something we could safely send across country any other way. We didn't tell you, because we didn't want you to worry. You must admit that you'd have been pretty nervous about it, if you had known."

"Is it much farther, Vincent? I'm freezing."

"No, dear. We're almost there."

Again there was silence. It was near midnight when Vincent brought the team to a halt in front of a small log cabin. He left the team in halter and opened the cabin door to get his family inside out of the cold. He lit an oil lamp that stood on a rustic table cluttered with maps and papers. The lantern light revealed a sparsely furnished interior – a table, four chairs, and long storage shelves. At the rear were an open kitchen, a cupboard, and a cook stove. Off to one side there was a closed door. The floor creaked with each step, and the cold wind swept up neat little rows of fine dust along the cracks between the boards. Vincent knelt on the hearth and brought forth a small flame from embers buried deep in the ashes. As he built up the blaze with kindling the light revealed the distress on the man's face. He arranged several pieces of firewood around the flames, then stood up to look at his wife and son. He seemed even taller now than he had when Stephen first saw him in the doorway at the landing. His boots were smeared with mud, and his woolen trousers were soiled. His heavy, fur-trimmed leather coat was scarred and black with wear. A wrinkled wool shirt protruded at the collar. He pulled off his leather gloves and laid them on the woodpile at the fireside. His hands were muscular and soiled, and he rubbed them together over the fire to warm them.

There was an apologetic tone to his voice when at last he spoke to his wife without looking at her.

"This will take the chill off the room. The bedroom's through that door. The linens are in the chest at the foot of the bed. The blankets are fresh – I had them out all morning." Then, turning to Stephen, he said, "You'll sleep in the loft. There's clean straw up there, and blankets."

A tumult of emotion prevented the lad from answering. He was embarrassed by his mother's silence, and by the pain it was causing his father. He could see the hurt in the man's eyes, could almost feel the pain himself. "Say something," he thought. "Please say something." His mother came to him, fear in her eyes, and clutched his arm.

"Goodnight, Stephen," she said, her voice cracking. She gave him a peck on the cheek with icy lips and abruptly turned him toward the ladder that led to the loft. He went quickly up to his assigned place and bundled himself in the blankets that were there for him. Had it not been for the whistling of the wind through the rafters, their conversation would have been distinct. As it was, only the tones of feminine outrage and masculine forbearance reached him in his nest of straw. The exchange was brief, followed by the sound of movement from the bedroom, and the latching of the bedroom door. He heard his father go out into the cold again to tend to the horses, and soon after his return Stephen could hear him snoring. Peeking over the edge of the loft, he could see the man, still in his heavy coat and covered with a blanket, curled up on the floor in front of the fire. The night sounds were different here. He could hear the howling wind, and his father's noisy sleep. But he could not hear his mother's sobbing, although he knew she must have been crying bitterly in her disappointment and her exhaustion, all in the darkness unheard.

*   *   *

Stephen's life in the wild new world began cautiously. He awoke to the sound of chirping, and the fluttering of wings outside the vent at the point of the roof. Through the shutters brilliant bands of sunlight fell across the floor and stretched to the ladder at the very edge of the loft. He rose to his knees and brushed the straw and the dust from his clothes. Still on his knees under the sloping ceiling, he crept to the ladder, and peered down into the cabin. His father was busy rekindling the fire, and in a moment the lad caught the odor of pine smoke. He ducked back out of sight as his father looked up and called up to him:

"Come down here, Stephen! Rouse yourself, lad."

Slowly he turned his back to the ladder, groped for the topmost step with his foot, and descended.

"Good morning, sir," he said haltingly.

"Good morning, son. The privy's this way," he said, flinging open the door. The blinding glare of sunlight and a blast of cold wind greeted the boy as he stepped gingerly outside. "That way," said his father, pointing to the outhouse.

The morning air was clean and invigorating. Stephen breathed deeply as he waited for his father. Looking around at his new surroundings, he saw that the cabin stood upon a wooded knoll, and below stretched a plain dotted with a dozen or more frame buildings. At the fringes of this small settlement stood several conical tents.

"Indians," his father explained as he approached. "Sioux from a village nearby. They come here for handouts and to scavenge. They think we're all crazy, cutting down the trees and floating them on the river. Maybe we are, but there's no use in trying to explain it to them. Come this way." Stephen followed him to an improvised wash stand, a plank laid across two sawhorses, near the cabin door. Next to it stood a rain barrel, the water covered by a thin layer of ice. "Go to it," Vincent said.

Stephen laid his coat aside, pushed up his shirt-sleeves, and unbuttoned his collar. Daintily he dipped his fingers into the frigid water, and dabbed at his face.

"Now how are you going to wash the sleep from your eyes like that?" his father asked, grabbing him by the neck and dunking his head into the water. The lad struggled and gurgled and at last broke free and staggered away from the barrel, coughing and sputtering. Vincent watched him with an air of uncertainty, but when Stephen came up grinning, and shaking his head like a drenched dog, his father laughed uproariously. Bleary-eyed and shivering, Stephen laughed, too, and caught a towel Vincent tossed his way.

"That ought to wake you up," his father said, chuckling affectionately. Then he plunged his hands into the barrel and swished the icy water over his face, and through his hair and beard. When they were both washed and dried, he led Stephen to a vantage point and gestured toward the shantytown below them.

"What do you think of it?" he asked, nodding toward the scattering of rude buildings.

"Is that St. Anthony?"

"No. St. Anthony's on the other side of the river. They're calling this Minneapolis."

"That's a strange name."

"I thought so, too. I held out for Albion, but most favored Minneapolis. It's a made-up name. *Minne* is an Indian word for water; *polis* is Greek for city – water city. I guess it's all right for a city by the falls, and there are lakes around. But it's the falls that are important. That's where the power will come from to put this town on the map. North of here there are pine forests that go on forever, and rivers to bring the logs to Minneapolis. And here the falls will generate the power to cut those logs into lumber. Can't you hear them roar? Just listen to that power. It'll make this shantytown into a great city one day, mark my words."

Eleanor came out of the cabin, carrying a chamber pot. Vincent nodded to the privy, and she walked on by without a word.

"We're on the verge of a great era, son. This town will cut the boards that'll build the homes across hundreds of miles of prairie between the Mississippi and the great mountains that lie to the west. And we're on the cutting edge, so to speak. I'm building a mill now at the falls. We'll cut the trees, float them down river to St. Anthony Falls, and cut them into lumber with our own saws. This will be a Shevley Lumber Company that will put my father's business to shame."

"Or make him proud," said Eleanor, joining them. "That's what this is all about, isn't it? Showing your father what you can do on your own?"

Vincent eyed her coldly. "I only hope he lives long enough to see it," he said evenly.

Eleanor gave him a knowing smile and went into the cabin to prepare breakfast.

The atmosphere at the table was stained. Eleanor remained deliberately aloof, an impregnable fortress of silence, ignoring her husband's attempt at conversation as if it were the persistent pawing of an annoying pup. As Vincent's frustration and bewilderment grew, Stephen squirmed in embarrassment, desperate for his mother to respond. When she refused, he tried unsuccessfully to fill the void with muttered monosyllables.

"Bet that was the experience of a lifetime," Vincent said, "traveling half-way across the continent in a railroad car."

"Yes, sir," said the lad after a brief silence.

"Well, today we'll take a little ride," said Vincent, still directing his words to Eleanor, "and you'll see that the trip was well worth it."

Again, silence.

"Yes, sir," Stephen responded hopefully.

"It's time to get acquainted with your new home. I think you'll agree it's beautiful here."

"Yes, sir."

Eleanor sipped her tea and asked, "Will you have another griddle cake, Stephen?"

"Yes, sir...ur, yes, m'am."

Vincent settled back in his chair, fingering his beard and brooding. Suddenly his eyes lit up, and he leaned toward his wife, pushing his plate to one side.

"I've got a surprise for you!" he said enthusiastically. "I surely have – a real surprise!"

Eleanor looked at him with some exasperation.

"I have shopping to do," she said. "I presume there's somewhere we can buy groceries. You certainly don't have much here."

"Of course, there is!" said Vincent. "And then we'll take a little ride. You'll love it!"

Eleanor studied him impassively. "Your sleeve is in your plate," she said.

Vincent heaved a sigh and scratched his head. Then his fist came down upon the table with such force that the pottery danced and a fork clattered to the floor.

"You may think you're too grand-elegant for this town," he said with a raised voice. "Well, I've got a few things to say about that, and you're both going to hear me out."

Eleanor was startled by his outburst; Stephen was relieved.

"This isn't the Penobscot Valley, and it isn't Boston. It isn't neat and trimmed, and it isn't cut and dried. It's a new land, but it's a rich land, full of beauty and promise. If it's a little wild, well, that's why we're here – to tame it. It may call for hard work, and it may call for some discomfort, but by God that's a small price to pay for the rewards it offers. We're sitting here in a wilderness today where tomorrow a great city will rise. But it won't grow a like a tree. It will be built – board by board, nail by nail – with muscle, sweat, and sacrifice. People like us will build it. And if the people, and the work, and the life, and the land are a bit rougher than you're used to, so be it. Right now it's the work that's important, and we don't have much time for refinements. But don't stick up your nose and reject the land or the people. We're the ones on trial here, not them."

He paused, slipping his thumbs in his suspenders and frowning at the floor. When he had regained his composure he spoke in a softer voice, though no less forcefully.

"If you'll forgive a man his pride, I'll ask you not to reject me, either. A lot has changed since I left Maine. But I haven't changed. Oh, I know I may have taken on a few rough edges, but I've been living a rough life. I haven't forgotten how to behave like a gentleman, and I haven't forgotten my duties to my family. But I also have taken on new responsibilities. When I left Maine, I set out to make a way for us all. I have found the life I was looking for, and despite appearances to the contrary, it isn't a small life enclosed by these four rustic walls. It's a grand life, broad, and fresh, full of adventure, full of riches, like the land itself. I've taken a lot from this land, and I plan to take a lot more. I'm in its debt; I owe it a lot in return. It's my duty – our duty – to build, to make it a great land. We're doing more than creating a home for ourselves, more than building a great city. We're writing a whole new chapter in the history of this country. Thousands of people will follow us. We're not building just for ourselves. We're building for them, too. We're building for the future."

His voice rang with conviction and authority, dedication and strength of purpose. How different he was from his brothers, Stephen thought. Old Williams had been right – Vincent Shevley had been cast in his father's mold, and it was no wonder that they had clashed. Strong-willed, self-assured Vincent needed his own challenge, and he had found it. It was his destiny to shape this land, to give heroic form and substance to his ambitions. The force of his personality was awesome to the boy, his strength frightening. It made him wonder about another of Williams's pronouncements: *"You're like your Pa, boy, and like old man Shevley before him. You're made of the same stuff, danged if you ain't."*
He could not believe that there was anything about him, even the smallest particle, that was like his fearsome father. He was so different from what Stephen imagined he might be, not at all like the portrait in his mother's locket, and nothing at all like his mother represented him to be. Vincent was embodiment of her deepest dread, a man tainted by the wilderness, hardened by the rigors of the frontier. How disappointed she must be, Stephen thought, that her fears had become reality. He remembered how she had wept in the solitude of her room at night, and he wondered now if she would ever cry again, or if there were simply no tears left in her.

Chapter 4

Eleanor responded to her husband's call for hard work and sacrifice by submerging herself in household chores, insofar as the limits of their humble log cabin permitted. But her industry was motivated by spite and hampered by the lack of anything but the barest necessities.

"I am fully prepared to accept the rigors and responsibilities of our new life," she announced sarcastically, "but I lack even a broom with which to sweep away the last traces of my idle and self-indulgent existence."

Vincent was quick to schedule a shopping trip to St. Anthony. At the general store he turned them both over to the proprietor, instructing him to comply with Eleanor's every wish, and to prepare a bill for him.

"As for the lad," he said, casting a disparaging glance at Stephen's clothes, "see that he's outfitted properly. He can't do a day's work in those clothes." Turning to Eleanor, he added, "I'll be back later this afternoon. I have business at the land office, and some personal matters to attend to. You may want to take a walk around village, if I'm late in returning. Then we're going for a ride. I have a surprise for you."

Eleanor remained aloof, refusing to show the least bit of interest in any surprise he might have for them. But she made good use of her time at the general store after Vincent departed. For Stephen she selected flannel shirts, sturdy trousers made of heavy sailcloth, woolen socks, cotton underwear, a jacket, boots, cap and mittens. She picked out two housedresses, an apron, and a sturdy pair of shoes for herself. For the cabin she collected bedding and blankets, yardage for curtains, tableware, pots and pans, dishes, soap and brushes, a broom and even a hemp mat to put at the front door. Resisting a vengeful impulse to totally disregard cost, she drew the line at frills, content to merely inspect for future reference such bric-a-brac as might someday brighten their rustic home. When the essentials all were listed, wrapped, and packed for the trip home, she paused to admire a display of glassware. The piece that caught her eye was a green vase. It had a simple octagonal base and a tapered stem supporting a fluted bowl. Carefully she held it up to the light, pleased by the kaleidoscope of colors it reflected. Its simple beauty brought back memories of Shevley House, where the influence of Vincent's late mother preserved the gentility of another era, and of her home in Boston, and its parlor where Vincent first came to court her. She remembered him now as he had been in those days, tall and handsome in a tailored frock coat and polished boots, the eager young gentleman her father had taken into his business, and whom she had taken into her heart. She saw him that same way again as she gazed toward the door of the frontier store where the light of the late afternoon sun flooded in upon her like those precious memories, as if it all were only yesterday. Tears welled in her eyes.

"I'd planned to look like this when I met the boat," said the figure in the doorway. "But the river ice broke up before I had a chance to get myself ready."

He was the man of yesterday, the man in her parlor, the man in her locket. He was a little grayer now about the temples, but the black beard had been shorn to reveal his weathered cheeks, and his moustache neatly trimmed. His hair had been cut, and the scent of cologne was strong about him. A thin cravat graced his spotless shirtfront, and under his opened coat could be seen a colorful vest from which dangled a gold watch chain. His pipe stem trousers folded perfectly at the instep of his highly polished boots. He nervously fingered the brim of his felt hat as his wife studied him in amazement. She shook her head weakly, at a loss for words, as a tear eased itself down her cheek.

"Now, now, what's the matter?" he asked. "I don't think I look that bad."

He came to her and put his arm around her as the shopkeeper hurriedly led Stephen toward the rear of the store.

"Come with me, son. I've got a saddle in the back room that'll make your eyes pop out. You can climb on it, if you want to."

*   *   *

Once the wagon was loaded and the bill paid they descended the slope to the ferry and crossed back to the west side of the river. There the wagon groaned up the grade and rumbled through the shanty town, past their cabin and through a meadow to a small pond where Vincent halted to water the horses.

"Where are we going?" Eleanor asked.

"We're going to see that surprise I promised you," he said, settling into a smug silence.

Eleanor sat smiling beside him, cradling the green glass vase in her lap as the wagon lurched over the muddy, rutted trail. The sun was low on the horizon, casting a bawdy burst of red across the pale blue sky until its brilliance faded into soft lavender streaks that stretched like graceful fingers into the darkening eastern sky as if to grasp the edge of night. They rode through groves of oak where evening shadows already lurked in the underbrush, and in a moment they heard the rumbling of another wagon approaching on the trail. It pulled off to one side to allow them to pass, and Vincent gave a nod to the driver and the gang of workmen he carried.

"Now," Vincent said, "you both close your eyes, and keep them closed until I say to open them."

The wagon swayed and rocked along for another fifty yards or so before it came to a halt. Stephen squeezed his eyes tightly and squirmed in anticipation.

"All right, now you can look."

Ahead of them on a knoll loomed a mansion made of huge red stone blocks. It was rimmed by stately oaks and towered three stories into the evening sky. A broad stairway fanned upward from the muddy surroundings to a magnifi-

55

cently carved door that hung on hinges as long as a man's arm. Eleanor gasped at the sight of the building.

"Gosh!" Stephen exclaimed. "Whose place is this?"

"Ours," said Vincent proudly. "I hoped to have it finished by now, but we had a bad winter and work was delayed. We got the roof on just before the first snows last fall, but a lot of finishing work needs to be done inside. In another few months we'll be able to move in."

"All these things!" Eleanor laughed in delight. "All these things I bought for the cabin. Whatever will I do with them now?"

"You'll put them to good use. We're still a long way from taking up residence in Shevley House West."

"Shevley House West?" Stephen asked.

"That's what I call it," said his father. "It's not as large as my father's house, but it's more our size – and it will be just as elegant. There's not another home in the territory like it, and I promise you there will be none as grand."

"But this morning – all that talk about hardships and sacrifice, about building a great city..."

"I meant every word of it. One elegant home doesn't make a civilized community. It's only a beginning. We'll lead the way, set the example. Others will follow. You'll see."

"It's so big!" Stephen exclaimed. "Will we have to close off the top floor?"

"No, my boy. We'll get your mother all the help she needs to run this place. It'll be the finest, most envied home in the territory. It's only fitting."

"Fitting?" Eleanor asked.

"Well, you know..." Vincent stammered, blushing. But in his eyes the answer glowed bright and clear: Fitting for the leader of the new community; fitting for the giant pride that dwelled within him; fitting for Vincent Shevley and his family.

*   *   *

As the long wet spring stretched lazily into summer the pace of life in the village quickened perceptibly. Each day brought new arrivals – hundreds of wide-eyed and eager immigrants, confident that their strong backs and faith in God would be all they needed to build successful lives in the territory. Vincent looked upon it as an omen of his personal success. Here were the hardy Scandinavians, Irish, and Germans who would join the Shevley workforce for winters in the woods. They were the men who would fell the trees, move the logs to the riverbanks, and ride the rafts of timber to the mill at St. Anthony Falls in the spring. These same men then would clear the stumps, till the soil, and raise the crops that would sustain the territory's burgeoning population. Theirs would be a cycle of labor and production to match the lumbermen's own, which was about to bear fruit.

Raft pilots who had guided barges loaded with sawn lumber down river were beginning to return with receipts that turned paper fortunes into gold. A land rush was under way as the lumbermen raced to convert that gold into more forest land – all but Vincent Shevley. He could watch from the sidelines, for he already had staked out the choicest claims, using the land warrants his brothers had sent from the East. He had snatched up the best sections of the Rum River pineries, enough land to serve his lumbering operations for years. His tracts, marked out on a surveyor's map on the wall of his mill office, stretched up the Rum River valley to Mille Lac, and from there northward along the major streams and rivers where the sound of the woodsman's axe had not yet been heard. His land cut through the richest forests, and straddled the best streams. Let the others scrap over the leavings; Vincent Shevley was one jump ahead of them from the start.

While his competitors used their cash to buy land, Vincent was free to spend his to expand his mill at the falls where the plunging waters turned the saws that cut logs into finished lumber for the local market, and for the lucrative trade down river. He welcomed his competition, for many of them would be dependent on his mill – and they would pay his prices. He could turn his attention to the completion and the furnishing of Shevley House West and have enough left over to dabble in real estate. He had enlisted his brothers as partners in an enterprise they called The Minnesota Territorial Association, to take advantage of the land boom. While Thaddeus and Gideon cultivated the support of New York investment houses, their agents were equally busy on the waterfront. Each arriving boatload of immigrants was informed by means of handbills printed in German and three Scandinavian languages that Minnesota had the richest farmland in America, and that land could be purchased from the association for ten dollars an acre – slightly more for city lots. No mention was made that the same land could be purchased at government land offices for a dollar and a quarter an acre. Nor was it revealed that much of the Shevley land had been bought with military land warrants for which the association paid only a few cents on the dollar. The hand bills promised that the Shevley Lumber Company was prepared to offer the immigrants jobs so they could afford to settle the land, good paying jobs that would buy ploughs, and seed, and livestock, and the food and clothing necessary to see the settlers through until their first crop came in.

For those who preferred city life, the newcomers were offered free maps of Pompantium – The City of the Future. The maps showed a well-ordered metropolis near the confluence of the Rum River and the Mississippi. In addition to residential lots, the plats showed a city hall, churches of several denominations, an opera house, stores, parks, lakes, mills and manufacturing facilities, and wide thoroughfares. Anyone familiar with the Shevley Company's operations could pinpoint the area as the site of the past season's logging, land that was nothing more than a denuded area of pine stumps and churned earth. But the handbills accompanying the maps proclaimed it the crossroads of the west, soon to become the crossroads of the world, a center of beauty, culture, and wealth – with lots ranging upward from fifty dollars. This dream of the future was available today to

the far-sighted investor, the handbills proclaimed, for cash
on the barrel head.

*   *   *

In their first weeks in the cabin Stephen felt strange
in his new boots, his coarse, heavy trousers, and bright red
flannel shirt. He drew on these clothes each morning as an
actor might don a costume, but he was unable to warm to his
new role. His duties were assigned each day – inside chores
dictated by his mother, outside chores by his father – and he
did his best to perform his simple tasks promptly and well.
But the backdrop was unreal to him. The cabin was just a
cabin, the muddy village just a muddy village. The other
characters in this drama were equally foreign to him – Ben
McAlpine, a frequent visitor; the foreman of construction at
Shevley House West, and his workmen who were sent by to
deliver requests for supplies; the superintendent from the
sawmill, and the gang boss of log rafts. They were a coarse
breed, not at all like the Shevleys of Maine or the Crafts of
Boston. Stephen moved among them in constant fear that his
costume could not conceal his alien airs and instincts. There
were no boys to talk to, no contemporaries with whom to
share his thoughts. The few lads who lived in the village
labored alongside their parents from dawn to dusk, building
shelters, clearing land, burning brush, hacking at tree stumps,
carrying a man's load despite their years. They had no time
for socializing, certainly not with Stephen, whose own labors
were markedly less demanding than their own. So it was that
after the first few weeks, when his own chores were done –
the firewood cut and stacked, the hay changed in the loft, the
water buckets filled, the horses fed, the small stable cleaned
– only then did Stephen take to wandering down the trail that
led to the marshy pond at the foot of the knoll below Shevley
House West where he could watch the workmen from a safe
distance, and dream of the day when life again would
approximate the comfortable existence he had known in
Maine, away from the threatening frontier, alone and apart

59

and secure. It was there at the home site that Stephen first heard of Pompantium. Two workmen, carefully fitting slabs of marble for the grand stairway that led to the front door, stopped in their labors to take long drinks of water from a burlap-wrapped jug.

"This stone is very hard to work with," said one.

"It's very heavy," agreed the other.

"And brittle."

"And expensive."

"They say the streets of Pompantium will be paved with marble."

They both laughed heartily.

"Maybe with gold!" cried the first stonemason.

"Aye, maybe with gold. But more likely it will be like the road that runs by my lot, which is paved with mud and swamp grass."

"Or mine, which just runs – it *is* the swamp."

They laughed again, this time with a note of bitterness.

"But it's our swamp; we hold the deeds."

"And one day it will be a great city, the capital of the world."

"So says Vince Shevley, and yet he builds his own home far from Pompantium."

"Maybe it's a joke. Maybe he believes Minneapolis will be the real capital of the world. Why else build such a palace as this?"

"Why, it's to give us work so we can pay for our lots in Pompantium!"

"Ah! A very kind and generous man." The workman's voice was heavy with sarcasm.

"But for now this stone must be set in place. If we do a good job, maybe he'll let us pave the streets of Pompantium."

As they turned again to their work, they were laughing heartily.

Stephen heard of that imaginary kingdom again at his father's mill where he and his mother had gone to observe the celebration marking the opening of the expanded facility. The ferry had crossed the surging river three times carrying celebrants from St. Paul and St. Anthony. The ceremonies lasted nearly an hour and forty-five minutes, with several speakers rising to pay tribute to Vincent Shevley, to the Territory of Minnesota, to the future of statehood, and to God Almighty that this grand event had come to pass. Vince was the last to speak, modestly accepting the accolades of his fellow citizens, and bidding all within the sound of his voice to follow his example, to work diligently, to look to the future with confidence, and to trust in the opportunities offered by this rich new land. When his last words had echoed over the roar of the mighty Mississippi, the mill-wright engaged the gears that set the huge paddle wheels in motion, impelled by the power of the surging waters, and in moments the giant circular blades began to turn ever faster. Then the raft foreman in the river below led the first log into place, and steadied it as it was caught and dragged by loudly flapping conveyor belts to meet the teeth of the saw. As the shiny steel blade ripped its way through the water-soaked log, it sent up a deafening scream that drowned out the cheers of the crowd. And as the first piece of cut lumber fell away, and then the next, and the next, the celebrants crowded around Vince Shevley to shake his hand before they departed. In time only one observer remained. He was a short, bespectacled man with curly hair and squinty eyes and the rumpled appearance of having slept in his clothes.

"Well, Whitcomb," Vincent greeted him, "there's a piece of news for your paper."

"Quite so, quite so, Vince. It's a prophecy come to pass. Another step toward statehood, as I see it, an advance toward national leadership. It's a omen, a sign of a future of unlimited prosperity," the little man pontificated.

"Write it down, Whitcomb! Don't waste your fancy words preaching to a believer. Put in down on paper for the rest of the world to read. But while you're here, I want you to meet my wife and son, Stephen. This is Charles E. Whitcomb, editor of The Frontiersman."

"It is my great pleasure, Mrs. Shevley," he said, bowing to Eleanor. "You must be very proud. And I'm pleased to meet you, my boy," said Whitcomb, extending his hand. "I presume you'll be heir to all this someday. I hope such a prospect doesn't humble you."

"Humble him!" Vincent laughed. "He's my son, Charlie. He's a Shevley. It's not in him to be humbled by anything, and certainly not by a challenge. He's here to watch, to work, and to learn. Don't you worry, he'll be ready to meet any challenge when the time comes."

"A grave responsibility," Whitcomb mused. "It may be left to you to realize some of your father's ambitions, young man."

"Nonsense! He'll have his own ambitions, unless I miss my guess. And I'll realize my own – say, what are you driving at?"

"I was just thinking, Vince, thinking about Pompantium. There are rumors going around."

"What kind of rumors? Who's doing the talking?"

"Certain people, I have no names," said Whitcomb.

"What do they say?"

"They say that Pompantium is more scheme than dream, Vince Shevley's scheme to make money selling pie in the sky."

"Damn their hides, Whitcomb. You know me better than that. You've helped me promote Pompantium. You've been in on it from the start. You wouldn't dare print unfounded rumors."

"You're right. I won't print rumors. But there's no law says I can't print your denial of the rumors. I figure it's my job to keep the public informed. As you so justly point out, my own reputation is at stake here."

"I don't have to answer slander. My record speaks for itself. Schemes, speculations – they're not part of that record. If I were scheming, why in hell would I be building my own home here? I'd fleece 'em and run, if I had a mind to. This is my home, Charlie, and you know me and my intentions."

"I know you as an honorable man, Vince, but your home is one of the points in question. Intentions, even honorable ones, can be misunderstood. The question going around is, Why are you building your home here in Minneapolis, instead of in Pompantium?"

"Why, damn it, because my work is here just now, that's why. And you can tell that to the world, if you have a mind to. No, don't tell 'em a damn thing. It's none of their business. I won't dignify petty gossip with any sort of response."

"They're curious about Minneapolis, too," Whitcomb went on. "The land office records show a lot of deeds in your name. You seem to own most of the land on the west bank."

"I was here first, I acted first. There's nothing illegal about that. Look, Whitcomb, I also bought nearly the whole Rum River valley, and timber land farther north than those tongue-flappers have ever dragged their lazy asses. Print that, if you want. Tell 'em I'll buy the backside of the moon, if I want to, and they can take their rumors and go to hell!"

"Then Pompantium remains a part of your plans?"

"Of course, it does."

"You've sold several lots – how many people have settled there so far?"

"None yet, that I know of. But that doesn't mean any-thing. Damn it, a man needs a stake. It takes money to settle a piece of land, money and hard work. I've done a lot more than my share, and I don't feel I need to explain my every move. I cleared that land, I platted that town, and I sold those lots. I've even given jobs to some of the folks who bought land up there to help them get on their feet. God Almighty, Charlie, do you expect me to go up there and build their houses for them? Maybe I should buy 'em each a cow and a mule, and raise their kids for 'em. This isn't a lazy man's country, Charlie, as you well know. I've done more than my share to establish Pompantium, and you know it."

"All right, Vince, don't get riled. I just wanted to hear you say it for the record. Rome wasn't built in a day, and

Pompantium won't be either. If I print anything at all, that's what it will be."

"Well, that's more like it."

"But there's one story I want to write..."

"What's that?"

"I want to tell the world about the first settler in Pompantium. I want to write about that man and his family – where he came from, what his dreams are. That's what will sell more property in Pompantium. Someone's got to break the ice, and that's the story I want to tell. But no more about that now, I want to know how your new home is coming along."

"Slowly, Charlie, but surely. It won't be long now and we'll be moving in. I'll throw a big party then, and you'll be invited so you can write about it in your newspaper to let everyone know that Vince Shevley's no fly-by-night speculator. He's here to stay."

"I'd be delighted to do that, Vince. And Mrs. Shevley, I hope the prying ways of a journalist haven't alienated you on our first meeting. It has been a pleasure to meet you and your son. Minnesota will expect big things from you, young man."

"Yes, sir," said Stephen, extending a trembling hand.

*　　*　　*

Charles E. Whitcomb was born in New Hampshire, the son of a prosperous merchant. He was reared in comfortable surroundings, and educated in public schools until his twelfth year when he was taken into his father's shop to learn the practical economics of retail trade. However, since he evidenced more talent for talk than for labor, his father sent him away to study the law. At fifteen he was admitted to Harvard University, and in two years established a reputation for eloquence, pugnacity, and a taste for strong drink. He saw little of his professors until his third academic year when he discovered politics. It was then that his activities were brought forcefully to their attention. He was summarily expelled after a political rally that degenerated into a street brawl, and his formal education came to an end. He decided to work his way west, and at eighteen found employment in St. Louis as a printer. His lively intellect and facility with words soon brought him to the attention of the publisher who soon entrusted him with limited editorial responsibilities. The young tyro seized the opportunity to suddenly and surreptitiously reverse the newspaper's policy by publishing a front page editorial espousing the Whig abolitionist stance and its opposition to war with Mexico His initiative was not appreciated by many in St. Louis, where tensions over the slavery issue already were at a fever pitch. Nor did his bold stroke endear him to his publisher, whose political ambitions evaporated before the ink was dry. A violent quarrel erupted between the two, ending in a single pistol shot that penetrated only Whitcomb's pride and his coattails as he fled the city on a hastily borrowed horse. His intention was to return the horse the next day and make amends, but when he discovered how horse thieves were treated in that western outpost he opted instead to seek sanctuary and blessed anonymity as a private soldier in the ranks of the United States Army, which was then seeking volunteers for an invasion of Mexico.

It was not a wise decision, but one neatly balanced by fate, for within weeks the green recruit found himself marching resolutely into Mexico under the command of General Zachary Taylor. The young journalist's impulsive nature was well suited to the battlefield where his outbursts of temper and total lack of discretion were interpreted by his commanding officers as acts of extraordinary valor that left him with a ball in his thigh and a medal on his tunic. He was honorably discharged and sent back across the border where he resumed his career as an itinerant journalist. Trading on his reputation as a war hero, Whitcomb easily gained a position on a pro-war New Orleans newspaper. His immodest tales of heroism made good reading for the citizens of that cosmopolitan city, but his zeal for humanitarian causes soon sent him fleeing northward on the Mississippi – carefully avoiding St. Louis – toward the more liberal climate of the sparsely settled northern territories. Over the years of his migration he held an assortment of editorial jobs and managed to accumulate a flatbed press and several cases of type, his sole possessions when he disembarked at last in Minnesota Territory where he published the first edition of The Frontiersman in the then-unnamed village at the Falls of St. Anthony.

It was Whitcomb's nature to be an advocate, and he did so with enthusiasm when it came to Minnesota. He set aside a portion of each edition for distribution via steamboat to the river towns down stream, exhorting his unseen readers to quit their lives of travail and wandering and hasten to the Promised Land, the bounteous northland blessed by riches bestowed by a benevolent God and crying out for the brave and the strong to meet its challenges. One such editorial, more glowing than all the rest, was illustrated by a map, across which was emblazoned in large type the name Pompantium. Accompanying the map was a long, gray column of print, the dullness of which belied the colorfulness of its message. It was the editor-publisher's extravagant endorsement of Vincent Shevley's plan to build the greatest city in the West on a patch of denuded timberland at the junction of the Mississippi and the Rum Rivers.

*   *   *

Stephen was curious about Pompantium, but he had no desire to visit the site. He knew that it lay at the edge of the pineries, and that beyond it was wilderness, an area that held no allure for him. He preferred village life and its conveniences. He liked working at the mill, where he could test his manliness and adaptability without venturing into the great unknown. He cringed at the thought of going into the woods, of subjecting himself to the rough and tumble life his father often spoke of as a great adventure. Stephen remained unconvinced. He lived in dread of the inevitable, and it came all too soon.

"Ben and I are going into the woods next week," Vincent announced as they opened their lunch pails at the noon break. "We'll be heading up toward Mille Lac, and I want you to come along. You'll have a chance to swing an axe and see for yourself what this business is all about."

"How long will we be gone?" Stephen asked.

"Oh, two or three weeks. Ben cruised the area last spring. Our job will be to stake out a site for the camp, and plan the winter's cut. You could be a big help."

"I don't know anything about it."

"You'll learn. We leave Monday," he said emphatically.

Stephen fell silent. There was nothing he could say, but his fears were impossible to hide.

"Oh, I won't insist on it," his father relented. "But I want you to think about it. Take the afternoon off. Go on down to the pond and have a swim. We'll talk about it at dinner."

Stephen left the mill quickly and ran out to the edge of village and through a meadow thick with clover. He raced along in a panic, his long legs flying, his arms pumping, his chest heaving painfully. He ran until the village was far behind him, and when he could run no longer he collapsed in the sweet clover and rolled over on his back and lay clasping his aching breast. Sweat ran down his cheeks, mingling with his tears. The sun had begun its descent when at last his fears subsided, and he arose and looked around him. To the west a hill loomed, reflected in a quiet pond. He was immediately seized by an urge to climb that hill, and he set off in long, easy strides, stopping only to skip a flat stone across the mirrored surface of the water.

Chapter 5

From the top of the hill Stephen looked back on the village with a sense of relief. He was free for the time being, and there was a trail beckoning him southward. For an hour he followed the path through the wooded countryside until he came upon a swamp at the edge of a sun-filled glade. He rested briefly, then arose to creep stealthily after a frog that hopped among the cattails. Hidden among the reeds and engrossed in the chase, he neither heard nor saw the horsemen until they were nearly upon him. There was no time to escape. He crouched in the marsh grasses, his boots sinking into the mud. As the first horse approached he saw that it carried two Indians, riding hard along the edge of the swamp. They galloped within yards of him and after they passed he bolted out of the marsh and raced for the cover of the woods. He was only halfway to safety when a shot rang out, freezing him momentarily in the open. He saw two other horsemen bearing down on him, and saw a puff of blue smoke rising in the air over their heads. In panic he fell to the earth and covered his head with his hands as one of the horsemen reined up, spraying him with dirt. The other charged on in pursuit of the Indians. Cautiously Stephen raised his head and looked into the barrel of a Colt .44. Behind the weapon he recognized the begrimed face of Jonathan Wells.

"If it isn't young master Shevley!" the office exclaimed. "Wait right here and keep your head down. I'll be back for you."

At the far end of the swamp another shot rang out. The horse carrying the two Indians was thrashing about in the water. It reared and pitched its riders into the swamp. A mounted soldier waited for Wells at the water's edge, a rifle leveled on the struggling Indians as their horse wandered off toward the tree line. Then Wells stood guard while the soldier dismounted and rounded up their prey. He tied them each with a rope wrapped securely behind their backs and around their necks. As he led the captives off through the woods, Wells went after their horse before returning for Stephen.

"Up you come, young man," he said, grasping Stephen's hand and hoisting him astride his horse. "You're a long way from home."

"Yes, sir," the lad acknowledged, his heart still pounding as a result of the excitement. He noticed that the officer was quite a different person from the fair skinned, neatly groomed gentleman he knew aboard the Galena. His dark blue uniform was splattered with mud, his face burnished by the sun and covered with the stubble of a beard. A ring of sweat banded his cap; his hands were dirty and leather-tough. His manner was brusque.

"What are you doing out here?" he asked.

"Hunting frogs," Stephen replied.

"You'd be wise to hunt frogs nearer the village."

A long silence ensued as the horse trotted back over the trail that Stephen had followed to the swamp. Riding behind Wells and clinging to his waist, the boy was alternately heaved to the left and right as the animal's hindquarters jolted him. He was still in a state of excitement over the chase.

"Those Indians," he asked, "why were you after them?"

"They killed a man."

"Where...when?"

"Yesterday at the fort."

"Why did they kill the man?"

"They're beggars, and they got into a fight. One of our scouts tried to run them off. They killed him and stole his horse."

"What are you going to do with them?"

"They'll face charges," Wells said, "for stealing government property and murdering a government employee."

"How'd you catch 'em?"

"We followed their trail to the Indian encampment down by the lake. The chief claimed he didn't know anything about the killing, so we left. We hid in the woods all night, watching the village. This morning those two wandered in drunk leading the stolen horse. They had the scout's hat and his ammunition pouch. The big one had a fresh scalp on his belt. We took off after them."

"What will you do to them?"

"That's for the colonel to decide."

They were at the outskirts of the village now, Stephen taking a sudden pride in his uncomfortable perch. The village boys stared at them as they passed, and Stephen tried to look nonchalant as he directed Wells to the Shevley cabin. Eleanor came to the door as Wells lowered Stephen to the ground.

"My regards, Mrs. Shevley," Wells greeted her. "I found your boy a bit far from home. It's not really safe alone out there."

"Stephen! What..."

"They were chasing two Indians! Murderers, they were. They were shooting!"

"Who was shooting?" Eleanor gasped.

"Wait, please. The boy's a little excited, Mrs. Shevley," said the officer, removing his cap. "Allow me to say how pleased I am to see you again. It's been several weeks since we last spoke."

The light of recognition shown in Eleanor's eyes.

"Why, Jonathan Wells!" she exclaimed happily. "I didn't recognize you. Is it really you?"

"I apologize for my appearance. I've been on duty in the field."

"And he caught these two murderers in the swamp after shooting at them, and..."

"Wait, Stephen. Let me tell the story while you calm down. You see, Mrs. Shevley, I ran across him down near the swamp. He was just chasing frogs, but I suggested that he confine his adventures to areas nearer the village. It's not entirely safe for him to be so far away alone."

"I'm very grateful to you, Mr. Wells. It seems I'm forever in your debt. I have things on the stove, and my husband will be home soon. Won't you please stay and have dinner with us?"

"I'm sorry, but I can't. I have to report back immediately."

"Later then?"

"Yes, perhaps later. Meanwhile, Stephen can tell you what he saw after the excitement wears off."

"Yes, I understand," she said.

"Good day, then," said Wells, the hint of a smile in his tired eyes. "Stay closer to home, young man," he called back over his shoulder.

At dinner Vincent corroborated Stephen's story, filling in with his own account of the murder at Fort Snelling the day before.

"Damned thieving Indians," he grunted, shaking his head.

"But what about Stephen?" Eleanor asked.

"What about him?" Vincent asked.

"I'm shocked at your lack of concern. Think what might have happened to him."

"I am thinking about it, and I don't see that anything so awful could have happened to him. That young officer is competent, and I don't think a horse would run a man down, if it could avoid him. But you'd have been smarter to stay hidden in the cattails, instead of trying to run away. No use sticking your neck out."

"Vincent! You're actually encouraging this sort of behavior. You seem to forget..."

"Forget what?"

"You forget that he's not used to this sort of thing."

"You mean this sort of life? Well, he'll have to get used to it. And I'm glad you brought it up. I plan to take him into the woods with me in a week or so. It'll help him get used to frontier life."

"Vincent, no!"

"Oh, yes, my dear. Aren't you, Stephen? He's looking forward to it. There are many things for him to learn."

Stephen glanced apprehensively from one to the other. His mother had a silent plea in her eyes, a helplessness that reminded him of their long years together at Shevley House when her protectiveness had become an obsession, when her dependence on him had been her fragile anchor during severe emotional storms. Their mutual reliance on one another had been their salvation, and he saw that she had not changed. They needed each other now more than ever. In contrast, his father's expression was hard and determined.

"You're looking forward to it, are you not, Stephen?" he demanded.

"He's too young, Vincent. He has his whole life before him. Why rush into this?"

"He is big and strong. Other youngsters his age shoulder the responsibilities of grown men. He's old enough. A week or so in the woods will do him no harm."

There was a sense of self-assurance in his tone that brought a steely glint to Eleanor's eyes, forcing a trump from Vincent's hand.

"And he's much too soft, too bookish," he said.

"I think we should discuss this later," Eleanor said.

And so they did. From his bed in the loft Stephen heard their muffled voices, the cold, clipped sound of his mother's determination, the resonant insistence of his father. But while her attitude was unwavering, his anger rose to a fiery pitch, before falling at last into smoldering resignation. The slam of the bedroom door brought sudden silence, but Stephen found it difficult to sleep.

*   *   *

Vincent was up before dawn on the appointed day. It was still dark when Stephen heard the horse and wagon draw up in front of the cabin. Ben McAlpine called out and in minutes the wagon departed. During his father's absence Stephen busied himself around the cabin, and on a sunny morning his mother packed a lunch of fried chicken and buttered biscuits and they walked the mile and a half to

Shevley House West for a picnic. The structure was even more impressive as it grew near completion. The yard had been tilled and planted and gardeners were installing infant shrubbery at the carriage entrance and along the driveway approach. Several grand oak trees had been left in place, including an especially large one that shaded the veranda where they sat to enjoy their lunch. Inside they found that the parlor's mahogany walls were being polished until they gleamed. The room was dominated by a massive fireplace dwarfed only by the piles of packing crates in the center of the room. The markings and bills of lading bore such names as New York, Boston, and New Orleans. One intriguing crate was stamped with bold letters proclaiming it had been sent from Paris, France. The boxes contained the furnishings and decorations for the mansion whose hardwood floors still were strewn with sawdust and shavings, and tracked by the dusty footprints of carpenters, cabinetmakers, and masons. Eleanor marveled at the immensity of the kitchen where a black iron range had been installed. She delighted in arranging each room with imaginary furniture, making it plain to Stephen that his music lessons would be resumed just as quickly as she could get a piano installed in the parlor. At one point she sank exhausted onto a crate and exclaimed, "How will I ever be able to care for it all! I wish Hannah were with us. I'll never be able to do it alone." And when she saw the long table in the dining room she planned their first dinner party, showing precisely where each guest would sit, and how the table would be laid.

"Good heavens! Who will we invite? Let's see, there's Mr. Whitcomb, of course. He's such a learned man. And Jonathan Wells...but your father hasn't even met him yet! A military officer and a journalist – that's pretty good for a start. I suppose there will be others as time goes on, lawyers and judges and businessmen. Your father has mentioned business associates, and they must have wives. My, Stephen, won't it be wonderful to have a home of our own?"

It was only a matter of days before she arranged for a young lady to call at their cabin. She seemed a prim little thing with her jet-black hair pulled neatly into a pug and pinned tightly at the back of her head. Her eyes were snappy and alert, while a smile played enticingly at the corners of her mouth as if she were about to laugh out loud.

"Stephen, this is Miss Fairchild. She is to be your piano teacher."

"I'm very pleased to meet you, Stephen," the young lady said. "I must admit that I expected someone much younger."

"How do you do, m'am," he said, quickly withdrawing his hand from her warm, gentle grasp. "But we don't have a piano yet."

"I like a practical young man," she said, smiling happily. "But I *do* have a piano. It is old and somewhat the worse for wear, but I tune it myself and you'll find it adequate until yours arrives."

It was arranged that he would call at her house in St. Anthony village each Wednesday afternoon from three until four o'clock until such time as an appropriate instrument was installed in Shevley House West. The ladies then embarked on an animated discussion about the new Shevley home until at last it was time for Miss Fairchild to depart. She took Stephen's hand briefly at the door, again expressing her delight that he was to be her student.

"I must invite Miss Fairchild to our dinner party," Eleanor said the moment the young lady was gone. But Stephen paid no attention, preoccupied as he was with his new teacher's bright blue eyes that lingered hauntingly in his memory.

*   *   *

Vincent returned on a Sunday night. He was alone in the rig, which he left at the door; the horses still in halter. He came in without a word, and collapsed into a chair. He was filthy and red-eyed and smelled of sweat and pine smoke and tobacco. His leather jacket and leggings were smeared with pitch. His beard was thick and his moustache scraggly. He threw his hat in the direction of the coat hooks by the door and let out a groan that spoke eloquently of a week of labor under the hot summer sun, of short, restless nights in the open, of meals over campfires, of pesky mosquitoes and aching muscles. He offered no greeting as such. His first words were, "God, but I'm tired."

Eleanor studied him with a mixed expression of pity and distaste.

"We're pleased that you're home safely," she said. Stephen feared that she would say how happy she was that her son had not gone along and returned in such a state, but she seemed to swallow the words, digest them and allowed them to emerge in quite another form. "Stephen has been quite helpful since you left."

Vincent looked at him with dull eyes and an expression that that seemed contemptuous.

"I'll put some water on for a bath," Eleanor said.

"Fine," Vincent replied. "A bath, a shave, a good dinner – and some sleep. That will be welcome."

"You shouldn't have worked so hard," she said tentatively, as if treading on treacherous ground.

"It was the long drive back," he said. "We worked until late into the evening, then drove all night. I had to be back to attend to business. Have to see Whitcomb about advertising for a crew. God, the timber up there is unbelievable. The forests go on forever. Have to think about another expansion at the mill. Stephen, see to the horses." He stood up, heavy with weariness, and stretched. Stephen could hear his shoulders crack. "And trim my lamp," he added. "I have work to do tonight."

At supper he was a different man. Bathed, shaved, and with an hour's nap, he was now alert and clear-eyed. He listened attentively to Eleanor's plan for a dinner party. His enthusiasm grew, and he even offered another name for her guest list, Dr. Ames, saying he was a friend from his earliest days in the territory.

"Is there a Mrs. Ames?" Eleanor asked hopefully.

"There's a shortage of women. I've asked Grace Fairchild to attend. I can pair her with Jonathan Wells."

"Yes, there is a Mrs. Ames. Who's Jonathan Wells?"

"He the officer at Fort Snelling who rescued Stephen the day those Indians were captured. He befriended us on our journey from Rock Island."

"Oh, yes, I remember. And who is Grace Fairchild?"

"She lives in St. Anthony. She's to be Stephen's piano teacher."

"What?" he asked with a disdainful glance at his son.

"Stephen will resume the lessons I began at Shevley House."

"That's nonsense," Vincent snorted.

"Your brothers were both accomplished musicians."

"What do they have to do with it?"

"They were taught by your mother. They told me so. Gideon played at Christmas. Surely you remember."

"Of course I remember, but they have nothing to do with Stephen. He'll learn the lumbering business, and music be damned."

"Vincent!"

They finished the meal in silence. Vincent spent the rest of the evening at the table poring over his maps, while Eleanor quietly washed the dishes and Stephen dried them. The clatter of a single dish drew a disapproving frown from his father. When Vincent at last arose from the table and headed for the bedroom, he announced:

"You're going to the mill with me in the morning, son. You'd better turn in soon."

"Yes, sir."

*   *   *

With great relief Stephen threw himself eagerly into his work at the mill. His enthusiasm soon warmed the cold heart of his father, although it was not to please him that Stephen labored so industriously. No task would have been too large, no challenge too great. He was nearly fifteen years old, after all, and ready for a man's burden and the pleasures it might bring. He was ready for anything, all childish fears miraculously behind him. He smiled readily, laughed idiotically at the slightest provocation, tore down the wall of deference that other workers built up against the boss's son. He cast off the shell of self-consciousness that enclosed him, and charged hell-bent into his tasks. Vincent watched from the sidelines, plainly pleased, but Stephen was oblivious to him. The bright blue eyes and the alabaster skin, the alluring smile and the warm and tender hands were vivid in his memory. The only thing that mattered now was Wednesday afternoon. He worked as usual that morning, then rushed home for lunch. He ate sparingly, impatiently, then studied the music book for half an hour, humming quietly to himself as his mind roved far more harmonious fields. He scrubbed, combed and polished, all under his mother's watchful and curious eye, and then dressed in his best trousers, his white shirt and his black shoes, all of which seemed a bit snug since he'd last worn them. At the door his mother felt compelled to adjust a few strands of hair that he had carefully arranged. Then she sent him on his way.

In no time at all he found himself standing on the porch of a tiny white frame house, nervously fingering the brim of his cap. Though the toes of his shoes sparkled in the sunlight, he bent his lanky frame and brushed the glistening leather with his cap. He adjusted his belt buckle so it was exactly centered, and spanked his trousers to dispel imagined dust. Then he ran his fingers slowly, carefully through his hair, smoothing it above his ears as he turned this way and that, observing his reflection in the brass knocker. Then, suddenly self-conscious, he whirled about and looked up and down the street. Some children romped at the end of the road and far off in the distance a horseman loped down the hill toward the St. Paul road. No one had witnessed his display of vanity. He reached out with trembling hand and raised the knocker, pausing midway as his pulse raced and his throat swelled. Then the knocker fell with a clang. He leaped back and had but an instant to regain his composure before the door opened.

"Yes?" she said with a pleasant ring to her voice. "Oh, Stephen, it's you. Won't you please come in?"

The way she said his name thrilled him. She gave it a romantic aura, a heroic quality that it had never had before. He stared at his shoes, his feet leaden.

"How nice to see you again," she said, holding the door wide. His eyes began traveling upward, timidly at first, then boldly until they met hers. He could feel his cheeks grow hot as he stepped quickly past her into the small, neat parlor. She closed the door behind him, still smiling brightly, and extended her hand. He grasped it gently, allowing her fingers to engage his full attention. They were long and shapely, the nails trim and pink; light blue veins shown faintly through the down-soft skin on the back of her hand.

"Well, we meet again," she whispered.

"Yes'm, ur, m'am."

"Your mother is such a charming woman."

"Yes, m'am."

"She said you studied for two years at home in Maine."

"Yes, m'am. She taught me."

"So she told me. She said you were on minuets."

"Yes, minuets."

"Well, then, let's begin by having you play something for me so I can see where to begin. Suppose you come over here to the piano, sit down on the bench, and leaf through the music book until you find a familiar piece, one that you like."

There was a musical quality to her voice, almost a lilt. It was the tone an adult might use to talk to a child, as if the words must be especially modulated in order to be understood. It was a false tone, and it disappointed him. In the parlor window he could see a sign that read, *Miss Fairchild's Nursery, 8 a.m. to noon. Piano Lessons, Afternoons.*

"This may be a battered old instrument," she said, "and it's far from new. But its tone is true, and I'm sure it'll do." She chuckled pleasantly at her unconscious rhyme, running her fingers along the keys in a gay tinkle of delight.

It was a delicious, exhausting hour, measured by the constant click, click, click of the metronome atop the piano. Thoughts raced madly through his mind, the sound of the music lost in a veritable stampede of emotion. The purring, caressing voice aroused him, enticed him. The soft hands sent a thrill of desire through him as they gently guided his own awkward fingers over the keys. The atmosphere in the warm room soon became oppressive. His hands grew moist and trembled. Her leg stirred beside his as her foot worked the pedals.

"No, no, here – like this."

She stood over his shoulder, leaning forward to reach the keys, guiding his hands as they pawed the keyboard. A wisp of her hair tickled his cheek, tantalizing him nearly beyond endurance. Then came a vigorous passage and the fullness of her bosom nestled warmly against his back in soft, fluid movement. A strange stirring arose in him, a sensation he had never known before.

When the hour was over he ran all the way to the river and stood mesmerized by the swirling waters as the ferry made its crossing. Then he walked slowly home, his heart still beating in time with the persistent click, click, click of the metronome.

*   *   *

"Be careful with that pottery, Stephen. Use plenty of straw. That's the way – into the barrel gently. We'll have to wait for your father. We can't possibly lift it. We'll pack it gently, but firmly, and wait for your father."

"We could tip it a little and roll it to the door," he suggested.

"Oh, I think not. It might shatter everything. What if it should slip from your grip? It would be a disaster. I don't know why I worry about pottery. There's fine china awaiting us at home. No! Not that green vase! I'll carry it on my lap. There I go again, treating a piece of inexpensive cut glass as if it were fine crystal. But it's important to me, nevertheless. I couldn't bear to see it broken."

She took the vase from him and held it up to the light as she so often did, turning it slowly, and watching the light shine through it. She placed it on the table and looked about the cabin.

"What a dreadful place this has become – so empty, so plain. I don't know how we survived. What have you left in the loft? Better look again. We'll not be coming back, thank the good Lord."

Next morning as the church bell echoed dimly across the river from St. Anthony they loaded the wagon, and left the cabin forever. Stephen sat with his back pressed against the barrel, bracing it as the wagon jolted down the road. Eleanor cradled the green glass vase in her lap, while Vincent guided the team toward Shevley House West. It stood majestically in the clearing, its topmost gables at eye level with the neighboring oaks. He stopped at the foot of the marble stairway and handed Stephen the latchkey.

"Help your mother down, and open the door for her. I'll take this load around to the back entrance."

The huge door swung open silently on well-oiled hinges to reveal a bright, spacious entryway. The dust and litter of construction were gone, and the floors glistened. To the right a curved stairway ascended to the upper floors. To the left a gingerbread arch led from the front hall into the high-ceilinged parlor, beyond which lay the dining room, its beamed ceiling and paneled walls giving it the appearance of ancient elegance. Behind the dining room were the kitchen and pantry, and another doorway that led down a side hall to the entryway again. Also through this door were the back stairs, and along the side hall a row of doorways opened into storage rooms and one larger room outfitted to serve as living quarters for household help. On the second floor Stephen and his mother explored the master bedroom which stretched across the front of the house. The huge room was complete with a tiled fireplace and French doors that opened onto a balcony overlooking the grounds. Down the hall in the rear was a second bedroom that Eleanor said would be Stephen's own. He saw with satisfaction that his door was just at the top of the back stairs, a mere skip and a hop from the kitchen below. His windows faced west and overlooked a hillside covered with oaks. Beyond lay the large pond where he remembered skipping a flat stone the day of his Indian adventure. In the distance he knew lay the village of Minneapolis, hidden now by the heavy foliage of the grove of oaks. He especially liked the oaks. They reminded him of Maine, and in his reverie he thought he heard old Williams chuckling.

*   *   *

Each day during those first weeks in Shevley House West wagons laden with crates and cartons lumbered up the trail to deposit the trappings of a palace. Vincent supplied the services of two strapping workmen from the mill to help with the heavier objects, but those two worthies – and one perplexed youth – were no match for one frantic woman. By the end of the first week Eleanor pleaded for help of another kind.

"Vincent, I'm ever so grateful for their help, but how wonderful it would be if only another woman...let's see, how can I explain it...if only I had a woman with whom I could discuss things. I can't talk to these men, as kind and polite as they are. A woman would understand."

"I know how difficult it must be," Vincent acknowledged. "I will see what I can do."

The very next morning, as Eleanor and Stephen stepped out the front door for another assault on the gathering pile of furnishings they found perched atop a crate a skinny waif of no more than nine or ten years. She had blond curls that hung to her waist, and wore a blue bonnet that shaded her face from the early morning sunlight. She got down from the crate, smoothed her skirt, and held forth a bouquet of wild flowers.

"How do you do, m'am," she said, curtsying prettily.

"Sarah, for heaven's sake, I told you not to lift the knocker!" said a round, red-faced woman wearing a quaint straw hat. She clutched a moth-eaten shawl about her shoulders as she hurried up the steps to the entry. "I asked her not to disturb you m'am. I was just takin' a look around back to see if there was a servants' entrance, but there was no one to answer the door. You see, Mr. Vincent Shevley said we were to come out this mornin', but I didn't know but what you'd still be abed, and not wantin' to be disturbed just yet. This here's my girl, Sarah, and I'm Mrs. Mathilda Carpenter. Mr. Vincent Shevley said we'd find plenty to do hereabouts, if you found us to your likin'. We work hard, we do, and we believe in moderation in all things. And Sarah's mannerly, she truly is, mannerly and quiet, and she can sew and wash dishes, and make a bed, and dust..."

Eleanor fairly reeled with this introduction, recovered quickly, and grasped Mrs. Carpenter's hands, which had been waving this way and that as if to orchestrate her cantata of words.

"Mrs. Carpenter, we are very happy to meet you and Sarah. I am Mrs. Shevley, and this is my son, Stephen. We were dreading yet another day of opening boxes and hanging pictures, and arranging furniture, and so it is a delightful surprise to discover you here at our door. You are most welcome, and must come in for tea and toast while we get acquainted. Have you had your breakfast yet?"

"As a matter of fact we have not," said the talkative Mrs. Carpenter, "and a cup of tea and a bit of toast would be most welcome, indeed. But you mustn't trouble yourself, for we came to be a help, not a hindrance. Follow along there, Sarah, and let Mrs. Vincent Shevley lead the way."

"Take Mrs. Carpenter's bag, Stephen. I presume that you'll be living in."

"That was the understanding, m'am, if you should find us acceptable. That's what Mr. Vincent Shevley had in mind, or so he said. Such a kind and generous man he is. Comin' to our rescue in our moment of need, grievin' and destitute and trustin' in the Lord God for our daily bread ever since He called my dear husband to His side, He did, the Lord God, I mean."

"Oh! How terribly sorry we are to hear..."

"It's past now, m'am, and poor Michael's found a better life, I'm sure, poor hard workin' man that he was. But he trusted in Mr. Vincent Shevley, and advised us to do the same, and the Lord has shown us the way. So generous he is, Mr. Vincent Shevley, I mean."

"Yes, yes, indeed. But just now let's have a cup of tea while we chat a bit. Stephen, take Mrs. Carpenter's bag to the maid's room and pump some water so she and Sarah can refresh themselves."

For more than an hour they sat engrossed by the rambling account Mrs. Carpenter gave of her life. She preceded each segment of her story with protestations of embarrassment and humility, in deference to her new patrons. Her home, she said, was in Ireland, but the famine had driven her and her sisters to emigrate to the land of plenty. They had settled first in the slums of New York, which she described as more dreadful years of poverty, before moving to Chicago where she had lived most of her life, and where she and her sisters earned their reputations as honest, hard-working and reliable household help.

"We worked some of the grandest homes on the North Side, we did. The O'Brien girls, they called us. Oh, my sisters and I were much sought after, we were. Mary Margaret was in charge, she being the oldest; Kathleen and I learned everything from her. Started as cleaning women, we did – you can imagine how it was for poor Irish girls alone in a strange land – and ended as serving women the likes of which you've never seen. Every night we were called upon for one party or another, being picked up by hansom cabs and delivered home again when cleanup was done."

She would stop now and then to nibble at her toast and marmalade and to daintily sip her tea before continuing with her story.

"But Mary Margaret was the stable sort, and after a time got tired of traipsin' here and there, despite the pay and all, so she finally took to livin' in. I guess it was an easier life for her – she was crowdin' forty and single yet and still is – single, I mean, God bless her soul. Then Michael came along, and a devilishly handsome husky he was, all full of talk about movin' west and makin' his fortune. Oh, it all seems so long ago, so many long years ago. And lovin' his daughter, the light of his life, as he so often said."

Her bright, blue eyes softened, and she shook her head sadly as she gazed into the past. She paused, tears welling in her eyes, and brushed her daughter's curls gently, as if seeing her again as a baby in her father's arms.

"I'm so sorry," Eleanor said quietly, her hand touching Mrs. Carpenter's.

"Oh, don't be feelin' sorry for us, Mrs. Shevley. Michael warned us that his work was a danger, but it paid well, and he tried to do his best for us. He had a tidy sum put aside when – well, it's all over now, and Mr. Vincent Shevley has been so kind."

"Then your husband worked for Mr. Shevley?"

"Oh, yes, m'am. He did until the good Lord claimed him and he crossed over to a far better place. He's been gone for several months now, and it's not easy here for a widow and a child these days. But Mr. Vincent Shevley was always askin' after us, and never let us go hungry, not on your life. And now this – work to do, and a roof over our heads. It's almost too good to be true. Of course, with your own generous approval, m'am."

"I'm sure we will get along very well, Mrs. Carpenter. So come, let's get you settled into your room – you and Sarah. Such a lovely child, such a little lady."

Sarah preceded them down the hall, her curls bouncing, and stood demurely aside as Eleanor and Mrs. Carpenter entered the maid's room. Stephen stopped at the doorway and nodded politely for Sarah to enter the room. But she blushed and stood aside, so he shrugged and stepped in ahead of her. As he passed her he felt a sharp pinch in his ribs which caused him to gasp.

"Stephen, what is it?" Eleanor asked.

"Nothing, Mother. It was nothing," he said, as Sarah giggled quietly in the hallway shadows.

Chapter 6

Eleanor's dinner party was to be on the second Saturday in August, and she could hardly contain her excitement. It would be her first opportunity to meet Vincent's friends, and to share with him the only friends she could claim as her own. She enlisted Stephen's help in carrying an invitation to Grace Fairchild on his weekly visit to her home for his piano lesson. He was thrilled when Miss Fairchild indicated her delight, and the following week he happily carried home to his mother his teacher's neatly penned acceptance. Getting an invitation to Jonathan Wells was another matter. She would need Vincent's help.

"Of course I know who he is. I made it a point to find out after you said you knew him. But as for carrying an invitation to him, I don't know. It would be highly irregular. We haven't even met. I'm not exactly on good terms with the officers at Fort Snelling. My dealings with the army have not been pleasant. Do you realize that the military claims the property on which this house is built? As far as they're concerned, we're squatters. Can you imagine? I've been trying for months to get them to recognize the rights of settlers like us. When I first staked a claim here they tried to drive me out with bayonets! It's been a running battle ever since, figuratively speaking. They claim thousands of acres more than they need, but do you think they'd give up a parcel of it without a fight? That's not likely. I don't take kindly to entertaining an army officer under my roof, but if you feel you must invite him in order to pay a debt of gratitude, then I'll take it with me on my next visit to the fort, and I'll see that he gets it."

*   *   *

A dirge-like roll of drums silenced the crowd of observers as a guard detail marched onto the plain escorting two stumbling Indians chained at the ankles. The drumbeat stopped, and an officer faced the Indians and read aloud the charges against them. Then the chains were unlocked the prisoners stood proudly erect, ignoring the crowd that had come to witness their execution. A group of tribesmen in colorful dress moved to the forefront to watch the proceedings. Some fifty yards distant stood two poles connected by a red ribbon pulled taut at chest level. The officer, standing abreast of the hapless convicts, raised his sword into the air while the firing squad took aim at the prisoners' backs. When the officer's sword swept down, the Indians galloped off with a wild yelp, racing toward the ribbon, zigzagging and raising a cloud of dust. The troopers wavered, attempting to hold their aim. The instant the first Indian struck and snapped the ribbon in his flight for life, a volley rang out. The second Indian leaped into the air with a cry and fell onto the dusty plain. The lead Indian continued his run toward a distant line of trees at the edge of the plain, haltingly now as if dragging an unseen burden. Finally he slowed to a stagger, then stopped, whirled about to face his executioners, and emitted a defiant, blood-curdling whoop. Then he sank to his knees and pitched forward into the dirt. A murmur ran through the crowd. The stern-faced Indian delegation marched resolutely out onto the field to attend to their dead, while the officer led his troopers off toward the barracks.

"Well, that was quite an exhibition. Perhaps now Lieutenant Wells can spare me a moment of his time," Vincent said as he made his way through the crowd.

*　　*　　*

Charles Whitcomb arrived early, even before Eleanor had descended to greet her guests. Vincent let him in and led him into his office for a whiskey and water. Stephen could hear the men talking and laughing when he came downstairs in his best suit of clothes. He ambled into the parlor to plink at the piano keys. Sarah tiptoed in with a finger to her lips.

"Shhhh!" she cautioned. "I'm supposed to be watching the stove."

Stephen eyed her diffidently and shrugged.

"Are you ready to play?" she whispered.

"Sure."

"You're not scared?"

"No. Why should I be?"

"In front of all the guests?"

"They don't matter."

"I bet your father will be furious."

"He might be," Stephen acknowledged. "It's Miss Fairchild's idea, and it's supposed to be a surprise."

"It will be to your father; I've heard him carrying on."

"You should mind your own business."

"May I listen?"

"Of course not. You're supposed to be in the kitchen."

"I could leave the door ajar."

He continued to plink quietly at the keys, lolling on the bench, lost in thought.

"If you're not scared, what then?" she asked.

"Go away, Sarah. Leave me alone."

"You look fine, dressed up and all. Maybe that's it – Miss Fairchild will be here tonight."

Stephen whirled on her angrily.

"What do you care about that?" he demanded. "It's none of your business. Go back to the kitchen, and leave me alone."

"I didn't mean to make you angry. I'm sorry. All I meant was, its kind of scary, isn't it, with your teacher looking on? I mean, I'd be scared, I know I would."

"Oh, that's what you meant. No, I won't be scared."

"I know you'll do very well. I've heard you practicing. Can I listen? Can I leave the door ajar?"

"Sure, if you want to," he relented.

"Oh, Stephen, I just know you'll be wonderful!"

They both heard a carriage pulling up in front, followed by voices. Mrs. Carpenter scurried past the parlor door, hurrying to answer at the first knock.

"You'd better get back now," Stephen advised. "You don't want your mother to see you."

Sarah skipped out of the room with her blond curls bobbing. Mrs. Carpenter could be heard greeting Doctor Ames and his wife, and Grace Fairchild, who had ridden out from the village with the Ameses. As they entered Eleanor appeared at the landing where the chandelier bathed her in a golden light that sparkled in her eyes and upon the modest jewelry she wore. Vincent came out of his office at the same moment with Whitcomb on his heels, the editor peering over the top of his spectacles and out from under an unruly thatch of graying hair. Vincent was beaming with pleasure, bowing to the ladies and extending his hand to Doctor Ames. He introduced Whitcomb to the new arrivals.

"It is an honor to welcome you to our home at last. A debt of long standing now begins to be repaid," Vincent said, reaching out with both hands to envelop Doctor and Mrs. Ames in the warmth of his greeting. Grace Fairchild, whose pale beauty was enhanced by a gown of royal blue, demurely met the master of the mansion.

"Your presence fills this house with music that puts your pupil to shame, my dear girl," Vincent purred.

The knocker fell again and Mrs. Carpenter admitted Lieutenant Wells, an imposing figure in his dress uniform with its polished brass buttons. He bowed to Eleanor who came forward to welcome him, glowing with admiration as she introduced him all around. Next she ushered the party into the parlor where she introduced Stephen and offered sherry while they awaited the call to dinner.

*　　*　　*

George Ames was an improbable denizen of that rough frontier. A small man of cherubic mien, soft and somewhat pudgy, he seemed better suited as heir to his father's established medical practice in Philadelphia that he had left behind to settle in the rustic village of Minneapolis. But he counted himself among the earliest pioneers on the west bank of the Mississippi, having arrived in the spring of 1850 with his delicate bride at his side. He had built one of the first wood frame houses near the falls, and began immediately to provide medical services to the community. Though his talents were much in demand, he found time to indulge his interest in politics. He was a prime mover in the election of a territorial delegate to the Congress of the United States to plead the cause of statehood, and currently was a member of the constitutional convention in St. Paul, a convention deadlocked over how the proposed new state was to be formed and governed. The disputation brought parliamentary chaos to the convention floor and thus had been entrusted to a committee of compromise with George Ames himself as chairman. Statehood became a topic of conversation at Eleanor's dinner.

"Tell us, George," Whitcomb asked over soup, "what progress has been made behind those closed doors of yours? We have heard nothing since the convention was dissolved."

"May I correct you on one point, Charles? The convention was not dissolved. It was recessed so that a smaller and more manageable group of delegates might bring our differences to a speedy resolution. I can tell you – and you may tell your readers – that the constitution is very nearly a reality."

"My readers are interested in specifics, George, and are upset by the secrecy that surrounds your negotiations. I'm afraid that your reassurances, however well intentioned, will not satisfy them."

"The specifics of the convention as a whole, duly reported in your columns, failed to satisfy them either," the doctor noted with a twinkle in his eye. "Such honesty and accuracy as you displayed is to be commended, despite the wrath it brought down upon our heads."

"I was only doing my job," Whitcomb said. "There are many who felt that the quarrels that disrupted your initial efforts were somewhat petty in nature and quite beside the matter of establishing statehood. Those same readers now wonder if similar quarrels are being carried on in the privacy of your committee meetings."

"No, they are not. We are proceeding in a business-like manner, but we feel that the glare of publicity might rekindle the disputes that disrupted the initial proceedings. We will have a draft of a state constitution ready to present to the convention by mid-week, I promise you. Tell your readers this and counsel patience and trust in their representatives."

"What he's saying, Charlie, is call off your dogs," Vincent interjected. "Give them a chance to do their job. If you want to crusade, why not take on the army. Take up your pen against the generals in Washington, D.C., who refuse to let go of the very land we're sitting on. Splatter your ink on those brass-buttoned bounders who'd let land lie idle rather than see it properly developed."

Stephen glanced at Jonathan Wells, whose face reddened under Vincent's jibes.

"I have very few readers in Washington," Whitcomb allowed. "But perhaps Lieutenant Wells could enlighten us on the status of our claims."

"I'm afraid I have little influence on such weighty matters," said Jonathan. "I'm just a line officer. The land issue is well beyond my purview. I've heard it said, however, that it's only a matter of time before the boundary lines of the military reservation are redrawn and the land in question turned over to civilian claimants. Until the government acts, I believe the army will continue its generous policy of permitting limited settlement on military land."

"Generous!" thundered Vincent. "We're supposed to be grateful to them, is that it?" He reddened and began muttering and shaking his head, groping for words to express his indignation. At last it came to him. "You ascribe a certain benevolence to the army, Lieutenant. Your job here, I believe, is to protect the settlers and administer Indian affairs. I witnessed the army's benevolence and the manner in which it handles the Indians just this week. I believe you were directly involved in that incident."

"I was only carrying out orders," Jonathan bristled. "The two Indians who were executed were convicted murderers. Their conviction was ordered by a court martial. Their punishment was arrived at in consultation with the elders of their tribe."

"You shot them down like fleeing dogs!"

"They admitted to the court that they murdered an army employee in order to steal government property."

"Did it occur to the officers in charge that having them shot might bring on acts of retaliation against the civilian population?" His fist hammered the table as he cried, "You were inciting the Indians to war!"

Jonathan's patience reached its limit. Straining against an impulse to counterattack, he arose and bowed politely to Eleanor before addressing his tormentor.

"Sir, I am honored to be a guest in your home, but I can see that my presence antagonizes you. I extend my most sincere apology to all present, and beg your permission to be excused."

Flushed with embarrassment and fighting back tears, Eleanor arose and followed Jonathan into the hall. "Jonathan, oh, Jonathan, I'm so sorry – please!"

"My dear Mrs. Shevley, it is I who am sorry for spoiling your party. If only I had been aware of his feelings. Whatever his frustrations in dealing with the army, I'm afraid he's allowed it to prejudice his attitude toward me. I'm sorry, but there's very little I can do – except leave."

Mrs. Carpenter appeared and got the officer's coat from the hall closet. She nodded sympathetically to Eleanor, a tear in her eye, and opened the door for Jonathan. He left without looking back.

Vincent was profuse in his apologies.

"It was nothing personal," he explained. "I know the young officer can't do a thing about it, but it's a sore subject with me. I should have kept my mouth shut."

"Yes," Eleanor agreed emphatically, glaring at her husband as her dinner guests looked about in embarrassment. Stephen could plainly see the pain in his mother's eyes. The flower of love that he had seen struggle through the soil of neglect and indifference suddenly seemed to wither and die.

*   *   *

"Lordy, lordy, I've never seen the likes of it, never, never."

Mrs. Carpenter's voice awakened Stephen from a troubled sleep. He dressed quickly, listening to the shuffle of footsteps going up the back stairs, then down again to the kitchen. He could hear the clatter and clang of the stove plates and a stream of chatter. By the time he entered the hall Mrs. Carpenter was on her way up the stairs again with a tray and tea service.

"It's none of my business," she puffed as she plodded past him, "none of my business at all. But lordy, lordy why didn't she tell me?"

"Tell you what?" he called after her as she headed up to the third floor.

"Never you mind," she called back. "Your breakfast is waiting in the kitchen. Sarah can get you whatever you need. Now get on with you. Lordy, lordy!"

"What's going on?" he asked Sarah as she brought the cream for his oatmeal mush.

"It's your mother. She spent the night in that empty front bedroom on the third floor – no bedclothes, no fire. And with all that rain and dampness last night she been taken with the chills."

It all came back to him then. The scene at the dinner table had cast a pall over the party. Eleanor had forged bravely ahead, insisting that he present a short recital before the other guests departed. He did his best, but it was obvious that his audience was uncomfortable and eager to leave. Later in the darkness of his room he found himself unable to sleep. He welcomed the howling wind that blew in a downpour, for the sound of it drowned out the angry voices that echoed down the hall from his parents' bedroom. He remembered hearing the door slam and sound of footsteps

93

ascending to the third floor. The half-forgotten sadness was upon him again with all its oppressiveness. In the distance a church bell pealed, its ringing muffled by the dank morning air. The skies were gray and utterly cheerless, and it would have been easy to cry. Sarah took the chair opposite his and leaned forward until her chin nearly touched the table. Her eyes glowed with excitement.

"I loved your recital last night," she whispered breathlessly. "It was wonderful. Everyone said so."

"Do you really think so?"

"Of course I do. It was very, very nice. I was so proud of you! Mama caught me at the kitchen door and didn't say anything to me until you finished. Oh, Stephen, you were very good."

Her flattery snagged his pride and abruptly halted his plunge into melancholia. At the same time, it embarrassed him.

"You oughtn't to carry on that way," he said. "I just do it to please mother. What's a fellow like me doing playing the piano? My father's right. It's just a lot of nonsense. I'd be better off working in the woods."

"Gee, do you think you'll really be going into the woods?"

"Don't know why not. I'm big enough, and I'm strong, so they say. Why not?"

"I think you'd be good as any man."

"And you'd know, wouldn't you?" he asked hopefully. "I mean, your father was a logger, wasn't he?"

"Yes, he was."

"And he liked being a logger, didn't he?"

"He did, or so my mother says."

"How...how did he die?"

"Well," Sarah said in a conspiratorial whisper, "I heard my mother tell the saddle maker's wife that a whole pile of logs fell on him. She said he didn't have an unbroken bone left in his body. They carried him into town in a wagon and he was all bloody and staring off into space and not saying a word until Mama came and stood over him. Then he

just looked up at her and said, 'Thank God you're here' –
and then he died, just like that!"

She snapped her fingers with a startling crack that
made him jump. A chill went down his spine as her wide-
eyed stare transfixed him. He shook his head and pushed
away from the table, heading for the door.

"I've got to clean the stable," he said, pausing with
his hand on the doorknob. "Sarah?"

"Yes?"

"There's always school, too, you know. I mean, I've
got the rest of my life to work in the woods. And schooling
never hurt anyone."

"Schooling never did, that's true," Sarah agreed
sagely.

*   *   *

Vincent, in perverse exaggeration of his concern
about his wife's pleurisy, which lingered into the autumn
months, lavished money on the third floor bedroom where
she chose to languish. It was a spacious room with a large
fireplace and gabled alcoves with tall windows that looked
down upon the front gardens. He furnished it royally. Rich
tapestries were hung upon the paneled walls, while the
canopied bed was dressed in silk and lace. Velvet draperies
graced the windows and a carpet of intricate design covered
the floor. The long, narrow room easily accommodated a
couch, several comfortable chairs, a table and a writing desk
upon which Eleanor displayed her green glass vase. After six
weeks, when her cough had subsided and the tightness in her
lungs abated, she still appeared wan and wasted, her delicate
beauty enhanced by her pallor, her eyes the more startlingly
alive for the dark hollows into which they seemed to recede.
Her golden hair took on a sheen by virtue of repeated
brushings, for she spent much of the morning at her vanity,
staring into the glass and beyond. She came fully to life only
in the late afternoon, when Stephen visited her after his work
at the mill was done. He read to her, talked with her,

95

comforted her beyond the limits of boyish sincerity, while she braced her sagging spirit against him and drained from him a measure of his youth. During their hours together she seldom missed an opportunity to encourage him toward education, and to warn him against the dangers of life in the logging camps. She was jubilant when she learned that a school had been established, and that classes were scheduled for the winter months. She was determined that Stephen attend.

*   *   *

In 1853 an itinerant preacher stopped off with his family to try his luck with a plow in the rich soil of the Mississippi River valley. He failed miserably as a farmer, but he succeeded in drawing around him a congregation of earnest and devout souls hungry for the word of the Lord. These parishioners in turn succeeded in persuading the preacher to remain in the community in order to share his knowledge of the Bible and its teachings. He was, they convinced him, the only resident with sufficient intellect to undertake the education of their children. An abandoned cabin was appropriated to serve as a schoolhouse, and steps were taken to secure a stipend for the Rev. Mr. Tobias Tubman. Eleanor was quick to lend her support to the new school, and Stephen found it easy to share her enthusiasm, since the alternative appeared to be a winter in the logging camps. It was easy to convince Charles Whitcomb of the need for a school in the community, and he was quick to use the power of the press to secure funds to that end. Vincent also joined the ranks of contributors, believing it might in some way help to lure his wife from her aerie of illness back to the warmth of the conjugal nest. So it was that by the workings of subtle and well-intentioned conspiracies that the Rev. Mr. Tubman found himself seated at the Shevleys' dinner table one cold and blustery evening in early October. The price of his supper was to undergo an interrogation by the master of the house, while the mistress listened in a state of smug satisfaction.

"It has been a good year for the farmers, Mr. Tubman, a bountiful season, according to reports reaching my office. How is it that you are deserting the fields?"

The lean, sharp-featured guest cast his eyes heavenward as if in search of divine guidance, then looked Vincent square in the eye.

"The tribulations of Job were visited upon me, sir, and in my agony I saw the hand of God."

"How so, reverend?"

"I looked upon the Lord's earth with greed in my heart and He harvested my pride, cut me down as with a scythe. Each to his own calling, sayeth the Lord."

"So you're responding now to God's calling."

"I am, sir. On the one hand He has shown me that I am not a farmer, for He has allowed others to prosper and caused me to fail. On the other hand He has sent me a flock of the faithful that has gathered around me as to a shepherd. Though God has punished me for my earthly ambitions, He has shown me the way to redemption. 'Stay and lead,' is His commandment to me, and it is mine to obey."

"Then you have decided to remain to lead your flock and to educate the children."

"Yes, but there are certain considerations..."

"Considerations?"

"The Lord has not asked me to prepare an altar before Him in order that I might offer up my family as sacrifice. I am charged with the care of a wife and six sons."

"Indeed!" Vincent exclaimed, trying to hide his amusement. "You mean you are obliged to support them."

"Yes, I must. It was the good Lord who blessed me with a large family. He certainly did not intend that they should starve."

"No, I'm sure He didn't. But did He also endow you with special qualifications for your new calling?"

"I bring what poor knowledge He has given me, plus a certificate of graduation from the Haley Institute of Higher

Learning in Atlanta, Georgia. It attests to my mastery of the various fields of knowledge which are deemed important for the instruction of the young and inexperienced."

Tubman reached inside his long, black coat and withdrew a yellowed document and handed it to Vincent.

"Hmmm, I see," said Vincent, examining the paper. "And have you gained any worldly experience which might prove that God's trust is as well-placed as this degree would indicate?"

"My past experience is a matter of public record, sir, as recounted most recently in Mr. Whitcomb's journal, the same article in which he revealed that you have been elected to the school board."

"Yes, yes, well I must have missed that item. But then you'll have ample time to prove your merit, and I see no reason why we can't come to some sort of financial arrangement so you can proceed with this glorious experiment. As a matter of fact, Mr. Whitcomb and I will be meeting at three o'clock next Tuesday at my office to conclude these arrangements. If you will be so kind as to join us, we will establish a sum sufficient to support you and your family and ask for your signature to seal the bargain."

The somber preacher relaxed into the barest glimmering of a smile, although his pleasure scarcely showed in his stern eyes.

"There is one more matter," he said. "I will need permission to use the schoolhouse on Sundays to minister to my flock, and funds to keep it warm during the cold winter months."

"Of course, we will include your request in our deliberations on Tuesday."

"Tuesday at three, then," Tubman said with an air of relief.

Eleanor, whose feeble amiability had neared its limits as Vincent toyed with his prey, also breathed a sigh of relief. And thus was Stephen spared a rigorous winter in the woods.

*　　*　　*

Vincent's election to the school board brought him the admiration of the community, but succeeded only partially in restoring domestic tranquility. Eleanor began taking dinner with the family once again, and occasionally spent an hour or so after dinner in the parlor. But in her weakened condition she tired easily and generally retreated early to the comfort of her own room. Her only other excursion from her high haven was a daily walk with Stephen upon his return from school. When weather permitted they strolled in the garden; once the snow fell they walked the halls of Shevley House, Eleanor always leaning lightly on her son's arm for support. This modest evidence of her improved health was no indication, however, that she had returned to the mainstream of family life. Her relationship with her husband remained strained. Dinner table conversations were particularly difficult, much as if she walked a tight rope where one false step might plunge them all into quarrelsome chaos. The tension was enough to knot Stephen's stomach and spoil his appetite. Evenings in the parlor were no less onerous to him. He would try to lose himself in a book, but he was forever being interrupted by their curt exchanges. And later, when Eleanor was safely in her room, and he had nestled into his own bed, he would hear his father's footsteps as he climbed the stairs, halted at the door to the master bedroom briefly, then resumed his upward march to the third floor. In a moment Stephen would hear the latch on his mother's bedroom door rise with a sharp metallic clack, followed by a deathly stillness. Then came a fierce clattering that jarred the house and rattled his nerves as his father shook the bolted door with impotent fury. Next came his stomping descent, all the way downstairs, ending with the explosive slamming of his office door.

Autumn was mild, and frost was late in coming to the river valley. The afternoons grew shorter, but remained sunny and warm and the rose bushes gave forth an extra set of blooms as if in gratitude for their extended lease on life. The weather might have been blamed for an incident that occurred in early November when Eleanor lingered in the garden later than usual. Stephen had returned from school and was in his room studying. Mrs. Carpenter was in the kitchen preparing dinner. Sarah was in the parlor dusting when Jonathan Wells came up the drive on horseback, dismounted, and knocked at the door. Sarah answered and informed him that Mr. Vincent Shevley was not expected home for dinner.

"Then with Mrs. Shevley's permission, I'd like to speak to her. I have some important papers to deliver and she could convey them to her husband when he returns."

Sarah wrapped a shawl around her shoulders and led him around to the rear garden, tarrying just long enough to hear him explain to her mistress that the documents he carried were from army headquarters in Washington, D.C. They concerned the immediate release of certain lands within the military reservation to settlers with otherwise unencumbered claims. Those lands included the Shevley property, and Wells had volunteered to personally deliver the papers to Vincent in hopes of improving his opinion of the army. At this point Eleanor suggested to Sarah that she might make better use of her time elsewhere and the child heard nothing more of their conversation. A half-hour later Jonathan Wells suddenly appeared at the kitchen door, his face ashen, his eyes wild. He held Eleanor's frail body in his arms. From the parlor Sarah heard her mother gasp and as she ran into the kitchen she saw the officer striding up the back stairs with his burden while shouting orders back down to Mrs. Carpenter.

"Take the buggy and fetch Mr. Shevley quickly!" he commanded. "Tell him to bring Doctor Ames."

Mrs. Carpenter, with Sarah's help, managed to hitch a horse to the buggy and off they raced for the mill, with Mrs. Carpenter at the reins, fretting all the way. It was nearly an hour before they returned with Vincent, who had rejected their plea to bring Doctor Ames. As Vincent charged up the stairway he ran headlong into Lieutenant Wells as he emerged from Eleanor's bedroom. In a fury he struck the officer in the face, sending Jonathan reeling down several steps where he nearly collided with Mrs. Carpenter and Sarah. The officer got up slowly, blood streaming from his nose. He stood dazed for a moment while Vincent hurled imprecations at him, then threw down the papers he carried and stormed out of the house. Eleanor, who apparently had suffered little more than a fainting spell brought on by exertion, awoke later to find that the bolt had been removed from her door. That night there was a loud, emotional scene in her bedroom that sent Stephen scurrying for his room where he hid under his blankets to muffle his father's rage and his mother's tearful defense of her honor. The noisy quarrel nevertheless filled the lad with shame and heartbreak and was destined to change his relationship with both parents.

The incident also brought about a major transformation in Eleanor. At first she gave the impression of being a frightened, whipped animal, cowering and desperate for escape. There followed a brief period of moody silence in which she moved ghost-like through the house as if she were in the grip of some secret resolve. At last there began a period of blossoming as she slowly increased her involvement in the family routine, and finally a full flowering as her strength returned and she reached out into the community to take on new roles.

One noticeable result of her regeneration was an easing of tensions in Shevley House. Stephen was relieved to see his parents conversing without quarreling, seeming to enjoy each other's company. Eleanor even assumed an active role in Vincent's public life, penning the speech he delivered at the opening of the first suspension bridge across the Mississippi, and entertaining his business and political associates at dinner. Together with Amanda Ames she helped to establish the Athenaeum Society to promote the study of classical literature, and to work toward construction of a public library. She became a charter member of the Lyceum and its first secretary, and joined the new Episcopal parish, persuading Vincent and Stephen to join, too. Before long her several activities were keeping her away from home for many hours each week, and all with Vincent's blessing. Theirs was a very civil arrangement, polite despite an obvious lack of affection. She still maintained her own bedroom, although it no longer was a barred sanctuary. Occasionally in the dark of night Stephen would hear his father's footsteps on the stairs, hear the latch rise and fall, the door open and close. Outside crisp winds tugged at dying leaves and there was the smell of winter in the air. But Stephen slept warm and secure.

Chapter 7

When the land was covered with snow, and the farm children released from their labors to cultivate the no less fertile fields of the mind, Tobias Tubman opened school for a varied lot of more or less willing pupils. The preacher/teacher's personal contribution to the class was six sons, the youngest only ten years old, the eldest seventeen. At their father's bidding each laid aside his tools and took up his books for a three-month assault on the walled citadel of ignorance. Tall, raw-boned and hard in their father's image, they plodded through the winter drifts to the one-room cabin that served that year as a schoolhouse. Invariably the first students to arrive, one replenished the wood box while another hauled out the ashes of yesterday's fire. The third kindled the blaze for the new day and the next arranged the rustic benches. The fifth swept up the remnants of the previous day's battle – crumpled pages from copybooks, the newsprint wrapper of some country lad's sour cream sandwich, the inevitable spitballs, and in one corner a chewed piece of pork rind that had satisfied the late-afternoon hunger of some young frontiersman. The last and youngest of the Tubmans, being the least able to assert himself against the others, was assigned to walk a quarter-mile beyond the school to a nearby farm where water was drawn from a well to slake the thirst of the students. Returning, his water bucket glazed with ice, he would place it beside the cast iron stove, which by then held a roaring fire, presided over by seventeen-year-old Jeremiah Tubman, who was called Jerry by all who feared him, and therefore by all but his father.

The aspiring students, boys and girls of the village, and that portion of the rural population able to arrange for the trip into town, filed into the drafty building, hanging caps, coats, and mufflers on wooden pegs in the wall. The six Tubmans lined either side of the room, eyeing the newcomers sternly, silently bullying them into submission.

When all were seated the six took their permanent seats amid the throng, each positioned strategically so as to assist the schoolmaster in the discipline of the unenlightened mob.

A lecturer of ingratiating tone and condescending manner, Tobias Tubman was a careful administrator of his wards. Troublemakers were quickly identified and subdued by fearsome glares, with the exception of one country lad who had come armed with a large stick. He sat defiantly in the rear of the classroom throughout the first morning's lessons while six eager young Tubmans were restrained by their father from attacking him in force. The righteous Tobias called upon the Lord to witness the evils done unto him in his secular ministry by the agents of the devil, and bided his time with the rebel until noon. Then, caught unaware in the rush for coats and freedom, the defiant one was seized from behind by one of Tubmans, disarmed by another, and carried kicking and screaming into the schoolyard where he was beaten unmercifully by the terrible Jerry, to the delight of the student body. From the school steps Tobias Tubman looked upon the arena and called upon the Almighty to give him strength to chastise the wicked among them and to lead them into the ways of righteousness. He also admonished them all to be back at their benches promptly at one o'clock. By then the insurgent's blood stained the crusted snow, and he was ready to take his place among the meek and the penitent.

The beating served to establish Jeremiah's reputation as the mightiest in the class, in strength if not in wit. Disciplinary problems that arose thereafter needed only to be referred to the grinning brute in order to be speedily and peacefully resolved. Stephen remained the Tubmans' only cause for concern. Although apparently tranquil by nature, his height, his broad shoulders and the quick, easy movements of his well-muscled frame were an unspoken challenge to the peace of that tiny community. Now fifteen, he was more than two years younger than the sergeant-at-arms of the clan Tubman. His skin, lightly tanned by the past summer's sun, was soft and delicate, and his bright blue eyes seemed never to harbor a malicious thought. But under that unblemished skin rippled muscles honed by his labors at the mill, and behind the clear blue eyes lay an air of self-confidence that the Tubman boys found disconcerting and vaguely threatening. Their suspicions led them to a firm distrust of Stephen, who was assigned a seat on the aisle immediately in front of Jeremiah. There he sat each day, square-shouldered, erect and not in the least intimidated, displaying an unruffled mien that set him apart from his classmates. As the weeks passed, Jeremiah's curiosity could not be contained. He had to try this soft-spoken Titan, the last apparent challenge to his superiority. Recitation offered just such an opportunity.

"In all God's earth," intoned Tobias Tubman, "there exist several continents and many seas." He paused, and a deathly silence fell upon the room as his cold eyes scanned the frightened assemblage. A Mitchell's Atlas fell to the floor with a deafening crash somewhere in the rear of the room. No one dared breathe. A fidgeting passed among the students like ripples from a stone cast into a still pool. "Which seas, Master Shevley, are connected by the Dardanelles?"

Stephen leaned forward and stood slowly erect, gathering his thoughts. All eyes turned toward the victim, who appeared unperturbed by the schoolmaster's attention.

"The Dardanelles, sir, connect the Aegean Sea and the Sea of Mamara. In addition, sir, the Dardanelles separate European from Asiatic..."

"That will do," Tubman interrupted him. "Take your seat."

Jeremiah's loud whisper rasped in Stephen's ear in whining mimicry.

"In addition, sir, it also connects European and Asiatic..." He emphasized the phrase from the atlas, but Stephen ignored him. Suddenly a thumb jabbed him in the ribs and he uttered a startled gasp. Tobias Tubman stared down on him in amazement.

"What's this? What's this?" he stammered with comic rapidity. "Does young Master Shevley wish to speak further?"

"No, sir," said Stephen.

"Rise when you address me, rise!" exploded the outraged instructor. Stephen stood and met his angry gaze.

"I beg your pardon, sir. It was nothing. A chill must have come over me, that's all. I'm sorry."

"And I suppose you'd have me displace one of these tender young ladies that you might sit nearer the stove! Crass, crass youth. No chivalry, no decency. A sudden chill indeed. You will remain after school today." He paused, awaiting some sign of protest, but there was none.

"Yes, sir," said Stephen.

"Take your seat!" Tubman roared. "I'll tolerate no more disturbances from you." He shuffled papers furiously for a moment, then collected himself and resumed his questioning. "God has seen fit to raise up a mighty range of mountains extending over three-quarters of this great continent..."

*   *   *

"Go sit with the girls, Shevley, if you're so cold!"

Stephen paused on the school steps and heard his tormentors, looking beyond them to watch evening descend upon the snow-covered village, the dark dusk of winter. A scattering of lights dotted the east bank of the river. His eye followed the icy path that led away from the school, a black trail through the white drifts to whatever comfort might await him at home. The six Tubmans, ranged according to age and height, stood before him. Behind them, looking away when his eyes met theirs, were his schoolmates, eager to witness a threshing. Some turned away; others urged peace upon the Tubmans, half-heartedly, so as not to rile them further.

"He sits with Miss Fairchild. He sits with Miss Fairchild!" cried the youngest of the Tubmans excitedly, goading

106

him for some sort of response. "The nursery school, the nursery school, Shevley goes to the nursery school!"

Stephen cringed at the reference. It sickened him to hear her name so used. He glared at the urchin who quickly cowered behind his next oldest brother.

"He doesn't go to the nursery school," said Jeremiah. "He goes there for *piano* lessons!" He wheezed the word contemptuously. "Come here, piano player," he ordered.

Stephen's pulse quickened. He felt a tingling in his fingertips and his long arms twitched nervously. His face was flushed, the skin tight, his lips flattened against his teeth, his jaw set.

"Come here, sissy boy," Jeremiah taunted him. "Are you scared of me? I just want to talk to you."

Stephen cautiously stepped away from the school-house door. The crowd surged forward, closing a circle around the two and drawing up the slack. He took several more slow strides, the crowd shouting encouragement – not to him or to Jeremiah, but to the fight itself. He felt their hot breath on his neck. He was cold, stiff. His nemesis stood with his arms folded, his head tossed back.

"Come closer, sissy boy. I won't hurt you. Ha, ha, look at him, would ya!"

Stephen halted, fists clenched at his sides. Suddenly the youngest Tubman brother threw himself at Stephen's feet while another pushed him from behind. He stumbled headlong against Jeremiah as the crowd roared with excitement. The older boy struck him with a glancing blow to the head, knocking him onto the hard-packed snow, his long legs flailing the air. He lay panting there on the ground, leaning on his elbows, watching his attacker paw the air above him.

"Jump me, will ya! Who do you think you are, piano player? Miss Fairchild's caller. You jumped me, didn't you? Well, now get up and I'll show you a thing or two."

Stephen pulled himself up and stood breathing heavily as the older boy danced around him, casting wild punches toward him, inviting him to attack. Stephen felt his blood rise. He dashed suddenly at Jeremiah, lowering his head and butting his opponent in the midsection. Jeremiah crumbled, expelling a cloud of vapor into the frigid air. The crowd drew back in stunned surprise, gasping with excitement. Bent over, clutching his stomach, Jeremiah glared at Stephen. Then his left hand whipped out, the fist catching Stephen full on the nose. This sent him reeling back into the arms of his schoolmates, who quickly shoved him back into the fray. He swung wildly at the face of his startled opponent who was too slow to avoid a series of blows. In his moment of fury, Stephen barely realized he had struck Jeremiah. He could only feel the biting pain of his knuckles, warm blood sticky on his fingers. Then a powerful hand clutched his throat, pulling him away from Jeremiah and holding him at arms length. He looked into the angry face of Tobias Tubman.

"What's this? What's this?" stormed the schoolmaster. He held both combatants in his grasp at each end of his wide reach, shaking them vigorously. "What is the meaning of this riot, this rebellion against common decency. Lord, witness my tribulations!"

There was no victor, no vanquished, no cheers, no cries. But there was a good deal of pain, humiliation and injured pride. Jeremiah was scarred, two front teeth gone forever. Stephen's face was bruised. Fear still reigned in the classroom, but now Stephen was above fear. He did not have to win, only to survive without defeat. Henceforth they left him to his solitary ways.

*   *   *

He looked upon his black eye and bruised chin as evidence of his heritage. His wounds would have gladdened the heart of old Williams, who would have pointed proudly to similar incidents in Ephraim Shevley's past, and in Vincent's. Although his father examined his son with a gleeful smile he contented himself with asking how the other fellow had fared. But his pride, his relief, were unmistakable.

He paraded Stephen at the mill that all might see what stuff his son was made of, and never passed up an opportunity to relate the story to anyone who would listen. In time Stephen began to share his father's pride, and to garner from it a measure of self-confidence. As he stood on the edge of adolescence contemplating maturity, he could not but wonder at the monstrous role trivial events played in the lives of men.

The school term ended abruptly with the Rev. Mr. Tubman's announcement in April that he was answering a divine call and would leave within a week for California. For Stephen this meant a return to the mill at its busiest period, for the spring thaw was underway and the first rafts from the pineries were headed toward the falls at St. Anthony. Their arrival brought him to his second meeting with the red-haired man in buckskin who had haunted his arrival in the territory. The rafts from the Rum River already were in the boom to be sorted, and the sweet scent of sawed pine was wafting from the mill when Ben McAlpine appeared. He was like a creature from the wilds that had arisen from the raft of logs that lay in the slough behind Nicollet Island. His leather moccasins and leggings were black and slick from the icy waters of the Mississippi, and his fringed jacket smudged and stinking of sweat and wood smoke. His face, burned brown by the cold and the winter winds, was framed by strings of greasy hair that he brushed aside as he walked about the mill, inspecting the expanded facilities. As he drew near Stephen caught the stench of him.

"You remember my boy, Ben," said Vincent.

The blue eyes danced, quickly taking in the youth's frame, his well-muscled arms and callused hands.

"Grown some, ain't he," he commented, extending his hand.

"I've got him working as a sawyer's apprentice," Vincent said.

Stephen knew what was expected of him. He swabbed the sweat from his brow with a dusty forearm and thrust out his hand.

"Glad to see you again, Mr. McAlpine."

Ben took his hand, smiling. His grasp was surprisingly gentle, his hand cold and hard.

"Got you to work, I see," said the woodsman. "About ready, ain't he, Vince?"

"You can bet he is," said Vincent, swelling with pride. "We'll take him cruising with us come summer. Then you can see for yourself."

As they passed on Stephen measured them with his eyes, noting how the fat rolled at his father's waist, how soft he looked next to the lithe, cat-like Ben McAlpine. It made him feel all the more confident.

"I'm ready whenever you are," he thought.

*   *   *

His first trip into the woods was the cause of much commotion in Shevley House. There had been no objection to his venture, since it was understood to be of short duration. His mother assented with what Stephen took to be unseemly haste, but Mrs. Carpenter worried enough for both of them.

"Lordy, lordy," she cried, "I pray you'll be safe."

Sarah looked forlornly across the kitchen from the stool at the sink where she sat peeling potatoes. Stephen pretended to be unconcerned as he loaded kindling into the brass box beside the stove.

"Heavens, Mathilda, he'll be perfectly safe with his father and Mr. McAlpine," said Eleanor. She was standing on her tiptoes, peering into the cabinet, her shopping list in her hand.

"I'm sorry, m'am. I was just thinkin' about my poor Michael, rest his soul."

"Now, Mathilda, this will quite a different sort of outing. Oh, goodness, look at the time! I must hurry. Stephen, will you please hitch up the rig for me? I have to be in St. Anthony by noon, and it's after eleven o'clock already."

"You ought to have the lad drive you into town," said Mrs. Carpenter. "What do those fine ladies from St. Anthony think about you drivin' yourself all over the countryside?"

"If it concerns them, they conceal it very well. And I'm sure Stephen has things he'd rather do than wait upon his gossiping mother at a gathering of hens."

Stephen paused at the back door. "I wouldn't mind," he said.

"I wouldn't think of it. No, no, I'm quite capable..." She hesitated, then held up a shopping list as if she'd just discovered it in her hand. "See! I also have some shopping to do on the way home. It would only make you restless and impatient. No, if you'll just hitch up the rig for me, I'll manage for myself."

A solitary person, Stephen often spent his free hours exploring the nearby forests and meadows, the hills and vales that lay on the outskirts of the growing village. He had managed to find places to fit his every mood. There was the tumultuous roar and the radiance of the Mississippi as it raced through canyons of sandstone toward its junction with the more placid Minnesota River at Fort Snelling. There were several quiet, mirror-like lakes and ponds and meandering creeks to inspire his reveries. There were sunlit fields of wild flowers and the cathedral calm of the hardwood groves that beckoned him to take his ease and commune with his inner being.

Sarah envied his freedom to roam the shrinking wilderness, but when her duties at Shevley House permitted, she was allowed to tag along, even when Stephen clearly wanted to be alone.

"My mother said I could," she insisted when he found her following him.

"I don't want to be responsible for you," he argued. "What if something should happen?"

"Nothing's going to happen. Besides, I can take care of myself."

He had gone over a mile now. To take her back would cut short his afternoon. So he relented.

"All right, but you have to do exactly as I say, and take care that you don't get hurt."

They wandered along the military trail that led to the fort. The sun drifted lazily across the sky and fell in a burst of glittering rays through the heavy foliage, bringing their path to life with myriad dancing shadows. The cool shade of the hardwood groves contrasted pleasantly with the dust and heat of the fields where tall grass had gone to seed and was browning in the afternoon sun. The air all about them was aflutter with butterflies and in the scant breeze the fluffy seeds of dandelion and milkweed wafted aloft in search of new beginnings. Near the shores of Lake Amelia, where pillars of birch and poplar shaded them, they stopped to rest.

"I'm thirsty," Sarah said.

"I know where there's a spring. We could go see if it's safe."

"Whatever do you mean?"

"It's a spring the Indians use. There may be some around."

"I thought we were on military land."

"We are, Sarah. But it's a spring the Indians use all the time. We can go there, just so we don't disturb them. We don't want to be seen or heard."

They made their way quietly through the underbrush next to the trail until they neared the spring.

"Be very quiet," Stephen cautioned her. "I'll go on ahead to be sure it's safe."

Sarah sat down and rested against a tree, chewing on a stem of sour grass while he slunk away, absorbed in his daring game. He'd passed this way several times before, and had never seen an Indian. But his father referred to it as the Indian spring, and one couldn't be too careful. He peered over the trunk of a fallen tree and surveyed the glade at the lake's edge where he knew the spring to be. There were no Indians, but what he saw caused a hot rush of blood to surge through him. His eyes smarted from a sudden outpouring of sweat that ran down his brow. When his vision cleared he looked again in shock and disbelief. But it was true. He was not imagining it. Composing himself, he rolled into the tall grass and slithered back to where Sarah waited. She began to rise, but he caught her shoulder with one hand and clapped the other over her mouth. They lay there without a sound, his arm forcing the terrified girl hard against the ground. Then a horse trotted by on the nearby trail, raising a cloud of dust that filtered through the brush and enveloped them. As the hoof beats receded into the distance Stephen rolled over on his back and breathed a sigh of relief.

"Stephen! There really *were* Indians!" Sarah whispered.

"Shhh! There may be others around," he said. He sat up, feeling cold and empty inside despite the heat of the day, and looked down the trail toward the fort, and up the trail toward the village. "It's all right," he said. "Let's get a drink and head for home."

"Are you sure it's safe?" asked the frightened child.

"Sure it is – now. But not a word of this to anyone, or they'll never let us go wandering again. Do you understand?"

"Yes, of course I do. I wouldn't dare tell a soul. Are you really sure it's safe?"

Stephen stood up, studying the trail in the direction of the fort where Jonathan Wells was already out of sight, then toward the village where his mother's rig was just disappearing around the bend.

"Yes," he said. "It's safe now."

*   *   *

It was good to get away from Shevley House, to get away from her voice and her eyes – especially her eyes. He had caught himself staring at her in pain and disbelief. Their rapport, forged reluctantly on the anvil of his young heart during the years of loneliness, had vanished. The helpless, pleading look was gone from her eyes, leaving only a furtiveness that suggested shame. Now that he knew she was concealing a secret life even from him, he saw guilt in her eyes, and it disgusted him. He was glad to get away.

It was far better not to think about her. It was better to sprawl in the bed of the wagon as it bounced over the rutted trail, watching the clouds that mottled the sky, seeing the plummeting hawk in its deadly descent, the rhythmic swaying of the tree tops forming a graceful panoply as they lurched their way into the pineries. On the driver's seat Ben and his father exchanged infrequent comments, their voices lost in the persistent squeak of the wagon wheels. As they traveled he was as good as alone, and he liked it that way. Only the dumb packhorses trailing the wagon at the end of their tethers were there to keep him company, their eyes dull and indifferent.

At first the men gave him little to do. He gathered firewood and rubbed down the horses and fetched water from the stream. But except for the smelly bedroll they gave him and the plain fare they provided for him, there was no indication that his first outing was to be the trial of manhood that he had anticipated. They asked no more of him than might be expected of any inexperienced hand. They may have laughed as he battled the clouds of mosquitoes that plagued them along the way, but they suffered the same discomfort and made no issue of his frustration. He noticed that Ben suffered the least from the insects, smearing his face, neck and hands with bear grease to discourage the pests. But the palliative made the woodsman smell even worse than usual, and Stephen declined his offer to share the stinking balm.

They made camp when they reached the banks of the Rum River. It was nearly dark when they ate a meal of baked beans, corn bread and venison jerky, and later as they relaxed around the fire Stephen saw the lights of several other fires in the distance.

"We're not alone," he observed.

Vincent looked up and frowned, saying, "Homesteaders. There are a couple of spreads over that way."

Ben chuckled and mumbled something that put Vincent on the defensive.

"There'd be a damn sight more of them if it weren't for those rumor mongers in St. Paul," he declared. "And there will be more, you'll see. Most of the crew I've line up for winter will be taking half their pay in land, and Charlie Whitcomb tells me he gets inquiries at the newspaper office every week. It's a natural place for a town. It may be a little damp during the spring thaw, but there's never been a real danger of flooding. You'll see. Someday they'll be thanking me for my far-sightedness."

Ben did not respond, and his solemn glance kept Stephen silent, too. After dinner he followed Ben to the river's edge for a lesson in washing tin plates with sand and cold water. The lights across the way were more distinct in the darkness.

"What is it, Ben?"

"That's Pompantium, kid, or so your dad calls it. He claims to be building a city there, though some say it's better fit for ducks. It gets a might wet there, and a couple of the settlers think he may be trying to pull the wool over their eyes. I don't know about that, but I know your pa's a bit touchy on the subject. I guess we'd better let it go at that, if you know what I mean."

The next day they passed through the cut-over lands until they ran out of road. They left the wagon at an abandoned logging camp and continued on foot, with the pack animals carrying their gear. For several weeks they cruised the rich timberland that bordered the river, calculating its wealth by pacing it off in sections, measuring the trees in a given area and multiplying the figures to arrive at an estimate of the board feet each section contained. Before they were finished they had covered many miles and dozens of acres, plotting the winter's cut and selecting sights for two camps near the riverbank. Only then did Vincent announce that it was time to return to Minneapolis with their notes and map books, while Ben continued northward to pass the winter at Mille Lacs.

"There's a Chippewa village there," Vincent explained after they had parted company. "His squaw's there. His mother was a squaw, you know. Ben's as much Indian as he is white, more so, probably. He'll be back in the spring when he comes down river with the drive."

Once they began their homeward journey the landmarks went by quickly. In three days they reached the wagon, and in another they were approaching Pompantium. It was here they discovered a rustic camp near the settlement, a camp that wasn't there when they passed by on their way into the woods. It consisted of a lean-to of tamarack poles covered with marsh grass, a covered wagon and a cook area built of river rock. At the edge of the clearing two oxen and a horse grazed amid the tree stumps, while a lone cow lazed in the warm afternoon sun. As their creaking, rattling wagon signaled their approach, a woman came out of the lean-to and stood watching them. Four little children quickly gathered around her, clinging to her skirts. Vincent halted the team at a respectful distance and looked over the site, noting a furrowed field not far from the lean-to.

"Kitchen garden," he said, nodding to the small plot. "Looks like they plan to stay awhile."

At that moment Stephen spotted something moving in a clump of birch near the river.

"Look there," he whispered.

A tall youth emerged from the trees, a squirrel rifle cradled in his arms. His boots and trousers were covered with dirt and his shirt soaked with sweat. The summer sun had bleached his long hair and burnished his face and arms. He studied the visitors carefully.

"Just passing through," Vincent explained. "We're on our way back from the pineries. Hadn't noticed your camp before."

The woman reached out protectively and gathered the little children closer about her. The youth left the thicket and strode slowly, cautiously to the wagon.

"Welcome," he said quietly.

"You been on this land long?" Vincent asked.

"More'n a month," said the youth.

"You've done a lot of work in a short time."

The flicker of a prideful smile crossed the lad's face and he nodded.

"Guess we have," he said.

"You part of the settlement yonder?"

"We are," said the youth. "We held paper for some lots, but they turned out to be marshland. It wasn't fit for farming, so we moved up here to higher ground above the river. Didn't figure it mattered much."

"But it's a bit beyond the settlement," Vincent noted.

"Reckon it is," he said. "Made one trip back to town after we put in a garden, but the land office said the owner was out of town. Lost almost a week, all tolled."

Another boy appeared from the birch thicket, a boy not more than ten years old. He was a stocky lad, barefoot and carrying a stick. He made a wide circle beyond the wagon, never taking his eyes off the visitors.

"Could we trouble you for cool drink?" Vincent asked.

The older youth lowered his rifle and nodded toward the lean-to.

Stephen and his father got down and followed him to a shady area where he pulled a burlap-wrapped jug from the bushes and offered it to them. Vincent hoisted the vessel to his shoulder, turned his head and took a long drink, then passed it to Stephen who did the same.

"Thanks," he said, wiping his mouth on his sleeve.

"You're welcome," said the youth, displaying a slight accent."You the man of the family?" Vincent asked.

"I guess I am," he said shyly.

"Then you hold the paper you mentioned?"

"I do. It bears my father's signature, but he's dead."

The woman stood motionless, the little ones hanging on to her tightly. Suddenly the youngest, a girl of two or three years, broke away and scampered toward them, her little feet raising dust as she came. Without slowing down she slammed into Stephen, grabbing his leg and jabbering happily at him, her blue eyes sparkling.

"Hildy, Hildy, behave yourself," said the youth, prying loose her grip on Stephen's leg.

"She all right," he said, mussing her curly blond hair. "Don't scold her."

The youth picked up the toddler and carried her with him as he followed Stephen and his father back to their wagon.

"We're the Koenigs," he said. "You're welcome to stop by, if you pass this way again. I speak English, the others are learning."

"Pleased to meet you," said Vincent, extending his hand. "We'll remember your hospitality. Gotta move on now to reach the falls by nightfall."

As their wagon trundled down the river road, Stephen asked, "Is that your land they're on?"

"Yes, I guess it is."

"Will they have to move?"

"Oh, probably not."

"He's tilled an acre or more."

"Yes, he has."

"Will he have to work it off in the camps?"

"I suppose he will."

Stephen tried to visualize the mother and her younger children with her oldest son gone and winter setting in. His father seemed to anticipate his concern, and shifted uncomfortably, snapping the reins.

"There's the younger boy coming up," he noted. "And they've got a garden planted. They'll get along. But if the big kid's smart, he'll get a cabin up before the snow."

Chapter 8

The streets of St. Anthony were swarming with people, horses, and rigs of every description. As Vincent Shevley's wagon approached the new bridge he spotted Charles Whitcomb elbowing his way through a small knot of men near the land office, squinting at them through his spectacles as they drew near.

"Well, Vince," he called out, "what's the news from the pineries? What can I report on next season's prospects?"

"Hi, Charlie! Tell the men there's work to be had, if they're willing to break a sweat. I plan to set up two camps, and I'll need men who'll work hard for good wages, room and board."

"The prospects are good then," said the journalist. "Hello, Stephen! I hardly recognized you. You're looking quite the grown up man. I guess you've been initiated into the fraternity of foresters."

"I guess I have, Mr. Whitcomb."

"He's born to it, Charlie. He did well."

Stephen beamed proudly.

"You liked it then, lad?"

"I liked it very much," he said. "It was...it was just what I expected."

"Good, lad, good! And what are your estimates of the cut, Vince?"

"Don't push, Charlie. You don't have to print everything in that paper of yours. Just say I'll fill the Mississippi from bank to bank and my rafts will stretch from Mille Lacs to the falls. Squeeze that somewhere between the Lyceum notices and the snake oil ads. It'll give your readers something to talk about."

"Maybe and maybe not. All the talk these days is about the new political party, the Republicans. They've organized locally and Ramsey's leading the parade. They make sense to a lot of folks."

"They make sense, all right. Free the slaves, and start a war," Vincent grumped. "I hope you have the good judgment to report them for what they are."

"I give credit where credit is due."

"So, you're printing a Republican rag now!"

"I didn't say that. But let's discuss politics later over a glass of whiskey. Meantime your good wife can bring you up to date on the Republicans."

"My wife! What in hell has she got to do with politics?"

"Nothing directly, Vince. Ask her about it. You come and see me soon, ya hear? I want the whole story on this winter's timber crop before next week's edition. Now you better get a move on, if you're going to get across that bridge."

They had reached the tollbooth, paid their fare, and led their team across the solid new wooden structure. It was sunset, and both were exhausted when they reached Shevley House. It was good to be home. Stephen relished the steaming tub, the clean clothes, the air of excitement their return created, and the rich aroma of dinner that permeated the house. He was ravenous, having had nothing but dry corn cakes and wild berries to eat since breakfast. At his elbow Sarah quietly came and went, laying on the plates and platters, and removing them each in turn. She managed to brush close to him each time, catching a glimpse of him out of the corner of her eye. Stephen basked in her adulation, unselfconsciously assuming a mature demeanor, seeming to ignore her. He was much more interested in his mother and the candlelight playing on her flaxen hair. How beautiful she seemed to Stephen. His heart went out to her, then quickly retreated before that terrible image from the past – his own mother in the arms of Jonathan Wells. Her guilty secret was there in his memory, and would be there forever. The tension between her and his father had eased. Vincent sat at the head of the table exuding a sense of well being. He spoke glowingly of their weeks in the woods, liberally praising his son. He was confident of a good winter's harvest, and anxious to plan another expansion of the mill. He spoke of growth and business, business and growth – and finally politics.

"I understand the Republicans have organized locally."

"Indeed they have, just last month. I read Mr. Whitcomb's account of their convention. It sounded thrilling."

"That's strange."

"What is?"

"That you should mention Charlie. We saw him in St. Anthony late this afternoon, and he also mentioned you."

"Whatever do you mean?"

"We were talking about the Republicans, and he said, 'Ask your wife about them.' Just when did you become involved in politics?"

She smiled knowingly. "I'm afraid Mister Whitcomb was having a bit of fun at my expense. No, I have nothing to do with politics. He apparently was referring to my role as secretary of the Lyceum. I was responsible for securing speakers, as you are well aware. When some of those speakers appeared at the Republican convention to espouse their various humanistic philosophies, Mister Whitcomb was quick to associate me with their presence here. It was just good-natured bantering. He was making sport of me."

"I suppose the humanitarians you refer to are those damned abolitionists who drew up the Republican platform."

"Please, Vincent," she appealed quietly. "The convention took a stand against slavery, if that's what you mean, and rightly so. It is wrong for one man to own another."

"What does it have to do with the territory? This is a new frontier, timberland and farms, not some Southern plantation with cottons fields and gin mills. Slavery has nothing to do with us or what we do here. You women are meddling in the affairs of men without realizing the dangerous consequences of your actions."

"Meddling! You may call it that, but you'll find that the Republican Party speaks for many people, perhaps even the majority."

"A majority that includes women? Women do not vote, so I'll not concern myself with their pronouncements."

"You misunderstand me, Vincent. If I failed to explain myself, I'm sure you'll understand once you've read Mister Whitcomb's thoughts on the subject."

"So, he *has* turned Republican. I might have guessed."

"I don't think that's a fair statement. He has not said that."

But Vincent brushed aside her response. He was upset and rambling.

"The solid citizens of this territory, yes, and its statesmen – Rice, Sibley, the backbone of this community – are Democratic, and they'll remain so. You won't find them flirting with war over such a trivial issue as slavery. I'll read Whitcomb's scribbling, all right, and I'll have a talk with him, too. Could be it's time for another newspaper to make its appearance in town."

*　　*　　*

The mill had run at full capacity all during their absence, but still the boom above Nicollet Island was carpeted with logs. Stephen watched from a sawmill window as the scalers and tally boys went about their dangerous jobs. Nimble and quick in their spike-soled boots, they moved rapidly over the wet, slippery logs, cutting out specimens to be sliced into boards as a cowhand might cut cattle from a herd. Other workers then guided the floating logs to the sluice where they were snagged by conveyor chains and dragged up the incline and into the mill. The piercing scream of the saws created a constant din and the sweet scent of pine permeated the atmosphere.

Stephen headed for his father's office at lunchtime, but found him engaged in a heated conversation with Charles

Whitcomb behind the closed door. As he waited a young man approached and paused to inspect the map of Pompantium that hung on the outside wall of the office. It was the young farmer, Koenig, whom they had met up Rum River way. He noticed Stephen, nodded to the map and smiled.

"Magnificent, isn't it?" he asked pleasantly. "But you and I know differently."

"You're Koenig, right?"

"Johannes – no, *John* Koenig. We met a few weeks ago when you came by our farm. I've come back to see Shevley. I want to strike a bargain with him. I hope he's in a generous mood. Have you looked at this map? All the lots are well marked, municipal buildings are shown – city hall, a library, courthouse. But they don't exist, you know. It's all a fantasy. We're here, near the river's edge, here at this bend," he said, pointing. "It's good soil, once I get the stumps pulled up. Such a grand city will need food, and I'm a farmer. But I'm told the land doesn't belong to me; it belongs to Shevley."

"You're determined to keep your farm?"

"Of course. It was my father's dream. He was a farmer in the old country. It was the only life he ever knew, and he loved it. But he lost his land, so he came to America."

"He settled your farm?"

"No. He settled in Wisconsin, then in Iowa, then headed for Minnesota. The soil was always richer in another place. He worked hard, saved his money and bought land script. We were on our way north when he died. We buried him along the way."

He mounded a bit of sawdust with the toe of his boot, then leveled it.

"I'm the oldest – my brothers and sisters were born here in America. I hold the script my father bought. It represents two lots in Pompantium. But there is no Pompantium, and the land is better where we settled. I've come to strike a deal with Shevley." He smiled ruefully, then asked: "Do you work here?"

"Yes, I do." The voices in the office grew louder as the office door opened. "And I'd better get back to work. Good luck, John Koenig." He hurried away as his father and Whitcomb said their farewells.

"You make damn little sense, Charlie," Vincent was saying, "but if you say you're not a Republican, then let your paper say it, too. Statehood is our issue now, and there's no time to play politics with it. If you're not for us, you're against us. It's as simple as that."

"You're a difficult man, Vince. The Republicans aren't against statehood. They're as much in favor of it as you and I. They just want to be sure it's a free state – free of slavery. But we can talk about it at dinner. Thank you again for the invitation."

Vincent noticed John Koenig, half hidden by the opened office door. "Well, what in hell do you want? Don't stand there with your hat in your hand. If you've got something to say, come in here and say it."

Stephen saw the young man later as he was leaving the mill and called after him.

"Koenig! Wait! How did it go?"

"Well, if it isn't young Mister Shevley," he said indignantly.

"Sorry, but I didn't have the courage to tell you who I was."

"I can understand that, after meeting your father." A smile punctuated his statement.

"You were successful then?"

"If you call becoming an indentured servant a success, then yes, it went well. Your father is a very straight-forward man..."

"Stephen. My name is Stephen," he said, extending his hand.

"Yes, a very straight-forward man. He told me I was a fool to pay for cut-over pine land, when there's rich prairie still in the public domain."

"Will you'll move on?"

"Oh, no. I like it where we are. We have moved once too often already. It's time to put down roots. In exchange for two winters in the woods, I'm to get one section of land. Two more winters, one more section."

"You must be quite a bargainer, Koenig. My father is not easy to deal with."

"I know what you mean. I think he summed it up best when he called me a stubborn, god-damned squarehead while he shook my hand!" He laughed and waved cheerfully as he departed.

*   *   *

"Prohibition, abolition and demolition – don't tell me about those damned Republicans, Charlie. I know their goals, and they'll reach them only over the corpse of statehood, and at the cost of everything we in this territory hold dear."

The odor of whiskey and cigar smoke mingled in the parlor with the aromas emanating from Mrs. Carpenter's kitchen. Whitcomb, his vest smudged with cigar ash, his spectacles resting precariously close to the end of his nose, shook his head and smiled.

"You've got to give credit where credit is due," he said.

"What in hell is creditable about a platform like that?"

"That isn't what the platform said, Vince. Take prohibition, for instance. The Maine Law was defeated by the convention delegates. As for abolition, the convention's stand against slavery was essentially a moral issue, not a political one. And I don't know what you think they demolished."

"Charlie, I'll not argue slavery. I don't own slaves, and I never will. I only know that if slavery is left for the individual territories to decide, it will become a national political issue. I say let the clergy argue the moral issues, and keep the politicians out of it. Because if it's left to the politicians to decide, it will lead to war, and war will demolish this nation."

Eleanor entered the parlor and placed a saucer on the table at Whitcomb's elbow. He nodded gratefully and laid the butt of his cigar in it.

"It's these political neophytes who are driving us toward war," Vincent added, staring hard at Eleanor.

"We neophytes stand on the side of common decency," she said defensively. "Slavery may indeed be a moral issue, but it cannot be ignored by the political system. It's an infection that lies at the very heart of our national institutions, and it demands political attention lest it begin to spread its rot and spoil our most cherished institutions. It is an innate evil, and it cannot be ignored. It must be attacked and destroyed in order to cleanse the whole country."

Vincent stared at her incredulously.

"Well, I'll be damned! A firebrand, right here under my own roof. And who is going to do battle against this evil? Are you going to take up arms? Yes, why not? Women in politics, women in war. You and I can sit at home, Charlie, and sew uniforms for the ladies."

He laughed alone.

"Eleanor is right, in my estimation," Whitcomb said. "Slavery is an abomination. It is wrong not to stand against it."

"Slavery is an issue to be faced in those territories where it is an economic factor," Vincent said testily. "It has no economic bearing on this territory, and therefore it has no valid place in our politics."

"It is not solely an economic issue," Eleanor countered. "As God-fearing people, we have a duty to oppose it. The Republican Party took cognizance of that in its closing statement. It said, 'In administering the Government, Man and Morals first; interests of property afterwards.'"

"That's pulpit palaver, not politics!" Vincent stormed. "The two just don't mix."

"Why not?" Whitcomb asked facetiously, trying to defuse the situation. "Why not preachers in politics, seminarians in the Senate, clergymen in Congress?"

Stephen, who had come into the room and watched quietly as the clouds of controversy billowed through the parlor like so much cigar smoke, laughed out loud at Whitcomb's word play.

"You see," said the editor. "Someone appreciates me. The lad has a quick mind and a good ear. Perhaps you're both wasting your time debating the petty issues of our times. You have a genius in your midst, one of obvious discernment who must wonder at the irrelevancy of our remarks. Groom him, my friends, groom this lad and let the world await his coming of age, for I expect great things of him."

"I swear, Charlie," said Vincent, "to hear you talk anyone who'll laugh at your silly jokes is fit for public office."

"Dinner is on!" Mrs. Carpenter called from the dining room.

"Ah ha!" Whitcomb responded. "Let's gather at the groaning board and allow the magnificent meats thereon to mellow our mood and mend our manners. Madame, my arm."

Eleanor placed her hand lightly on Whitcomb's forearm and they led the way to the table. Vincent followed, his arm around Stephen's shoulder. "Don't encourage the old fool," he whispered. "He's drunk."

Whitcomb needed no encouragement. Conversation at the dinner table quickly grew loud and acrimonious. Stephen was by turns embarrassed, impatient and bored. As the great clock in the front hall chimed nine he asked to be excused and went to his room. He was tired of it all, and wanted desperately to get away. As he undressed he noticed his boots gleaming in the lamplight. Sarah must have oiled them, he thought. Good girl, Sarah. He sat on his trunk at the foot of his bed and fondled the cloth-soft leather. Through his open window came the night breeze, heavy with the rich smells of the summer land. There was a call on the breeze, a lure and a promise. It set his heart to aching, yearning to be free of Shevley House and the tensions there. Suddenly he could stand it no longer. He quickly pulled on his work pants, his boots and a flannel shirt. He took a change of clothes from his chiffonier and crammed them into his rucksack. Listening in the hall, he could hear his parents bidding goodnight to Whitcomb, and in moments his buggy was rattling down the drive and off into the night. Below stairs the occasional clatter of china told him the kitchen work was nearly done. He went back to his writing table and composed a brief note. Later he crept up the stairs to the third floor and down the dark hall to his mother's door. As he came near he could hear them quarreling.

"We've got to be tough!" Eleanor shouted. "Isn't that what you've always told us? We've got to be tough, you said, because this is a tough land and it's our job to tame it. Well, I *am* being tough. I'm doing things that I would not dream of doing in any other place, in any other time. I have set feminine scruples aside and entered the fray with all that is in me. I cannot wield an axe in the woods, but there are other struggles within my powers. I have never been a political person, but I have a grasp of these issues, and the will to fight for what I believe in. And fight I shall!"

"Damn it, it's unseemly, Eleanor. I won't have it! You're making me the laughing stock of the town. Not only that, but you're on the wrong side of the fence. You're out to destroy the very things we came here to fight for. Your 'grasp of the issues' is no grasp at all. You're mistaken; you misunderstand. You're gambling with everything you hold dear – and you don't realize it."

"No, Vincent. It's not my political immaturity that galls you; it's my Republicanism. You're angry because we differ politically."

"You're straining the very bonds of our marriage!"

"What do you mean by that?"

"I mean that I rule this household and I intend to as-sert that authority vested in me by the marriage vow. You *will* obey me! I insist that you cease all these ridiculous activities immediately or suffer the consequences.”

“Tough you said, and tough I will be! Straining the bonds of matrimony, indeed! You have made a mockery of our marriage and tattered those bonds long ago. Rant and rave, if you will; I am your wife, not your slave.”

“Eleanor, I’m warning you...”

“Get out! Get out of my room!”

Stephen made it to the back stairwell and cowered there momentarily until he heard his father’s bedroom door slam. He tiptoed downstairs and past the kitchen where Mrs. Carpenter was putting away the last of the dinner dishes. In the dark hallway he found Sarah’s door ajar and slipped inside. She sat up in her bed, startled.

“Shhhh!” he said, placing a hand gently over her mouth to quiet her. “Take this note,” he whispered. “Give it to my mother as soon as she comes down in the morning. Do you understand?”

“Yes, but...”

“I’m going away for awhile. It’s all in the note. I won’t be far away, and I’ll be safe. But you must see that she gets this note.”

“I will, Stephen, but...”

He leaned toward her in the darkness to hear her whisper and she grasped him about the neck and gave him a fleeting kiss, her young lips brushing his cheek like the wings of a butterfly. “Be careful,” she said earnestly.

“I will, Sarah. Goodbye. I’ll be back – someday.”

He went quietly into the hall and secluded himself in the shadows until Mrs. Carpenter put out the kitchen lamps and passed him in the dark hall on her way to bed. He crept into the kitchen and rummaged around in the cooler where he found some bread and meat, which he stuck in his rucksack. Then he let himself out the back door and fled into the night.

Late in the afternoon of the third day of his flight he came to the deserted campsite near the junction of the Mississippi and the Rum River. He was tired and stopped to rest. His scant provisions were gone, and his stomach ached with hunger. Nearby a patch of wild raspberries lured him off the wagon trail. He gorged himself on the succulent berries, then stretched out in the shade to sleep. It was sunset when he awoke and hurried on his way, seeking the stand of birch trees that marked the Koenig farm. It was nearly dark when he found it at last. Wading into the shallows, he crossed the river and climbed the steep bank. He had gone only a few steps when he went sprawling to the ground, his legs entangled with a stick. In a flash someone fell upon his shoulders and began to cry out in excitement. Recognizing his assailant in the dusk, he began to laugh hysterically. John Koenig quickly arrived on the scene and joined in the merriment.

"Let him up, August," John said to his younger brother. "It's only young Mr. Shevley come to pay us a visit. Sorry, Stephen, but August fancies himself an Indian fighter."

John helped him to his feet and led him off to the cabin, while his brother brought up the rear, lugging a two-gallon jug of milk he'd retrieved from the cooling cage in the river.

"What brings you this way alone?" John asked. "Are you meeting someone coming down from the camps?"

"No. There wasn't much work at the mill, so I thought I'd see if you could use a hand here on the farm."

"You've come to help?" John asked with a laugh.

"There's plenty to do, isn't there? I'm not asking for pay."

"Of course there's plenty to do, but what do you know about farming? And how can we make you comfortable here?" he asked, gesturing to an unfinished cabin.

"I don't need to be comfortable," Stephen said. "I spent time in the woods this summer with little more than this bedroll."

"Forgive me, my friend. Your offer is generous, and I accept it gratefully. You will be treated like one of the family. Come in and get acquainted."

The widowed Bertha Koenig was a sturdy woman, buxom and thickset. Her graying hair was done up in a bun, and her cheeks were ruddy and seemed to glow as she knelt close to the fire. The sleeves of her dress were rolled above her elbows until they pinched her large, fleshy arms. She smiled and nodded as her eldest son introduced Stephen, offering him her strong hand and a heavily accented greeting, bidding him "Velcome." John introduced the children next.

"This is our Indian fighter, Augie, who is going on eleven and knows everything there is to know about life, except perhaps fear and caution."

Augie extended his hand and an apology. "I didn't mean to hurt you," he said.

"And you didn't," Stephen assured him. "I am pleased to meet you."

"Anna and Lotte here are their mother's right and left hand. Anna is eight and Lotte seven."

"I will be nine soon," Anna said, curtsying daintily. "Lotte is only seven."

"I will be eight next spring," Lotte said defensively.

"And the babies," John continued, "are Martin and Hilda, if they can interrupt their eavesdropping long enough to come forward."

Lotte scampered out from behind a flour barrel and ran to her oldest brother's side. She was barefooted and smudged with dirt from head to foot. One soiled finger was stuck shyly in her mouth, which was ringed with bread-crumbs firmly cemented in place with honey. She smiled flirtatiously at Stephen.

"After her evening bath in the creek, you'll see that this is Hildy, who is three years old." Then, looking around the barren cabin, he asked, "Where is Martin? Martin, come here. We have a guest."

From the window a small head appeared from behind a blanket that was tacked to the window frame. He appeared to be lying down, which indeed he was. With the blanket pushed aside, Stephen could see that the Koenigs' wagon had been backed against the outside wall to serve as a bedroom for the smallest children. John went to his youngest brother and lifted him into the room.

"This timid child is Martin, who is five."

The boy said nothing, but stared wide-eyed at their visitor, who smiled and nodded politely.

"How do you do, Martin. I see you have a fine room there."

"I still have much work to do," John explained. "Another room to add, and I must get the roof up before cold weather sets in. It is not a job that I could do alone, so your offer to help is most welcome. That will be our first job, to raise the beam into place and set the rafters."

"I'm not a carpenter," Stephen apologized, "but you can teach me."

"I only know what I learned from my father, but together we can do it. We built two cabins together, my father and I."

Mrs. Koenig made a clucking sound and raised her eyebrows by way of exclamation.

"She hopes this home will be our last," John explained. "I've tried to assure her that I have no desire to move on, as my father did. We are tired of moving; we've had enough of it. We'll settle here, and the fate of this land will be our fate. The soil is rich, and we are happy here."

They ate boiled potatoes and cabbage for dinner, and shared a large sausage sliced between two pieces of bread. As Mrs. Koenig cleaned the dishes, they laid their bedrolls on the floor snug against the wall. A line strung across one corner of the cabin guarded the only bed, a crude cot, and gave John's mother some privacy. Once she had put the youngest children to bed in the wagon, she left Augie in charge of his siblings, she hung a blanket over the line and went to her bed. John and Stephen spoke quietly in the darkness.

"You've done a lot here since we first passed by," Stephen said.

"We've worked hard," John conceded. "It was not the fear of winter that prodded me. I've longed for years for just such a challenge. We always looked upon our other efforts as only temporary. Soon my father would get that faraway look in his eye, and we knew we'd be moving on."

"You were different sorts, weren't you," Stephen noted.

"Yes, but I don't blame him for his wanderlust. I could never understand what he wanted. Maybe he never knew, either. He was the youngest of three brothers, and had no chance of an inheritance. He joined the army at 15, the Kaiser's guard, and traveled a lot. I think he got into the habit of traveling here and there, never settling down. But then he met my mother, and soon ran away from the army. After I was born he ran away again, bringing us to this country. He ran all his life. I don't think he knew whether he was running after something or away from something. It seemed to me that he was a dreamer, dreaming of a better life, better land, and better times. But he was never able to settle down long enough to realize his dream. It was hard for all of us. If he had not died, we'd still be running. My mother used to laugh and say he thought the Kaiser was after him for running away from the army. I don't know what it was, but I know I was glad when he died. Not that I didn't love him. I buried him, after all, and I wept at his grave. But his death freed both of us. Neither of us had to run any longer, and I was free to realize my dream. There's no time to weep now with so much work to do."

Work, Stephen soon discovered, was a religion to the young farmer. He asked nothing more than the opportunity of labor and to earn a reasonable living from his toil. It was an attitude that ennobled him. Stephen quickly learned to respect him and was proud to be his friend. John was older by several years, but they were close enough in age that they could speak easily to one another, share their private thoughts.

"Why did you run away?" John asked him one hot afternoon as they rested in the shade of the birches by the riverside.

"What makes you think I ran away? No one has come looking for me."

"No, they haven't, and I think you are disappointed."

"Sometimes I am."

"You shouldn't be. I have met your father, remember? He is not the type to come running after you. He will wait you out."

"He'll have a long wait."

"I don't think so. You will go back sooner or later."

"Maybe much later. I may move on, go to California. They don't seem to care anyway."

"Why should they worry? You said you left a note telling them where you would be."

"But I thought my mother might care."

"She probably does."

"I don't know. There was a time not long ago when we were very close, but that's all changed – *she's* changed. She has other interests now."

"I can see that something's bothering you. What is it?"

Stephen stared at the river flowing by, mesmerized for a moment by the rippling current. Then he took a deep breath and unburdened himself.

"There's another man in her life – not just my father."

"How do you know this?"

"I saw them together."

John thought a moment, then offered an embarrassed observation: "She is only a woman, a frail woman. No less the credit, no more the blame."

"When I was young she used to weep alone at night in her room, and I felt sorry for her. My father was here and we were in Maine. She needed me then, but not anymore. There are other things in her life – even politics. She's – well, she's a Republican!"

"Ah ha!" John exclaimed jocularly. "And what's worse, her love affair or her politics?"

"You're laughing at me, but I tell you it's no laughing matter. They quarrel a lot. It used to frighten me, but now it just makes me very unhappy. Once we could talk about things, like you and I talk about things. But not anymore."

"You mean they won't put their problems aside to come running after you, is that it?"

Stephen looked a little sheepish. John grasped his shoulder and shook him gently.

"It was good of you to come to help us," he said with a kindly smile. "Whatever your reasons, we are happy to have you here."

"You have a way of twisting my words..."

"Into something like the truth?"

"You see? I can't even get the words out, and you twist them! Come on, let's put those last two rafters in place, or the first snow will catch you out in the open."

By the end of September not only was the roof in place, but they had added an extra room with bunk beds for the little children and a loft for Augie. A root cellar had been dug and covered with poles and sod, and a small shed put up to protect the animals and their winter feed. While they were haying the first wagons carrying supplies to the logging camps passed their way. That gave John an idea.

"The camps will need supplies all winter. Why couldn't I be the one to carry those supplies? That way I could keep up with my chores here and look after my family. Let's get this hay stacked, and we'll take a wagonload of produce down into town. I've got to talk business with your father."

Chapter 9

"Well, I'll be damned! If you two aren't a sight!"

Vincent stood in his office doorway, looking his visitors up and down. Stephen was conscious of his own appearance for the first time in weeks. His boots were scuffed and worn, his trousers and shirt ragged, his jacket stained and out at the elbows. A cap that Mrs. Koenig had fished out of a trunk for him to wear was perched on the back of his head, holding his unshorn hair in place. The trace of a silky beard graced his cheeks and chin. As his father sized him up Stephen felt suddenly taller and inexplicably pleased with himself. He smiled and extended his hand.

"It's good to see you, sir," he said.

"You've grown a foot, I swear!" Vincent exclaimed. "And you, Koenig, are you ready to go to work?" He shook John's hand, addressing him in a businesslike manner.

"I'm ready," said John. "But first I've a proposition for you."

"A proposition, huh? Well, it'll have to wait until dinner. Take him home, son, and both of you get cleaned up. We'll discuss business at dinner. I've still got work to do." With that he strode off through the mill, leaving John chuckling.

"What are you laughing at?" Stephen asked.

"He acted as if he'd last seen you at breakfast."

"That's just his way. He seemed pleased, don't you think?"

"He seemed pleased, yes, but not nearly as pleased as you. I can tell that you're glad to be home."

Stephen *was* glad to be back, and eager to see his mother once again. The weeks of separation had eased his troubled heart, and he was more than willing to forgive and forget. He grew more excited as they made their way toward Shevley House, while John grew more apprehensive.

"My mother did her best to teach me manners," John explained, "but I never had time to practice them. I've never been a guest in anyone's home. I'm not sure I'll know what to do or what to say."

"Just be yourself. That's what I did at your house," Stephen said.

"Yes, but you didn't understand what my mother was saying when she spoke to me in German. In fact, she was telling me what a gentleman you were, and asking why I couldn't act the way you did. She never let me forget that you and I are different. I can only wonder what your mother will think of me."

"There's nothing for you to worry about."

"I remember being told once that it is polite to bring a gift when one is invited to another's home. I should have brought some of my mother's preserves."

"It's enough that you have been a generous friend. She will appreciate that more than any gift. Turn up the hill there on the right."

John guided his wagon off the road and up the drive through the oak grove until suddenly he caught sight of the towering grandeur of Shevley House.

"Gott damn!" he whispered in astonishment. He had to be urged to follow Stephen up the marble stairway to the front door, which opened as they stepped onto the porch.

"Come in, Stephen, come in!" Mrs. Carpenter cried. "I saw the wagon coming up the drive and I couldn't believe my eyes! Oh, just look at you! What a man you've become. And who is this?"

"This is my friend John Koenig."

"How do you do, Mrs. Shevley. It is a pleasure to meet you," said John, bowing stiffly.

"No, no, this is Mrs. Carpenter," Stephen explained. "She is the maid and the cook and the conscience of this place. Tell me, Mrs. Carpenter, where is..." Two small arms suddenly gripped him from behind. "There she is! Dear Sarah, how good it is to see you again," he cried as she buried her face in his side. When she finally looked up at him her eyes sparkled with tears of joy.

"We missed you, Stephen," she said emphatically. "You should have sent us word."

"But there was so little time. Where is my mother? Is she home?"

"She is in her room," Mrs. Carpenter said. "She has not been well lately. It's like it was before – the pain in her chest, the coughing and the headaches. But she'll be fine, now that you're here."

"Has she been ill since I left?" he asked in astonishment.

"No, only for the past two or three weeks. But you must go up to her. It will cheer her. What she needs most is a big, happy smile on her face."

"I'll tend to the horse and wagon," said John. "You go and see your mother."

"I'll show you the way," Sarah said to John. "The stable is around in back."

"Meanwhile I'll put some water on the stove," said Mrs. Carpenter. "You both could use a bath."

*　　*　　*

Eleanor's room was eerie, dimly lit in the dusk. The elegant trappings of her high retreat were ghostly, ethereal, like the setting of a medieval painting. Only her writing desk showed any signs of life, an inkwell standing open amid a clutter of papers. The bed was draped with a white brocaded coverlet, its mahogany posts standing like mourners over her diminished form. She had not stirred as he entered. Her flaxen hair was spread upon the pillow, her head turned slightly away, her eyes closed. She was very pale, her lips thin and gray. Dark circles ringed her eyes. He stood for a moment at her bedside, studying her closely, and was relieved at last to see her breathe ever so weakly. He leaned down and kissed her forehead. Her eyes fluttered open and suddenly confronted him, eyes full of fleeting expectation followed by vague disappointment and sad resignation.

"Hello, mother. I've come home."

"Stephen, oh, Stephen!" she gasped, taking his brawny hand in her delicate fingers and holding it gently. "You've been gone so long, and I worried so."

"Not so very long, Mother. I'm sorry if I caused you to worry. I didn't know you were ill."

"It's nothing," she said, coughing lightly and rolling her eyes heavenward. "It's a touch of pleurisy, nothing more."

"How long have you been ill?"

"I don't know; I've lost all track of time. What day is it?"

"I'm not sure," he admitted. "I've been living from sun-up to sunset for so long – but I do know it's not Sunday. We've just come from the market."

"We?"

"I've brought a friend home. His name is John Koenig. I've been living with John and his family. They've been very kind to me. I helped build their cabin and they gave me room and board. John had to come to town on business, and it was too late to start back. I felt I owed him a favor and asked him to stay the night with us."

"How nice," she said without enthusiasm. "Will you be going back with him when he goes?"

"I hadn't thought about going back. I don't know what I'll do."

"I suppose your father will have some ideas on that subject. It's growing dark – the sun has set. He'll be home soon." She spoke with little inflection, as if reciting lines.

"I've already spoken to him."

"He's home?"

"No, I saw him at the mill."

She turned her head away, withdrawing from him.

"How nice that you found time to visit me," she said, her voice heavy with sarcasm and self-pity. He found himself unable to resist a feeling of contempt verging on anger.

"Will you be coming down for dinner?" he asked tersely.

"Oh, no," she said, turning to look at him with dull, accusing eyes. "I haven't been down for days. I'm not well, as you can see. I take my meals alone in my room. You'll have to extend my apologies to your friend."

She closed her eyes as if too weak to abide his presence any longer. He lingered a moment by her writing desk, staring at the open ink well. He replaced its silver cap, noting that the nib of her pen was still wet. He smiled ruefully and headed toward the door.

"And Stephen," she called after him, "please drop in to say goodbye, if you should decide to leave again."

He closed the door firmly behind him.

*   *   *

Bathed and dressed in clean clothes, the young men joined Vincent in the parlor. Mrs. Carpenter had rummaged among some of Vincent's cast off clothing and managed to outfit John Koenig tolerably well. Sarah had even found time to brush the young men's work boots.

"You lads look better than when I last saw you," Vincent observed as he poured them each a whiskey. "Here, have a drop to settle the dust."

They took the glasses and winced as the fiery liquid seared their throats. Vincent laughed.

"That ought to clear the cobwebs," he said. "Now what's that proposition you had for me, Koenig?"

"I offer myself for the winter as set forth in my father's agreement with you," John said. "In addition I offer my wagon and team. I propose that I work as a teamster for Shevley Lumber."

"I've got all the teamsters I need. What I want are strong young men to fill out my crews in the woods."

"Those crews have to be fed," John pointed out. "I could make regular trips between the camps and town. And as I passed by Pompantium, I could look in on my family to be sure they are safe."

"Ah ha! So that's your motive."

"John is the man of his family," Stephen put in. "He's responsible for his mother and five younger children. They depend on him. If he were in the woods..."

"So the truth is that you want me to offer *you* a deal!" Vincent's voice had a sharp edge to it and he allowed it to cut for a moment before withdrawing it with a warm smile. "I don't see why we can't make some sort of arrangement. But you'll be on the road a lot with two camps to supply."

John's face brightened and he took a nip of his whiskey. "That would suit me very well," he said.

"Then you'll start tomorrow," Vincent said. "No sense in dragging an empty wagon back upriver. After breakfast you can come down to the mill with me. We'll go over the maps together and round up a load for you."

At dinner it seemed they couldn't get enough to eat. Sarah buzzed about the table, bringing an apparently endless variety of food to sate their appetites. The child's presence, the familiar sounds of Mrs. Carpenter bustling about the kitchen, the warm glow provided by the whiskey, the flickering candles that made shadows dance upon the walls – it all combined to give Stephen a comfortable sense of well-being. He was glad to be home, if only it weren't for..."

"Sarah, have you taken a tray up to Mrs. Shevley?" Vincent asked. "There won't be a bone left to chew on, if you don't get moving."

When the young men had eaten their fill, John's eyes grew heavy and he begged to be excused while father and son went into the office, closing the door behind them. Vincent poured himself another whiskey and nodded to indicate Stephen was welcome to do the same. Then he went to the window and leaned against the frame, sipping his drink and gazing out over the front yard where the grass lay under a cover of golden oak leaves.

"There's the scent of winter in the air tonight," he said quietly, as if talking to himself. Then he turned to his son and asked, "What about you, what will you do now?"

"I don't know," Stephen said. "I haven't given it much thought."

"As I see it, you've got several options. I could put you to work at the mill again, or I could send you into the woods. Or you could go off to school – your mother's keen on sending you back east. She thinks you're well suited for college."

"What do you think?" Stephen asked.

"I think it'd be a god-damned waste of time. I've seen what an education can do to a man. Oh, it's fine for a doctor or a preacher. But you don't need it. You've got a career cut out for you, a career in the lumber business. The day will come when all that I'm building today will be yours. You can't learn the lumber business in any college. You learn by doing."

"What did you have in mind?"

"I want you at the mill. I want your nose in the books – Shevley Company books. I want you to learn everything there is to know about the business, so that when the time comes you can step into my place. I'll teach you myself. And if there's anything I can't teach you, I'll find someone who can."

"What does mother say?"

"I don't care what she says," he flared. "She says good day, if she feels like it, and damned little else. What she says or what she thinks has no place in this conversation."

"I see," Stephen said, taking a sip of his whiskey. "Well, a business education would be worthwhile, I guess."

"Worthwhile, you guess! It's critical, critical to you and critical to the times we live in. I'm offering you the opportunity to move in the company of men who are building this country. You'll learn from the experts."

Stephen mulled the options, weighing them carefully against their alternatives, and concluding, "I guess it would be agreeable."

"Agreeable, is it? Well, I'll be damned!" Vincent exclaimed with a laugh. "You give a seventeen-year-old kid a career with a built in fortune, and he says it would be agreeable!"

They shared a laugh, with Vincent grabbing his son's shoulder, as if the matter had been decided.

"What I meant was, it sounds a lot better than going off to school somewhere," Stephen said seriously. "I don't know if I'd like that. I know what mother thinks. By the way, what's wrong with her? Has Doc Ames been around to see her?"

"Hell, yes, he comes around every few days. He goes along with her complaints and tells her to keep out of drafts, but let me tell you, son, there isn't a damned thing wrong with her. She's no sicker than you are. The doc says she has a weakness in the lungs, but it's nothing to lie abed over. Fact is..."

"Yes?"

"I don't know how to tell you this, but I've got my suspicions about her. You remember that soldier boy, Wells? I think there was something between those two, but I could never put my finger on it. I think they might have been seeing one another on the sly. Can you imagine that? But lately things seem to have cooled between them, if you know what I mean. She'd been running all over town, going to temperance meetings, and abolition rallies, and what have you, and you can bet Wells was in the picture somewhere. Then about a month ago she suddenly stopped going out and took to her bed, complaining of a cough. When I heard rumors that Wells had a lady friend, I mentioned it to her, and she raised a terrible storm, cried and carried on as if I'd hit a sore spot."

"What kind of rumors?"

"I've got no right to repeat the stories I hear without certain knowledge of the facts. But one thing I can tell you for sure – just as I told her – the day she took to her bed was the same day Whitcomb's newspaper printed a gossip item about Wells planning to marry that little Fairchild woman."

"Grace Fairchild," Stephen mused. "Then there was no escape."

"What's that?"

"Nothing, father. But I think she's really ill."

"No!" Vincent exploded. "She's run up to that room to hide her jealousy and her shame. She's made a fool of herself, and she's up there hiding from the truth."

Yes, Stephen thought, she's run away to hide – to hide from a husband who doesn't understand her, from a life she can't abide, from the pain in her heart, and now even from the son she once loved and depended on. And she'll lie there and pity herself, because no one else will pity her. And here's my father, angry, jealous and confused, and just as pitiful in his own way as she is in hers, trapped behind a wall of obstinacy and indifference that he's built around himself in his single-minded preoccupation with chopping down trees and cutting them into pieces. I don't understand either of them, but I pity them both. I pity her for the weaknesses that have turned her in upon herself to the exclusion of everyone else. But I cannot blame either of them. She needed him, and he couldn't see it. Nor can I blame him. It's like old Williams said, he is his father's son, and as much like him as – as I fear I am like my father.

"Well, maybe I've been a little hard on her," Vincent conceded, his eyes rheumy from liquor and longing. "Anyway, you think things over. There's no hurry about going to work. Take your time. Get reacquainted around town. Drop in on Charlie Whitcomb. He can bring you up to snuff on what's going around here. When you're ready, we'll get down to business."

"Good night, father," Stephen said in a voice made small by the weight of concerns too heavy for his years, a voice lost in the dark tunnel of helplessness where one crushing thought came echoing back upon him: *He is his father's son, and as much like him as – as I fear I am like my father.*"

*   *   *

He set out on foot in the dark, and an hour later arrived at a harness shop just off Bridge Square. He went around to the back of the building to peer through a dusty window into the office of The Frontiersman. By the light of an oil lamp suspended from the rafters he could just see the top of Charles Whitcomb's head. He appeared to be seated at a massive desk piled high with old newspapers, crumpled proof sheets, books and periodicals, letters and handbills. The clutter spilled from the desktop, inundated a battered waste basket and poured over onto the floor. Benignly safe from the deluge were the tools of the printer's trade, a small flatbed press, and a case of type, a serene island of order amid the general chaos of the room. Stephen noted that a bottle of whiskey and a battered tin cup rested safely atop a tall stool in front of the type case. With a wry smile he stepped away from the window and rapped lightly on the door. His knock raised a muffled flurry of activity inside the newspaper office followed by dead silence. Curious, he eased open the door and looked into the musty room.

"Hello!" he called out in a stage whisper. "Are you in, Mr. Whitcomb? It's Stephen Shevley come to talk with you."

Slowly the journalist's tousled hair, then his furrowed brow, and at last his eyes, wide with apprehension, appeared above the heaps of paper.

"Well, well," he said, "what a pleasant surprise! Come in, Stephen, come in."

"Did you drop something?" the lad asked as the editor struggled to his feet.

"Oh, no – why, yes, I did! My glasses. I seemed to have dropped my glasses."

"There they are," Stephen said, pointing to the editor's spectacles swinging from a ribbon around his neck.

"Yes, yes indeed," Whitcomb mumbled, grasping the glasses and rubbing them against his vest. "I hope you'll pardon me, but your knock startled me from my reveries. I don't usually get visitors this time of night – unless they come with some complaint."

"In which case you duck for cover?"

"Merely a precautionary measure," Whitcomb said as he adjusted the spectacles on his nose. "So, the prodigal son has returned to the bosom of his family. Your parents have been concerned for your safety, young man. Where have you been all summer?"

"I've been staying with friends up on the Rum River. They're farmers. But I'm home now, and my father says a lot has happened since I left, and that you can bring me up to date."

"Indeed I can, and it would be my pleasure," said the editor, hastily whisking away the liquor bottle and stowing it in a desk drawer. "I try to keep abreast of events, and can say in all modesty that I have seen much of what has transpired locally, and heard even more – some rumor, some reality. How would you have it?"

"I'd like the truth, of course. Isn't truth a journalist's stock in trade?"

"A journalist's job is to *seek* the truth. But few among us are able to sort out the facts, so often do they come to us commingled with fantasy. That is particularly true in the case of your parents – and they, I presume, are the true object of your inquiry, right?"

Stunned by Whitcomb's perspicacity, Stephen struggled to conceal his surprise.

"You see?" the editor went on, "Even trusting friends may try to hide the truth from one another. Acknowledge that, and you'll have some appreciation of the difficulties of my profession. I won't indulge in rumor or fantasy, which have been rampant. I will try to deal only with what I have personally observed. It will be up to you to interpret those observations. Here, sit down."

He hauled a chair from amid the clutter and offered it to Stephen, while he himself perched upon the typesetter's stool in the manner of a school master seeking to maintain vertical superiority over his student. While he spoke he dabbled with a printer's spatula, immersing it in a container of viscous black ink, twirling it carefully, and applying a glob to the paten of his press. Despite this nervous preoccupation he remained focused on his solitary audience. When he made a point of particular importance he would turn his face toward Stephen, cock his chin downward, then suddenly snap his eyes upward to peer over the rims of his glasses, fixing a steady gaze upon the youth as if to etch his words on Stephen's memory.

"These are challenging times," he began, "and this is a challenging place. Everything is new here – there is new work to do, new ideas to explore, new lives to lead. Five years ago only the fort was here – the fort and a scattering of shacks at the St. Paul landing. There was only one frame house in St. Anthony, and a dozen or so Sioux tepees near the government mill. This town didn't exist. It was a gleam in the eye of men like your father, men who could look at the wilderness and see a great city rising. It was a sight to inspire such visions – the roaring water falls, the endless flow of the river, the groves of oak and elm, the broad green meadows and the sparkling lakes. They were sights to inspire dreams in the minds of even the commonest of men. Who wouldn't dream great dreams in such a wonderland? I remember trading a bottle of whiskey for a tent of tamarack poles and animal skins in which to shelter my press. I printed the first edition of The Frontiersman in that tent, and did so once every two weeks for nearly a year. It was worth the struggle, for like your father I had seen the future, dreamed the dream. I had heard the call, received the invitation to greatness. But I needn't tell you that for you've witnessed most of it yourself."

"I did indeed," Stephen interjected, "but the price of such dreams runs high. I fear they have cost me my family." The editor squirmed on his stool, looking away as if seeking divine guidance, while Stephen continued. "You've seen what transpired here. I have a right to know."

"I'm coming to that. But first you've got to understand that the forces that drive men and women together can just as easily force them apart."

"They both dreamed of having a home of their own," the lad said dejectedly, "and all they got was a pile of rock."

"Let that be a lesson to you," Whitcomb said. "There's more to a home than walls and roof. A home, be it rude or grand, is a state of mind. Its whole existence is in the heart."

"Then I have no home."

"Frequently the child must bear the burden of his parents' unhappiness."

"We all had such high hopes," Stephen said, his voice quavering, his tears near to overflowing. "How did it happen?"

"The frontier demands certain things of people," Whitcomb explained. "Of your father it demanded success; of your mother sacrifice. Your father embraced success; your mother rejected sacrifice. They became strangers travelling different paths. I have watched it happen, but there was nothing anyone could do about it."

"What do you know of Jonathan Wells and my mother?"

"I know they were friends. That is a fact. The rest is only rumor. As I said, I deal in fact, not fantasy."

"I once saw them together. He was kissing her."

"The flesh is weak," Whitcomb said with an embarrassed shrug.

"They were seen together in public."

"An innocent confluence of interests – the Lyceum, the Athenaeum. They were literate adults, cultured individuals. One would expect them to attend the same gatherings."

"But my father never attended."

"He had other interests, nothing more."

"He blames it all on politics. I don't understand politics."

"Sometimes I don't either, but I'll try to explain."

Somewhat circumspect in his responses so far, Whitcomb seized upon the opportunity to expound upon what was obviously his favorite topic. He repositioned himself upon the stool, adjusted his spectacles on his nose, and otherwise composed himself for a dissertation.

"Politics," he explained, "has to do with the manner in which we perceive the world around us. Its fascination lies in the ever-changing issues that present themselves, and the diverse opinions those issues inspire in the public at large. Political parties come into being to represent those interests. Most of the men who first came into this wilderness – your father among them – called themselves Democrats. They came here to make their fortunes, and they wanted no interference in that pursuit – not even from the federal government that held most of the land we occupy here today. It is only recently that that contentious issue was resolved when the Army reduced the size of the military reservation, resulting in a victory for the founders of this burgeoning community. These first settlers were generally a rough and tumble crowd, an honest, easy-going bunch of rugged individualists, men who liked a drink now and then, but who were generally sober and law-abiding. However, if men tame the frontier, it is the women who civilize it. And if those women are able smooth some of the rough edges, they also can create their share of problems."

"By getting into politics, as my father says?" Stephen asked.

"Vince has his own way of seeing things," Whitcomb noted. "I think politics are incidental to the women's more commendable activities. Take the founding of the Athenaeum Society, for example. Who'd have thought that the society's discussion of Mrs. Stowe's book would result in the formation of a committee on the abolition of slavery? And the Lyceum – why, discussion of politics was usually left to the men who gathered at one of the local taverns. But with the Lyceum we suddenly had temperance speakers coming to try to close our saloons, to preach against the evils of slavery, and finally to tout the platform of the Republican Party! Never mind that hard working men needed a drink now and then, or that slavery was not even an issue in the territory. We don't pick cotton; we cut trees! Can you blame a man for getting his dander up?"

"I've heard my father say you were in cahoots with them," Stephen pointed out.

"That's nonsense!" Whitcomb insisted. "I may enjoy a nip now and then, but I'm a reasonable man. When the ladies of the Carson League began agitating for passage of the Maine Laws, I could see the wisdom of their temperance arguments. The same with the abolitionists. They made valid points, and I said so in my newspaper. And believe me I caught four kinds of hell for it. Things really got rough when the Republican Party decided to organize here and gathered all those contentious issues under their umbrella, and threw in liberal land policies to top it off. That really gave the old-timers fits – your father most especially."

"Is that why you duck for cover when you hear a knock at your door?"

"Discretion is the better part of valor, my boy. I have been shot at in the street, and I'm not anxious to be a target again."

"Politics sounds like a very dangerous business. How did my mother become involved with the Republicans?"

"Your mother is well known around town as a woman of intelligence and breeding. She was one of several local ladies who were called upon to serve as copyists for the party convention. It was they who put the men's ideas into words – drafts, resolutions, bylaws and the like – so they could be voted upon by the delegates."

"You're a printer; I should think they'd have asked you."

"Oh, they did, but I had to maintain my objectivity. My readers looked to me for an honest report on the convention's work. I had to admit in my editorial that I sympathized with some of the major elements of the platform – it favored statehood, increased settlement, growth in industry, encouragement of agriculture. But I stood four-square against the inclusion of moral issues in a political document, advising that such matters be left to the pulpit."

"Is that why someone took a shot at you?"

"A wild-eyed fanatic, a southern rabble-rouser, an ig-noramus incapable of discerning satire from slander."

"What did you say about him?"

"Absolutely nothing! I wrote a satirical piece on ra-cial intolerance. Somehow this scoundrel saw himself in my fictional portrayal and called me out. I was on my way to the livery stable to secure passage to St. Paul – I had a shipment of newsprint coming in – when he confronted me and demanded satisfaction."

"A duel?"

"Precisely so, although my anger clouds my memory of the incident. Iinitial breaching of an argument colors my temperament somewhat, and not wishing to act under the pressure of anger, and I rejected his demand and told him to go to hell. With that I turned my back on the lout and continued on my way. I hadn't gone five steps when I heard his call after me, 'Turn and fight, you cowardly nigger-lover!' His vulgarity was punctuated by a pistol shot and in an instant a ball ripped my coat sleeve and seared my left arm. I was furious, of course, but not blindly so. I faced the scoundrel, drew my own pistol and shot him in the knee. I reasoned that killing him would have given me no satisfaction and would undoubtedly have branded me as a hothead, possibly ending my career as the good conscience of this community. Maiming him, on the other hand, would give me great satisfaction, preserve my reputation for cool-headedness, and leave my professional reputation untarnished. Alas, my ball shattered his knee. The wound subsequently became inflamed, and his leg had to be amputated. I'm afraid I incurred more misery on the poor wretch than I intended or he deserved. He has since left the territory.

"But enough of my adventures; the incident was typical neither of the times nor of this community. My assailant was a peregrine predisposed to violence, probably a riverboat gambler holed up here temporarily to recoup his losses. I like to think that my response to his provocation was enough to discourage such outbursts in the future. Nevertheless, I find it prudent to take cover behind my desk when there comes a knock at my door in the dark of night. And of course I never go abroad unarmed," he concluded, his eyes twinkling mischievously.

"I'll keep that in mind," Stephen said with a smile, "and I certainly won't call again at night unannounced. Thank you for taking the time to talk with me."

"It was my pleasure, Stephen."

The young man arose and made his way carefully toward the door, trying his best to avoid the clutter of paper on the floor. He paused with his hand on the doorknob.

"There is one more thing..."

"Yes?"

"What can you tell me about Grace Fairchild."

"I frequently have seen Miss Fairchild and Captain Wells together. It is rumored they intend marry."

"I see. Well, thank you, and good night."

As he made his way in darkness along the road to Shevley House Stephen felt more alone than ever. Not only had Whitcomb acknowledged and explained the apparently unbridgeable gap between his parents, he also had confirmed that the mistress of his boyhood reveries, the object of his youthful yearnings, would belong to someone else. And while no hint of intimacy had ever passed between them, and no romantic feelings had survived his growing maturity, just to know that Grace Fairchild might soon wed to the man who was the object of his mother's affections – thereby destroying her impossible hope of escaping her doomed marriage – only added to Stephen's emotional burden. A strange result of his new understanding of events was that he found himself pitying his father, who seemed incapable of coping with either the loss of his wife's affection or her refusal to play the thankless role of dutiful wife.

Chapter 10

Ever since the territorial legislature approved the formation of a city government for Minneapolis, the only sound to compete with the whining mill saws was the ring of hammer on nail as a building boom began in the burgeoning borough.

"It's just like Chicago," Mrs. Carpenter proclaimed. "We're growing up just like Chicago. My, oh my, how it reminds me of my girlhood. And you, young lady, will see it all come to pass. You'll find yourself a good, solid man to marry and raise your family in a fine city – and no need to blush that way. It's none too early to start sizin' up the young fellas hereabouts. There's a new family moved onto the Benson property, Callaghan's the name, fine Irish stock, and four sons, they have. He farms and is a bit of a blacksmith, comfortable and well off they are, a respectable, church-goin' family. I might just take this old pot around to have the handle mended and make myself acquainted."

"Really, mother!" Sarah exclaimed just as Stephen poked his head in the door.

"No breakfast for me this morning. I'm late already. I'm going down to the landing with Mr. Whitcomb." He grabbed his muffler and heavy jacket from a peg in the hall and headed for the door.

"Stephen!" Sarah sighed plaintively. "You were going to take me into town this afternoon."

"Not today, Sarah. Maybe later. I can't be riding around town with you now. I've got responsibilities."

"My, ain't he growin' up though. You mustn't be a bother to him, Sarah. Your place is here in the kitchen, not traipsin' around town with your betters. Learn your place, and stay there. You'll be all the happier for it."

Sarah watched from the window as Stephen hitched up the team and raced down the driveway. It was not a look of sadness that crossed her young face, but one of patient determination.

*   *   *

"Tie up at the wharfinger's office, Stephen, and we'll go on foot to the landing."

Whitcomb strode confidently toward the riverboat, sizing up disembarking passengers as he went. When he saw a likely prospect his eyes brightened and he made directly for them. His "Ah, ha!" of discovery was like a command to charge, and the rapidity of his advance invariably threw his subjects off their guard.

"I am Charles E. Whitcomb," he began, "publisher of The Frontiersman. It would be my pleasure to report the arrival of..."

Here he would pause, pencil poised, allowing his startled quarry to blurt out his identity before he pressed his attack with more questions, all the while jotting furiously on his notepad. Stephen was amused by the editor's audacity, and amazed at how his technique elicited answers to some of the most impertinent of questions. He noted with glee the tactics Whitcomb used on his less than modest subjects. His technique was to dwell upon some bit of trivia, interrupting his victim's response and deflating him by sheer exasperation.

"Pomeroy, sir. C. Gladstone Pomeroy of the Pomeroys of Vicksburg. We're staying at the Winslow House in the village of St. Anthony. Allow me to present..."

"Pomeroy, hmmm. Would you kindly spell that for me?"

"Of course. P-o-m-e-r-o-y. It is a name prominent in the history of Mississippi. And this is my wife..."

"The usual spelling of Gladstone, I presume?"

"Yes. G-l-a-d-s-t-o-n-e. And this is my wife..."

"And the C, what does the C stand for, Mr. Gladstone?"

"The name, sir, is Pomeroy, not Gladstone. That is, I should be addressed as Mr. Pomeroy, not Mr. Gladstone. Gladstone is my mother's family name. As for the initial C, I prefer using it to my Christian name. It should appear in your newspaper as..."

"Thank you for your time, Mr. Gladstone. I do hope your sojourn in our fair territory is a pleasant one. And I am pleased to make your acquaintance, Miss Pomeroy. I trust our climate will prove stimulating to you both. Now if you'll excuse me..."

Whitcomb chuckled as he beat a hasty retreat.

"You cut him off rather nicely," Stephen observed. "I have an uneasy feeling we're about to be hit on the back of the head with that cane he was carrying."

"He was too eager," Whitcomb said. "He would have spent an hour telling me how important he is, and then stopped by the office to assure himself he'd be treated with due respect in the columns of The Frontiersman. I have no intention of publishing a history of the Pomeroys of Vicksburg, only a simple listing under the sub-heading 'Among arriving passengers,' et cetera."

They made their way through the crowd, stopping briefly to accost other likely prospects. Among the last to leave the vessel was a young man in eastern dress, wearing a beaver hat and a starched shirt over which bulged a silk cravat held in place by a diamond stickpin. He carried a dispatch case in one hand while his valise rested at his feet. Whitcomb, pausing at the foot of the gangplank, spotted the young man, and quickly strode up to him.

"Are you expecting someone, sir, or may we be of service?"

The fashionable young man's only response was an icy stare.

"My name is Whitcomb," the unflappable journalist went on. "I am the publisher of the local newspaper."

Only then did the young man display some interest.

"You might be helpful at that," he mused, looking Whitcomb up and down. "I have business in St. Anthony with one Vincent Shevley of the Shevley Lumber Company. Do you know him?"

Whitcomb guffawed and slapped his knee.

"I dare say I do!" he exclaimed. "Better than that, let me introduce my young friend, Stephen Shevley, Vincent Shevley's son."

Stephen extended his hand. "How do you do? Are you a friend of my father's?"

"You might say I am a business associate, here to represent his brothers. This is indeed a coincidence – or is it the result of your father's clever planning? My name is Roger Frasier," he said, shaking Stephen's hand. "I bring news from the Shevley offices in New York, not all of it good. It is my sad duty to inform you, young man, that your grandfather Ephraim Shevley is dead."

Frasier's blunt delivery of the news startled Stephen even more than the report of his grandfather's death.

"We hadn't heard," he said.

"I'm not surprised. Word of his demise came just hours before I left New York. Will you direct me to your father's office?"

"We're finished here," Whitcomb interjected. "Why don't you ride into town with us? Stephen, give Mr. Frasier a hand with his valise."

*　　*　　*

"You certainly didn't come all this way to tell me of my father's passing," Vincent said as he closed his office door to shut out the squeal of the saws.

"Indeed not," Frasier said. "Ephraim Shevley's death was coincidental to my departure, although the two events are in some ways related."

"How's that?" Vincent asked.

"For some time your brothers have been reluctant to become more deeply involved in your business affairs. They were mainly concerned about your venture into land speculation. They feared your father would have disapproved, and cut them off, too."

"What do you mean, 'cut them off, too?'"

"I mean that your father long since had written you out of his will, and they didn't want that to happen to them. Once his failing health placed him beyond the understanding of business matters, Thaddeus took over the family lumber operations in Maine, while Gideon opened an office in New York. There he hired me to assist him in the immigration business, as if were."

Vincent grinned broadly. "Pompantium! I see my brothers had no qualms about selling land script for property that an immigrant could homestead free. No, my father never would have approved. He was not a forward thinking man. But I'll get my share of the estate, of course."

"You've already gotten it. It's represented in your brothers' investment in your enterprises. They saw it as a fair way divide your father's estate without violating his business ethics or his last will and testament."

"You mean they used my inheritance to buy a partnership in my company? The hell, you say! I'll spend my inheritance any damned way I please."

"The money they invested was legally theirs. It not only will see you through these perilous economic times, but if your company succeeds, you will all enjoy your share of the profits. To assure that comes to pass, they sent me here to assist you."

"Assist me! Who in hell told them I needed assistance?"

"These letters will explain everything in detail," Frasier said impatiently, taking papers from his coat pocket. "But in brief they felt the need for more reliable communication. They want quarterly financial reports. You will see in my letter of introduction that I am an experienced administrator, and an expert accountant. My first duty will be to conduct an inventory and an audit. In the long term I will be available to manage the company in your absence."

"That's nonsense. I'm not going anywhere," said Vincent, his anger beginning to show.

"They were concerned about your long visits to the pineries. They cannot go for weeks on end without some word of the company's progress, and they have found your correspondence to be spotty and inadequate."

"What do they expect? I can't run a lumber company sitting at a desk all day penning fancy letters."

"Precisely so," Frasier said with a smile. "You will be free to conduct business as usual. I will attend to the more mundane matters of management, bookkeeping, correspondence, and the like."

"I'm grooming my son for that job," Vincent said with a scowl, nodding to Stephen. "Isn't that right, Stephen?"

"Yes, we've talked about it," Stephen conceded.

"I would be pleased to relieve you of that responsibility," Frasier said to Vincent. "Stephen seems a most promising student, and I am an accomplished tutor."

"Well, I'll be damned," Vincent said, slamming his brother's letters onto his desk. He studied Frasier with worried and suspicious eyes, then went to the window and looked out over the busy street below. "I never expected anything like this," he said.

"I was led to believe they'd forewarned you," Frasier said. "I was told..."

"They may have mentioned it. I don't always have time to read everything they send to me," Vincent said vacantly.

"You seemed to have no hesitation about asking for money, nor in accepting it without question."

"Money's in short supply, banks are failing. Don't they read the papers? I spelled it out in my last letter, or don't they read my letters?"

"They read them very carefully. It is you who failed to read theirs. But now it won't be necessary," Frasier said brightly. "I could also serve as your personal secretary and take care of such matters. At the moment, however, I am exhausted from my journey and want to get settled. Your friend Whitcomb was kind enough to arrange lodging for me close by the mill – a Mrs. Newby's establishment. Stephen has offered to guide me there. But I'll return first thing in the morning."

*   *   *

"I know the type, and mark my words he'll be a handful."

Mrs. Carpenter punched her floured fist deep into a ball of dough, then slapped its velvety surface until it regained its shape. "I knew it the minute Mr. Vincent Shevley came into my kitchen this morning. He was talking to himself, and mad as a wet hen."

"This Frasier fellow does that to a man. He just takes over," Stephen said. "I drove him to Mrs. Newby's boarding house last evening, and we hadn't been there five minutes before he was telling old Mrs. Newby how he liked his eggs in the morning and when he'd require absolute quiet in the house after dinner – from eight o'clock on, mind you."

"I'm just glad he's her problem, and not mine," Mrs. Carpenter said. "He'd not be tellin' me how to run my house!"

"He says I'm to pick him up promptly at seven every morning but Sunday, and he cautioned me not be late."

"He's close enough to walk to the mill," Sarah said as she carried Eleanor's tray into the kitchen.

"Mother didn't eat much," Stephen observed.

"Never does," said Sarah.

"Eats like a bird, she does. I don't know how she survives," said Mrs. Carpenter.

"She's sick, Mama."

"Well, that may be, but a body's got to eat."

"I've got to get going," Stephen exclaimed as the clock struck the half-hour.

"This Frasier person has really got you hopping!"

"He's just testing me, Sarah. He's going to teach me how to be an accountant, but he said the first lesson of business is to be on time." He gulped down the last of his

159

milk and headed for the front hall where he met his father coming downstairs.

"Tell him to bring back my ledgers!" Vincent demanded. "I'll have to scratch my tallies on the wall, if I don't have those books."

Frasier, ledgers in hand, was waiting for him when Vincent arrived at the mill office.

"Everything seems to be in order," he said, handing Vincent the books. "At least as far as these records go. I still must check your employment lists. I have no idea how many men you have in the camps or how much they are paid, when and by whom."

"Damn it, Frasier, the pay books are in the camps where they belong. How can I..."

"We'll need duplicates, of course. You pay through a bank, do you not? Certainly the bank demands records."

"The bankers do what I tell 'em to do," Vincent grumbled. "I won't worry about payrolls until next spring. We've got months to get the books in order. My mills are working overtime to keep up with the demand for lumber. I don't care whether a bunch of timber tramps have a dollar in their pocket or not. My crews went into the woods short-handed and the straw bosses were told to bring them up to strength as best they could. I don't even know how many men I've hired, let alone how much I'm paying them."

Frasier responded with a slow shaking of his head signaling his disapproval, and causing Vincent's blood to rise.

"What in hell is there to worry about? There's nothing in the woods to spend money on. The men know they'll get their wages when the timber rafts arrive in town after the thaw. I can't be worried about payrolls. I've got orders to fill, saws to replace, and booms to empty."

"Your foremen can fill orders, and any mechanic can replace a saw. What we need is better liaison with the camps. Perhaps an inspection trip would be in order."

"Don't tell me what to do!" Vincent exploded. "This is my business, and I'll decide when..."

"Wrong, sir," Frasier said quietly but firmly. "This is a partnership, and it carries with it certain well-defined obligations to your brothers. It was clearly spelled out in the papers that accompanied their investment draft. In accepting their money you also accepted the terms they laid down. They have asked for monthly reports, and it is my duty to comply with their orders."

Despite his haughty demeanor, Frasier was an excellent tutor. As each ledger was checked and corrected Stephen was set to work copying it in the fine hand he had learned at his mother's knee. Repetition, Frasier advised him, was a good way to fix information in the mind, and through his copy work, and Frasier's willingness to answer questions, the young student learned many things – how many logs floated in the boom, how many were processed each day in the mill, how much lumber was sold to buyers in town and down river. He learned how to read bark marks and stamp marks, and how to speak the language of the catch markers, sorters, scalers and tallymen. He learned how many barges the Shevley company operated on the Mississippi, and how much lumber each could carry, to what ports, to which consignees, and at what prices. Through it all he developed a close working relationship with his mentor that soon grew into a firm friendship. Before long even Vincent developed a grudging admiration for his new executive secretary – Frasier insisted on that title, and suggested a salary to fit it. Vincent found little reason to complain; the new arrangement not only freed him to carry on as usual, but also allowed him to devote more time to his growing interest in the political affairs of the day.

The 1850s were difficult years for the conservative founders of the city by the falls. The rising tide of immigration brought with it many new and contentious issues that soon manifested themselves in the social and political life of the frontier. Prominent among them was the issue of abolition, soon brought sharply into focus by the influx of southerners who came north in season to enjoy the salubrious climate of Minnesota Territory. With them they brought their slaves to attend to their needs, slaves whose black skin made them objects of curiosity among the white settlers, many of whom had never before seen an African. To some the black men immediately became objects of fear and derision whose right to exist in the pristine frontier community was subject to challenge. This despite the fact that the slaves' roots in America might well go back five generations or more, while many of the Caucasian settlers' boots still carried the dust of Europe. In society at large battle lines were drawn, and they were mirrored in Shevley House West.

"Slavery's none of our business," huffed Vincent. "Let's not go looking for trouble. We've got problems enough of our own."

"It's simply not right that one man should own another," said Eleanor in righteous indignation.

Fanning the flames of controversy were readers at the Athenaeum who introduced their fellow members to the emotional portrayal of slave life in the South as described in Mrs. Stowe's popular new romance. At the Lyceum touring abolitionists took the podium to further stir up sentiment against the iniquities of slavery. As if to give expanded voice to the abolitionists the Republican Party emerged to provide a political home to the anti-slavery faction throughout the country, including Minnesota Territory where the desire for statehood inevitably became mired in the free state-slave state controversy that raged on the national level. When delegates met in St. Paul to write a constitution for the proposed state of Minnesota the fledgling Republicans rallied under the banners of abolition and temperance, while the majority of Democrats held fast to their national party's pro-slavery position and its benign neglect of the temperance movement. The schism that developed led not only to a walkout of the minority Republicans, but to the writing of two separate state constitutions and the nomination of two opposing candidates to carry Minnesota's hopes for statehood to Washington, D.C. Vincent held fast with the majority Democrats, convinced that slavery was a southern problem that had nothing to do with Minnesota. He'd also had his fill of the Maine Liquor Laws put forward by temperance advocates, arguing that if the Republicans and dissident Democrats wanted to legislate against the honest thirst of hard-working men he would have no part of it. The Democrats' candidate was the Honorable Henry M. Rice, and the voters in the October election vindicated their choice. In due course Rice carried to Washington a statehood bill that reflected the views of the majority, including boundaries running north to Canada at the Pigeon River and west to the Red River of the North, boundaries that incorporated the vast northern pineries wherein lay the hope and prosperity of the Minnesota frontier and the fortunes of its founders.

*   *   *

Politics aside, life in Shevley House became a daunting challenge for Stephen. Although his mother's health slowly improved after Jonathan Wells and his bride left the territory, she seemed resigned to a lonely fate, feeding on her own inner resources, asking nothing, and giving nothing in return. Stephen pitied her. He wanted to help, to reach out to her with love. But she made it impossible. She was empty of emotion, a shadow person, a ghost of the mother he once had known. The color may have returned to her cheeks, the sparkle to her eyes, but it was ephemeral. She was a woman without substance, present in body but not in spirit, an apparition that floated through Stephen's life without touching him. He could find no joy in her recovery. Vincent, on the other hand, was elated at her improved health, seemingly content with the mere appearance of normal family life. He and Eleanor treated one another in a polite, even courtly manner, but there was never any display of affection between them. They were kind to one another, but only because it was more comfortable than quarreling. They adhered to social conventions and stayed together, because divorce would have been unthinkable. They walked carefully through their roles, because one slip might plunge them into ugly confrontation. Their lives became a sham, because there was no place for them to hide. They were constantly on stage and the curtain was up. They had no choice but to wear masks of domestic bliss. They fooled everyone except themselves and their son. And when each day's performance was over they went their separate, lonely ways to bed.

Deprived of a loving family life, Stephen directed his energies toward the marketplace where his training under Roger Frasier and his father led him to remarkable success for one so young. He worked with all his youthful enthusiasm to imitate his father, the rough and tumble trader, the cunning bargainer, and like Frasier, the cool, calculating intellectual. The results often sent his confidence soaring.

"I suppose you saw the item in The Frontiersman."

"No, I didn't," Sarah admitted.

"Mr. Whitcomb wrote that I was a chip off the old block, and said my father was very proud of me."

"We're all proud of you, Stephen. Will you take me to the Callaghans?"

"Why are you always running off to the Callaghans?"

"I'm not *always* running off to the Callaghans. Last week I took a pail to be mended, and today I'm going to pick it up."

"All right, come along. But let's be quick or we'll be late for supper."

She looked even younger than her twelve years as she left the blacksmith's shop, smiling coyly at the red-faced, raw-boned Irish lad who shuffled along barefoot at her side.

"I'm grateful for the service, Mr. Callaghan. You did a wonderful job."

"Gosh, Miss Sarah, I ain't Mr. Callaghan. He's my pa. I'm Patrick."

"Well, Mr. Patrick Callaghan, you could have fooled me!"

The boy blushed, wiping blackened hands on his leather apron.

"Come along, Sarah. We have to get home," groused Stephen impatiently.

"Goodbye, Mr. Patrick Callaghan," said Sarah. "I'm sure we'll be seeing you again soon."

As the rig lurched away from the smithy's Stephen was unable to contain his annoyance.

"Why all of a sudden do you break into that brogue? If ever there was a more obvious, more insincere..."

"My mother happens to be Irish, and I come by it quite naturally, especially when I hear it from a boy like Patrick. We surely must have a lot in common. That's the way with the Irish, you know. There's a kinship, as my mother says."

"Maybe Patrick Callaghan would be pleased to know that you were born in the north woods, and that your only truly Irish trait is your wagging tongue and your freckled nose."

"Why Stephen! I do believe you're angry. You must be hungry and anxious to get home to dinner. Really, sometimes I just can't tell which is bigger, your appetite or your head."

*   *   *

Thursday, May 13, 1858 began as any other day for the Shevleys. Up at dawn, Stephen and Vincent had their breakfast and by 7 a.m. were on their way downtown. As they drove along the avenue they paused before the nearly completed Nicollet House where the usual knot of onlookers gathered to evaluate the progress on the magnificent new hotel. The building in its grandeur and bright promise was a beacon of hope in ever-darkening economic times. Some claimed to have seen the doom descending like the ominous clouds of grasshoppers that had appeared during the fall harvest, stripping the fields of their abundance and devastating a large segment of the agricultural community. Then like a thunderbolt a financial storm struck beginning with the failure of the Ohio Life Insurance and Trust Company. That collapse set off a chain reaction among financial houses across the country. If the foundering of conservative institutions in the east was disastrous, the impact on the frontier's freewheeling wildcat banks proved even more so. Minnesota Territory, flooded as it was with worthless bank notes issued by these shaky institutions, was hard-hit. Real estate prices plummeted, the money market dried up. The volatile fuels of greed and land had fired the engines of growth and expansion until the boilers of boom shuddered and groaned. The banks, churning out script to support the frenzied activity in the market place, were driven to the wall when eastern creditors refused to accept their homemade currency. The impasse sent the scant supply of gold and silver scurrying into hiding. The panic left searing poverty in its wake, and land speculators were some of the first to feel the heat. In Minnesota Territory alone some 700 townships had been platted in the last few years. These maps now gathered dust in recorders' offices along with the dreams of the landholders and speculators alike. Among the many failures was Pompantium, and whatever Vincent had envisioned for its future. Some real estate ventures survived, to be sure, such as Minneapolis' newest hotel. The economic foundations of the Nicollet House seemed to be made of pure gold. Among its investors was Roger Frasier, who stood now in the crowd admiring the edifice as the Shevley rig passed by.

"It won't be long now, Roger," Vincent called out.

"No, indeed, sir," Roger responded as he and the hotel's builder, Henry Titus, stepped into the street to talk. "Mr. Titus and I have just been discussing a gala celebration, perhaps a ball, to mark the grand opening. What is your opinion?"

"I think it would be a wonderful idea!" said Vincent enthusiastically. "It would show we've got confidence in the future, despite the panic. It would help to calm the economic waters."

Their conversation was suddenly interrupted by the arrival of the morning stage from St. Paul. It rattled over the suspension bridge and charged down the street with passengers leaning out the windows, shouting and waving their hands in excitement. At the Nicollet House the driver reined up to announce the news.

"Statehood's here! Minnesota's become the thirty-second state of the Union!"

"When? How?"

"News came by steamboat just an hour ago. Those aboard said President Buchanan signed the bill on Tuesday."

The stage passengers swung down to the street and were immediately surrounded by excited citizens hungry for more information.

"I guess this will make your celebration all the more appropriate," said Vincent. "But if you want a good turnout, you'd better get your plans laid before the excitement wears off." He handed Stephen the reins, saying, "Take the rig on down to the mill, son, and tell 'em I'll be along later. I've got a lot of talking to do."

Stephen stopped briefly at the offices of The Frontiersman to alert Charles Whitcomb to the news. The journalist hurried to join the crowd at the Nicollet House, notepad in hand, and within hours his first posters appeared around town. They proclaimed the advent of statehood, and invited all citizens to an open house at 1 p.m. on Thursday, May 20, 1858, at the new hotel, "a monument to appropriately herald the admission to the Union of the great State of Minnesota, a symbol of its progress and its faith in its own future and the future of the United States of America. A Buffet and Grand Ball will follow at 6 p.m."

*   *   *

Roger managed to make the most of his boarding house accommodations, expanding from his sleeping quarters into an adjacent bedroom that he transformed into an office, and laying claim to a sitting room that now served as his dining nook.

"I can't stand eating in the kitchen with the other boarders. They don't dine, they feed. For an extra two dollars a week, Mrs. Newby brings me my dinner here in the privacy

167

of my rooms. This allows me on occasion to choose my own company. I know I am an unmitigated snob, but I find no pleasure in breaking bread with a teamster, a gambler and what I can only describe as a drifter. It's bad enough that I have to hear the drunken louts coming and going at all hours of the night, disturbing my work and my sleep. I explained to Mrs. Newby that if she weren't more discriminating in her selection of tenants this would become a common flophouse. I told her that by accommodating my needs – for a fee, of course, paid regularly and in advance – she would greatly enhance her reputation in the community. She was keen enough to see the wisdom in my proposition."

"Do you often invite guests to dinner?" Stephen asked.

"Infrequently. As a matter of fact, you are the first."

"Dinner in your rooms! You'll have her carrying you pick-a-back to work before long," Stephen laughed.

"No, no, no," Frasier protested modestly. "But I do wish that Mrs. Newby would polish her culinary skills. I already am tired of her weekly menu, which I've memorized. Tonight, for instance, we can expect a thick gruel made of dried peas; pork chops tough as your boot; huge baked potatoes hard as a rock in the middle; boiled turnips, which I detest, and a concoction she calls tea, but which I happen to know is brewed from some sort of dried leaves her imbecilic husband gathers in the adjacent wilderness. I shall count myself fortunate to survive until I can take a suite at the Nicollet House, this community's first respectable hotel and restaurant."

"What about the Winslow House?" Stephen asked.

"They cater to transients, what they pompously refer to as tourists. Besides, I find it difficult to converse with the Southerners who flock there. I find their manner of speech – well, rural."

They were enjoying a glass of sherry in front of a blazing fire, and Stephen was warmed inside and out. Frasier's furnishings were simple – a few books on a desktop, a braided rug on the floor, a linen tablecloth, small silver candle holders, crystal wine glasses, and matching decanter. It made Stephen feel quite mature to sip wine in the company of such a sophisticated companion. He stretched his legs, leaned back in his chair, and watched the flickering flames in the fireplace through the sherry glass.

"You've created your own little world here," he observed.

"My surroundings are a far cry from the grand castle you call home. What does it matter? It's all just scenery on the stage of life."

"Shevley House is my father's scenery, not mine. I spent last summer in a cabin, and found it suited me very well. I believe he built his castle to match his hopes for the future."

"I'm sure he did. It shows that he's a man of great ambition, a man who sets high goals for himself. Nevertheless, he will be judged on whether he achieves his goals, not on some edifice he is destined to leave behind."

"Then we all will be judged by how we perform, how we live our lives, not in the things we gather around us," Stephen said, eagerly grasping Frasier's line of thought.

"Yes, something like that. But it's not as if you will be standing at the Pearly Gates being judged by Saint Peter. I don't see it in religious terms. It's a personal thing. 'This above all, to thine own self be true,' as Polonius said. A man should strive to satisfy his own demands, not the dictates of one religion or another."

"He works hard, and he sacrificed a lot to reach his goals. I think, however, that he has caused a lot of harm along the way."

"That may be, but his life isn't over yet. Our lives are what we make of them. It's important to know ourselves, our strengths, our weaknesses, so we don't make a mess of things. You have reached a time in your life when you should look toward the future, set your own goals, and determine how you'll attain them."

"It's a little early, isn't it – at seventeen?"

"Not at all. You're on the verge of manhood. It's never too early, and it's frequently too late. One must have a plan."

"I don't know what good a plan would do. I might make all sorts of plans today, but tomorrow..."

"You miss my point, Stephen. A man cannot plan his life, but he can plan how he'll live that life. Do you see the distinction? The world is constantly changing, disrupting our plans, no matter how firm we are in our resolve. 'The best-laid plans o' mice and men gang aft agley,' as Burns put it. Your father, for example, dreamed of making a fortune in the lumber business, he did not *plan* it. What he *planned* was to work hard, and not be distracted or defeated by outside influences until he had achieved his goal. He even ignored his brothers' demand to form a partnership – or pay back what he owed them – so intent was he on achieving that goal."

"He had other distractions, too," Stephen observed darkly.

"But he had a singleness of purpose. We must ever be alert to the obstacles fate puts in our way. Every day could present a new challenge, any one of which might turn our dreams upside down. Life is a series of up-endings that test our resolve and our adaptability. That's why we must plan how we intend to live our lives. Your father is a pragmatist. He has been since he first ran away from home when he was much younger than you are now. He did not plan to run away to sea; it was a means to an end. He did not plan to become a good businessman; it too was a means to an end. Are you properly confused?"

"Not by what you say, but by my own circumstances. My father has planned my life for me, which in your terms is not only wrong, but also futile. What he should be doing is helping me plan how to live my life. That's the distinction, isn't it? He is wrong in the first instance, because fate may disrupt his plan for me. And he has failed in the second instance by not preparing me to cope with whatever life might hold for me."

"You go one step too far," Frasier cautioned. "You must never use philosophy – any philosophy – to disavow your personal responsibility. Your father's plan for your life is nothing more than an extension of his own dream. He expects you to carry it forward after he is gone. He has told me as much. You, and only you, can determine how you will conduct your life, how you will face each day, whether that day's activities are planned by your father or flung at you by the most contrary of fates. How you respond to each day's challenge is entirely up to you. Your response to life is uniquely your own, and cannot be blamed on anyone else."

"Nevertheless," Stephen shrugged. "I feel I'm a victim of my father's dream of success. I don't care about his dream. I want to find my own dream."

"Your dream will come in due time. You mustn't be impatient. This needn't be a difficult time in your life. After all, it's not as if you're facing a life of poverty and suffering. Look upon your father's plan as a quirk of fate, an up-ending such as we all must endure from time to time. Go along with his plan while you decide how best to live your life. You may decide his plan parallels your own, or you may reject it to pursue your own dream. He rejected his father's plans for him, didn't he? Perhaps you will make a similar decision when your time comes. I am not worried about you. You are intelligent and resilient. You will survive. Perhaps someday men will point to you and say, 'That fellow was born to a life of wealth and privilege, but he rejected it all to follow his dream – and he succeeded!'"

Stephen smiled ruefully, uncertain whether or not it was bitterness that he detected in Roger's humor.

Chapter 11

A cadre of ambitious young boys made a thriving business of attending to the horses and rigs of the hundreds who came to take part in the gala opening of the Nicollet House. They charged five cents for each horse, and an additional ten cents for a rig. In return they promised safe tethering spaces for the animals and a parking area for the carriages, coaches and wagons that jammed the streets of Minneapolis. In exchange for his twenty cents Vincent received a paper ticket with a number scrawled on it that identified the young entrepreneurs and the location of their parking area. The leader of each team collected the fee, while his partners took charge of the animals and conveyances and hastened them away. Their initiative brought an admiring grin to Vincent's face.

"It's that kind of enterprise that will build this state," he chuckled as he pocketed his claim ticket and guided Eleanor toward the hotel. As they neared the door Eleanor paused, a frown of anger and dismay darkening her face. "What is it?" Vincent asked.

"Just look at that!" she exclaimed, pointing to a crowd that was gathering across the street, apparently to watch a fight that was raising dust amid a ring of onlookers.

"Ruffians," Vincent commented. "It's none of our business."

"Well, it should be!" Eleanor exploded. "That man is beating his servant, and those fools are cheering him on."

"It's not our..." Vincent began, but by now Eleanor had stormed into the street toward the melee. "Wait, Eleanor! For God's sake wait!" he called, hurrying after her. By the time he caught up she had elbowed her way through the crowd, and grabbed hold of the cane that a portly, red-faced man was using to beat a cowering black man who groveled in the dust.

"If this woman is yours, sir, call her off for God's sake!" the portly man puffed. "I've never seen such unseemly behavior."

"My woman!" Vincent shouted. "Unseemly behavior! How dare you speak that way of my wife?"

"She is interfering with the discipline of my slave, sir. Call her off, I say. Let go of my stick, woman, and cease that abolitionist cant! He is my property, and I will discipline him as I see fit."

"He is not property, he is a human being!" she screamed, tugging on the cane with all the strength she could muster.

"Eleanor, please," Vincent urged, gently prying her fingers from the stick and leading her away through the crowd of jeering onlookers. "There, there, now, let's collect ourselves. This is a day of celebration, not politics."

"It's not a matter of politics," she muttered through clenched teeth. "It's a matter of common decency. You wouldn't stand by while a man beat a horse like that. Why do you look the other way when a man is being beaten?"

"Because it's none of my business," he said calmly, "nor is it yours. You know my feelings on the matter. We are not a party to slavery; it has no place in our lives."

"But cruel, barbaric behavior does have a place, is that it?" she asked as she straightened her skirt and adjusted her hat. "Someone must speak up for the defenseless."

"Perhaps, my dear, but not today. Please, not today," he begged as he guided her into the hotel.

They came upon Roger Frasier near the end of the receiving line and exchanged pleasantries. As a major investor in the six-story brick structure, Roger exuded a sense of self-satisfaction.

"Welcome to a new era in this fair city," he said.

"Such a beautiful ballroom!" Eleanor gasped.

"Made all the more so by your presence, Mrs. Shevley."

"We are indeed coming of age," Vincent said, aglow with the opulence of the place. "It's magnificent. How I wish

I'd had the foresight to buy into it when I had the chance. This is going to be a real money-maker."

"You can't say I didn't encourage you," Roger said.

"I thought you were just trying to get away from Mrs. Newby's boarding house," Vincent laughed.

"And I did! I've taken a suite on the third floor and intend to make this my home," he said enthusiastically as he passed the Shevleys down the line toward the ballroom.

Cast adrift in a sea of humanity, Charles Whitcomb came to their rescue.

"How wonderful to see you both! Isn't this marvelous? Our fair city is on its way to becoming a sophisticated metropolis. Eleanor, you're looking absolutely radiant. Such a fine, healthy glow. I'm very pleased to see you feeling well again."

"My glow has nothing to do with my health," she began, but Vincent, fearing she was about to recount her confrontation in the street – and seeing the portly, red-faced man nearing the end of the receiving line – he interrupted her.

"It's spring, Charlie, and she blossoms with the flowers," he said, casting an admiring glance at his wife as he guided her to one side toward a chair.

"So it would appear," agreed Charles as he followed after them. "And where is Stephen? I expected he'd be here today. He's becoming quite a young man about town."

"He's growing up much too fast," Eleanor said.

"He'll be along shortly," Vincent said. "He didn't want to come with us for some reason."

"Typical," Charles observed. "He's not a child anymore. It won't be long before he'll be leaving the nest."

"For school in the East, I hope," said Eleanor.

"Now, now, my dear. His education is in good hands."

"I would have to agree," Charles said. "With his father to emulate, and with Roger Frasier as his mentor, he's bound to make his mark in this state. I wouldn't be surprised if he became governor some day."

At the moment, however, Stephen was barely able to govern his unruly hair. When at last each strand had been carefully placed, he examined the beginnings of a beard that he had been cultivating for more than a week. He rubbed his fingers ruefully over the downy whiskers and shook his head. In the mirror he saw Sarah peek around the doorway, a knowing smile on her face.

"I was thinking of shaving it off," he said. "Although it does make me look older, don't you think?"

"Oh, indeed it does," she said gravely.

"Still, it's rather a poor beginning. If only..."

"If only what?" she asked.

"If only I hadn't shaved off the beard I had when I came home from the Koenigs."

"My mother said it was mostly dirt."

"I don't want to look too young," he mused, ignoring her remark.

"Too young for what?" Sarah asked innocently.

"For the Nicollet House party, of course. There's a buffet and an orchestra and dancing."

"How could anyone who's seventeen look too young?"

"I suppose that's true," he agreed. "But it just doesn't look the way it should. I think I'll shave it off."

"You don't have a razor."

"I'll borrow my father's razor and his soap. Heat some water, Sarah. I've made up my mind."

While the water was on the stove he decided on a compromise. The cheek and chin would be scraped clean, but the soft fuzz on his upper lip would remain. As fate would have it, a slip of the razor upset that plan, and in the end the moustache also had to go. It was with a melancholy sigh that he presented himself in the kitchen.

"Well, just look at the perfect gentleman," Mrs. Carpenter exclaimed. "My, but won't you set the young ladies' hearts aflutter."

"I think you nicked your upper lip," Sarah observed dryly.

"It's nothing," he said, "a mere scratch."

Sarah raised an eyebrow, but said nothing.

"Hurry along, now," said Mrs. Carpenter. "Your father took the carriage, so you'll have to take the buckboard or walk. Watch out for the mud, and mind your manners."

"I can probably catch a ride down at the road," he said. "I see a rig coming now. Goodbye."

"Mind your manners!" Mrs. Carpenter called again from the doorway. He could still hear her admonition ringing in his ears as he stood in the doorway to the ballroom and surveyed the crowd. He took a quick glance at himself in one of the huge mirrors that lined the room. In it he saw himself looking quite elegant in a new split-tailed dress coat, pipe stem trousers and black boots gleaming in the light of giant chandeliers.

"Hello, Stephen," Whitcomb greeted him warmly as he emerged from the crowd with a glass of punch in one hand and a hefty sandwich in the other. "You're late, my boy. The receiving line dissolved a half-hour ago. Come let me show you the buffet. You've never seen such an array of delicacies, but they're going fast. And the young ladies – I never guessed there were so many lovely charmers in the entire state. And hear that? The orchestra is warming up, and you can't dance on an empty stomach."

"I would like a bite or two," Stephen allowed. It was nearing sunset, and he had primped through much of the afternoon without noticing the passage of time.

Whitcomb wolfed down his sandwich as he pressed greedily toward the tables. "Look at that!" he exclaimed, gesturing toward a pheasant that served as a centerpiece. "Have you ever seen anything like it?"

"I saw one in the taxidermist's window, or is this one alive?"

"No, of course not. It's just decoration. But look at that platter with sliced meat fanned out to tempt one and all." He selected a piece, devoured it, and daintily licked his fingertips. He was about to reach for another when suddenly he stopped. "Oh my God," he muttered. "Look who's coming this way. Excuse me, my boy, but I must circulate among the guests."

Stephen turned to look just as the imposing figure of C. Gladstone Pomeroy hove into view.

"I say, wasn't that Whitcomb, the local journalist? I did want to talk to him."

"Yes, sir," Stephen replied. "He said he..." But at that instant his eye fell upon the most beautiful girl he had ever seen.

"Don't I know you, young man?" Pomeroy asked. "Yes, I remember you from last season. You're Whitcomb's associate, if memory serves. I am C. Gladstone Pomeroy of Vicksburg. Allow me to introduce my party."

Stephen stood dumbfounded as Pomeroy presented his wife and their niece, Gaily Gladstone. What a perfect name, he thought. She was a tiny thing with a smile as big as all outdoors and she seemed in constant motion, fairly dancing in place as her sparkling eyes first flirted with him boldly, then glanced demurely away, a maneuver that nearly drew him off balance. All the while her fan fluttered like tiny wings, alternately concealing a bit of bare shoulder, then a glimpse of rosy cheek, drawing Stephen's eyes first one way then the other, tantalizing him, hypnotizing him. Although he had entered the room only moments before supremely confident and self-assured, he now found himself stammering perilously close to the end of his limited small talk. At last he could do little but stand agog, smitten dumb, totally taken in by this charming creature with her soft Southern accent and vivacious personality. It was Mrs. Pomeroy who saved him from making a fool of himself by suggesting that the young people enjoy the music and join others on the dance floor. Relieved, Stephen bowed politely and managed a gracious invitation, which Gaily shyly accepted. She was light as a summer cloud in his arms, a sweet-scented delight. Close to her, moving in time with the music, he found that a million thoughts were racing through his mind but not a single word with which to express them. Desperate, he whirled this bright and glittering jewel to the sidelines as the music came to a halt and guided her toward an open window. There they paused for a breath of fresh air and a view of the sunset.

"My, you certainly turned silent on me, Stephen Shevley," she said. "I don't know what's proper up here, but down home it's considered polite to chat with one's partner on the dance floor."

"I – I was waiting for you to speak," he stammered lamely. "I'm not used to dancing, as you probably could tell."

"Nonsense! You dance divinely," she gushed. "But this is wonderful, too, this cool evening air." She threw her arms wide and rose on the tips of her toes as she inhaled deeply. "It's beautiful. Is it always so pleasant here? I surely can see why Uncle Clarence enjoys these visits. How fortunate you are to call this home."

"It is beautiful, isn't it?" Stephen said in wonderment as if noticing for the first time the shadows that settled on the river at dusk, and the sweet aroma of spring on the evening breeze that wafted through the river valley.

"We have a spectacular view of the falls from our room at the Winslow House," Gaily said. "And when it's quiet in the street we can hear them roar just as if we were standing beside them."

"Have you seen them close up? Would you like to?"

"Why, that sounds exciting!"

"Good!" he said, guiding her quickly around the perimeter of the ballroom, searching for his parents. At last he spied them near the buffet engaged in an animated conversation with Charles.

"You see what I mean," the editor said to the Shevleys as the young couple approached. "Stephen seems to be doing very well with the young ladies."

"I'd like to present Miss Gaily Gladstone of Vicksburg," Stephen said. "This is my mother, my father, and our good friend, Charles Whitcomb."

"How do you do, Miss Gladstone," Eleanor said warmly. "Are you and your family staying at the Nicollet House?"

"No, we are at the Winslow House, Mrs. Shevley. We find it most delightful."

"It is a pleasure to make your acquaintance," Vincent said with a bow.

"I believe I know your uncle," Whitcomb said.

"Yes, indeed, sir. So he has said."

As the pleasantries continued, Stephen pulled his father aside and whispered, "We thought we'd enjoy a closer look at the falls. May I borrow the carriage for an hour?"

"What? The carriage? What's this all about?"

"Sh-h-h-h!"

"Oh, I see! A buggy ride."

"Father, please...oh, never mind."

"Have you tried the fruit punch?" Eleanor asked innocently, having heard nothing of their conversation.

"No, we haven't; that's a good idea," Stephen said, grasping at the opportunity to escape. "Let's try the punch, Miss Gladstone."

"Pleasure to meet you all," Gaily gasped hurriedly as Stephen rushed her away. "Well! What was THAT all about, Stephen Shevley? How rude to break away so abruptly. Your parents will think I've not had a proper upbringing."

"It was nothing – an idea, that's all. I thought if I could borrow the carriage for an hour we could drive down to see the falls at dusk."

"Why, I declare! Do you really think I'd entertain such an invitation? I would not, of course, although I do find it somewhat flattering." She smiled fetchingly, flicking her fan and peering over it with her bright flashing eyes. "The fact is, Mister Shevley, that my guardians would never permit it. After all, we've just met, and we know nothing about you. It wouldn't be proper."

"What would be proper?" he asked hopefully.

"It would be proper to make a formal call and ask Uncle Clarence's approval. And he would NEVER approve a ride alone with a young man. Never. It isn't done. But it was sweet and impetuous of you to think of it."

The thought of confronting the formidable C. Gladstone Pomeroy dampened the lad's enthusiasm considerably, but it was clear it was the only way he could see Gaily again. He would have to call on the Pomeroys before he could even think of paying his respects to their niece. As the music began again, a polite young man stepped forward with a bow, and in a pronounced southern accent asked Gaily to dance. She accepted, but not without rewarding Stephen with a squeeze of her dainty hand. Stunned at his sudden loss, but thrilled by her gesture, he set out to find the Pomeroys.

"Ah, I see. You want to call on us? That would be fine, would it not, my dear?"

"Why, yes, I think it would," Mrs. Pomeroy said hesitantly. "You could bring your card around. I believe we'll at home on Sunday."

"At two o'clock." Pomeroy added.

"Yes, sir!" Stephen exclaimed. "I'll be at the Winslow House at two. I'd like to take you all on a tour of the area – Gaily, too."

The music stopped at that moment and he hastily excused himself and set out to find the light of his life on the crowded dance floor. But before he could locate her, he bumped into his parents heading toward the lobby, his mother obviously in a fury.

"If you want a ride home, you'll have to come with us now," his father said glumly.

"Why? What's the matter?"

"It's that awful man," Eleanor fumed. "I can't stand to be in the same room with him."

"What man? Do I have to leave now?"

"You do, if you don't want to walk home in the dark."

"But what man?"

"A man that your mother saw caning a servant in the street. I don't know why it should spoil our evening, but it has. I'm afraid if we don't leave immediately there'll be another scene."

Perplexed, Stephen cast a final glance around the ballroom. Unable to see Gaily in the crowd, he reluctantly followed his parents as they strode toward the lobby and out onto the darkened avenue.

*   *   *

On Sunday morning Eleanor sat at her writing desk penning neat little calling cards in flowing script. She made six of them, each identical to the others, and in her drawer she found a small leather case to contain them. The cards read:

Stephen Craft Shevley, Esq.
Shevley House West
Minneapolis, Minnesota
1858

She presented the calling cards to Stephen along with a lecture.

"From your description, these are gentle people, the sort we might have associated with had we remained in the East. They are accustomed to the finer things in life; propriety is important to them. They are not like most of the people we are familiar with here in the West. I am confident that you have been properly trained over the years, but I want to remind you to heed your lessons well. It has been a long time since we've reviewed the rudiments of polite behavior, and we've had little opportunity to practice the social graces. In surroundings such as ours, such things are easily forgotten." She walked to the window, where she saw Sarah picking flowers in the front garden, a tiny bouquet of lilies of the valley for the parlor. "Yes," she said absently. "Yes, where was I? Oh, of course. Mrs. Carpenter pressed your trousers, and Sarah can shine your boots."

"I can do them, mother. Thank you for all your help."
He reached out to her and she took his hands gently in hers.
"I want you to meet the Pomeroys. I'm sure you'd like
them."

"That would be very nice, Stephen. Perhaps we could
ask them to dinner."

"I would like that. I'm sure we'd have lots to talk
about."

"Yes," she said, smiling wanly. He kissed her lightly
on the cheek and left her room.

*   *   *

The clerk at the Winslow House took his card and
disappeared up the stairs while Stephen waited patiently, if
somewhat apprehensively, in the lobby. The clerk soon
reappeared and without a word went back to his duties at the
desk. It was more than fifteen minutes later – fifteen
agonizing minutes for Stephen – when the Pomeroys paraded
grandly down the stairway, followed by the newfound light
of his young life. She was dressed in blue and wore a bonnet
tied with a huge bow under her chin. They graciously
accepted Stephen's offer of a carriage ride, with the
Pomeroys riding in the comfortable rear seat and Gaily
perched brightly beside him in front. Stephen offered a
running travelogue as they went, pointing out the modern
wonder of the city, the first suspension bridge across the
Mississippi, and its dominant natural feature, St. Anthony
Falls. Later he guided the open carriage south toward
Minnehaha Falls along a road where sunlight sparkled amid
the tamaracks and the birches, the shady oaks and stately
elms. The leafy green canopy rang with bird songs as they
wended their way to the banks of Minnehaha creek and up to
the falls where the grass was damp with mists that arose as
the tumbling water raced over the rocky ledge and splashed
into the moss-lined pool below. Stephen tethered the horses
and spread a blanket on the grass where his guests could rest
in the shade and enjoy their idyllic surroundings. The scene

reminded Clarence Pomeroy of a similar scene in rural Mississippi, and he began to tell of his childhood days on his grandparents' cotton plantation.

"I was a city boy, myself," he confessed, "and it was my great good fortune to spend many days at Gladstone Gardens – that's what granddaddy called the estate – little knowing then that someday my beloved sister would marry her third cousin and raise her family there."

"That would be Gaily's mother," Angelica Pomeroy interjected. "May God rest her soul."

"I'm sorry..." Stephen began.

"I never knew her," Gaily said to spare him embarrassment.

"No, she died in the birthing bed. And imagine, after giving life to three strapping boys with nary a problem..."

"Hush, Angelica," said Pomeroy, obviously uneasy with his wife's comments. "Listen to that whippoorwill. It must be growing late in the day."

"Are your brothers at home?" Stephen asked, equally eager to get off the subject of Gaily's birth.

"They manage the plantation," she said, "carrying on the family tradition. William is in charge, of course, while Henry's a judge, and Evan is in the state legislature. But just listen to me going on without a hint of modesty. I do hope you'll forgive me, Stephen Shevley, but I am duly proud of my family and sometimes this little old country girl just gets carried away." She blushed and flashed him her most enchanting smile, and he virtually wilted at her feet.

It was the closest they came to intimacy, relaxing there amid the lush greenery and the veil-like beauty of the falling water, the whispering rush of the stream. Their eyes met often and each time a dream formed in Stephen's imagination, formed and flowered and flowed away again as a leaf upon the waters. On the ride back to town she again was allowed to sit next to him and at each bump in the road their knees would touch, thrilling him to the point of ecstasy. His reverie at last was dashed as C. Gladstone Pomeroy launched into his own musings about life on the plantation in that other world so far away. The older man's words were to plague him all the way back to the hotel where he bid them a sad farewell. He arrived home at sunset, glum and speechless, and drove directly to the stables where Sarah found him just as darkness fell. He had combed the horses and then slumped into the fresh straw, his head upon his knees.

"What's the matter?" she asked gently. "Why don't you come in?"

"I'm not hungry."

"Did you have an awful time?" There was a hopeful tone to her voice, then an eagerness as she asked: "What went wrong?"

"It's the Pomeroys."

"Don't they like you?"

"They live on a plantation, Sarah. They grow cotton – and they own slaves!"

"Oh, my goodness! And your mother plans to ask them to dinner. What will happen when she finds out?"

"I don't know. I just don't know."

*   *   *

"I want it understood that Saturday's dinner party will not degenerate into another of your Lyceum meetings. The subject of slavery is not to be broached. I'll tolerate nothing that might embarrass our guests."

Eleanor, standing at her bedroom window, whirled about crimson with rage.

"Am I to understand that you fear I will misbehave?"

"Now see here," Vincent cautioned her. "You know I am not good at things like this. I can't stand beating around the bush. I'm appealing to your intelligence."

"And in so doing you are displaying your own ignorance!" she flared. "Do you really think that after all we've been through – do you really think I would do anything to embarrass you?"

"You're becoming emotional. Try to control yourself."

"I don't need such advice from you of all people!" she screamed. "I have never been guilty of driving guests from our home. Can you say as much? I have played the dutiful wife, been a gracious hostess to your friends without exception. Can you say as much? I have encouraged our son in social pursuits; I have tried to make him a gentleman. Can you say as much? Yes, I am becoming emotional. I am angry and hurt. You are a callous, unthinking man, and I live in fear that your son will turn out to be just like you."

Stung by her words, Vincent bowed his head, rubbing his temples wearily with his fingertips, staring at the floor. When at last he spoke again, he spoke quietly.

"I am sorry," he began, "but Stephen expressed his concern to me, because he was ashamed to mention it to you himself. He knows how you feel about slavery and he did not want to offend you. I took this upon myself at his urging."

Eleanor stormed to her writing desk, snatched up a handful of plain white cards and flung them to the floor at his feet.

"I sat at this desk and penned his calling cards myself," she said in measured tones. "I am fully aware of the Pomeroys' probable attitude toward involuntary servitude. As southern planters I know they must be slaveholders. I also am aware of Stephen's attraction to this Gaily Gladstone, and I am fully prepared to overlook the probability that Mr. Pomeroy will turn out to be a self-centered bore, and that his wife may be a vacuous piece of fluff that can most charitably be described as amusing. Despite my suspicions I never thought it would be necessary to assure you that I would mind my manners. But I see now that it would have been asking too much that you show a little trust in me."

"Trust? You dare to speak to me of trust? You who had the audacity to sneak around behind my back..." Vincent stomped to the door where he paused, glaring at her in disgust and frustration. "Charlic told me that Pomeroy complained to him of being attacked in the street a week ago by a female abolitionist while he was disciplining a servant. I thought you ought to know that before he knocked at our door as an invited dinner guest. How do I know what you might have done when you recognized one another? Trust? I can't even trust you to walk down the street without losing control of yourself."

He shook his head slowly, despairingly, then slammed the door and stomped down the stairs to his office.

*　　*　　*

Eleanor involved herself in all the preparations for the dinner to be certain that everything would be perfect. Then late Saturday afternoon she was overwhelmed by an attack of the vapors and took to her bed, leaving Vincent to make her apologies. He in turn was relieved by her evasive action, but Stephen was torn. On the one hand he was grateful she had avoided a confrontation; on the other he knew it was only a matter of time before the truth would be known. He feared that his dreams of a life with Gaily Gladstone were doomed unless he took drastic action. Dozens of daring plots crowded his imagination, but his favorite involved a midnight elopement, an escape across the plains and over the mountain ranges to California where they would begin their lives anew in the West. The dinner itself was not nearly as exciting as Stephen's imaginings. There was an instant when the two men first met at the door that a look of puzzlement crossed Pomeroy's face. But Vincent assured him that they'd never met and that seemed to defuse the situation. The rest of the evening went off like a well-rehearsed drama, albeit dull beyond description. Though the participants played their roles with stiff precision, Eleanor's ghostly presence hovered over every scene, stultifying conversation and reducing it to absurdity. There would be no applause for these actors, no cheers for the author of this play. There would be only deep relief when the curtain came down at last and the homely sounds of kitchen clatter brought a welcome return to reality.

What stuck in Stephen's mind was a comment by Pomeroy that he and his family planned to stay in Minnesota through the Fourth of July, if the weather remained agreeable. Time enough, Stephen resolved, to press his suit for the hand of his lady love before she and her beguiling charms were ripped rudely from his grasp. It was a major challenge, for the formalities of courtship were impossibly complicated by the Pomeroy's protectiveness of their young ward. As for Gaily, she behaved in her usual flirtatious manner, oblivious to his feelings for her as well as to his predicament. It did not help that she exuded charm like deadly venom, apparently oblivious to its devastating effects on Stephen. These unfortunate circumstances, and the long, hot summer days, inflamed his passion to nearly intolerable degrees, causing him to invent ever wilder schemes to win her heart.

*   *   *

The Independence Day parade began in front of the Nicollet House and marched through Bridge Square to the beat of a brass band. Old Glory, hastily revamped to incorporate its thirty-second star – proud Minnesota – led the procession. As the marchers crossed the suspension bridge they were joined by the contingent from St. Anthony, including guests from the Winslow House. The Shevleys' rig trundled across the bridge near the head of the parade, and when Stephen caught sight of the column approaching from the east side of the river his heart began to pound. Gaily was not hard to find regally ensconced in an open carriage, twirling a parasol that alternately revealed and then concealed her lovely smile. As the lines of march converged and turned down the road toward Nicollet Island the Pomeroys' carriage was swept on ahead and Gaily was lost from sight. Near Blakeman and Greenleaf's jewelry store Stephen spotted their empty carriage parked at the side of the street. Gaily and the Pomeroys were lost amid the hundreds who thronged the island playground for the celebration. Vincent rounded the corner at Nash's drugstore and reined up.

187

"No use taking the rig over; we can carry what we have from here," he said. "Lend a hand with these picnic baskets, Stephen."

Together the family crossed the narrow bridge over the river channel and found a shady spot under an oak tree where Sarah and Mrs. Carpenter spread their blanket. As they made themselves comfortable Stephen excused himself and hurried away toward the dance platform where the Melodeon Troupe was offering a lively rendition of "Beulah Land." At the very edge of the planking stood Gaily Gladstone, swaying to and fro as if she might at any moment float out upon the boards. She was surrounded by a half dozen young admirers, all under the watchful eye of her aunt and uncle who lingered protectively a few feet away. As Stephen pressed closer he caught her eye and waved. Without interrupting her chatter she took a half step in his direction and raised an arm delicately toward him. As if by divine command the ring of admirers parted and Stephen came into her magical presence.

"Why, I was just saying, Mr. Shevley, how I wish the Miller string orchestra were playing. Y'all remember the night we danced at the Nicollet House ball. I can't remember when I spent such an enjoyable evening. Of course, y'all know Mr. Stephen Shevley."

Suddenly the center of hostile attention, Stephen ignored the scowling young men and directed himself solely to her.

"I've got to talk to you," he blurted out. "Can you spare just a few moments in private?"

"Is there something wrong?" she asked with a worried look as the other young men melted grudgingly into the crowd.

"We can't talk here," he said desperately. "Come with me."

"I couldn't possibly. Oh, Uncle Clarence," she called out. "Look who's come to pay his respects."

"Good day, sir," Stephen said as Pomeroy came to them. "I wonder if it would be all right if Gaily and I took a walk together – here on the island, with folks all around..."

"Why, I do declare!" said Mrs. Pomeroy as she joined her husband. "It's Stephen Shevley. How is your mother, Stephen?"

"She's better, thanks. She's here – over there under that big oak. We brought a picnic."

"Perhaps we should wander that way later, my dear."

"We should indeed. Meantime why don't you young people run off and visit with your friends. We'll pay our respects to your parents later on, Stephen," said Pomeroy.

They were alone at last, just the two of them amid the crowd of celebrants.

"Gaily, I'm so glad to find you."

"I'm happy to see you, too, Stephen. I was saying just the other day when Uncle Clarence came home with our tickets that it would be nice to see you again."

"Tickets?"

"The tickets for our passage. We'll be leaving Tuesday on the Delta Queen. Aunt Angelica is just dying to get home."

"That's why I've got to talk to you, Gaily. We haven't a minute to waste." He took her by the hand and led her toward the trail that rimmed the island and in moments they were alone and out of sight of the crowd. Stephen slackened his pace, hooked his thumbs in his vest pockets and strode along slowly with Gaily clinging to his arm.

"You're a bundle of worry and fret, Stephen Shevley. What could be darkening that handsome brow on such a sunny day?"

He shook his head sadly. Even now with time running short, he thought, she doesn't understand. Maybe it's best to say nothing, let her go home and forget about all his crazy schemes. But as he turned his downcast eyes upon her he found it impossible to suppress his feelings.

"Gaily, you've got to understand how I feel. This is probably our last day together. We might never see one another again, ever!"

His anxiety seemed to sober her briefly, as if she were trying to understand the earnestness of his plea. But then in a flickering the mischievous fire returned to her eyes.

"It never occurred to me, Stephen. After all we'll be back next season!" she exulted. "We'll be old friends then, and won't it be grand?" He stared at her in disbelief while she prattled on as if she had bestowed a ray of sunshine into his gloom and was intent on chasing the last shadows from the corners of his mind. "You could look forward to the next spring, and the next. Maybe you could even pay us a visit in Mississippi. I think Uncle Clarence and Aunt Angelica would be thrilled at the prospect of entertaining you and your parents over the Christmas holidays. We always spend Christmas at Gladstone Gardens. Why, I can see it now! It would be the social event of the season."

Suddenly infuriated, Stephen grasped her by the shoulders and shook her, glaring into her frightened eyes.

"Damn it, don't you understand? I'm not talking about next spring or next Christmas, or next year. I'm talking about here and now. I'm talking about forever, Gaily, you and I together forever."

His grasp tightened as he shook her to emphasize each word. Her neatly curled hair tumbled from beneath her bonnet, and tears of terror rolled down her cheeks. Suddenly her eyes rolled back and she fell limp in his arms. Surprised, he eased his grip and she slipped free and fell backward down the bank toward the racing river waters. He made a grab for her and went tumbling after her. Both would have plunged into the Mississippi and been swept away by the current, if her skirt hadn't caught on some blackberry brambles. He got hold of one flailing arm and with the other grasped the prickly brambles. He could feel the pain as the tiny thorns cut into his fingers, and with horror noted that her skirts already were billowing in the water. Unconscious and unable to help herself, her wet clothing dragging her further into the river, she was more than he could hold for long. Slowly but surely his fingers began to slip from the brambles, leaving him no choice but to leap into the river to try to save her. But her head slipped under water and together they began to drift downstream. The shock of the cold water brought her to consciousness, and as she felt his grip around her waist she began beating upon him with both fists. He tightened his hold on her with one arm and with the other stretched out and grabbed the exposed root of a riverside tree, holding on to it with all of his remaining strength. Gaily's hysterical screams attracted a crowd to the riverbank, and in a moment saving arms caught hold of her and jerked her from Stephen's grasp. He was relieved to see her being hauled to safety, but shocked to hear her cries: "He attacked me, he attacked me! He nearly drowned me! Oh, save me, please save me!"

In a moment she was wrapped in a blanket and hurried away in the arms of her rescuers, while Stephen was left to fend for himself. He rested a moment in the swirling waters, then summoned his strength again and hoisted himself hand over hand up the sturdy tree root, collapsing at last on the trail at the feet of several angry young men. In his exhaustion he barely heard their curses, but he felt the blow when one of them kicked him in the ribs.

"You ought to be horsed-whipped," said his assailant.

"I was trying to save her," Stephen gasped.

"Shove him back in the river," said another.

"No, let him be. We don't want to get involved," said a third.

"Maybe he's telling the truth," said another.

"Then just for good measure," said the first man, delivering swift kick to Stephen's midsection with the toe of his boot.

"Let him be," said another. "Let's look after the girl. She was pretty upset, after all. Let's be sure she's all right."

They left him alone there on the trail, while Gaily's rescuers guided her through the gathering, their passage sending a ripple of excitement through the stunned celebrants. Waves of rumor soon reached the farthest fringes of the crowd, and soon the Pomeroys were drawn into the vortex of the excitement where they were stunned to discover their dripping, bawling niece. Taking her into their arms, the Pomeroys led her away toward their carriage, with her uncle calling out in passionate fury for an officer of the law to see to this outrage.

Stephen meanwhile struggled to his feet and made his way to the picnic area, where the crowd parted to let him pass. He could see their menacing glances and hear more than one call out that he was the young woman's attacker. He soon found that his parents also had rushed to judgment. They were packing up their picnic paraphernalia and standing in pinched-lip anger as he approached.

"Get to the wagon," his father demanded tersely.

Stephen marched toward the bridge with his parents trailing behind him to avoid the accusing stares and curious glances of onlookers. Mrs. Carpenter and Sarah brought up the rear with their burden of baskets of uneaten food. Eleanor's frustration and embarrassment manifested itself in a peculiar fashion. All the way home she sat erect next to her husband, emitting occasional gasps that never quite formed themselves into words. Mrs. Carpenter fussed over the baskets and blankets, muttering to herself while Sarah sat close to Stephen studying him sympathetically. Stephen sat silently with his knees drawn up and his chin resting upon them, his eyes glazed with tears.

"Everything will be all right," she whispered.

He wanted to reach out to her, to anyone at this point, for understanding and consolation. But he could not, so he buried his face in his arms and squeezed out his tears on his wet sleeves. Vincent reined up in front of Shevley House and helped Eleanor down from the carriage.

"Take the rig to the stable," his father commanded sharply. "And while you're there get out of those wet clothes. I won't have you tracking mud into the house. You're filthy."

"Sarah, go get him a change of clothes," Mrs. Carpenter whispered. "He'll catch his death of cold."

*   *   *

Stephen stood nearly naked in the stall, the setting sun pouring in through the stable windows, the straw prickly under his feet. As the far off boom of the revelers' cannon marked the beginning of the torchlight speeches on Nicollet Island, Sarah appeared quietly and draped his dry clothes over the stall. He took them and quickly pulled them on.

"How is it inside?" he asked.

"She's taken to bed, and he's fit to be tied," she whispered. "He was supposed to give a speech tonight, you know."

"I guess I'd better stay out here," he said.

Sarah nodded gravely. "I'm *so* sorry for you," she said.

"Don't be. I guess I deserve it. I guess I really do."

She reached for his hand in the gathering darkness and gave it a gentle squeeze before heading back to the house.

Later as fireworks exploded over the river valley he crept into the darkened house like a whipped animal and tiptoed to his room. He lingered there in grief and shame into the early morning hours Tuesday when the distant whistle of the departing Delta Queen wafted through his window and wrenched from him a final spasm of weeping. He lay awake until midday and then, swallowing his pride, he returned in mortification to the cold atmosphere of Shevley House to live as a stranger.

193

Chapter 12

"There must be a dozen different versions of the story going around," Roger said. "Yours makes it thirteen."

He was stretched out in an overstuffed chair in his elegantly furnished suite. It was early in the evening and the heat was oppressive. The humidity hung like a pall over the city so that even the dust had to struggle to rise. Clouds above grappled for dominance, crashing into one another in a Thermopyleaen clash that sent flashes of lightning earthward followed by the loud, ominous rumbling of thunder. Each flash and clap quickened the pace of activity in the street, but only momentarily. It was too hot to flee from the inevitable. Stephen leaned against the window casement hoping to catch the first breeze that would herald the rain, longing for any relief it might bring. He did not look at Roger as he spoke.

"Strange that no one has asked for my version of the story."

"It's not strange at all. It's human nature. People don't want the truth; they prefer the vicarious thrill of innuendo. They want to create fantasies to suit their own morbid personalities. They crave excitement. They need villains and heroes to populate their myths. History's greatest heroes and most heinous criminals will live forever, because common men need them and refuse to let them die. To lose them would be to lose life itself."

"And at the moment I seem destined to be their villain."

"Precisely. What difference does it make? Be their villain and enjoy a bit of immortality."

"They're damned fools."

"All men are fools of one sort or another. Don't let it bother you. It's a sure way to let your life rule you instead of you ruling your life. As a philosopher once said, 'Life is short, nature is hostile, and man is a fool.' So ignore them and go on about your business."

Stephen slouched away from the window and slumped onto a couch with a sigh: "My God it's hot. Why doesn't the rain come."

"Because 'nature is hostile.' Best not to expect too much from Mother Nature; she is fickle at best. Besides, rain won't help, it'll only accentuate the humidity."

"It's even too hot to eat, but I *am* hungry."

"Come along with me, then. I have work to finish at the office, and you can drop off somewhere along the way for dinner."

They walked from the hotel through the darkening streets. The black clouds had defeated the white and now massed for an assault on the earth, sending a deceptively cool breeze ahead of the attack. Stephen relished the scant relief it brought.

"I'll stop here and meet you back at the hotel later," he said as they neared a small café. Since he couldn't afford to dine at the Nicollet, he often took his meals at this low establishment that catered to loggers and mill workers, clerks and shopkeepers. There were no fine wines here, but ample supplies of St. Louis beer.

"Don't wait up for me; I'll be late," Roger said, breaking out his umbrella as the first raindrops began to fall.

In the weeks since Gaily's departure life at home had been unbearable. Stephen had left that frigid atmosphere and taken a small room at the Nicollet House to escape his parents and to be near Roger's cynical sanity. He had turned eighteen, was being adequately if not lavishly paid, and his move had met with no objection. His father liked the idea of his being close to the mill, and his mother seemed almost glad to see him go. Strange, he thought, how much she had changed over the years. But his father had said it all at the very beginning: the frontier was a hard, uncompromising place where only hard, uncompromising people would survive. His mother had adapted in her own way, defiantly refusing to bend to the demands of her surroundings. To protect herself she developed an impenetrable shell of indifference, a cruel aloofness to all who might hurt her, including her son. It was clear to him that she no longer needed him, that he had failed her and thereby lost her love and understanding. So there was nothing to do but move out, not bitterly but resignedly. He was intent on proving, if only to himself, that he could get along without her or his father, although occasionally it took a pitcher of beer to get him through the lonely hours. He took a table alone at the rear of the café and placed his order. He had just asked for a refill when the splattering of raindrops turned suddenly into a torrent whipped by severe winds. Suddenly in through the door plunged a man in buckskin, laughing at his luck as he struggled to close the door against the storm. Once protected from the elements, the man paused, looked carefully around the café until he spotted Stephen, and came his way.

"Frasier told me I'd find you here. How ya' been, kid?" asked Ben McAlpine.

"I've been well, thanks. Good to see you, Ben! Have you had your dinner? Sit down and join me."

Ben's deerskin clothing was soaked black from the rain and he carried about him the smell of pine smoke and sweat. Ringlets of red hair protruded from under his broad-brimmed hat, and his gray beard had been crudely chopped as if with the knife he carried in his waistband. He removed his hat, slapped it against his leg, and laid it on the table. Slipping onto the bench across from Stephen, he leaned forward on his elbows and looked carefully at the young man.

"You growed, you sure as hell did," he remarked, casting a disdainful eye over Stephen's clothing. "When you goin' to get out of them linens and laces and come back to the woods?"

Stephen poured Ben a glass of beer while mulling over his question. The woods were one escape that hadn't occurred to him.

"Maybe sooner than you think," he said, "but timber cruising must be over by now."

"It is, and we've found trees enough to keep at least two camps workin' all winter."

"So you're looking for crews, are you? Who knows, I just might sign up. What's in it for me?"

"Twelve hours a day of back-breaking work and all the bacon and beans you can eat!" Ben laughed. "And I'm lookin' for men, all right. I might get me a dozen or so tonight when they're liquored up a bit. Too much hagglin' when they're sober. You could help me, lad. I'll talk 'em into signin' on, and you can write the work tickets and keep the list. What do you say?"

"Sure I'll help, but let's eat first. Can't work on an empty stomach," he said.

"Just stew left," said a gruff waiter as he placed in front of them a large bowl of venison and vegetables in greasy gravy, two tin plates, a platter of coarse bread and another pitcher of beer. "That's seventy-five cents."

"I'll get it," said Ben, fishing in his poke for a coin. "Your pa just paid me off." The woodsman ate with his fingers, Indian fashion, and smeared his bread with a concoction of grease and berries that he carried in a leather pouch on his belt. When they had finished he wiped his hands on his leggings and took a small bundle of labor tickets from his breast pocket. He then spent a few minutes making the rounds and led three men back to the table. While he extolled the virtues of life in a Shevley camp, Stephen filled out the tickets, and recorded the names and job designations on a master sheet. It was clear that Ben was looking for common laborers, men to cut tote roads into the pineries, to clear stumps for campsites and erect shanties. "No experience necessary," Ben told the curious as they crowded around the table for a free beer. They signed up four men, and Ben seemed pleased with their success.

"Two laborers, a blacksmith and a cook's helper! That's a pretty good start. Let's move down the street and see how we do."

For the rest of the stormy evening they went from café to tavern along Washington Avenue, plying prospective workers with beer until at last they ran out of applicants. Then they headed toward the Nicollet House, Stephen leaning heavily on Ben's shoulder. It was nearly midnight when a hotel employee summoned Roger Frasier to the lobby. He arrived in robe and slippers to find the towering Ben McAlpine, standing dripping wet at the registration desk with Stephen's limp form draped unceremoniously over his shoulder.

"This fella won't let us in," Ben complained. "I just wanted to put Steve in his bunk, but he won't let us in."

"What happened to him?"

"Drunk, I'd say. But we had a good night, no mistake about it. Signed up more'n a dozen men for the camps."

"I imagine his father would be pleased," Roger said sarcastically. "Well, put him down. I'll take responsibility for him, but you can't possibly stay here."

"Don't have a mind to," Ben said contemptuously as he dumped his limp comrade into a chair. "I'll put up at the mill. See you in the morning, Frasier."

*   *   *

Before the leaves had turned and begun to fall Stephen was going abroad two and three nights a week to drown his inner torment. Roger's diligence shielded his dissipation from his father's notice for a time, but nothing could stop the flood of gossip that had surged to the very steps of Shevley House that fall.

"You've got to get hold of yourself," Vincent said one Sunday afternoon. "Think of me; think of your mother."

"Oh, I do. I think about you often," he said with a faint smile.

"It's nothing to smirk about," his father flared. "There's the family name to consider. You have responsibilities. You have a future. I have plans for you. We can't have people talking."

"Who's talking? Roger? Charlie?"

"Never mind. The word gets around – carousing until all hours, drunk in public. How do you think your mother feels?"

"I don't think she feels anything at all," Stephen said bitterly as the irony of their discussion began to arouse his anger.

"That's unkind and unfair. She thinks about you a good deal. She thinks your behavior is due to the silly incident involving that southern girl."

"If it was just a silly incident, why was I treated like a criminal in my own home? Why wasn't I given a chance to explain? Why didn't you ask me what it was all about?"

"Some things are better left unsaid. Besides, it's all water under the bridge. Yesterday's not important. It's tomorrow that counts."

"No, yesterday is *very* important. Yesterday I was badly hurt and no one reached out to help me. Yesterday I was presumed guilty without anyone hearing my side of the story. But yesterday also held important lessons for me. I learned that "proper" people like you and mother expected me to accept my fate without protest despite the pain and the injustice of it all. Well, I happen to think that proper people are hypocrites who look the other way rather than admit any responsibility. That's why I find it ironic when their own hypocrisy brings embarrassment upon them."

"Hush!" Vincent cautioned. "Mrs. Carpenter might hear."

"Do you think she hasn't heard worse within these walls?"

"Then for your mother's sake keep your voice down."

"She hears only what she wants to hear."

"She hears the gossip, you can be sure of that. She wanted us to have this little talk. That's why she invited you to dinner today. She thought it was time to clear the air. We don't expect you to be a saint. You're young, impetuous. You're bound to make some mistakes, suffer disappointments in life. But we mustn't let them get the better of us. That's really all that I'm trying to say."

"Then it's time for me to go," Stephen said tersely, trying to conceal his exasperation. "I should get my horse back to the livery before dark."

"Don't forget to say goodbye to your mother."

"No, I won't forget."

He found her as usual alone in her room at her writing desk.

"I wanted to thank you for dinner," he said.

"Yes, well," she said, barely looking up, "I hope you won't forget Christmas Eve. We're expecting you to spend the night."

"No, mother, I won't forget."

"Well, then," she said with a practiced smile of dismissal. He closed her door quietly, his heart heavy with regret, even a touch of guilt as he wondered if somehow he was at least partly to blame for the seemingly unbridgeable gap between them all. Perhaps he could have tried a little harder, met them halfway. But no, she made it impossible. It was typical that she had left it to his father to speak to him – and unfortunate. His father would never be able to convey to her what he didn't understand himself. Understanding required love, and where had love gone?

In the stable the last rays of the setting sun fell through the frosted windows and landed on a dusty vase that held the dried remains of a summer bouquet. As he saddled his horse he remembered that his mother once had treasured that vase, and he despaired at its fate. On an angry impulse he snatched it off the windowsill and threw it against the stall. But it bounced off, landed in the straw, and failed to break. As he stared at it an idea came to him along with a glimmer of hope. He picked it up, shook out the dead flowers, and stuffed it under his coat. Then he went on his way.

*   *   *

The holiday spirit impressed itself upon him that season as it never had before. Months of living away from home had created an emotional distance that allowed him to fantasize about the joys of family life to the exclusion of his unhappy memories. Roger merely scoffed at his "attempt to recreate a boyhood that never was."

"No, that's not entirely true. I remember Christmases at the Crafts' in Boston when I was very young. It was a joyous time."

"And what about later in Maine?"

"It was different then. My grandfather was ailing most of the time. And then my father left for the West."

"Exactly! From what you've told me there were no *joyeux noëls,* not since your early childhood. No, my young friend, you're trying to cling to a past that never existed. I think you're really trying to avoid the future. Face it, you're not a child anymore. You're eighteen years old! You're a man, a man facing maturity with a good deal of trepidation. It's a big step to be sure, but you can't escape it, no matter how nostalgic you may grow over events that never occurred."

"No," Stephen insisted, "there were happier days, I'm sure of it. But something went wrong. I don't know what it was, but maybe I can do something about it. I've got to try."

So eagerly, desperately, he threw himself into a search for gifts for everyone, spending lavishly given his limited earnings. For his father he found a new pipe and a canister of imported tobacco. For Sarah he bought a leather-bound diary in which she could record her secret thoughts. For Mrs. Carpenter he purchased a fancy dress apron with lace trim. And for his mother he sought a large jewel box to hold the green glass vase that now stood upon his chiffonier at the Nicollet House. The vase reminded him of their first days on the frontier, days when they were both afraid and alone in the rustic cabin, days when she longed for some-thing of beauty to brighten their harsh new surroundings. He could see her again in the general store as the vase caught her eye. He remembered how she held it up to the light and watched the sun's rays play upon its prismatic surfaces. She was delighted with it then; he was certain it would inspire memories that would bring happiness to her again. As the holiday approached he grew more and more determined to find just the right box to hold the vase, and when he found it at last it was not in a fancy jewelry store, but in a pawnshop – for fifty cents. It was scuffed here and there, and one hinge was bent, but it was fashioned from inlaid wood, polished to a sheen, and it was lined with black velvet. To him it seemed the perfect setting for a most precious item – the hope of better times.

Once he had wrapped all his gifts, the days seemed to drag on interminably. Then a series of events seemed to confirm that he was on the right track toward holiday happiness. First his father asked him to join in the search for a tree, an adventure that began on a Friday afternoon one week before Christmas. They took their sleigh and headed west to Cedar Lake and tramped from tree to tree until they at last came upon a beautiful blue spruce standing alone amid the cedars as if it were a visitor from another forest. Once cut it still measured eight feet in height, and later after they had fashioned a sturdy stand to hold it erect it reached nearly to the twelve-foot ceiling of the parlor. The next evening Mrs. Carpenter prepared quantities of popcorn and Stephen, with Sarah's help and a sturdy needle, strung yards of the white puffs to bedeck the boughs. On Sunday he was invited to dinner and brought along his presents to place among the brightly wrapped gifts already under the tree. At midweek he again joined his father in cutting a Yule log worthy of the grand fireplace.

On Friday Vincent closed the lumber mill at noon and Stephen hurried to his room at the Nicollet to freshen up and change clothes in time to meet his parents at Gethsemane Episcopal Church for Christmas Eve caroling. Then it was off for home to light the Yule log and begin the Christmas festivities. Stephen experienced a growing joy as each little drama played itself out that evening, and after a light supper he went to his own room for the first time in several months and lay awake in giddy anticipation of the morning's adventure. It began with a scream of delight from

Sarah's room as she discovered her stocking laden with small surprises from a generous Father Christmas, which she knew with certainty was really her mother with a generous assist from Vincent and Eleanor. Stephen and his parents met in the upstairs hallway and hurried down to Sarah's room to see what all the commotion was about. When all had watched the child open each little stocking gift, they marched down the hall to the kitchen for a light breakfast of hot sweet rolls and coffee surrounded by the rich aroma of a huge goose roasting in the oven. Then it was arm in arm to the parlor where Vincent paused dramatically in the shadowy hallway before flinging wide the parlor door to be greeted by a brilliant burst of sunlight.

Stephen fell to his knees in front of the blue spruce and began reading the names on each brightly wrapped present and passing it to its recipient. Within moments they were all immersed in a colorful confusion of ribbons and wrapping paper. Sarah sighed in delight at the sight of her leather-bound diary and gave Stephen a peck on the cheek in thanking him. But it was the gift of a beautiful new dress that excited her most and she danced off to her room immediately to try it on. Vincent leaned back in his chair to admire his new pipe, while Eleanor sat demurely with Stephen's gift cradled carefully in her lap.

"Open it, mother, open it!" he urged.

Slowly she untied the ribbon and unfolded the wrapping paper to reveal the jewelry box with its cover of inlaid wood.

"Why Stephen, it's lovely," she said, "but look, it's scratched. And one hinge is bent."

"What's that inside?" Vincent asked.

She opened the lid all the way to reveal the green glass vase lying in its bed of plush black velvet.

"Well, let's see it," said Vincent impatiently.

"I think it's...no, it can't be." She lifted the vase to the light as she had done so many years ago, captivated momentarily by its simple beauty. Stephen's hopes soared as he studied her face for some sign of happy recognition, some glimmer of joy. But all he saw was a faint, bemused smile. "It is the same old vase, isn't it?"

He nodded, still hopeful, as she laid the vase aside and turned her attention to the jewel box.

"I do hope you didn't waste a lot of money on this box, Stephen. It's certainly not new, and if you bought it thinking it was, well, we'll have to take it right back where it came from."

"I know, mother, but the vase – you do recognize it, don't you?"

"Of course I do," she said. "I saw it a few weeks ago out in the stable. It's probably been there for months. I'd completely forgotten about it."

He studied her expression incredulously, crushed that the vase seemed to hold no meaning for her.

"You don't understand, do you," he said somewhat indignantly. "It means nothing to you."

"Stephen! Don't be silly. I'm delighted with your gift."

"It meant something to you once, I know it did. But it's all forgotten now. I'm sorry. I should have known. I've been a fool."

"Now, Stephen, don't talk like that," his father cautioned. "I'm sure I don't know what you mean either. Is there something here that we've missed?"

"I wouldn't expect either of you to understand. I don't know what I did expect," he said, sinking into a chair, head in his hands.

"I don't know why you're so upset," said his mother. "It was a clever gift, I guess. But after all it's just an old vase that's been around for years, a little old vase in a battered old jewelry box. If you think so highly of it, I'll find a place for it in my room."

"Never mind. What's past is past. I apologize for expecting too much."

"But you haven't even opened your gifts," she said.

At that moment Sarah returned to the parlor wearing her new dress, a present from Eleanor and Vincent.

"Sarah, it's beautiful," Eleanor gushed. "Come here and let me look at you. My, how grown up you look. Of course we'll have to take it in a bit here, and adjust this bow."

"You look very pretty, Sarah," Stephen said quietly.

"Oh, thank you, Stephen. Isn't it just beautiful?"

"And what's this?" exclaimed Mrs. Carpenter, holding up the fancy apron Stephen had given her. "What a fine piece of work, but it's not for today's kitchen, not with that goose splatterin' grease all over. Our thanks to you all, but now we've got a lot of work to do. Run along and change your clothes, Sarah."

"I'll be out soon to help," said Eleanor. "Now Stephen, you must open your gifts. You haven't touched a package yet!"

It was a struggle to keep up the appearance of delight as he opened his gifts and dutifully exclaimed over each of them. From his mother he got two fancy dress shirts with detachable collars, and a handsome cravat of fine silk. His father's gifts to him included a rugged winter jacket of the Canadian variety with leather protective patches, sturdy buttons and a collar that could cover his ears when it was turned up. There was also a pair of sturdy boots with thong laces, a can of grease to protect them from dampness and keep them supple. Sarah's gift to him was a perfect complement, a hand-knit pair of warm woolen socks. Mrs. Carpenter gave him matching woolen scarf which led him to imagine the two of them in their room at night when their work was done, the mother teaching the daughter to knit with the same loving patience she used to teach her to cook. These latter gifts brought him true joy and made him ashamed that he had felt it necessary earlier to feign his delight and gratitude. The simple goodness of the Carpenters' generosity mellowed his mood considerably and helped recapture the holiday spirit that was crushed by his mother's reaction of the vase.

"Well, I'm beginning to smell that goose, and it's making me hungry," Vincent announced. "Let's straighten up this mess and maybe there'll be time for some refreshments before the dinner bell rings. What do you say, lad?"

"I'll leave the parlor to you two," said Eleanor. "I think it would be nice if you spent some time together. I'm going to set the dining room table and then see if I can be of help in the kitchen."

When they had straightened up the parlor and disposed of the wrapping paper, the ribbons and the boxes, Stephen and his father closed themselves in Vincent's office for a snifter of brandy and talk of the lumbering business. As the day drew on there was time for several more brandies, and soon Stephen felt the warm glow they engendered. At dinner that afternoon there was a dry red wine to enhance the flavor of the succulent dark meat of the goose; cornbread stuffing with butternuts, sausage, cranberries and sage; bowls of string beans, beets and corn that Mrs. Carpenter had put up in the fall; and a heaping bowl of snow white mashed potatoes, and a boat of rich brown gravy to ladle over all. For dessert Mrs. Carpenter brought forth a fragrant baked apple for each, oozing caramel and awash in heavy cream. As the feast progressed the winter sun went into its early retirement and the candles' glow bathed the holiday table in an aura of opulence. Their conversation was warm and intimate and unaffected and so laced with nostalgia that it was easy for Stephen to forget for the moment the profound sadness that had dwelled deep inside him. For the first time in a very long time he felt very close to his parents, and it was a good feeling.

Eleanor soon left the table to help in the kitchen cleanup, and Vincent went to his office, ostensibly to go over some business papers, but really to nap. Stephen wandered back to the parlor and stretched out on the floor in front of the fireplace and wondered about the changes that had come about this day. The kitchen sounds were muffled, and soon he could hear snoring coming from the office. It wasn't long before he himself dropped into a deep sleep, only to be awakened later by the sound of heavy footsteps on the stairs and a whispered conversation in the upstairs hall. All he could make out was his mother's final words, "No, Vincent," followed by the latching of her bedroom door – and then the slamming of his father's door. Nothing had changed, he concluded bitterly. Roger was right. It was self-deception to long for a past that was gone forever, if it ever really existed. There was no bridging the gap between them, he knew that now, and no place for him in their unhappy world. A hushed voice at the parlor door interrupted his thoughts.

"Hasn't it been a lovely day?" Sarah asked.

"You have helped make it so," he said tenderly as she slipped into the room in her nightgown and robe. "You must promise me you'll never change."

"Oh, I can't do that! Mother says I've already grown a foot this year."

"That's what I mean!" he laughed. "You've grown a foot, but you really haven't changed a bit."

"I don't understand."

"Not now, but you will someday," he said, the sadness returning to his voice.

"What will you do?" she asked.

"Do about what?"

"About whatever it is that's troubling you."

"I'm not sure. Maybe I'll go away."

"Where?"

"I don't know. Maybe I'll go to sea. Or maybe I'll go to California."

"Why?"

"To get away. To be free. I don't really belong here anymore. I should go away and live my own life. I can't do that here. You can understand that, can't you?"

She nodded, but he knew she did not understand. He also knew that when he left Shevley House it would be a long time before he would see her again. It was his only regret.

*　　*　　*

207

It was one-thirty in the morning and only three men remained in the tavern. The barkeeper suddenly loomed over their table and snatched the empty pitcher away.

"It's cash now or out you go!" he growled.

The two older men looked sadly at one another, while their younger companion stuffed his hands into his pockets and brought them out empty.

"Wait," he said. "I know where I can get money. Come along with me."

The three reeled out the door and staggered down the street. It was icy and walking was difficult. A light snow was falling, dusting the frozen ruts in the street. One of the older men slipped and fell.

"Damn it, I cut my hand!" he exclaimed.

"Sh-h-h-h! Let me help you," said the young man, raising the man to his feet.

"Thanks, but no more for me," said the man with the cut hand. "I'm going home to bed."

"No, no," the young man protested. "I might need help."

"Help for what?" asked the third man.

"Never mind. Just follow me."

Outside the Shevley lumber mill they stopped. There was a light in the office.

"Let's get out of here," whispered the man who had fallen. "I don't want to get caught around here."

"We'd be in real trouble," agreed the third. "Come on, kid. You don't know what you're doing."

"Oh, yes, I do. Help me ease this gate open a crack."

The young man slipped into the yard and dodged among the stacks of lumber, heading toward the lighted office. The older men lagged behind.

"No, kid. We don't want no part of this," said one from the shadowy distance.

"Yeah, we don't want no part in stealing," said the other. "We might get caught."

"We're not going to steal anything," the young man insisted. "There's a fellow in there who'll loan me some money."

"Maybe so," said the man with the injured hand. "But we'll just wait here until you come back."

The young man shook his head, but continued on, creeping stealthily through the lumberyard, keeping an eye open for a guard. He reached the mill and pressed himself against the wall, edging toward the office door. As he reached it, it swung suddenly open and he fell into the light.

"What the hell is this!" Vincent hollered, collaring the culprit. "Stephen! For God's sake, what do you think you're doing?"

John Koenig leaned down and lifted Stephen to his feet and helped him into a chair.

"Well," Vincent shouted, "what do you have to say for yourself?"

"I...I thought I'd find Roger here," he muttered. "I came to talk to Roger. I wanted to borrow some money."

"Look at you!" Vincent stormed. "You're slobbering drunk."

"I was going to..."

"You were going to steal money, is that it?"

"No, I..."

Vincent's right hand shot out and struck him on the side of the head, slamming him into the wall. He grabbed his son by the jacket to keep him from falling and smacked him again.

"Wait, wait," John pleaded.

"It's all right," Stephen said. "Let him rant. Let him beat me. It doesn't matter."

"Shut up!" Vincent shouted.

"I knew you'd never understand," Stephen said, looking at his father with contempt. "Yes, I'm drunk, but you never asked why. Don't look for answers, you might find the truth. And the truth would be too hard for you to bear. So beat it down, trample it."

Vincent, in a fury, hauled him away from the wall, braced him briefly and then knocked him across the room. The blow split Stephen's lip and the hot pain of the blow blinded him as he slumped to the floor barely conscious.

"Get him out of here before I kill him," Vincent ordered. "Throw the drunken lout on the sleigh and get him out of my sight."

"What shall I do with him? Where shall I take him," John asked. "I've got to get to the camp by noon."

"Throw him off at the hotel. Throw him off the bridge. I don't give a damn what you do with him, just get him out of here."

John dragged his semi-conscious friend out the door to where his heavily laden sleigh and team stood waiting. He boosted Stephen into the back among the boxes and barrels and hoisted his legs in after him. Just then Stephen's hand reached up and grabbed John's arm.

"Take me with you!" he gasped.

"To the camps?"

"Yes, to the camps. You must take me."

Vincent came to the office door, his huge frame black against the lantern light.

"Well, get him out of here!" he roared.

"Yes, sir, Mr. Shevley. We're on our way."

Chapter 13

It was dark as John guided the sleigh to the door of a large shanty half buried in drifted snow. They had been on the road most of the day, stopping only once at the Koenig farm for a brief visit and to feed the horses. Mrs. Koenig prepared them hearty breakfast and sent them off with sour cream sandwiches and venison jerky to eat on the road. Then it was off again for the pineries with John saying little about the events of the night before. It was after six o'clock and dark when he halted at Shevley Camp No. 1. The shanty door creaked open on leather hinges and a flood of light illuminated the exhausted travelers.

"Hal-ooo!" called out the shadowy figure that emerged from the hut. "That you, John?"

"Hi, Hjalmer. It's me with a new man for the crew. Take him in while I unload my sleigh and tend to the team."

Stephen, stiff from the cold and the rough ride, eased himself down, and watched the sleigh groan into motion and glide toward the stables across a clearing.

"You're letting a lot of cold in," said Hjalmer indignantly.

Stephen stomped his boots on the stoop and stepped inside. The hovel was filled with the fetid odor of damp wool and unbathed bodies. Some thirty loggers sat side by side on a long bench, staring at him, while others looked up from a table where they were playing cards. Stephen's gaze ran the line of faces, coming hopefully to rest on two twinkling blue eyes that seemed the least hostile. A pipe protruded from the man's tobacco stained mustache and a thatch of yellow hair ringed his ruddy face. He took the pipe from his mouth and emitted a cloud of sweet smelling smoke.

"He's a young'un," the man said with a broad grin. He got up from his place on the bench and yanked Stephen's cap from his head. "Yah, look! He's young, but he's big, ain't he?"

The one room shanty rocked with a burst of laughter just as John came in through the door covered with snow that fell all around him as he shook himself like a wet dog.

"Where'd you find this one, John, in a schoolyard?"

Another round of laugher was interrupted by the appearance of a large man in a filthy woolen shirt who had been lingering in the shadows.

"What's this you've brought, Dutchman?" he asked quietly.

"Supplies, Neil, and a new man for your crew."

"I can see that, you dumb squarehead. I mean what's his name and what does he do?"

"My name is Steve Craft," Stephen said. "And I do whatever I'm told to do."

"Yah?" said the big man contemptuously. "That means you probably can't do anything."

"I'll work hard; I'll do my share."

"You work for me you'll do more than your share, and you'll start by hanging that coat on the wall and stop drippin' on my floor," Neil said with a scowl.

Stephen hurriedly did as he was told, revealing himself to Neil's scrutiny.

"A city boy, huh? You ain't dressed for the woods. And look at that face. Looks like you got a whippin'. You a street brawler, city boy? Looks like someone got the best of you and run you out of town." He stepped close to examine Stephen's split lip and swollen eye. "Whew! You stink a' whisky. You a drunk, too? No place here for a brawlin' drunk. You fight with my men, you'll get yourself killed. You got any whisky on you?"

"No."

"You better not. I don't allow it. No drinkin'."

"We could use a bite to eat," said John. "We've been on the trail all day."

"Sure, I'll give you a bite. Cookie!" he called out. "Feed 'em!"

Neil Amundsen was the camp boss. Big Neil, he was called, because he was an enormous man, bigger than any one of them and stronger than any two. Behind his back they called him the Black Norwegian, because of his black hair and beard and swarthy complexion, not at all like most of the other Norwegians, who were blond and fair-skinned. His word was law, and everyone obeyed the law. When he said, "Feed 'em!" two plates piled high with baked beans and two mugs of tepid tea appeared immediately on a crude trestle table at the elbow of the ell-shaped shanty. The beans were cooked to a mush and smelled strongly of salt pork, vinegar and molasses. Stephen followed John to the table and ate slowly, feeling the eyes of the loggers upon him. The beans puckered his mouth and his stomach rolled and grumbled as he forced them down. Big Neil towered over him, a sneer on his lips.

"We could use another man," he said, "but you sure as hell ain't it. Where'd you pick him up, Dutchman, in the gutter?"

"At the mill," John said.

Big Neil grabbed Stephen's hand, sending his fork flying across the room. He studied the trembling hand carefully.

"These ain't a workman's hands," he said. "You a goddam dandy? Dandies don't last long around here."

"No...no, sir," Stephen stammered.

"Stand up when you talk to me," Big Neil shouted, grabbing him by the collar with one hand and yanking him to his feet. "You eat like a man, let's see if you are a man." With his other hand he gave Stephen a sharp blow to the stomach that sent him reeling toward the door where he collapsed in a heap. His cheeks tingled and twitched, and he quickly cupped his hands over his mouth.

"Get him out of here!" Big Neil shouted, as two loggers leaped from the bench, flung open the door and tossed Stephen into the bitter cold. He sprawled headfirst into the snow and lay there retching and gagging as his tormentor loomed dark in the doorway hurling curses at him. He ended by spitting tobacco juice toward his victim and slamming the door, muffling the laughter that filled the shanty. Stephen buried his face in the snow to wait for the gagging and retching to end. When at last it was over, he rolled over on his back, staring into a black, starless sky. His heart ached even more than his stomach, and the bitter cold began to numb him beyond pain. He longed for some gesture of comfort, but could only see his father's red-faced fury and he knew that he was very much alone in a harsh new world. As tears welled in his eyes the door to the shanty opened and John came out to him.

"Better come in," he said. "You'll catch your death of cold out here. You'll feel better in the morning."

Inside the shanty the loggers were in various stages of undress. Some already had crawled into the communal bunk that ran the length of the room. Fronting the "breech-loading" bunk was the "deacon's seat," the bench on which they had been sitting. First the loggers placed their boots under the bench, then stacked their clothing on top of the seat. and finally they climbed headfirst into the loose straw that served both as mattress and insulation. Each man had his own blankets that marked his place in the long bunk, and used his poke sack as a pillow. John got four blankets from a bin near the kitchen area and gave two to Stephen. Then they stripped down to their long johns and woolen socks and climbed into bed at the empty end of the bunk. It was soon obvious why the others had shunned this area. The warmest end of the bunk was near the huge stone fire pit in which flames were roaring. The empty end was near the front entry where tracked-in snow never melted and a bitterly cold wind rattled the door. Stephen found himself between John, who had taken the end place, and the tall Scandinavian with the yellow moustache, who already was snoring loudly. The dusty straw caught in Stephen's nose provoking a sneeze.

"Sh-h-h!" John cautioned him, hoisting his blankets above his head and turning his back to him.

In the semi-darkness the mumbled conversations of the loggers subsided into whispers and then into silence. The blaze in the fire pit cast eerie shadows through the room while outside the wind howled. Stephen rolled up his shirt to use as a pillow, tucked his icy hands under his armpits to warm them, and shut his eyes. His face hurt from the beating his father had given him, and his stomach ached from the brutish camp boss's blow. All he could think of was the warm embrace of his mother when he was a little boy and she held him close and rambled on about what life would be like on the frontier. He could almost feel the soft caress of her hand, and hear her sweet voice lulling him to sleep. But the logger next to him coughed and stirred and his knee came up suddenly and jabbed Stephen in the backside, dispelling memories of his mother and leaving him shivering, cold and alone. It was a long while before he fell asleep.

*   *   *

John's rough jostling brought him out of a restless stupor and into the pre-dawn cold and darkness. Cramped and aching, he sat up cautiously as the big Scandinavian next to him muttered a curse and slipped out of the bunk. Lanterns were lit and the sullen woodsmen danced one-legged jigs as they pulled on their woolen trousers and staggered across the cold floor to retrieve their heavy outer clothing from the drying pegs in the wall. Thus bundled against the morning chill they filed out the door to the communal outhouse, then back into the adjoining wing of the shanty for breakfast. Stephen could see his breath in the frigid air. His nose and fingers and toes were numb as he fumbled with his buttons and pulled on boots. Then he staggered outside to join the line of grumbling, cursing men waiting their turn in the privy. It was breathtakingly cold and the line moved very slowly. He stamped his feet on the frozen earth when his toes began to feel numb, and flapped his arms vigorously in a vain effort to keep warm. He relished even the stinking outhouse for the scant protection it offered, then hurried back to the shanty so he could warm himself by the fire pit. In the dining area the loggers were taking their places at long tables amid the clatter of metal plates and cups. Beyond them lay the kitchen, dominated by

215

a huge iron range and divided from the tables by a broad serving plank. The kitchen wall was lined with shelves and in the corner a door opened into a pantry. Like the others the bull cook wore heavy woolen trousers held up by suspenders, and no shirt over the top of his long johns. His sleeves were rolled above his elbows, and over all he wore a huge apron that hung nearly to the floor and obviously had been used for many weeks. He was a big man, nearly the equal of the camp boss, with powerful arms and gnarly hands, a barrel chest and a small waist that suggested he ate sparingly of his own culinary creations. When he moved it became apparent why such a magnificent specimen spent his time in the kitchen. His left leg was missing, replaced by finely carved length of hardwood. On his right he wore a moccasin decorated with beads and fringes of leather. Around his forehead a beaded band restrained his wild gray hair that fell like a pony's tail down his back. He stood majestically behind the serving plank with a young assistant, ladling food onto their plates as the woodsmen filed by.

John led Stephen to the far end of the long tables where they picked up their utensils and joined the serving line. Like their bunks, their places at the table were far from the fire and the bitter winds whistled through cracks in the log walls.

"My God, it's cold!" Stephen exclaimed. "Let's sit near the fire."

"You may get a seat closer to the fire later on," John laughed. "But for now we have to eat here. How did you sleep?"

"I don't remember sleeping. I think I just shivered all night."

When their turn came their plates were heaped with flapjacks and molasses, baked beans, fried pork, and cold shuts, a doughnut-shaped roll that proved to be a challenge to his chattering teeth. As they started back to the far end of the table Stephen noted: "There's plenty of room there near the fire. Why can't we..."

"Here's why," said John as the front door blew open and in from the wind and the cold stomped Big Neil Amundsen. He doffed his cap and scarf and his heavy coat and hung them on the wall pegs, then marched to the head of the table and took his accustomed place nearest the fire. The bull cook came to him immediately with a platter laden with food like all the rest, but the flapjacks were topped with four fried eggs, sunny side up.

"Mornin', Rasmussen," he greeted the cook. "My, that looks good. I see the Dutchman brought us a supply of eggs."

"Yah, and a new hand. Wonder how he knew we were short a man?"

After he had devoured the huge platter of food Big Neil headed for the door, a signal to the crew that it was time to go to work. He paused as he passed the far end of the table where John and Stephen were just digging into their breakfast.

"Get enough beans?" he asked Stephen with a grin.

"Yes, sir."

"Better eat 'em all, or you might regret it later on," Big Neil said with an evil glint in his eye. "Got a job for you today. Get over to the blacksmith across the way. His name is Potter. Tell him I sent you to tend to the fire. He'll know what I mean."

"Guess you got a job," John said as Big Neil went out the door.

"What does he mean about tending to the fire?"

"I'm not sure, but just do as you're told. If you have any serious trouble, just tell him you're Vince Shevley's son."

"NO!" said Stephen in a whisper. "No one's to know that."

"Whatever you say, my friend. I've got to move on to the next camp. And I'd like to get back to the farm before dark. I'll be by here again next week to look in on you. Let me know if you need anything...and good luck."

Grimly Stephen shook John's hand. In bidding him farewell, he sensed that he was saying goodbye not only to his good friend, but to the world of his youth.

*   *   *

The sun was just rising when he left the shanty and went across the way to the blacksmith's shed, which stood next to the cabin that Big Neil Amundsen shared with his foremen. The rutted area that divided the camp was frozen solid and difficult to traverse. A pathway carved through the drifted snow at the entrance to the blacksmith's shop was nearly five feet high and the heavy door was closed tightly against the cold. Inside he could hear the sound of extraordinarily heavy breathing, a deep sucking in and exhaling of air. When there was a lull in this weird respiration he opened the door a crack and slipped quickly inside. It was dark but for the open bed of embers in a raised fire pit in the rear corner. There a man sat hunched over the embers, one arm rising and falling rhythmically as he pumped life into the glowing coals. The scarlet incandescence cast ghostly shadows that rose and fell with each stroke of his bellows. The walls were hung with rusted pikes and bars of iron of various lengths. As Stephen approached the Satan in charge of this miniature underworld he saw that the man's head was covered with a thatch of white hair that tangled into his beard and came to rest upon his shoulders. His back was humped but his shoulders were massive and under his shirt the muscles bulged with each movement of his powerful arms. He was seated on a stool with one leg braced firmly against the foot of the hearth. The stump of his other leg rose and fell along with each stroke as if it were a grotesque counterweight. Though his body was thus misshapen, the man's eyes were wild and luminous, fixed on the fire as if they could see what lay beyond the flames. Whatever they saw, it seemed reflected in the man's expression. His mouth, so far as it could be seen amid the tangle of white hair, seemed to turn down at the corners as if weighted by some infinite sorrow.

218

The skin of his face, taut and translucent in the fiery glow, seemed barely to confine some raging inner torment. Suddenly his eyes shifted toward his tall young visitor with a look that demanded some explanation.

"Big Neil sent me over to tend to the fire. I'm new here. My name is Craft, Steve Craft."

The man's arm continued its rhythmic pumping and in a moment he nodded to the bellows to indicate that Stephen should take over. He moved close by and at the top of the next stroke he grasped the handle without missing a beat. The blacksmith hoisted himself up on a pair of crutches and hobbled over to a cabinet from which he removed a battered coffeepot. He smiled at Stephen's ill-concealed surprise.

"No, Big Neil didn't send you over to heat my coffee," he said in a hoarse whisper. "He wants a fire of another sort. Have a cup of coffee?"

"No, thanks. I had tea at breakfast."

"Can't stand tea," said Potter. "They feed it to the crew 'cuz it's cheap. Koenig brings me coffee when I need it. You know Koenig?"

"Yes, he's my friend. He brought me here last night."

"If he brought you here, he's no friend," said Potter. "I see you're looking at my stump. You saw the bull cook? He lost his left leg; I lost my right. Sometimes when we get drunk he takes off his wooden leg and I lay aside these crutches and we try to walk together as one man, but then we fall down and the crew gets a good laugh. Be careful of your legs. You're not much good out here in the woods without your legs." As he spoke he sized up his visitor, looking deep into his eyes as if trying to read his thoughts. Then he looked away and asked, "Why in hell do you want to be a logger?"

"I need a job."

"Where you from?"

"Down river."

"St. Paul?"

"Minneapolis."

"Got a family?"

"No."

Stephen squirmed on the hard stool, and his host reached for a piece of bearskin and handed it to him to sit on.

"How much do you get paid?"

"I don't know."

"You don't care, then. That's good. You won't get rich here, that's for damned sure. Good thing you don't care. Some come to get rich, you know. They all come to make their mark, one way or another. I came to make my mark, but I got marked instead." He gave a hollow laugh that lifted the corners of his mouth a little.

"You were a logger?"

"I was a chopper, best there was – once. No man could swing an axe like I could – no man. I made the woods ring with the sound of my axe. I can still remember the thrill of it, the way the tree would make a snapping sound, then teeter for a second before plunging to the earth where it lay with it's life's blood oozing out of the wound I'd given it." His eyes burned with an unholy light and his lips spread in a grin. "It's a wonderment, lad, a wonderment. Oh, I had my day, and glorious it was. I did it with these two arms and a good axe, and there was no one better. I cut 'em in Maine, in Michigan and in Wisconsin Territory. I cut my last one over in the St. Croix River valley – the one that finally got me."

The woodsman's brow glistened with sweat as the coals alternately glowed brightly and then faded, only to glow again as Stephen pumped the bellows.

"But no more," the old man sighed, surveying his massive arms and slapping the stump of his leg. "I called them my trees then, lad, but they weren't mine. They were God's creatures, sure as you and I are. There's not a man alive who can kill the creations of God and go unmarked. Sooner or later His hand falls upon us all. You must be careful, lad, or you'll be marked, too, one day."

"How did your mark come?" Stephen asked.

"Directly from God!" he said, leaning heavily forward on his crutches and staring into Stephen's eyes. "What I killed that day was not only a living tree, it was the sacred

Balm of Gilead. That tree came from a seed of the living cross upon which the Lord Jesus was crucified. It was my fate to strike my axe into its very heart. That's why the vengeance of the Lord fell upon me. I took great pride in dropping that tree. I smiled with joy as it twisted and fell. But my joy vanished as I saw that it wasn't falling where I'd aimed it. It was falling directly at me. I tried to leap out of its way, but I was too late. Some say I tripped on some brush, but I know it was the hand of God that tripped me. Before I could roll out of its way, that tree fell across my leg and pinned me to the ground,. God had come to settle my account, and He did it in the most painful way He knew how. It took a team of oxen to drag that awful weight off me. I watched as that tree ripped my leg off and carried it away. It was God's punishment that left me with this useless stump to remind me of my sin." He paused for a moment looking off into the middle distance, mulling over his fate. "Course I'm better off than Henry McCloud – or maybe worse. Who's to say? Well, we'd better get to work."

He swung out the door on his crutches into the morning light, leading Stephen around to the rear of the shed to a cut-over clearing swept clean by the wind that had drifted the snow to one side revealing dozens of tree stumps. He paused near the drifts and began poking with the end of his crutches, marking a rectangle about two feet wide and six feet long.

"We want a fire to cover this area," he said. "You gather some tinder, some kindling and deadfall, then come for me and I'll give you hot coals to set it off."

"What's the fire for?"

"It's for Henry McCloud."

"Who is Henry McCloud?"

"That's Henry over there," Potter said, pointing with one crutch to a pair of boots protruding from the nearby snowdrift.

"You mean he's dead!"

"Hope so. It was pretty damn cold last night."

"But how long has he..."

"Day before yesterday. We would have taken proper care of him at the time, but Big Neil thought the sky pilot might be coming by today, it being Sunday, and he'd want to be in on the doings. He's quite a talker, you see."

"You mean we're getting set to cremate him?"

"Henry, you mean? Hell, no. He'll get a proper Christian burial, but the ground's frozen down about four or five inches and we got to thaw it out and dig him a proper hole. You lay a good fire, and come and get me when it's ready."

"How did he die?" Stephen asked, not really caring, but not eager to be left alone with the corpse.

"He was greasin' the skids – putting a layer of snow on the skid road and packin' it down to move the logs along. He slipped and fell just as a big tree came slidin' his way. Flattened him like a pancake. We'd have buried him on the spot, but Big Neil said haul him back and wait for the preacher to come by. So they hauled ol' Henry back and stuck him in the snow to keep him fresh. Well, it may be fine for old Henry, but it's too cold here for the living, so I'll head back and let you get to work."

As Potter hobbled away Stephen set about gathering what tinder he could find, keeping an uneasy eye on the boots of Henry McCloud. He stripped quantities of paper-thin bark from the birches and mounded it in a long row the length of the cleared area, filling in the gaps with fistfuls of pine needles. Then he tugged at gray, lifeless branches that jutted out of the snow and leaned them against the tinder pile. When everything was in order he returned to the blacksmith's shed.

"Around back of the outhouse there's a woodpile," Potter told him. "You'll find a sled there. Load the sled with firewood while I fetch some coals. I'll meet you out by old Henry's resting place."

As he loaded the sled Stephen noticed that the loggers were gathered around several bonfires in the common area apparently taking their Sunday ease. But then he saw huge kettles suspended over the fires filled with water coming slowly to a boil. Scattered all about were small piles of dirty clothes. Sunday, he realized, was wash day. The loggers ignored him when he first came by, but when he returned dragging the sled full of firewood they fell silent and stared as he passed. When he arrived at the burial site Potter was already there, scattering glowing red coals from a bucket over the tinder and kindling to set the pile ablaze. Stephen began adding the firewood until a huge blaze was sending a column of black, sweet-smelling pine smoke heavenward. He huddled close to the flames, trying to dry his cold, wet clothing.

"That all the duds you got?" Potter asked.

"Yes."

"Won't be near enough."

"I'll have Koenig bring me more."

"Meantime, you might find some in McCloud's turkey."

"His what?"

"His turkey. His poke. His bag of belongings. He won't need 'em now."

"What about his family?"

"Never spoke of kin. Might look for a letter or something among his things. But he never spoke of kin."

Potter left behind a pick axe and a spade along with orders to keep the fire spread over the area until the ground was soft enough to dig.

"You'll want to go four, five feet deep in order to keep the wolves away."

"Wolves didn't get him last night," Stephen noted.

"Froze solid. No smell, probably," Potter said in departing.

By mid-morning when the ground was covered with embers Stephen tested the earth with the pick and found it thawed. The coals steamed and sizzled as he loosened the soil with the pick, then took the spade and began digging. By noon he was three feet into the grave, leveling the bottom and striving for sharp corners. His shoulders began to ache as he was forced to heave each shovel full of dirt higher and further away to keep it from sliding back into the hole. At noon he heard the clang of the bull cook's bell, and the talking and laughing of the loggers as they filed inside the shanty. But since no one came for him, he kept on digging. By mid-afternoon, aching with hunger, arms, shoulders and back numb with fatigue, he at last was satisfied that he had done his best for the late Henry McCloud. It was not a moment too soon. As he hoisted himself out of the hole he saw coming toward him a strange procession led by a short, fat man in a long black coat with a black fur collar turned up around his face. A fur cap covered his head and ears and his porcine eyes peered solemnly out from this mask of animal hair. His hands were concealed in a fur muff that rested on his belly and from his bearing Stephen suspected those hands were clenched in prayerful respect for the deceased. This surely was the itinerant preacher Potter had spoken of, for behind him followed the entire camp crew led by the towering Big Neil Amundsen. All were properly silent and respectful except for the last men in line who were grinning in blissful detachment from the event at hand. As the loggers ringed the grave Big Neil ordered the two stragglers to retrieve the stiffened corpse from its resting place in the snow bank and to lay it at the feet of the preacher. When the body was properly positioned the preacher daintily brushed the snow from the face of the leading character in this dismal drama.

"Get on with it," ordered Big Neil impatiently. "It's cold out here."

"Just wanted to see who I'm praying over," said the preacher. "What's his name?"

"McCloud. Henry McCloud," said Big Neil. "Now get on with it, for Christ's sake."

"Oh Lord," the preacher intoned, lifting his eyes to the heavens, "we are gathered here today to commend to your eternal care the soul of our dear departed brother, Harry McCloud."

"Henry," Big Neil corrected him.

"Henry McCloud, a devout and hard-working laborer here in your earthly vineyards. He's gone from us, Lord, and we are his only known family. We grieve at his parting and mourn here at his grave. But we trust, most merciful Father, in your wisdom and goodness to take him to a better land to labor in your golden fields in peace and happiness, in sunshine and warmth forever. We'll miss Henry, Lord, for he was a good friend and companion and his empty place at our table..."

"Amen, God dammit," Big Neil interrupted. "You two, get his boots off. No use buryin' a good pair of boots."

When the boots had been rescued the camp boss gingerly placed his foot on the body and nudged it into the grave where one leg caught on a protruding root, leaving the dear departed resting at an awkward angle. Big Neil snatched the spade from Stephen and with two vicious strokes jammed the body flat into the bottom of the hole. While the preacher resumed his oration, the two men who had fetched the body sat down on a nearby log to try on Henry McCloud's boots, one the left boot, the other the right. This led to an argument over which man had made the better fit, and thus should be the rightful inheritor of this bounty. As the argument grew louder, the preacher raised his voice in competition. This inspired some giggling among the mourners, which was soon drowned out by great stomping of feet and flapping of arms as the mourners sought to ward off the bitter cold. The preacher, unhurried, shouted on, his voice ringing in the vast cathedral of the forest, rising into a darkening sky where it mingled with the flurries that heralded a snowstorm.

"Oh Lord, we pray that having opened to Henry McCloud the gates of larger life, Thou wilt receive him into Thy joyful service. For God we are all but dust; man's days are as grass: as a flower of the field; so he flourishes and the wind passeth over and he is gone. Take unto Thy bosom, God, the soul of Henry McCloud. Dust unto dust..." he said as he kicked some loose soil into the grave.

"Amen!" shouted Big Neil. "Let's get the hell out of here."

"Amen!" shouted the mourners thankfully.

The camp boss jammed the spade into Stephen's hands.

"Fill it up, kid," he said as he hastened away.

*   *   *

It was dark when Stephen put the last dirt on the grave and tamped it down with the flat of the spade. He stretched his aching back and stood for a moment in silence, not in respect for the departed, but more in wonder of death itself. He remembered Old Williams in Maine, stretched out cold and dead and alone on the table in his cabin, waiting for strangers to bury him. It was no worse than the fate of Henry McCloud with his cadre of reluctant mourners, an itinerant preacher to pray over his remains, and an icy grave in the middle of nowhere. He decided he'd come back to this grave with a marker of some sort, so future passersby would know that here a life had ended and that someone, stranger though he might be, had thought enough of the deceased to mark the site. Then he turned wearily and made his way back to camp. He left the sled by the woodpile, stopped off at the outhouse, and finally made his way to the shanty door. He stood for a moment with his head reeling, weak from hunger and fatigue, too tired to lift his hand to the door latch.

"Are you all right?" asked a kindly voice behind him. "Let me open the door for you. I think we're just in time for supper. We'll get out of the cold and have some hot stew and a mug of tea. It'll make you feel much better."

The logger guided him into the shanty and over to the roaring fire. The men of the crew were gathered around one of the tables where several were engaged in a game of cards. They barely looked up. Stephen shucked off his heavy jacket and sank to his knees by the fire. He held his numb hands near the dancing flames and squeezed his eyes shut as tears rolled down his cheeks. His teeth chattered involuntarily and his whole body shook.

226

"Get him a blanket," the kindly logger ordered and in a moment one was draped over his shoulders. Stephen stared into the fire mesmerized as the tears continued to flow, tears of relief, of pain, and of sadness. The loggers fell silent and he knew that they were watching him.

"Come and get it!" yelled Andy Sweet as he laid out the platters and bowls of food on the serving plank.

"You can sit by me," said the kindly logger as he helped him to his feet. "We can talk and get to know one another."

He guided Stephen through the line and saw that he got a goodly quantity of venison stew ladled over doughnut-shaped rolls.

"I'm Peter Shaw," he said as they took their place at the table nearest the fire. "What's your name?"

"Steve Craft."

"You've had a tough initiation, Steve," said Shaw.

"I never thought I'd have to bury a man on my first day."

"Neil was seeing what kind of stuff you were made of," said Shaw. "I think he was pleased with what he saw."

"I worked as fast as I could – had to or I'd freeze."

The men of the crew, who had only pretended not to be listening, laughed heartily as this. The oldest among them got up, came over to Stephen, and put his hand on his shoulder.

"I'm McClintock," he said. "Where are you from?"

"Minneapolis. I worked at the mill until I had a run-in with my boss."

"Was he the one who gave you the beating?"

"Yes."

"How old are you?"

"Nineteen."

"Have you ever spent a winter in the woods?"

"No, but I spent a summer cruising."

"You happen to run into a man called Ben McAlpine?"

" I was cruising with Ben."

"Well, then," said Peter Shaw. "We'll have to see that you get a better impression of us than you have so far. Ben McAlpine is very highly regarded here. He's a woodsman of the first rank."

"We've all been a little touchy," said another logger from his place at table. "We saw Henry get smoothed out and it didn't sit too well. Bad enough to look death in the eye, but to have to listen to the sky pilot, too!"

Over the laughter of the others, McClintock responded, "You were angry because the preacher interrupted your Sunday binge."

"Who was interrupted?" asked the logger. "Besides, look here, I got a new pair of boots out of it!"

"All right," Big Neil's voice boomed over the laughter. "Craft, when you're finished with your supper, come down to my cabin. We've got some papers to fill out."

Big Neil's cabin was a sturdy structure well caulked against the winds that seemed intent on whipping up a blizzard. A fire blazed cheerily in his fireplace, the logs snapping and filling the air with sparks that fell harmlessly on the dirt floor. The boss had a table on which an oil lamp burned, three chairs, a commode and wash basin, a double bunk against one wall, a single bed on the other. Big Neil sat at the table as Stephen entered.

"Pull up a chair, Craft. This will only take a minute."

He had a work ticket in front of him and a ledger in which each man's name, specialty and wages were recorded, along with the date of hire. They were like the papers he had filled out for Ben McAlpine the night they were recruiting in Minneapolis.

"Spell your name for me," Big Neil began, a pencil poised over the work ticket.

"S-t-e-v-e," Stephen began.

"Wait! Not so fast. I got to write it down," said Big Neil.

"If that's a work ticket, I can fill it out," said Stephen.

"You know how to write?"

"Yes. And I can fill out the ledger, too, if you'll tell me my job and pay scale."

"Well, I'll be damned. You done this before?"

"Yes."

"That's why the soft hands. You worked in the mill office."

"Sometimes," Stephen admitted, taking the work ticket and the pencil and filling it out, then the ledger, asking, "What's my job and what's it pay?"

"I'm taking you on as a swamper at three dollars a week."

"Shevley usually pays five," said Stephen.

"Maybe next year after you learn the job. You'll be in Shaw's crew and you'll do as he says. You'll be paid off when the drive begins, unless you work the drive. Then you'll get your pay when the raft arrives at the Shevley mill."

"I understand," said Stephen, pushing the ledger back to him.

"You'll need more clothes. You can buy some things in the storeroom. See Cookie about it. They'll be deducted from your wages. Meantime take this." He reached under the table and brought up a canvas bag with a drawstring. "Belonged to McCloud. Go on, take it. Might be a few things you could use. What you don't want, maybe some of the others will. It was stupid to come up here without any gear. You come on the run? The law after ya'? Hell, I don't care; it's none of my business. My business is cutting timber. If you work hard, like today, and don't complain, that's all I ask. If you decide to hit the tote road before I dismiss the crew in the spring, you'll leave without your pay."

"I understand," Stephen said. And then he went out the door, a dead man's bag over his shoulder.

Chapter 14

The men were up, dressed and fed in the dark of night, stumbling and mumbling and paying only harsh heed to one another. In his own groggy state Stephen relished being left alone; isolation within the crowd was the only way to preserve the last lingering moments of privacy one brought from the world of dreams into the world of wakefulness. Only when they had drunk their last cup of tea did the loggers face up to the realities of the new day. Gulping the bitter liquid, each was fortifying himself against the cold and hard labor that awaited him. It was time to share a last moment of warmth and to rekindle the camaraderie that hardship forges among men who suffer together. By the time they stooped through the doorway into the frigid pre-dawn they again were treating one another as human beings.

Across the way Potter stumped about on his crutches in front of the shed, helping to load the lumberjacks' tools aboard sleighs that would carry them to their work site. Peter Shaw, foreman of Stephen's gang, took him by the arm and guided him forward.

"Find a brush hook for our new friend, Potter. He'll be taking McCloud's place today."

Potter lifted the curved blade, tested its keen edge with his blackened thumb and flipped it about, presenting it to Stephen.

"Not a good omen," he said darkly, "taking a dead man's place.".

"Someone's got to," Stephen said defiantly. "I figure I'm entitled since I helped bury him."

There were eight men in each crew and from the comments they exchanged as they boarded the sleighs it was obvious that the day's labors were to be a competition and that the choppers were to be the featured players. The grizzled John McClintock was the chief chopper in Shaw's crew. Their teamster was Charlie Huffman, a quiet man who communed more easily with his oxen than with his colleagues. A Maine man, Joe Pettibone, was the chainer; Jacob DeGroot and Jon Svendson were barkers, and the swampers were Ole Lundberg and Stephen. Another gang under Big Neil's command boarded a second sleigh and the logging crew set out for the work area just as the sun was rising. Their trail led through a devastated forest littered with piles of brush, dotted with oozing tree stumps and scarred by deep ruts that all ran in the general direction of the Rum River. At a cleared and well churned area the sleighs came to a halt and after a brief consultation Big Neil led his crew on foot some one hundred yards to the west and Shaw led his men north some fifty yards where their work for the day would begin. As they neared the work area the loggers paused near an icy area stained with blood, the skid road where Henry McCloud had met his unfortunate end. Shaw led the loggers up a small rise, turning often to gauge the distance to the skid road that led to the river, then set about giving orders for the day's cut. His swampers were last to get instructions.

"We'll be dropping our trees on either side of this draw," he explained. "You clear it of all brush, heavy limbs, large stones – anything that might block the movement of logs between the top of the draw and the skid road down below. Ole, you show him what I mean."

"Come along, young fella'," said Ole. "I guess I'll be your nursemaid today."

Ole showed Stephen how to grasp the brush hook firmly with both hands, slip the sharp blade around the stem of a shrub, sever it with a quick yank, and heave it out of the way.

"We'll clear the draw down to the skid road. The crew will be dropping trees up on that rise. The barkers will trim each tree. Then Charlie and his ox team will chain it to the go-devil, drag it into the draw and down to the road. The first couple of logs will pack the snow, and pretty soon they'll be sliding along pretty as you please. Now let's get to work so we can stand clear when the first logs come our way."

They worked on opposite sides of the draw. Stephen labored in silence, sinking into the deep snow and swinging the sharp blade with all his might. It was exhausting work performed under the pressure of the thump, thump, thump of the chopper up above. When the thumping ceased there followed a cry of warning as the tall white pine crashed to the earth.

"You better pick up steam," Ole called back to him. "They'll be on top of us soon."

Stephen quickened his pace, but the veteran logger raced on ahead of him, completing his side of the draw and then working back up along Stephen's side. The young man's arms, shoulders and his back began to ache. The brush hook became a dead weight in his hands. His legs turned to rubber with fatigue as he stumbled through the deep snow. His clothing was sopped and clung to his skin. Sweat poured from his brow and stung his eyes. He targeted a shrub ten yards off and staggered valiantly toward it, only to stumble and sprawl into the snow as Ole reached it first and felled it with a swift stroke of his hook.

"You sweat like a fat whore," he said with a grin. "And you swing a hook like one, too. When you finish with your nap, go back to the sled and get a shovel and start packing down the snow. I'm going up and help that Norwegian trim the branches from that tree."

As the thumping of the choppers resumed in the distance, Stephen set about compacting the snow, stomping it, smacking it with the back of the shovel, smoothing it – and always looking up the draw, thinking about the fate of Henry McCloud. When the sun was at its zenith the bull cook's wagon arrived with the noon meal. Both crews gathered at the skid road when the bull cook banged an iron bar against a barrel hoop and sent the signal ringing through the woods. Andy Sweet, a boy about fifteen, helped dish up steaming plates full of baked beans and salt port, with a cold shut and tepid tea on the side.

"Why's this called a cold shut," Stephen asked Ole as they settled into a snowdrift to eat.

"A cold shut's an iron link for mending a broken chain," Ole explained. "Try a bite, you'll see why. But don't chip a tooth."

Stephen ate quickly, greedily, gulping down the warm food before it froze. The beans, which had gagged him when he first tried to eat them, now tasted delicious and warmed him deep inside. He cleaned his plate and went back for seconds, and when the time came to get back to work, he did so with renewed vigor. Only late in the afternoon when it began to grow dark did he notice the cold again and feel his aching muscles and blistered hands. On the ride back to camp he grew numb from the cold and fatigue, but endured the discomfort proudly for it was a bond he shared with all the others. In the shanty the banter still bypassed him, and his glance caused the others to avert their eyes. But this was the natural shyness of simple men. Despite their reluctance to draw him into their tight little fraternity, he was undeniably one of them now. He felt it in his aching back and he relished the pain as if it were a right of passage. He was determined not only to endure, but also to succeed.

*   *   *

Late January brought a sudden warm spell and a thaw that turned their clean white world in a muddy morass. But it was only a momentary relaxation of winter's grip. By February they again were locked in frigid temperatures and fighting frequent blizzards that slowed their labors. There were days when the blinding snow made them all afraid, days when they found themselves peering into the white swirls for a reassuring glimpse of a crewmate, when each lonely step invited disorientation and the panic of being lost in a tight cell of snow behind thick black bars of tree trunks that towered into pale infinity and vanished from sight. Blinded, they feared the loud "Hal-loo-loo!" that signaled a falling tree, feared they might unknowingly be in its path, uncertain which way to run for their lives. But work went on, and the wooden wealth of the wilderness grew in great piles at the river's edge to await the spring thaw.

Stephen was well satisfied with his lot. The hardships of life in the logging camp were a welcome relief from the confusion and pain of life at Shevley House. When occasional spells of loneliness or remorse threatened to overwhelm him, he threw himself even more energetically into his work. Hard labor became a solace to him, a narcotic that brought him instant relief and blessed forgetfulness. But some reminders of the past were unavoidable. John Koenig brought news from the city with each weekly delivery of supplies. His appearance frequently led to questions about what was going on at the mill, and that would lead to talk of payday.

"I'll make the drive to sweeten my poke," Ole said one night. "I'll make enough money to stay drunk all summer."

"Why don't you save your money and buy a farm?" asked Peter Shaw. "It's foolish to work as hard as you do and earn nothing for it but a summer-long headache. You'll end up begging for coins on the street by fall."

"He'll be lucky if his earnings buy him a weekend drunk," said Charlie Huffman. "There's no money to be made here. The money lies down there at the riverbank, waiting to be floated to town and into Shevley's pockets. He'll grow rich, but we never will."

"Why shouldn't he?" asked Jacob DeGroot. "They're his trees, aren't they?"

"Some are, some aren't," Huffman responded. "Who's to say when we cut beyond Shevley's land?"

"Big Neil, that's who," Jon Svendson exclaimed. "Big Neil knows very well where the line is. He's in tight with the mill bosses. He's got the books and the maps."

"I suppose you think the big bosses don't steal from one another," said Jacob. "It's a matter of pride with them. If they can't steal a man blind without his knowing it, they've got no business being in business."

The banter drew chuckles from the loggers who lined the deacon's seat in front of the communal bunk. The shanty was warm. Odors of musty straw, sweat, pine smoke and the sweet aroma of pipe tobacco hung heavily in the air. Potter, whittling idly at a stick so that the chips flipped neatly into the fire pit, picked up the thread of the conversation.

"They're not Shevley's trees," he said. "They don't belong to any man. They're God's trees. They belong to God."

"If that is true, then those clothes you're wearing belong to God, too, because they're made from the fibers of His plants and the skins of His animals."

Potter's dull stare indicated Shaw's point was lost on him.

"I'll concede that the earth is indeed the work of God," Shaw went on. "But so is man. Certainly He didn't put us here to wither and die. He gave us 'dominion over the earth,' or so the Bible tells us. So it must be His plan that we use nature for our needs. This forest, for example, provides fuel to keep us warm, shelter to protect us from the rain, snow and cold. It also provides work for us so we can earn wages. Surely there is no sin in that."

"Greed is a sin," Potter insisted, "and it will spell our doom."

"I still say we cut down trees beyond Shevley's land and drag them to our landing," DeGroot maintained. "Whether that's God's will or just plain greed, I'll leave it to the devil to decide."

*　　*　　*

When the bitter cold and violent storms of winter were over the loggers began talking about the spring drive. There was a quiet excitement about the prospect of big money and danger. From the more experienced loggers Stephen gathered that the drive was a test as no other in lumbering. It seemed to represent hardship beyond imagination, even the possibility of death.

"We lost a man last year," Shaw said. "Broke a wing jam that had tied us up for most of a day. Clem Brooks was his name. He fought that jam for hours and when he finally found the key log, damned if he wasn't standing on it!"

"Ya," said Ole, "you only get one mistake, that's for sure."

"Ya, you betcha," Jon agreed. "One mistake and you come up wet – or dead, maybe."

"Clem didn't come up at all," said Charlie the teamster. "I was watching him. He pried loose the key log and the whole jam broke loose. I saw him go under, but he never came up. The way that river was runnin' he was probably in New Orleans by morning."

"But he was makin' five dollars a day," McClintock pointed out. "I'd wrestle the devil in hell for that kind of pay."

Orville Potter, long silent on the sidelines, looked now upon the aging John McClintock with baleful eye and made the sign of the cross.

Stephen had no such reservations. As with most young men his age, he felt indestructible, and the prospect of adventure thrilled him. He could imagine himself leaping across the flotilla of logs until he stood tall at the head of the raft as it neared the city, the wayward son arriving home as a conquering hero, guiding the raft into the boom above the falls to greet his parents as a son who had met the test of manhood. By now he could work from sunup to sundown with little pause, his muscles hard and his strength at its peak. Though he still stood at the bottom rung of the camp hierarchy and had not yet been allowed to wield an axe, he was expert in the use of the brush hook and the cant dog and a respected member of the crew. For all his acceptance among his colleagues he still loved to wander alone through the woods under the towering pines rather than join in Sunday card games, the surreptitious drinking matches or the tall-tale contests of his crewmates. With the frozen river as his guide he could cover several miles in an afternoon of solitary wandering, relishing the crunch of snow beneath his feet, at peace under the ermine-draped branches of the white pine, enraptured with the company of the winter wrens that lived along the frozen river and chirped in alarm as he invaded their territory. At the river's edge he would sit with his back against a fallen tree to rest and dream. Above him the sky was clear and blue and through the branches wafted a breeze that stirred the woodland to lazy life, bringing with it memories of old Williams. He had been right, after all. He was indeed his father's son, and like old Ephraim Shevley before him, fit for the forestlands and all they might demand of him. As the sun lowered he arose and stared into the darkening immensity of the woods and knew no fear. He was a part of it now, comfortable and at ease. On his way back to camp he went to a huge white pine, slapped its rough bark with affection and hugged it as if it were a human thing.

In early April the season's last snow fell. The air was warm and the snow pack turned soft and sticky. The ice along the river's edge became delicate and lacy as the sun eroded it from above and the racing waters ate at it from below. Even the hard packed skid road grew mushy and began to sink as rivulets of melted snow undercut it and whittled at its flanks. As the land shrugged off its pristine mantle it exposed a scene of utter devastation, the wounds and scars of a winter's logging – brush piles, ragged tree stumps, and churned earth turning rapidly to mud. Gradually the work shifted from the cutting areas to the riverbank where the winter's cut of logs lay in huge piles waiting for the stream to burst its bonds of ice. As the southernmost of the Shevley camps, Big Neil's men were to play a key role in the drive. Theirs would be the lead raft in the journey down river to the mills at St. Anthony Falls. To prepare for the drive a daisy chain of logs was stretched across the frozen river and anchored on either bank, each log connected to the next by a short length of chain secured with a spike. This device would guard against release of the logs in case the softening earth should collapse and spill them prematurely into the raging river. While Charlie Huffman's ox teams dragged the last logs from the skid road to the riverbank for the stacking crew, Stephen and Ole were put to work clearing brush at the river's edge so that nothing would impede the final toppling of the stacks into the river. All was in order when the big bosses from the mill arrived aboard John Koenig's supply wagon to sign up the rafting crew. They were led by Vincent Shevley.

It had been only a little more than four months since Stephen had seen his father, but to him it seemed like a lifetime. So much had happened; so much had changed since his father had beaten and banished him. He knew full well that John had kept Vincent apprised of his circumstances. And yet, according to John, his father had never inquired about him. When John asked him for clothes for his son, Vincent gave them to him. When John asked for a few dollars for Stephen to spend in the wanigan for personal items, he got them.

"But he never asked about me?"

"I would have told you, Steve. You know that."

"I don't know what to say to him."

"Then let him speak first, if he even recognizes you. Here, give me a hand unloading the wagon. You'll want to go back and hear what he has to say about the drive."

"You don't think he'll recognize me?"

"He might not, Steve," he said with a smile. "Have you got a mirror? Have you looked at yourself recently?"

John was right, of course. His hair came to his shoulders. A beard, a real man's beard, not the soft down of his youth, covered his face. He felt larger somehow, not the skinny youth that passed his idle hours in the taverns of Washington Avenue. He was bigger, heavier than ever before. Indeed, Stephen thought, Vince Shevley might *not* recognize his own son. The idea amused him, strangely enough, and he was willing, if not eager, to put it to the test.

He stayed on the fringes of the crowd as the loggers gathered around a tree stump that Vincent had mounted to speak to them. Standing nearby, a ledger in his hands, was the faithful Ben McAlpine, dressed as usual in his buckskin jacket, leggings, and moccasins, and with a feather stuck jauntily in his hatband. Stephen stepped slightly apart from the other loggers as Vincent began his talk. After a few minutes their eyes met, but Vincent gave no sign of recognition. Later their eyes met again, and this time Stephen thought he saw a glimmer of recognition, a slight nod, the flicker of a smile. He quickly looked down, avoiding his father's eyes, and immediately regretted it. What harm would it have done to return his smile? What a fool to have been so cold and unforgiving. Stephen felt a twinge of guilt. For the first time in weeks he felt like a child again, bitter and ashamed. A simple smile might have bridged the gap between them. Wait! That look again. Was it a look of pain he saw in his father's eyes? He shouldered a bit closer through the crowd, wondering if there would be another chance. He wanted to call out to him, run to him and clasp him, as he must have clasped him in his uninhibited childhood, to cling to him and draw from him the strength and security of his love. Now as Vincent spoke his eyes seemed to dart past him, avoiding him.

"It's been a good, productive winter," he was saying to the men. "I see the results of a lot of hard work and I'm pleased and proud of you all. It's getting near time to get these logs to the mill. The days are getting longer and the snow is going fast. The river ice is thin and the runoff will be heavy. That makes for good, fast water, and a tough drive, make no mistake about it. We don't want anyone who'll quit half way. That's why we're paying five dollars a day – payable at the mill when the raft is safely in the boom."

The men shuffled their feet and mumbled quietly.

"You know I'm a man of my word. And I know the kind of men you are. Your work here speaks for you. You're the kind of men I want on this drive. Now who's with me?"

A cheer arose and Vincent stepped down from the stump as Big Neil dragged forward a rustic table and chair for Ben.

"Ben here will sign you up or take your mark," Vincent continued. "It may be a week before the ice goes out, but rafting pay begins tomorrow."

This brought on another cheer as the eager loggers formed a line and chatted happily as they waited their turn to sign up. Only a few held back, making plausible excuses to one another for not challenging the river, trying more than anything else to convince themselves that five dollars a day was not enough to keep them any longer from hearth and home. There were fields that needed tending, children too long without a father, wives lonely and forlorn at their absence. And for the inexperienced, there were dangers to life and limb on the river for which no amount of money could compensate. The wanderers also held back. They were lured by rumors of even grander forests to the west and the certainty of a warm summer in which to make the journey.

But most of the loggers were going through the line, subjecting themselves to Vincent's scrutiny as he questioned them on their skills and past experience. It would take all their talents to move more than a million feet of timber seventy miles along a treacherous, rampant river to the mills, he warned them, but none backed down. Stephen took his place at the end of the line, as fearful of facing his father as he was of the unknown perils of the drive. As he slowly approached the table he caught Ben's eye and gave him a wink. Ben smiled broadly, and suddenly Stephen was standing alone at the table under his father's gaze.

"What about you, young fellow," Vincent asked, "have you ever been on a drive?"

"No, sir."

"What do you do?"

Big Neil stepped forward with his own ledger, flipping through the pages and finding Steve Craft's name.

"We picked him up in early January," he said. "His name is Craft. He was a swamper. He's a good, hard worker, Vince. He's strong and he does what he's told to do."

Stephen scuffed his mud-caked boots against one another and shyly raised his eyes to meet his father's.

"That's good to hear, Neil," Vincent said. "I like a young man who can make his own way. And a man's got to start somewhere. I'm glad to hear that, son."

Stephen's heart leaped at the sound of the word, and he looked up warily to see if any of the loggers had caught it. No one seemed to notice, and Vincent smiled mischievously.

"I'm going to put you on the sacking crew," he said. "John McClintock will be your foreman. Your job will be to help round up the strays that get away from the raft and keep them moving down river. If you have any questions, McClintock will answer them. He's a good man with a lot of experience. But mind you, be careful."

His tone was unexpectedly hushed as if he meant his caution for Stephen's ears alone. Then without waiting for a reply, he took Ben by the elbow and hauled him away toward the wagon.

"Come on, Ben. We can make the next camp by nightfall."

*　　*　　*

"Hi! Hi! See what I got here!"

The loggers looked up from their work and watched as Andy Sweet struggled up the slope into camp with water sloshing from the buckets he carried. Big Neil strolled out of Potter's shed and squinted in the sunlight.

"What's going on," he asked.

"The ice is breaking up," Andy shouted. "Come and see for yourselves."

He put down his buckets and raced back down the slope again with the others after him. The river looked much the same as it had all winter with ice from bank to bank, only now there was a dark streak down the center where brown water swirled and foamed like so much cold beer. Andy went carefully out on the ice, testing it with his foot at each step. As he neared the center the ice became rubbery and he had to throw himself backward and stretch out flat to keep from breaking through. The men cheered as a chunk of ice from somewhere upstream bobbed by in the current and was carried away.

241

"You see!" Andy called out as he crawled toward the riverbank. "You saw it! It's ready to go, I tell ya!"

"By golly, you're right," Big Neil agreed. "Shaw, have one of your men run the length of that daisy chain to make sure it's secure. We'll be toppling these stacks sooner than I figured."

Shaw sent Stephen to the blacksmith's shed for drag lines, and checked the daisy chain himself, walking the precarious path of logs to the far bank and back again.

"What's all the commotion about?" Potter asked when Stephen arrived.

"Shaw sent me for the drag lines. The ice is breaking up."

"Not yet, it ain't," said Potter scornfully. "It'll be a couple of days yet."

"But Shaw wants the drag lines," Stephen insisted. "I don't know why, but he wants 'em now."

"He wants to topple the stacks," Potter explained. "The drag lines are to pull the stakes the piles are resting against. He'll loop the lines around the stakes and Charlie's ox teams will pull on the lines, jerk out the stakes and the logs will roll down the bank onto the ice. That way no one gets hurt."

"All I know is, he wants 'em now."

Potter smiled indulgently. "You going on the drive?"

"Yes."

"What's your job?"

"Sacking crew. I'll be with McClintock and Deauville, the Frenchman from Big Neil's crew."

"That's some gang," Potter muttered. "A greenhorn and that worthless scum Jacques Deauville. McClintock's age must be catching up with him, getting a job like that."

"I don't know what you mean."

"Probably the old man's last drive, and they give him you two to look after."

"I don't think that..." Stephen began to protest.

"Don't get your dander up, kid. You'll do all right. It's that Frenchman who'll be a problem. He's a filthy one, he is, always talkin' dirty about women. And he's lazy, too. The old fella will have to keep ridin' him same time he's trying to educate you. Helluva way for a fine lumberjack to go out, but you just do as he says, and don't let the Frenchman pull the wool over your eyes. Here, gather up that rope in the corner. It's heavy, so use the sled out back to haul it down to the river."

That very day the ropes were looped around the restraining stakes and tied securely to the harness of the ox team. Then Charlie prodded the team into motion, and slowly the ropes grew taut and the stakes began to inch free of the soft riverbank. Suddenly one stake and then another burst out of the muck with a sucking sound and flipped into the air with drag lines flying. At first the huge stack moved not at all. But gradually the lead logs began to lose their battle with gravity, settling slowly down the bank toward the river. Then with a mighty roar the entire stack tumbled onto the ice, crushed it and plunged into the frothy water. At the rear of the stack lumberjacks wielding cant hooks and pikes kept the logs moving toward the river. Other loggers leaped atop the bobbing logs to shepherd them snuggly against the daisy chain where they'd form the leading edge of the raft. Stephen marveled at their agility as they leaped from log to log, balancing themselves with their pikes as they herded the logs into position. Upstream the drive crew already was at work to free the next stack, which soon toppled into the river. And so the work continued until after sunset when it grew too dark for such dangerous work. There was no grumbling when Big Neil ordered a final check of the daisy chain and then it was back to the shanty for supper.

The work continued for several days until the riverbed was carpeted from bank to bank with logs. Then the freshet came. It was in the early afternoon after the sun at last had driven off the night chill and the sky had cleared and the air was warm with the promise of spring. It came silently at first with the river swelling as if a huge paddle had stroked it. The flotilla of logs rose, rocked gently, and repositioned itself in the broadened streambed. When the second wave came it came with a roar that echoed down the river valley. The mighty surge lifted the entire raft and tossed the massive logs about as if they were mere sticks in a pond. The river swept up the banks, inundating the brown marsh grasses and gathering everything that was loose – branches, tangles of reeds, rotting leaves from the tamaracks that lined the river – and deposited them several feet higher along the slopes. Then the log raft settled quietly within its newly enlarged bounds. The river gods had shaken off their winter stupor, stretched their mighty muscles, and yawned in the face of spring. The sudden surge was followed by a mad dash to the daisy chain to be certain it had withstood the pressure.

"All's fast on the far bank," called out one logger.

"We lost a few over the chains at mid-channel," shouted another.

"How many gone?" Big Neil hollered.

"Five or six. They're headin' down stream to show us the way to town!"

"The hell they are! Get after them before they get hung up and block our way," Big Neil ordered. "Let's get this raft ready to move. We've got a wide stream and fast water – and money waiting for us at the end of the line."

The raft began to move first with its daredevil drivers dancing deftly over its undulating surface, poking it along, keeping it tight. Long before the last logs had drifted past McClintock and his sacking crew helped launch the wanigan, a crude barge with a cook shack on top. The wanigan carried Big Neil, Rasmussen the bull cook, and his helper, Andy Sweet, and two drivers whose job it was to keep the barge moving and on course as it floated down stream behind the raft. The barge also carried the belongings of the river drivers, tools from the logging camp, and enough food to keep the crews well fed during the drive, which might take as long as three weeks. Men and tools that weren't to be used on the drive were loaded aboard a wagon and headed south along the tote road, leaving Shevley Camp No. 1 a lonely and deserted place. Only the three-man sacking crew was left to bid the camp farewell.

"Well, that's the end of it," said McClintock, giving a casual salute. "We'd best be getting on our way."

"We're well rid of it," said Deauville. "It's not a fit place for a man. Leave it to the timber wolves, and hope for a better camp next season."

"There'll be no next season for me," McClintock said sadly. "I'm through."

"None too soon," said the Frenchman. "You're too old for this kind of work."

"I can still swing an axe, and I could still work the drive, if they'd let me," he said.

"Then why are you bossing a sacking crew?"

"To make five dollars a day for my retirement, that's why. So let's be on our way."

"Five dollars a day! I'm only getting three," Deauville protested.

"And you're not worth that, if you don't get a move on. You got that boat packed, Steve?"

"Yes. Everything's aboard."

"Then we'll start in that backwater across the way. I can see a bunch of strays from here."

They worked from their stable flat-bottomed boat that Jacques called a bateau. It carried their personal belongings and a supply of food, for it was unlikely they'd catch up with the wanigan for several days. In the backwater on the east bank they found dozens of logs that had drifted out of the mainstream or been tossed there by the freshet. Stephen and Jacques waded waist-deep in the icy waters, prying loose the stranded logs with their sturdy pikes and setting them adrift. Standing in the bateau, McClintock guided the freed logs to the river and into the main channel to begin their trip downstream. As it grew dark he pulled his crew aboard and found a good campsite along the riverbank where the first order of business was to build a fire for his men to warm themselves and dry their wet clothes. They dined on skillet bread wrapped around chunks of fried port and washed it down with cups of piping hot tea. After they had eaten they sat close by the fire to absorb its warmth, and while

McClintock sat quietly sucking on his pipe, Jacques regaled Stephen with tales of his sexual conquests in the dimly remembered past.

"Oh, the women, how I have missed them," he sighed. "And the poor dears, how they must have missed me these past months. The lumberjack's life is a hard life, but it is even harder on the women who are left behind."

Impatient with the Frenchman's boasting, McClintock said to Stephen, "I should teach you two how to handle the bateau tomorrow, so I can take my turn in the water."

"I don't mind being in the water," said Stephen.

The old man fixed him with a sad stare.

"Good," said Jacques, "then I'll take the bateau."

"But John's the boss," said Stephen. "He should be in the bateau."

"You think I'm too old to go in the water?" John asked him.

"No. I don't think I could handle the bateau. I've never done it before. What if we came upon rapids?"

"Fine," said Jacques. "Then it's settled. I will take the bateau."

"You may be right," McClintock said to Stephen, ignoring the Frenchman's offer. "Maybe it's best that I am in the bateau, in case we do hit some rapids."

"He's afraid of the cold," Jacques said to Stephen as if McClintock weren't there. "He's too old for the cold water."

"You're right," McClintock said. "I am too old. I've known it all winter long. The cold gets into my bones and won't go away."

"The water is very, very cold," Stephen agreed.

"It would stiffen me; I'd be useless. If I were younger..."

"How old are you?" Stephen asked.

"Let me see," he said. "This is April of eighteen hundred and sixty. That makes me fifty-six years old – fifty seven come May."

"So we must freeze so that you'll live another year," said Jacques. "It's not fair. I would like to live to be your age and still enjoy the ladies. How can I enjoy the ladies if I shrink up with the cold?"

"Is that all you think about?" McClintock asked.

`"Mais, oui! What else is there to think about?"

"If you want to be in the bateau, you can think about being the boss, about guiding the bateau through the rapids, about finding all the stray logs."

"Oh, no, I don't want to be the boss. You be the boss."

"The boss directs the men and the boat. So it's settled. I've spent many winters in the woods, and many springs in the cold water, wet for weeks at a time – wet and cold. But now it's over. I'll take the bateau."

"You've got to stay well so you can tell us what to do," Stephen said, trying to lift John's spirits.

The old man looked from one to the other with his sad, searching eyes. Then he looked away from them, poking a stick in the fire and watching the end of it burn.

Later they checked the clothing they had stretched over the underbrush to dry, then tipped the bateau and braced it against their pikes to form a lean-to. They gathered pine boughs to protect themselves from the cold, wet ground, and lay down under the protection of the bateau to sleep. Stephen, shivering and clutching his blanket tightly around him, listened to the rushing of the river and the whisper of the breeze through the branches overhead. In the distance he could see a patch of moonlit sky, vast and filled with thousands of stars. He loved the sights and sounds of the wilderness and although it grew very cold during the night he remained warm inside and slept a deep, deep sleep.

Chapter 15

After several days of fast water and hard work the riverbed spread out and the water flowed at a more leisurely pace. They had left the pineries and were drifting through the flatlands above the Rum River's junction with the Mississippi. Here they found but a few stragglers that had floated away from the rear of the raft and were making their way independently downstream. All three rode in the bateau. McClintock stood in the rear, poling the boat through the quiet waters. Stephen and Jacques, shifting from one side to the other, used their pikes to prod the bobbing logs into the mainstream to speed them along. Another two days of such relative ease and they came suddenly upon a barrier of logs stretching from one bank to the other with no apparent forward motion.

"Looks like we've caught up with the raft," said Stephen.

"It means trouble," said McClintock.

"It's a log jam," said Jacques.

"Either that or they're having trouble keeping the raft together at the Mississippi," said McClintock.

The bateau had nowhere to pass, even at midstream where the fast-running water dove under the logs to follow the main channel.

"Nothing we can do here," said McClintock. "We'll head for shore and hike on ahead to see what's up."

As they walked downstream the extent of the problem became apparent. Where at first the logs had formed a veritable carpet covering the riverbed, the raft soon became a jumble of logs piling one upon the other, forming dams where water spouted into the air as if from little fountains, or forced its way to the edges of the raft to carve gaping holes in the riverbanks and cut new channels to ease the immense pressures of the river. They had chosen to walk the east bank, and before long Stephen saw on the opposite shore a familiar grove of birch trees that marked the Koenig farm.

From the distance he could see a flurry of activity as John and his brother August struggled to create a buffer of logs to lessen the erosive impact of the water as it carved away at the land. Already two the birches had fallen, their roots exposed and washed clean by the raging river water.

"That's Koenig's place over there," Stephen said, pointing. "We ought to help him, if we can."

"You go first," said Jacques. "If you make it without falling in, then maybe I will try."

"Best way to help him is to get these logs moving again," said McClintock. "Let's push on and see where the jam is."

"I want no part of a log jam," said Jacques. "I've seen men vanish in them. I've seen others broken or chewed to pieces."

"I don't know anything about a log jam," said Stephen. "But if the Koenigs need help, we ought to help them before they're washed out."

McClintock eyed him with a stony stare.

"You agreed that I'm in charge. You signed on to work the drive, and that's what we're going to do. Let's find out what's going on, then we'll tell Big Neil about the Koenigs' place. If he can spare the men, he'll do what he can for them. Now let's get moving. I think I see the wanigan up ahead."

At the wanigan the bull cook told them that Big Neil had gone on ahead to take charge of clearing a log jam, probably at a narrow cut through a sandstone bluff near the point where the two rivers merged. They continued on foot, noting that the river had spread out and flooded the marshland near the site of Vincent Shevley's ill-fated Pompantium. As the river plunged through the sandstone gap they saw on the bluff above them a knot of men who had gathered to discuss the problem and hurried to join them.

"You've got a bad one here," McClintock said.

"Another hundred yards and we'd have been clear of the Rum, damn the luck," said Big Neil. "But the water was too fast for us. At least we didn't lose anyone."

"There's only one way to clear a jam like that short of blasting it," said McClintock. "Mind if I take a look?"

The men watched as the old man climbed down a jumble of logs to a point at the face of the jam. There several river drivers, dwarfed by the mountain of logs, were poking ineffectually at the pile of timber. One would grip a log with his cant hook while another pried at it with his pike. Some refused to budge; others fell away without impact on the pile. The haphazard wall of logs remained firm. McClintock, his silver locks flowing, made his way to a central point in front of the jam and crouched down to study the crosshatch of logs.

"We may have to blast it," said Peter Shaw up on the bluff.

"We're not turning these logs into kindling wood," said Big Neil emphatically.

"It's too much for the old man," Shaw whispered to Stephen.

"The trip's been pretty hard on him already," Stephen said.

"The whole season's been hard on him. He's not as young as he used to be."

"He says this is his last drive. He didn't want to spend it on the sacking crew."

"We could have used him on the raft, if only he weren't..."

"Too old?" Stephen offered.

"Yes, and more agile. It wouldn't have been safe for him."

"He's only fifty-six."

"That's old in this business."

"Does he have a family?"

"A grown son and daughter – somewhere. His wife's dead."

"Too bad."

"He stayed too long. It was his own fault. Now he'll have to leave without his pride."

As they spoke McClintock shifted from one position to another across the face of the towering logjam while jets of water spewed out here and there soaking him to the skin. Now and then he would crouch down to study the jam from every conceivable angle. After a while he stood up and waved to the men on the bluff.

"He thinks he's found the key log," said Shaw.

"The key log?" Stephen asked.

"It's like a game of jackstraws. If he can dislodge the key log, they'll all come tumbling down."

"And then?"

"Then he'll have to run like hell."

McClintock climbed part way up the slope and called out.

"I think I can break it. May take a couple of hours."

"That'll give us time to clear the channel and form boom down the line," Big Neil called back. "How many men do you need."

"None. Too dangerous. I'll work it myself, if you can keep the channel clear."

"Go ahead," said Big Neil. "Take charge down there."

McClintock ordered the river drivers to move out of the way, borrowing a cant hook from one, a pike from another. Then he began picking through the maze, rolling away the tangled logs one at a time and guiding them into the main channel. As he cleared a large area at the base of the jam, he became more cautious. Poking and shoving here and there, all the while keeping a wary eye on the towering mass, looking for any sign of weakening. But the pile remained immovable. Occasionally as he loosened a log and set it adrift, a new flume would burst out showering him with icy water. As nightfall neared, he called out again to Big Neil.

"I can see the key log!" he yelled. "Gotta make a runway, so when it goes I can get out of here."

"How about roping the key log and pulling it from shore?"

"No. Angle's wrong; wouldn't work."

"Then come on up get a good night's rest. We can pull the key log in the morning."

"We could have this whole mess lying in the boom by morning," McClintock protested. "If you can build me a steady runway, I can make it."

"You're puffin' like a bridegroom already," said Big Neil.

"Look there," said McClintock, pointing. "See where those logs are jammed in the mud? If you could have your drivers secure them, maybe staking them, or pulling a layer of smaller logs on top, I could make a run for it before they get washed out. It'll be a close one, but it's possible."

No one disputed the veteran logger. Big Neil gathered some of his men who began arranging the logs to form a solid runway to the shore. If the jam broke, the rush would take out the runway one log at a time, allowing a split second between each log to make an escape. A fast runner, sure of foot, could traverse the disintegrating runway as it collapsed behind him in the roar of cascading water and logs. On reaching the base of the bluff, he could be hoisted to safety.

"He could never make it," Stephen muttered angrily.

"He has to try," said Shaw. "He has to prove himself once more before he's through. Besides, there's a worse fate."

"What's that?"

"He might still be picking at that pile when the sun comes up. He might be wrong about finding the key log."

Big Neil lowered one end of a rope to McClintock, then watched as he tied it under his arms and around his chest. "At least we'll be able to retrieve his body," he said quietly.

Everyone on the bluff watched in fascination as the aging woodsman played out his lonely drama on a lantern-lit stage of wet, slippery logs. He studied each move carefully, then approached the log and sank his cant hook into it. Applying every ounce of the strength he had developed over a lifetime of hard labor, he wrestled each log away from the pile until he had cleared a path to the key log. Then he crouched before the cavernous mass and thrust his lantern into its dark recess. After a while he set the lantern upon a steady log and called for Big Neil to take up the slack in his rescue rope. Positioning the lantern so that its eerie light fell into the black hole where the key log lay he began to test the logs immediately in front of the key log. Finally he jammed his pike between two that seemed solidly entwined in the pile and tested them cautiously.

"The man's skills are equal to his courage," Shaw noted. "He's going to use a lever log to dislodge the key."

When all was ready, McClintock walked the length of the runway, testing its rigidity at every step. At the base of the bluff he looked up.

"We're ready to jerk you up," Big Neil assured him.

With the same caution, McClintock made his way back to the area of the key log and tested the pike he'd jammed between the logs. Satisfied with its position, he once more looked back along his path to safety. Then he picked up his cant hook and jabbed it into the lever log next to his pike. Grasping both tools, he braced his legs and began applying a slow, steady pressure. The log began to rotate slightly, releasing a spray of water that nearly knocked him over. Next he repositioned the pike and gripped the cant hook with both hands, took a deep breath, and pulled downward with all his might. The log suddenly broke free, sending out a great squealing sound as dozens of wet logs began moving against one another, releasing tons of water. McClintock kept a close eye on the giant moving mass, while continuing to exert pressure on the cant hook until the lever log flipped loose, jerking the cant hook from his hands. The sudden shift knocked him backwards and his lantern went dark as the huge jam gave up its cohesiveness in a thunderous roar. He leaped to his feet and began a wild dash along the runway toward the riverbank, shouting as he went, "Pull me up! Pull me up!"

"Hang on," Big Neil shouted as he and several of his river drivers bent their backs to the rope. "Pull, you bastards, pull!"

Above the roar of the freed waters and the crashing of logs Stephen could hear the cheers of the loggers on the bank who were running to avoid the deadly rush of water and tumbling logs. In a moment John McClintock lay stretched out on the top of the bluff ringed by a circle of lanterns. He looked up at his rescuers with a haggard smile.

"I'll be damned, you old son-of-a-bitch," said Big Neil. "You did it."

"I move pretty fast for an old son-of-a-bitch," McClintock gasped. He closed his eyes slowly then opened them again to peer out from the depths of his fatigue. "But I owe you my life."

"You owe me a cant hook and a pike," said Big Neil with a smile.

"Find that lever log and you'll find 'em both. I had a bite on it that must have been six inches deep."

"Are you sure you're all right," Shaw asked.

"Can we get you anything?" asked Stephen.

"You can get me a ride into town. One of those logs hit me in the back while you were hauling me up. I think it snapped my stem. I can't feel my legs."

*　　　*　　　*

Vincent Shevley arrived at dawn after an all-night ride from Minneapolis. The raft was overdue, and he was concerned and very unhappy. Ben McAlpine accompanied him, and stood aside while Big Neil explained the delay. The tale of McClintock's heroism failed to impress him.

"I've got crews standing by at the mill waiting for this raft!" he stormed. "I can't afford to pay crews to do nothing. Why couldn't you get the raft underway last night?"

"It was late and too dark to do a proper job by the time the jam broke. We had a hell of a time just holding the logs, let alone trying to form them into a raft. Half the cut would have been floating downstream and over the falls. We'd be chasin' logs all the way to New Orleans. Not to mention the men we'd lose, if we sent 'em out in the dark."

"Where do we stand now?" Vincent asked impatiently.

"We can be ready to move in an hour."

"Damn good thing. The rafts from upriver will be on your backs, if you don't get clear soon. Let's get hopping."

Vincent's fury was real, and his confrontation with Big Neil took place aboard the wanigan where all could hear.

"Listen to him rant," Stephen muttered. "You'd think it was the end of the world."

McClintock only smiled; his gaze fixed on the horizon. A glint in his eye said the sun was his today, the sun and the sky and the whole world were his, and the petty events of the moment could no longer touch him. Stephen, who had helped carry McClintock's stretcher to the wanigan, made himself useful by helping Andy Sweet scrub the pots and pans from breakfast. He tried to keep clear of his father, but to no avail. Vincent soon came into the kitchen area to see McClintock.

"For Christ's sake, haven't you heard? We carry blasting powder for jams the size of the one you tackled. Were you trying to kill yourself?"

"Didn't figure you'd want a batch of splinters. You're paying us for logs."

"Well, that was a hell of a fine job. There isn't another man in the crew with the brains or the guts to do what you did. You've got my personal thanks, and my promise that the company will get you a doctor and see that you're properly cared for. Well done, old timer."

McClintock glowed.

Then Vincent turned on Stephen.

"What the hell are you doing here?" he demanded. "You're supposed to be chasing strays."

"I stayed with my foreman," he replied defensively, nodding to McClintock. "I've been trying to help out the best I could."

"I want every able bodied man on the river. I'm not paying you to wash dishes and play nursemaid. Now get out of here. McClintock isn't going to run away. Let the bull cook watch him."

Glowering, Stephen began to leave the wanigan. Big Neil, who had heard the exchange, grabbed him by the arm.

"You take charge, and take the Frenchman with you. Now hop to it."

"All right, you river rats," Vincent was hollering. "Put this raft together and get it moving. I'll give you two days to get it into St. Anthony or there'll be hell to pay."

His father's shouting echoed in Stephen's ears as he returned to work, trying to control the fury that rose within him. He found Jacques already at work pulling strays from the muddy riverbank, along with two other river drivers.

"Big Neil gave us some help," Jacques explained. "He put me in charge."

"That's funny. He just told me that I was to take charge."

"Well, somebody had to show these fellas what to do," Jacques said sheepishly. "You want the bateau?"

"No, not yet. I've got a powerful peeve I want to work off. We'll take turns."

Hard labor, which usually helped him forget his cares, now only fed his anger as the day drew on. Near noon Ben McAlpine rode by on a brown mare, waving as he passed.

"Where's he headed?" Stephen wondered aloud.

"The woodsman? He's going up to the Ojibway village at Mille Lac," said Jacques. "His squaw's there. That's where he spends his summers, eating dog meat and riding his squaw. He's half Indian himself, you know – Indian and Canuck."

"French?" Stephen asked.

"No, no, his father was a Scot – no French blood. See his red hair?"

"Don't Frenchmen have red hair?"

"None that I've ever seen. Of course, I don't see many Frenchmen."

Stephen looked up and watched as Ben disappeared down the trail. He felt a sudden urge to follow him. Looking around at the devastation wrought by the floodwaters, his mind wandered to the Koenig farm and John's desperate efforts to keep it from being washed away.

Finally he tossed his pike into the bateau, and said, "I'm quitting."

"What? You can't quit now!" Jacques exclaimed. "You're supposed to be in charge."

"You're doing just fine. Keep your eye on the wanigan, and you'll be all right."

"But in a day or two you could be in town with money in your pocket, beaucoup d'argent."

"No matter. I don't give a damn about Shevley or his money. I don't care if these logs rot. I'm chucking it all."

He struggled through the marsh waters and pulled himself up the bank, his boots sucking mud until he reached dry land.

"Where will you go?"

"North."

"When will we see you again?"

"When hell freezes over."

"Ah, ha! Then we'll see you next winter in camp. We'll watch it freeze together."

*　　*　　*

"Sometimes I have doubts about your sanity," said John Koenig as Stephen sprawled in the shade of the birch grove, plucking sour grass and nibbling on the yellow stems. He smiled, enjoying the indulgence of his friend.

"What will you do next?"

"I don't know. I've thought about it, but I just don't know. Maybe I'll go to California."

"What will you do there, dig for gold with a cant hook? I think you *are* insane."

Stephen rolled over in the grass and stretched out. "I may just lie here and sleep for a week or so."

"You'll have to earn your keep, if you stay here. This is a busy time for us since the flood. We were in the middle of preparing our fields. We have to plant..."

"I'll help with the planting."

"Can you follow a plow?"

"I don't know. Where is it going? Wait! I can milk the cow."

"My mother can milk the cow. You're being a fool. I'm going into town in a day or two. I'll take you home."

"I'm not sure I want to go home."

"Then to the mill; you must at least collect your pay. You can't let a winter's wages slip by. We'll go to the mill, and if you don't want your pay, you can give it to me. I'll buy another cow. Why leave your pay in your father's pocket, if you're so angry with him?"

So it was that Stephen, who had dreamed of riding triumphantly into town at the head of a giant raft of logs, instead bounced into Minneapolis in a rude farm wagon, half hidden among a pile of sacked potatoes. At the mill he went directly to the paymaster's shack where a stern little clerk in rimless glasses thumbed through his ledger for the name of Steve Craft. The record showed he had earned nearly one hundred dollars after his debt to the company store had been deducted.

"You're late," the clerk said suspiciously. "Most of the others have been paid."

"I stopped to help a friend," Stephen explained. The clerk made no reply, but counted out his earnings – Shevley Company notes payable at the Bank of St. Paul – and laid them in Stephen's hand. As he signed the ledger he said, "I'm looking for a friend, John McClintock." The clerk turned the ledger around and ran his finger down the list of names.

"Oh, yes," he said. "Red-lined. Means he won't need his pay. He's dead."

Stunned, Stephen walked slowly away from the paymaster's shack and walked aimlessly through the lumberyard. Then he heard his name called, and John Koenig's wagon pulled up beside him.

"Hop up and I'll take you home."

"No...no, thanks. Have you heard about McClintock?"

"Just now at the mill office. That's why I came looking for you. Let me take you home."

"No. How did he die?"

"He died as they were carrying him off the wanigan."

"Then he made it back," Stephen said. "I'm glad of that."

"What will you do?" John asked.

"I can't go anywhere like this. I'm going to Washington Avenue to buy some new clothes and get a haircut and a bath."

"When will I see you again?"

"The next time I'm desperate, I guess," Stephen said with a sad smile, extending his hand. "Thank you, John."

"Goodbye, my friend. Good luck to you."

Less than two hours later he stepped from the barbershop – bathed, shaved and trimmed. In his new clothes he looked very much like the young man who had fled the city nearly six months before. His hair and beard glistened with a light application of pomade, and his face stung with sweet-scented lotion. His new denim trousers were stiff and smooth, his blue flannel shirt soft to the touch. Before moving on he stuck his head in the door.

"What time is it?"

"After six o'clock," the barber said.

"What day is it?"

"It's Saturday, twenty-sixth of May."

Six o'clock on a Saturday in May – his mother might be in her garden now, looking after her first crocuses. Sarah and Mrs. Carpenter would be in the kitchen, beginning the evening meal. His father would be in his office, poring over records of the spring drive. He wanted to ask him about

McClintock. He wanted some comfort as he dealt with the death of a brave and determined man. He also wanted a home-cooked meal. His stomach churned at the very thought of it. So he walked down Washington Avenue to Nicollet and south along that muddy thoroughfare where construction seemed to be in progress everywhere. At the edge of town where the street turned to a rutted trail he walked rapidly but carefully along the grassy center strip so as not to muddy his new boots. He passed the Callaghans place on the old Benson property and through the grove of oak trees now shadowy in the dimming light of the setting sun. The closer he came to Shevley House, the stranger he felt. So much had changed in his life in such a short time. He felt alien amid these familiar surroundings, feeling that he didn't belong there. When finally he came within sight of the imposing mansion he was filled with a sense of foreboding. It was bathed in the fast fading rays of the sunset and the reddish blocks of stone seemed darker than he remembered them. The front lawn was neatly clipped, more than an acre of soft green grass highlighted by small gardens of rich black dirt studded with an assortment of sprouting plants. He went forward hesitantly, harboring an irrational fear of being discovered. Avoiding the graveled driveway, he circled around to the rear of the house, tried the back door and found it unlocked. The kitchen was empty. There were no signs of dinner preparation, no aroma of cooking, no sign of life. He crept quietly down the hall, noting in passing that Mrs. Carpenter's room was empty. So was his father's office across the hall from the parlor. He paused in the front entry hall, still as death, and listened. Hearing no sound, he tiptoed up the stairway, past the second floor landing to the third floor, where his mother's door stood open. In the dusk the last light of day fell through a gap in the draperies and dimly illuminated her writing desk. On her dresser stood the green glass vase that held a dusty spray of dried flowers. The beveled edges of the glass caught the fast-fading light of day, splintered it and scattered a splash of color over the white silk coverlet of her bed. In a moment the sun dropped below the horizon, plunging the room into darkness. Overwhelmed by sadness and a sense of longing, an emptiness and despair, tears came to his eyes and fell to his cheek. He stepped quietly out into hall again, pausing to remember the sounds of the past – the tramp of footsteps on the stairs, the slamming of her door, the angry voices that tore at his heart. He was a child again, cowering in his bed, burying his head in his pillow to stifle the sounds that robbed him of his childhood. How he had loved them once, he thought, and how he hated them now for what they had done to him and to themselves. In the depths of his despondence he heard the distant sound of horses' hooves on the drive and was seized with panic. As the sound drew nearer, he fled down the back stairs and out into the night.

*   *   *

"You have an uncanny instinct for doing precisely the wrong thing," said Roger Frasier. "Ridiculous, entering your own home by stealth, fleeing from your own family, lurking about the street at night. I'm surprised the townspeople haven't set upon you."

Roger was one thing that hadn't changed. Cool, urbane, haughty – even cruel – he took it upon himself to scold Stephen as if he were a child.

"I couldn't face them," Stephen said. "I couldn't go back to that life."

"But it's your life! There's no escaping it."

"No, it's not my life any longer. I've made my own way for months. I can make my own life from now on." He languished in the overstuffed chair and sipped his whiskey and water.

"Still the romantic. When will you realize that a winter in the woods does not make one a different person? A few months in a camp doesn't make you a logger, any more than a few nights of carousing doesn't make you a hopeless derelict. You cannot escape who you are, or what you are. You're play-acting, over-dramatizing everything you find distasteful. It's childish. You now know what it's like to work like a man, but that doesn't make you a man."

"A friend I admired greatly died on the way down river. He died heroically," Stephen said by way of protest.

"Logging is a dangerous business. You must face the unpleasantness in your life and come to grips with it. Then perhaps you can call yourself a man."

"I've grown up, I've changed. And I like my new life."

"Horse feathers! You haven't grown up. You're a child running away from his responsibilities."

"You made your own way in life, you told me so yourself. Why can't I do the same?"

"There's no comparison between us. I sought responsibility; I didn't shun it. I was not born to good fortune; I had to create my own. I'm sorry for the death of your friend. But I find your posturing exasperating. I was not brought up in a mansion surrounded by wealth and comfort. I was a child of the street. I survived by begging for my bread. I was an urchin with no other home than whatever doorway I happened across at nightfall. I couldn't spend my youth in paroxysms of self-pity because my friends died, or my parents quarreled. I had no parents. I was arrested at the tender age of eight for stealing a carrot from a dray as it passed in the street. That led to the first warm bed I can remember – in a foundling home. The discipline was severe, the food abominable, and the schooling limited. But by the age of twelve I had managed to master the rudiments of mathematics and was apprenticed to a bookkeeper on the East River wharves. I have labored for years to realize my dreams of affluence, and I am still laboring."

He put his drink on the mantle and continued his pacing about his room. His words had come in a torrent, as if they'd been dammed up for some time awaiting a chance to burst forth. Now he seemed angry and embarrassed that he had revealed the deepest secrets of his life.

"Perhaps now you can understand my impatience with you. You seem prepared to turn your back on an opportunity for which I would sacrifice everything. I intend to see that my own fortunes rise along with those of the company, Stephen – and I assure you they will rise, with or without you. I will not stand idly by while you waste your youth in the logging camps and the taverns. But you would be well advised to cultivate a more mature outlook. I would like to succeed because of you. But I warn you, I shall succeed even in spite of you."

Stephen flushed in embarrassment as a burden of guilt and responsibility began to settle unseen on his shoulders. His impulse was to flee, but instead he had another whiskey and another until in anger and frustration, Roger asked him to leave.

*   *   *

Jacques Deauville dragged a woman over to their table, kicked a chair aside and plopped her in Stephen's lap.

"This one's for you!" he exclaimed. "You're lucky you ran across me tonight. Give me some money for another bottle."

The woman grinned lewdly and mashed her heavy lips against Stephen's cheek, as he picked up the bottle and tilted it to his lips, only to find it empty.

"Gimme some," the woman said, taking the bottle from him.

"It's empty," he said, standing up and dumping her to the floor. He dug into his pocket and pulled out a handful of coins and a rumpled wad of bills.

"Come on," she whined. "Let's go out back."

"Need a bottle," he said, spreading the money out on the table. Immediately a hand reached for it and in a flash the blade of Jacques' knife pressed into flesh of that hand.

"Back off," said Jacques. "It's the kid's money."

As the hand slowly withdrew from the table the point of the knife dug a shallow red line in the stranger's flesh. As the would-be thief disappeared into the crowd, Jacques gathered up the coins to buy another bottle, stuffing the bills into Stephen's shirt. The woman, getting up off the floor and brushing the sawdust from her dress, eyed the bills and pleaded, "Let's go out back."

"My stomach," Stephen muttered, pushing her away and staggering away from the table. The woman grasped his arm and guided him toward the back door.

"Out back!" he called out to the crowd, triggering a gale of laughter through the bar. Jacques appeared at his side, a tight grip on a new bottle of whiskey.

"Go on, kid. Have yourself a time."

"Out back!" Stephen shouted again.

The crowd cheered their encouragement and the woman shoved him out the door. They stumbled headlong into a canvas-topped crib not three steps from the door and sprawled into a nest of stinking blankets. There was a furious grappling and tearing at his clothes, and in a moment he was lost in a mound of flesh. When it was over his head throbbed and he was becoming sick. The woman quickly shoved and kicked him out into the dirt, cursed him and stepped back into the tavern. He awakened several hours later, his new clothes thrown over him, his money gone. The tavern was closed and all he could hear was the croaking chorus of frogs against the distant roar of the falls. In the darkness he pulled himself together and walked through empty streets toward the river.

Chapter 16

The southwestern edge of Mille Lac was a marshland that defied close approach to the open water. But above the reeds the lake could be seen stretching north as far as he could see. Late in the day when Stephen came upon it the water shimmered in the sunlight, a glistening silvery vastness. The marsh appeared impassible, but nearby lay a stony beach where whitecaps lapped and noisily retreated again. Above the beach a clearing in the pine forest stood an Indian village where smoke arose from a dozen fires and the aromas of cooking wafted his way, making his empty stomach churn. He walked around the marsh to the beach where a group of women were cleaning fish and held out his arms to show he carried no weapon. The women glanced at him, then began making a clucking sound to alert the village. Men taking their leisure in the shade of the trees stood tall and acknowledged him with curious stares. He stopped about halfway to the nearest hut and called out, "Ben! Ben McAlpine!"

Upon hearing Stephen's cry, the men immediately lost interest in him, as if calling out Ben's name was enough to explain his presence. His call also seemed to have coaxed a little girl from her hiding place among the huts. She appeared to be about seven years old. She was barefooted and dressed in a buckskin skirt with a fringe at the bottom and wore a ragged flannel shirt that hung to her knees. She stopped short of Stephen, sized him up, and then shyly looked away while one foot massaged the other reassuringly. Not wishing to startle her, he stood silently for a moment until suddenly she looked up again, smiled broadly and skipped away a few yards. There she paused and looked back to see if he was following her. He took a few steps in her direction, and again she skipped off and paused for him to follow her again. The women of the camp averted their eyes as he passed, and in looking at them he momentarily lost sight of the little girl. Then Ben emerged from one of the huts, the child peering shyly from behind him.

"Stevie! I'll be damned. What brings you here?"

"I came looking for you, Ben."

"Does your dad need me? Did he send you?"

"No. I haven't seen him since the drive."

"Well, come on in. We're about to eat a mess of fish, caught this morning. Come and join us."

In the rear of the small hut an Indian woman kneeled over a bed of coals where two large fish were cooking on a grill of green willow branches. Ben lowered himself onto a bed of deerskins and blankets and sat cross-legged as Stephen sat down opposite him.

"What brings you up this way?" Ben asked as the woman broke the fish into portions with her fingers and served it to them in bark dishes.

"I didn't like being in town after a winter in the woods."

"Hmmm."

"You heard about John McClintock?"

"Yes. Good man, John. Too bad. You plan to stay awhile?"

"Do you mind?"

"No. You're welcome here."

"No fuss. I can manage."

The little girl came in and sat down next to Ben cradling her dish in her lap.

"This your daughter?" Stephen asked.

"Yes. I call her Marie. This is her eighth summer."

"She's very pretty."

The woman at the fire looked up at them and seemed about to call the girl away, but Ben gave her a nod and she said nothing. The child smiled at Stephen and went on eating her fish.

After supper they left the woman and her child behind and went for a walk along the lakeshore. The breeze off the water was cool, the sky clear.

"Fine people," Ben said of the Indians. "Smart and hard working. Been around these woods for a couple a hundred years, or so their stories say. Came from the east over the top of the big lakes and chased out the Sioux. They were better armed. Been in contact with whites for hundreds years back east. Used metal weapons, pots and pans. More advanced than the Sioux. More peaceful, too – so long as you're not a Sioux. They'd as soon kill a Sioux as look at him. Always keep a camp here. They think it's a sacred place. Their medicine man tells them their ancestors fought a big battle here once and put the Sioux on the run. So the land is theirs now. Good fishing and hunting – deer, otter, beaver, squirrel. Along the edges of the lake the women harvest swamp grass seeds that make for pretty good eating."

"How long have they lived here on the lake?"

"Hard to say. They move the village occasionally if the fishing turns bad, or the hunting. They have to eat. But this is a good place to come back to, so they do."

"Do you plan to be here all summer?"

"No. Just a couple of more weeks. Vince wants me to cruise the woods south of here. He'll be pushing his way further upriver in the fall."

"I've been following the river trail for days now and saw good timber all the way."

Ben smiled. "You want to join me?" he asked.

"Sure, why not?"

Ben paused and studied the calm surface of the lake, thinking before answering. Finally he asked, "Your dad know you're here?"

Now it was Stephen's turn to ponder an answer, knowing full well that Ben already suspected the truth. All he could come up with was an excuse.

"I'm nearly twenty – old enough to be on my own," he said.

"Sure. I was thinking of Vince, thinking he'd like to know."

"I don't think so."

"I wouldn't want him to blame me."

"He doesn't have to know."

"You know damn well he'll find out. I know he can be tough sometimes. Is that the problem?"

"It's my problem. I'll work it out."

*　　*　　*

He spent the first night in the hut with Ben and his family, but determined that he would make his own shelter. The hut was sturdy and simply built. Saplings, abundant along nearby streams, were cut and trimmed to make the frame. The heavy ends were buried deep in the ground in parallel lines. Then the supple tops were bent toward the center and tied with leather thongs forming a long arch. Strips of birch bark were threaded between the uprights, overlapping from bottom to top to create waterproof walls and ceiling. The open ends of the hut were covered with deerskin flaps for privacy and protection from the elements. In Ben's hut there was ample space for the three family members and their meager belongings. Observing the family in close quarters, he noticed that their communication was minimal. He spoke quietly to his squaw and she usually responded with a nod. If he called her by name, Stephen failed to discern it. She had a kindly face with high cheekbones and wide-set eyes. Small of stature and thick of limb, she was muscular and sturdily built. Her sleek black hair was long and she bound it to her head with a leather band decorated with beads and quills, which were her only adornment. Her dress was of soft deerskin tied at the waist with a thong. She went barefoot, though a pair of elaborately decorated moccasins were placed neatly near her sleeping mat. When it was time to retire she flung a blanket around her shoulders, unrolled the reed mat and lay down on it, stuffing her feet under Ben's pack and clutching her blanket close about her like a cape. Marie, shy of the stranger in the hut, daintily laid out her small mat beside her mother's and knelt on it. Her mother opened her blanket wide and with one arm gently enclosed the little girl in it. Stephen watched the embers of the fire fade, shooed away an occasional mosquito, and soon allowed fatigue to envelop him as the mother's blanket had enveloped the little girl.

*   *   *

The following days were spent in a wilderness idyll. In the early morning they fished from a bark canoe, using drop lines and bone hooks and freshly netted fingerlings for bait. They chewed dried venison during these early hours, and when they returned to shore they found awaiting them a pot of gruel made from bitter acorn meal seasoned with dried berries and crunchy butternuts. While the woman cleaned the catch and laid strips of fish over a rack to dry in the sun, Ben and Stephen studied maps Vincent got at the land office in St. Paul when he laid claim to the pineries along the Rum River. Later Stephen, with Marie's eager assistance, began work on a small hut for himself. The child showed him where to find saplings and how to place them in the ground. She led him to a birch grove and showed him how to cut and strip the bark and weave it among the poles. Her shyness faded and she chattered winningly as they worked, bombarding him with a mix of English and Chippewa dialect that amused him even when he found it incomprehensible. She seemed very proud to help their visitor and delighted in playing the role of a grownup woman serving her man. Her playmates in the village were greatly impressed and crowded close by to watch them erect the hut. Marie studiously ignored them or sent them scampering away with a scolding.

In late June Ben loaded their gear onto his mare and the two men left the village with little ceremony. Ben explained briefly to his squaw where he was going and why, and when he would return. She listened carefully and nodded. Stephen fished in his pocket and withdrew a shiny flat stone he had found on the beach. It had a strange marking that suggested a lightning flash, and he had drilled a small hole in it with the point of his knife and threaded a thong through it. He placed it around Marie's neck as a parting gesture.

"This is to thank you," he said. "I will miss you."

She smiled and clung to her mother, waving as the men walked away. At some distance Stephen turned to wave goodbye, but in the village the Indians had gone about their business and Marie was nowhere to be seen.

They traveled south and east, following deer trails and streams and pausing at beaver ponds to rest in the shade of the pine forest, to listen to the sound of the tumbling waters and the excited chirping of the birds that nested nearby. They ate dried venison and tough acorn cakes that they brought with them and munched on delicate watercress that grew wild at the edges of the pond. They slept at night beside the stream on beds of pine boughs and as he watched the glittering heavens through the treetops and breathed the cool fresh air Stephen felt a sense of peace and contentment. On the third day the stream they followed led them to a lake of remarkable clarity, a blue gem set amid the rich green of the forest. At its outlet they made camp and at sunset watched a water ballet of leaping fish.

"Let's gather some river rocks and build a good fire pit," said Ben. "We'll be here for a spell."

They began next morning to cruise the pineries that surrounded them, section by section, charting the virgin timber on their maps and noting in a ledger the riches of the stands. When after several weeks their survey was completed they built a monument of stones to mark the site of a logging camp and followed the stream south and west to its junction with the Rum River. Here they marked off another campsite and began another survey, working their way through the blistering heat of July and into the sultry dog days of August. Then Ben announced their task was completed; it was time to return with their report to the Shevley Mills in Minneapolis.

"I'll wait here and guide the camp crew," said Stephen.

"What about your old man?"

"Tell him the truth. Tell him I'm here where I expect to work all winter on the Shevley payroll. And tell him I'm well."

Leaving Stephen with the remainder of their food supplies, their fishing equipment and a trap for small animals, Ben climbed up on the mare and headed down the river trail with the report on their cruising operation. Stephen immediately set to work building himself a shelter to escape the afternoon heat. He also sought relief in the cool river from the sultry atmosphere, the mosquitoes, and the horse flies. It was his pleasure to loll naked for hours on end, letting the water massage and relax his lean, muscular body. He was at ease here, truly happy in the wilderness with the cares of the world far away. When boredom set in he occupied himself by marking off the site for the new logging camp, calling on his memory of last season's Shevley Camp No. 1. When in the midst of his solitary existence he began talking to himself, he picked up the pace of his work, felling small trees with the hand axe in order to make a clearing for construction of a shanty. He was thus occupied when the construction crew finally arrived and its leader called out to him.

"Ho, there, Steve Craft! That's no axe for a real logger."

"Peter Shaw! Well I'll be...what have you brought to eat?"

"Not even a 'good day' from the lad. Tired of roots and berries, are you? You'll be pleased to know we carry three barrels of salt pork, six sacks of dried beans and a barrel of molasses. We could whip you up a shanty banquet in no time."

"Even shanty banquet sounds good to me. I was on the verge of eating grasshoppers, if only I could catch them. How are you, my friend?"

"Broke! Why else would I be here? It's another winter in the woods for us. And this year I'm the boss. Big Neil's taking a crew to Camp No. 1. You stick with me, young man, and I'll make a chopper out of you."

Shaw brought a dozen men with him, and when all the canoes had landed he lost no time in putting them to work building the shanty, a blacksmith's hut, a cabin for himself and his straw bosses, a stable for the oxen, and of course, an outhouse. His style was just the opposite that of Big Neil Amundsen's, who led by instilling fear in his men. Shaw, a bright and educated man, won the respect of his loggers through his reputation for fairness and intelligence, and his prowess with an axe. Stephen thrived under his wing. He relished the long, hard hours in the woods, enjoying the heft of an axe in his hands, relishing the thrill of felling the tall white pine. Only a few of the men knew him from last season when he was the green and puking kid who had stumbled into their midst without confidence, experience or reputation. But all that had changed during his months in the camp and on the drive down river. His summer with Ben McAlpine, who was highly respected by the loggers, also stood him in good stead. He now had the confidence he once lacked, the experience, and – for better or for worse – a reputation. Jacques Deauville never tired of telling the tale of Stephen and the whore and of his capacity for strong drink.

"He wandered off drunk as a lord with his trousers around his knees, and I didn't see him again until I found him here in the middle of the woods, eating grasshoppers and dying for a drink of whiskey. And if the next wagon over the tote road carries a little brown jug, it's best to keep it out of his reach or there'll be none for the rest of us. As far as I'm concerned, he can have my share – of grasshoppers."

*   *   *

It was a bitterly cold winter, but with scant snowfall. The puny patches of it on the ground were insufficient to meet the loggers' needs. As the crews moved further from the camp, the job of dragging the logs to the riverbank became a major challenge. Charlie Huffman found his two-ox team unable to keep up with the cut. Soon four others and two more teamsters arrived trailing John Koenig's supply wagon. To compound the loggers' problems, the January thaw proved devastating. It began two weeks of steady rain that turned the forest floor to mud. Streams swelled and overflowed their banks. The torrent that followed toppled one log pile and a portion of the winter's cut was lost.

It was a season of learning for Stephen. Shaw taught him to use an axe so that the strength of its hickory handle became an extension of his own strong arms. He developed a great respect for the cold, blue steel, and also a sense of dependency. For the axe was more than a tool to him, it was a release of the stresses that had driven him to the woods. Six days a week he wielded it with enviable skill and precision. On Sunday's he could fling it thirty feet and imbed it three inches deep in a tree trunk at center target to win a competition. He learned other things from Shaw as well; for second only to his love for logging, Shaw admired the men who followed that trade.

"Look at them," he would say. "A filthy lot of lying, ignorant braggarts. But how they do work! Their labor ennobles them. They are princes of their realm. They are the engines that turn the wheels of civilization, that drive the cities forward and turn back the wilderness. It's a lesson you should learn, Steve. One hears so much talk of the railroads — the steam engines will build the country, the rails will link a mighty nation. But look at the facts: Iron rails, belching engines, even tall trees and vast forests never built anything. Men build nations, men like these. Progress rides on the their backs, spurring them unmercifully and kicking them aside when they can work no longer. Yet they are the ones who build the engines, who lay the rails, and who cut the trees. And mark my words, it is they who will fight and die to save this nation."

"Have you heard some news?" Stephen asked in surprise.

"Not for weeks, but there was talk of secession, talk of war, this past summer."

Stephen arose from the table in Shaw's cabin and peered out its only window. Outside the world was soaked and dripping with rain, the earth a muddy slough.

"It's all seems so very far away," he mused. "It's so quiet and peaceful here."

"It's not so far away," Shaw said. "There's anger in the air."

"My father warned that it would happen sooner or later."

"Your father?"

Stephen turned and met the man's gaze. The question lingered there in his eyes, but it was not demanding. He did not seem suspicious.

"Yes, my father argued that it was insanity to fight a war over slavery, but that the abolitionists would bring it down on our heads."

"That was accurate, as far as it goes," Shaw said. "The fact is that war is inevitable. It's a matter of economics. The entire plantation economy of the South would perish without slave labor. But men prefer to fight wars for moralistic reasons, emphasizing the immorality of slavery rather than the economics of it. That way they can send men off to die and still live with their consciences."

"The backwoods philosopher," Stephen said. It was his turn now to be curious, but Shaw merely smiled.

"Someday perhaps we can share our secrets," he said.

"Maybe someday," Stephen conceded.

He found his talks with Shaw interesting and pro-vocative as he did his conversations with Roger Frasier. They were very different types. Frasier was a pragmatist, Shaw a humanist. But his discussions with both could be unsettling to a young man seeking his way in life. They both made him think, even when there were many times when he did not want to think. But he had the perfect escape – the wilderness, where now he always felt at home. Neither the miserable cold nor dampness of winter, nor the torrential spring rains could dampen the sense of security he enjoyed in the woods. The camaraderie of the logging crew, the mind-numbing labor, the cozy familiarity of the shanty at night, the aroma of the constant baked beans, even the flea-infested blankets and his filthy bed roll were warm not only to his body but to his soul. He belonged in the woods, he decided, and no hardship could discourage him, no discomfort destroy his sense of belonging. And the hardships and discomforts were many that spring of 1861. The snow, what little there was of it, had vanished by March under the pounding of the interminable rain. On the point where the camp stood, the placid little stream of summer became a raging terror, while on the other the Rum River was equally as wild and unpredictable. Moving logs became a monumental task, even with three teams of oxen working from sunrise to sunset. But the loggers surmounted all difficulties, and managed to topple enough logs into the river to form a raft behind the daisy chain and report they were ready for the drive. As the drive date neared Stephen felt the recurring reluctance to return to Minneapolis. No strength of arm or manly reputation could protect him from the pain and sorrow he had known there. He despaired of leaving the comfort of the woods, but as fate would have it, he had to leave even before the raft. It was Ben McAlpine who brought the news.

"Your pa wants you, now. He says to take the first wagons back and to see him right away. And he's fit to be tied as it is, what with the size of the harvest, and you don't want to be rilin' him."

"What's so urgent that it can't wait for the drive?"

"He didn't say, and I know better than to ask. Just git!"

*   *   *

The trip over the tote road took three days, three very unpleasant days for Stephen as it turned out. Jacques Deauville had managed to seriously injure one hand as he helped to topple the stacks of logs into the river, and was deemed unfit to make the drive. Shaw ordered him to ride back with Stephen and the one-legged smithy Orville Potter.

275

To ease the burden of Potter's depressing company Stephen encouraged the voluble Frenchman, even though his conversation frequently embarrassed him.

"You'll never know, *mon ami*, when you'll stumble across a kinsman in the woods. When you sleep with Indian women, you never know how many children you left behind."

"You're a rascal, Jacques. I didn't sleep with Indian women; I bunked alone."

"Perhaps, but you must have had visitors, special friends who came to keep you warm at night. You said you lived with Ben McAlpine and his squaw."

"First of all, it was a very hot summer, and I had no need of help keeping warm. Secondly, I spent only one night with Ben and his wife and their daughter, Marie."

"Ah ha! So there was a young woman named Marie!"

"Marie was an eight-year-old child."

"The very best! A child bride. I envy you such pleasures. You must tell me about them."

"It was nothing like that. She was only a child. She helped me build my own hut."

"Your private place. Wonderful! Tell me, did you swim naked together? I can recall one summer I spent on the big lake among the Chippewa. I dreamed of just such an opportunity, but they gave me only an old squaw that no one else wanted. She was all right, but to have an innocent child! You were indeed fortunate."

"You make a mockery of manhood," said Potter bitterly.

"At least I am a man," Jacques retorted, "not half a man, like you."

Potter's muscular hand gripped the pike that lay beside him in the wagon bed, his knuckles whitening.

"Take it easy, you two," Stephen cautioned. "Let's try to get back to town without killing one another. We survived the winter together, let's try to survive the spring."

The journey ended too soon for Stephen. Reluctantly he drove the wagon to the mill, less than enthusiastic about confronting his father. But Roger was alone in the office.

"You'll find him at home," he said. "I presume Ben found you."

"He did. I still don't understand the urgency."

"That's rather callous of you. I know you're in no hurry, but take my horse. I've got a lot of work to do."

He rode through town with feelings of dread, but he was determined to see it through and not run away as he had done once before. He was a man now, after all, a man capable of making his own decisions, of leading his own life. They might do what they like; he would not give in to them.

"To hell with them," he said to himself as he turned up the drive. The shades of evening had fallen and the windows of Shevley House were dark, empty sockets in the shadowy skull, the doorway a black and forbidding cavern. He preferred to enter by the rear door, stopping only to lead Roger's horse into the stable. His father's carriage was there, the horse still in harness. Out across the yard toward the oak grove he saw him on the knoll. He was kneeling. Stephen went to him in slow, cautious strides. Then he saw a mound of fresh earth and polished stone with an inscription.

Eleanor Craft Shevley
January 1822 – April 1861

Vincent had not turned as Stephen approached, but remained on one knee, his head in his hand, concealing his features. Shocked speechless, Stephen laid his hand on his father's shoulder. Vincent looked up slowly. His eyes were red and tears rolled down his cheeks. There was helplessness in his expression, and a deep, nearly incomprehensible grief. His voice cracked as he spoke.

"I wanted you to be here," he said. "But she went fast."

"I came as soon as I could. I didn't know. What was it?"

"Her old complaint, the pleurisy, but sudden. I prayed
you'd get here in time. She asked for you."

"I should have..." His words were lost in an overwhelming sense of guilt.

"I know," said his father. "We all should have."

*   *   *

"He tries not to show it, but he's taking it awful
hard," Mrs. Carpenter said. "He comes home early every day
to visit her."

"I've never seen him cry before," Stephen said.

"He kept his head," she acknowledged. "I sent Sarah
into town to fetch him – Lord knows I was in no condition to
break the news – and Mr. Vincent Shevley had enough
presence of mind to pick up Dr. Ames, and to make
arrangements with the undertaker."

She scraped the bacon drippings from the big iron
frying pan into the crock, replaced the lid, and put the crock
back in the cooler. The aroma of the hot grease made him
think of fried chicken, and to wonder about the strange
workings of the human mind: His mother was dead, and he
was thinking about fried chicken.

"How did she go?" he asked.

"Just as we always feared," she shrugged, as if some
facets of existence are simply beyond explanation. "There
wasn't a thing anyone could have done. She was alone in her
bedroom. I didn't like leaving her alone, but she'd sent me
away, wanting to be alone. She'd been sick so much over the
years, but I never thought it'd be the death of her. We were
all so used to her coughing. I don't know what made me
suspicious – yes, I do to know. It was quiet all of a sudden,
like the wind had died down before a storm. There was an
awful stillness in the house. The coughing had stopped. I was
clankin' away, cleanin' the stovetop. I remember stoppin' to
listen, and there wasn't a sound, any sound, for the longest
time. I just knew it was all over."

She rambled on as she scrubbed the breakfast dishes.

278

"It was you who found her, then?"

"I galloped up those stairs like I was a kid again, and raced down the hall to her room. There she was, lyin' there as if she was sound asleep. One arm was just so, I remember, with the palm up and her fingers ever so delicate and lady-like. She was so beautiful."

Stephen wept.

"Oh, dear boy!" she gasped. "I'm sorry, but you asked..."

"I'm grateful to you, Mrs. Carpenter. I had to know, and I thank you for telling me."

He got up from the table and went up the back stairway and down the hall to his mother's room. There was a cold tidiness to it. The bed was unwrinkled, its flounces cascading to the polished floor. Her writing desk was immaculate, the ink well and pen holders neatly in place. And there on her chiffonier was the green glass vase. It made him think how really little she had asked of life in this wild new world. He picked up the vase angrily, yielding to a sudden impulse to fling it into the fireplace. The sound of a voice stopped him.

"She spoke of you often during her last days," said Sarah.

"I should have been here," he said remorsefully.

"You had no way of knowing. She understood that."

"I might have been able to do something, anything," he said, placing the vase back on the chiffonier.

"There's plenty to do here now," she said.

"You think I should settle in?"

"It's your home. You can't spend the rest of your life in the logging camps."

"What is there to do?"

"First off, the windows need washing."

"Right now?"

"Why not? It's better than moping around all day. I just brought home a bottle of vinegar. You can get the ladder and work on the outside; I'll work from the inside."

Despair was no match for Sarah. She had a way about her that dispelled gloom, chased the shadows away and let the sunlight in. She had grown tall during the months since he'd last seen her. Her hair was its winter brown, soft and flowing. She carried herself with unusual grace. The gangling girl of yesterday seemed to have come together at last into a manageable, reasonably attractive package. It was difficult for him to realize that "little Sarah" was nearly fifteen and obviously not a child anymore.

Part II

War and Recovery

1861 to 1872

The war came to Minneapolis on a quiet Sunday afternoon. Vincent returned from lunch at the Nicollet House with the news that was spreading throughout the town. Fort Sumter had fallen to southern forces on Saturday, and Minnesota was the first state to answer the call to arms in defense of the Union.

"Governor Ramsey's in Washington. He went right to the president and offered a thousand Minnesota men to put down the rebellion. The news came in just a few hours ago."

"One thousand men?" Stephen asked. "That ought to be enough to end it right there."

"Oh, there'll be more. All the northern states will flock to the colors, you can be sure of that," Vincent exclaimed. He was in a state of high excitement, relishing the drama of the event.

"Then it surely will be a very short war," Stephen said.

"You can bet it will. There'll be a quick end to this nonsense. What foolishness; what absolute insanity."

"It's just as you predicted."

"But I never dreamed it would actually come to this."

"There won't be much to it. If every northern state sends one thousand men..."

"You're probably right, son. It will be a brief encounter, but a tragedy nevertheless if even one man's blood is shed. What an absurd reason to start a war!"

"A sickness at the soul of our nation," Stephen mused.

"Your mother's words. I thank God she didn't live to see this day. Her soul would cry out in anguish to see what that damnable abolitionist uproar has brought down upon our heads."

On Monday Stephen went downtown himself to witness the excitement. Charles Whitcomb was going about placing newly printed posters informing all that, in the absence of the governor, Lt. Gov. Ignatius Donnelly had issued a call for volunteers, and that the call was meeting with enthusiastic response throughout the state. Despite the tumult, Stephen could not be aroused. He remembered his mother's abhorrence of slavery, and his father's dire predictions. It all seemed to be coming to pass, and he wanted no part in it. But he also remembered Peter Shaw's assessment that the whole slavery issue had its roots in economics. And Stephen decided he would never be so foolish as to kill – or die – for another man's financial gain. It was the ultimate folly, and he would not play the fool. From the mood of the crowds in the street, however, he was in the minority. An air of patriotic hysteria seemed to have gripped the entire community. He was shaking his head in disbelief when he caught sight of John Koenig who wore a troubled expression.

"I'm glad to see I'm not the only one shocked by this madness," Stephen said by way of greeting.

"Madness is a good word for it, Steve. I'm looking for Augie. He's run away and we're afraid he's come to town to join the army."

"But he's not old enough."

"He's fifteen, and he looks older. I must find him and fetch him home. I'm told they're enlisting recruits at the fort. Will you come and help me look for him?"

"Of course I will. But Augie can wait until tomorrow. No one is going to march off to war today. Come home with me for dinner. We'll have a good night's rest and ride out to the fort in the morning. Augie may even have changed his mind then."

"Or we'll change it for him," John added.

The stolid farmer was quiet throughout dinner while Vincent vented his fury over fighting a war over slavery, of all things. But over brandy John broke his silence.

"It may be 'damn foolishness,' as you say, but I can't quarrel with my brother's actions, only with his motives. He goes off to the war for adventure, not to preserve the Union. I doubt that he knows the meaning of the word. On the other hand I don't pretend to understand your argument, sir. I don't think I've ever seen a slave, although I have seen black men here in town before. Nor do I understand your talk about economics, Stephen. What I do know is that an armed rebellion threatens this country, and this is my country. I have a good farm that feeds us well and provides us with a small income. That farm is part of America, and it is my duty to defend it. I'll not have it said that I stood by and allowed my younger brother to do my fighting for me."

"How do you propose to get him out?" Stephen asked.

"How can they keep him? He's underage."

"Good point," said Vincent. "I heard late today that so many high-spirited kids have flocked to the colors that families are suing for their release – so many, in fact, that old Judge Chatfield has been called out of retirement to help hear the cases."

"Who's he?" Stephen asked.

"An able jurist and honorable man, highly respected by all who know him. He came here in 'fifty-three to serve as an associate justice of the territorial supreme court. I understand he's practicing law down in the Minnesota River valley with his son-in-law."

"I must find him and see if he will help me get August out of the army before he marches off to war," John said.

"There's no hurry," Stephen observed. "The war is a long way from here. My guess is that it will all be over before any Minnesotans get there."

"Even so, I'll go to the fort tomorrow and look for August. He doesn't belong in the army. I am the oldest man in my family. If anyone goes off to fight, it should be me."

*   *   *

Much of Fort Snelling, home to only a token force of men for many years, had fallen into disuse over the years, but this day the grassy plain that stretched away from a

285

cluster of dilapidated barracks was crowded with young men. A small detail of soldiers stood in military formation at the base of the old round tower and a fresh new flag fluttered from the pole that rose high above them. Nearby a battery of cannon, whose booming could be heard all the way into town that morning, were arrayed overlooking the plain where volunteers milled about in eager anticipation. John and Stephen plunged into their midst in search of young August Koenig, who blanched when he spotted his brother approaching.

"What are you doing here?" he exclaimed.

"Did you think your mother wouldn't notice you were gone? I've come to take you home. She's very worried about you."

"You can't! I've enlisted. I signed the roll this morning. They're going to give me a uniform and a musket."

"Then they'll have to erase your name from the list, because you are not old enough to join the army."

"You can't do this, Johannes! Think how my new friends here would laugh at me. You can't!"

"Oh, yes, I can. I have read the recruitment posters. You must be twenty-one years old to enlist. You are fifteen."

"Half the fellows here are not yet twenty-one," August protested. "They don't care how old you are. You can tell them anything. They just wink and write down your name."

"They'll take your life in a wink, too, if you let them, my dear brother. War is not a game, it's a very dangerous affair."

"I signed my name; I took the oath," he said adamantly. "I've been ordered to stay here, and here I'll stay."

"Here in this field?" Stephen asked. "Where will you sleep? What will you eat?"

"We slept on the ground last night. But they've promised us food, blankets, even tents. But they're not ready yet," the lad explained.

"Then let's see if we can do something for this brave young fellow," Stephen said, giving John a nudge. "We can find some food and blankets for Augie and his friends and bring it back tomorrow night.”

“Fair enough,” John said, sensing the gist of Stephen’s plot. “We will be back tomorrow, Augie. Meantime, I’ll tell our mother that you are warm and well fed. It will make her feel better.”

They bid the youth a manly farewell and left the field.

When they returned after dark the next night the plain was dotted with campfires around which groups of volunteers clustered against the chill. They parked their wagon and went from one group to the next until they located the young enlistee.

“We’ve brought supplies for you and a few of your friends,” said John. “Come with us to the wagon and help carry things. The guards won’t let us bring the wagon down here.”

At the wagon John unloaded a crate of food supplies and passed it down to Augie. As the delighted youth accepted the gift of food, Stephen snatched a blanket from the wagon and suddenly slipped it over his head. John hurriedly wrapped him round and round with rope and tied it at his ankles. Together the two conspirators lifted the wriggling lad into the wagon bed, stifling his muffled cries.

“Quickly now, let’s get out of here,” Stephen said, “before one of the guards hears him.”

“You go,” said John. “I am going to stay.”

“You’re what?”

“When they call the Koenig name in the morning, I will answer,” he said, picking up the box of supplies.

“But you can’t! Who’ll tend the farm? Who’ll take care of your mother, the children?”

“August will, of course. Take him directly home and tell him the family it is his responsibility now. I’ll take his place here.”

With that he slapped the horse’s hindquarters and the wagon lurched away into the darkness, the startled Stephen at the reins. When they were a safe distance from the fort

Stephen halted the rig and loosened the blanket around Augie's head.

"Let me go!" he yelled. "Let me go, I tell you!"

"I admire your courage, Augie, but your brother said to take you home, and that's where you're going. Shout all you want, there's no one to hear you out here at this time of night."

"I'll just run away again," he cried. "I swear I will!"

*   *   *

Stephen returned the wagon to the mill the next morning, and went to his father's office to explain his absence.

"I can't understand you young people," he said, shaking his head. "What must Mrs. Koenig have thought when she found her son missing? And what must she think today with John gone? For that matter, how do you think I felt last night when you didn't come home? You young people must take others into consideration. It's selfish of you not to think about your families before you act."

"Give credit where it's due," Stephen argued. "John's action was not selfish and inconsiderate. It was a magnanimous patriotic gesture. I think he's a fool, but I'm proud to call him my friend. When August tells his mother about it, I think she'll agree."

"Let's not quarrel. You're exhausted, and I'm in no mood to argue. Go home and get some rest, and let's have no hard feelings. Why not have dinner with Charlie and me tonight at the Nicollet House? Frasier's invited us, and I'm sure he'll be happy if you come along. Take my rig home, have lunch and a good nap, and meet us at the hotel at seven. Agreed?"

"I'll be there."

He was warmly greeted when he arrived at the hotel, where Whitcomb was holding forth on the subject of war.

"You can't imagine it, if you have not experienced it first hand. As a veteran of the Mexican expedition I can tell you it is an unforgettable experience. It is man's most grandiose display – the long lines of uniformed troops; the artillery arrayed upon the field, raining death and destruction on the enemy; the legions advancing into the face of death; the distant clash of arms; the pounding of hooves as the cavalry charges into the fray, and the clouds of dust and smoke that rises to enshroud it all. Magnificent!"

He leaned forward to bask in the fascinated expressions of his audience, cocking a wily eye and flashing a knowing smile.

"On the other hand there are other impressions never to be forgotten by men who have known battle. There's the drudgery of the march, the gnawing hunger and damn little food. He'll forever wonder at the abject fear that threatens to immobilize him when he's ordered into battle. Nor will he forget the unbearable weight of the musket that grows heavier with every step, or the unreasonable hate he feels for an enemy he's never met and cannot even see until the fatal moment of encounter. He'll recall the weird exhilaration as his comrades begin to fall around him, the inexplicable sense of invincibility that drives him forward. He'll vividly recall for years and years the look of astonishment on the face of a man he's just killed – a man who felt just as invincible as he only a moment before. And the sudden realization of how thin is the line between life and death. When it's all over there'll be the unbelievable carnage of war, the stink of death and rotting flesh, the searing pain of a wound, and the dismal sense that he may die among strangers in an alien land. These, gentlemen, are just some of the sensations of war, and you can have them. It is man's most magnificent moment, and his ultimate insanity. I'll never again want any part of it."

"You're a fine one!" Vincent roared. "A decorated, authentic hero by your own evidence, and yet you talk like a coward. Be honest now, you're a real fire-eater, and you know it."

"Not so, not so. I'd renounce my country first, sell my soul to the devil, before I'd go to war again."

"I prefer to think of you as a hero, Charles," said Frasier. "You make a most unconvincing coward."

"But much more alive, and much less the hypocrite. The glories of war are half lies and half faulty memories, and hence don't really exist."

"Then why do you exhort young men to join the army?" Stephen asked. "The Frontiersman sounded a battle cry this week."

"I can't allow my personal cowardice to overcome my sense of responsibility to my country. The cause is great; only I am not."

The older men laughed, but Stephen smiled ruefully. They enjoyed another whiskey, a sumptuous dinner, followed by brandy and coffee. Vincent and Charles left at half-past nine, but Stephen lingered.

"You mustn't let that old codger fool you," Roger said. "He's a bona fide hero and still a fighter, as his profession attests."

"I think he speaks great truths," Stephen said. "Some small lies, perhaps, but also great truths. I'd like to put them to the test."

"I'm not sure what you mean by that, but you have a look in your eye that I've come to recognize. If you're contemplating another escapade, let me warn you not to temp fate in the matter of war. People die in wars."

"Some people die on river drives. Others die alone in their beds."

"We all die, Stephen. But people die by the hundreds and thousands in war. There is no glory in such a waste of life."

"Many more survive, if history be the guide. I doubt that putting down a rebellion of a few plantation owners will result in many casualties."

"I understand that one axiom of the military is not to underestimate the enemy. Don't be a fool, Stephen. Your place is here, your future is here."

"This sounds like your usual lecture: Don't seek a new path, settle down to a life that holds little interest. Why should I, when an opportunity for adventure is at hand?"

"I remember when you relished such a life, when you played your role to the hilt."

"And I suffered your criticism then for that very reason – playing a role."

"Play-acting still infuriates me," Roger conceded. "It means being something you're not, and I believe that is self-defeating. It means running away from your fate instead of facing up to it with courage and vigor. That's really the best way to make something of your life. If you spent just half as much energy living your life as you do in running away from it, you would be a great success."

He snuffed out his cigar as Stephen finished his brandy. They watched the smoke curl into the air and disappear.

"I've gotten to know your father very well," Roger said. "It's easy to see the similarities in your characters. But he is a man who eventually outgrew his childish impulses and settled down to deal with the gifts that had been laid at his feet. I suppose I should be more patient with you as you mature."

"It's encouraging to know that you think I'll grow up someday, but you see only what you want to see in my father. To 'deal with his gifts' as you put it cost him his marriage and drove his wife to her death. It ruined our family. Did he tell you how often he failed in his younger years, and how often he had to run away? 'Going west,' he called it at last. In truth it was his refusal to live the life others had cut out for him. Yet when I embark on a similar course, you accuse me of running away from my responsibilities. You're not being consistent."

"What are you pursuing?"

The question caught Stephen by surprise. After a moment's thought he replied, "Freedom. I'm pursuing my personal freedom. I am not running away from my responsibilities, I am running after the freedom to do what I want with my life."

Roger abruptly got up from the table, obviously angry.

"Running away, running after – you are like a mad dog chasing your tail. I'll not waste another moment watching you devour yourself. *Bon appetit.*"

*   *   *

He came upon the field in the wee hours of the morning and made his way among the lines of ebbing campfires. It was a clear, cool night and the long walk from town had helped him get over his anger at Roger's impatience with him. In the shadows he could make out the rows of sleeping men and briefly imagined walking among corpses on a battlefield. He quickly put the idea out of his mind and concentrated instead on the thought that this was the beginning of a great adventure. He tripped at last over the outstretched leg of a sleeping recruit and fell sprawling into the wet grass. He lay there motionless as the man whose sleep he had disturbed tossed and grumbled and then fell silent again. Stephen rolled over on his back, put his hands behind his head, and stared into a clear sky filled with stars. He felt giddy. There was a new day coming, and he was eager for the sunrise. In a moment he surrendered to his fatigue and fell into a deep and restful sleep.

*   *   *

They were among the first to enlist, and they carried themselves proudly and boasted of their unit, D Company, First Minnesota Volunteers. The regiment grew rapidly in the next few weeks as young men from the towns and the countryside, some of whom had traveled as much as one hundred miles or more on foot, arrived at Fort Snelling to answer the call to arms. All spoke bravely of war and adapted willingly and readily to the dull routine of discipline and drill. When they were ten companies strong the state

292

supplied each man with a red flannel shirt, a pair of socks, and a blanket. As they wheeled about the drill field, each company responding to its own cadre, they began to take on the appearance of an army. While they drilled they grew ever more impatient to join the fray, for they were eager to get the job done and return to their families. A few months, they were certain, would be all it would take; they could be home by harvest time. But when the order came demanding three years of service or the duration of the war, many a brave voice fell silent and vanished from the ranks. But there was no shortage of volunteers to replace them, men who were certain that the war would be short and the honor great.

Soon the men of the First Minnesota were issued black felt hats and black trousers to go with their red flannel shirts, giving them the essence of military mystique: the uniform that offered anonymity and a sense of invincibility. Thus attired they were marched into St. Paul nearly one thousand strong to receive the praise of their state and an official flag to carry into battle. The ceremony stirred within each man a fierce personal pride and set Stephen's head awhirl to the extent that he failed to notice his father standing tall and proud as his son passed by, his teary eyes betraying the fears and doubts in his heart. Beside him, also unnoticed, Sarah Carpenter jumped and waved and called Stephen's name, while her mother attempted to restrain her, a look of wonder and worry clouding her usually serene features. After a grand ceremony on the steps of the state Capitol the regiment returned to the parade field at Fort Snelling and resumed more long weeks of drill.

In June when the men began to be released on overnight leave, Stephen returned to Shevley House.

"Oh, my but you're a handsome sight!" Mrs. Carpenter greeted him at the door.

"This uniform could use a washing," Stephen responded shyly.

"Welcome home, son," Vincent said, embracing him warmly for the first time since he was a little boy. The loving gesture led to an awkward silence, and Sarah took full advantage of it.

"The parade was thrilling!" she gushed. "You looked so grand. We were all so proud of you. The flags and the drums and the music – we called out to you but I don't think you heard us."

"We had to keep our eyes straight ahead," he said. "I couldn't look if I wanted to."

"It was all very professional," Vincent said. "How long will you be home?"

"I have to be back tomorrow, then I suppose it's back to drilling again. The war's going to be over and we'll still be drilling."

"Don't be impatient," Vincent advised. "I've heard that the regiment will be moving out soon."

"We hear such rumors every day, but we're still here."

"Count your blessings," his father advised. "They say it'll be a short war, and the sooner it's over, the sooner you'll be home to stay. We've been worried about you, worried you might really get into the war. I don't know what possessed you, but you're a grown man with a mind of your own, and I'm proud of you. You know I've always been proud of you, well, with some exceptions. If you're joining the army had anything to do with...if you feel that I..."

"I felt that it was my duty," Stephen said helpfully.

"Then that's as it should be," Vincent said.

"We're all so afraid for you," Sarah said.

"You mustn't be, Sarah. We'll go and do what must be done and then we'll all come right home. You look after things while I'm gone and don't be fretting about me. I can take care of myself."

"Lordy, lordy," Mrs. Carpenter exclaimed. "Look what time it's getting to be. I've got to get dinner on."

"Don't go to a lot of trouble," said Stephen. "I'd like it best if we could all eat together at the kitchen table."

"Why, that's a good idea," his father said. "After all, we're all family."

At the table Stephen told them how he and John Koenig had vowed to stay together and help each other, and how they resolved to look out for one another and come home safely. Vincent brought him up to date on what was going on in town, how business had picked up after the war news came, and how anxious both he and Roger were for him to come back to work at the mill. Mrs. Carpenter brought them all up to date on the town gossip, and Stephen teased Sarah by asking if Patrick Callaghan was still her best beau. When they were all talked out, Vincent settled down in the parlor with the latest edition of The Frontiersman, leaving Stephen to browse through the library where he dipped into long forgotten tomes, nostalgically reabsorbing passages that had inspired his imagination many years before. Finally he returned to the parlor and sat down at the piano. His fingers reached tentatively for the keys and suddenly the long-dormant strings filled the room with a chord that startled Vincent's uneasy quiet. He looked up at Stephen over the rims of his reading glasses.

"Sorry," Stephen said with a smile. "Guess I should be getting to bed."

"Nonsense. Go ahead and play. It's all right."

"Another time, maybe. It's been a long day."

"What time do you have to leave?"

"I don't have to be back until noon tomorrow."

His father laid the newspaper aside and came to him, pawing his shoulder tenderly and coughing as his words caught in his throat.

"We'll have big breakfast for you. I don't have to be at the mill right away. I'll drive you out to the fort."

"I'd like that, Father," Stephen said. "Good night."

"Good night, son," Vincent said as he turned away and left the parlor. Stephen heard him cough again and clear his throat, then ascend the stairs to his bedroom and quietly close the door. Stephen plinked at the piano keys for a time, thinking how ironic it was that both father and son learned the true value of their relationship only when it was in danger of being lost forever. His own bed felt very good that night, and it had nothing to do with the discomfort of sleeping on the ground at Fort Snelling.

Chapter 18

At 5 a.m. on Saturday, June 22, 1861 the men of the First Regiment, Minnesota Volunteers, formed 1,080 strong on the parade field that had been their home for two months. They were fed and formed into ranks, prayed over, and marched down the bluff to the landing on the banks of the Mississippi River below the fort. There they were loaded aboard steamboats. Stephen noted with a touch of irony that his own D Company was assigned to the War Eagle, the same river packet that had chased the Galena upstream seven years before. The War Eagle and its sister vessel, the Northern Belle, carried the regiment down river to the St. Paul landing where the troops disembarked to be paraded through the streets before a cheering throng of citizens. Since he already had bid his farewells, Stephen was sure there would be no one in that crowd to cheer especially for him, so he assumed a stern military bearing and inured himself to the clamor and the excitement, marching like an automaton until at last his boots resounded on the docks where they again boarded the War Eagle for their journey into the unknown.

"Come to the rail, Steve," John urged him. "Listen to them! They're still hollering. Can you beat that?"

"They cheer because it is we who are going to war, and not them."

"Why so cynical on such a joyous occasion? Where is your patriotism? Didn't you hear the chaplain's prayer? We are the chosen ones. We go with the special blessings of God. Don't deny yourself this honor."

"You may be right. I admit I've an urge to cheer right along with them, but somehow it didn't seem proper. After all, we haven't done anything yet to earn such cheers."

"Nonsense. This is our moment to enjoy. Cheer right back at them. Tell them that, by golly, you're Steve Shevley and you're a soldier going off to give the rebels hell."

Stephen allowed himself to be pulled toward the railing while emotions so long subdued began to swell within

296

him. The excitement of the moment brought tears to his eyes, obscuring the crowd that worked its way along the riverbank to cheer their departure. In the din he shouted madly back at the well wishers with a hysterical chant of his own:

"Free, free, free, free, free!"

It was three o'clock in the morning when they arrived at Prairie du Chien where they disembarked to board a train to Janesville. There they changed trains for Chicago where a cheering throng greeted them at Northwestern Depot. In the dark of night they boarded yet another train for Pennsylvania. Along the route to Harrisburg enthusiastic spectators cheered them as heroes, swelling their pride to the extent that they were indignant to learn they'd be jammed into common cattle cars for the journey into Maryland. It was an even greater shock upon reaching Baltimore to be met not as heroes, but as invaders. They were marched through streets thick with tension and pierced by glares of hatred from the population of secessionists. They carried loaded muskets with fixed bayonets and their hearts were filled with fear and dismay. They left that troubled city with a feeling of relief, and arrived in Washington, D.C., at ten o'clock Wednesday night, June 26. They made camp in a field a half mile from the Capitol while their officers reported to officials of the federal government that the First Regiment, Minnesota Volunteers was reporting for duty and in need of military supplies.

The men of D Company were ready for action, but pragmatic in their outlook.

"Well, we're here," said Pvt. Ernest Drescher. "Let's get on with the war."

"It can't be too soon for me," Stephen agreed.

"I'm in no hurry," John Koenig confessed. "I'm not eager to kill, and I'm certainly not eager to die. But I am eager to get home, so I too say, let's get on with it."

"I'm anxious to get home, too," said Drescher, "but I never again want to see the inside of a cattle car." He stretched out in the grass, breathing a sigh of relief, gazing happily at the clear summer sky. "Once we take care of the rebels I'll walk home, if necessary."

Pvt. James Malloy, who had listened nearby, joined in their conversation. "They may send us all home in boxes, if we can't get a jacket to cover these red shirts."

"What's wrong with red shirts?" Stephen asked.

"They make us easy targets," Malloy responded. "I've fought Indians and I know. In these red shirts we'll stand out like priests in a whore house."

"May God forgive such blasphemy!" said Drescher.

Stephen looked down at his shirt. It was the first time he had thought about being hit by a bullet, of bleeding and perhaps dying. The thought made him shudder, while simultaneously giving him a perverse sense of excitement. Only by looking out over the surrounding acres, and seeing more than a thousand red shirts, did he feel reassured.

"Had you thought about being shot?" John asked.

"I'm thinking about it now," Stephen replied.

"Are you frightened?"

"Of course, I am. I am worried, too."

"About dying?"

"No, about how I will do when the shooting begins. It's hard to imagine what it will be like, how I'll react."

"Don't worry, every man on this field is thinking the same thought. As for me, I'm more concerned about killing another man than being killed myself. I really have no desire to kill anyone."

"Strange, but I've not thought much about killing, only about dying. Even now I can't really imagine killing anyone."

"Then you're in the wrong army," said Malloy. "You can bet the rebs want to kill you, and if you're going to survive, you'd better think about killing them first."

"God commands us not to kill," said Einar Jacobson, a pious Finn from the village of Fair Prairie in the Minnesota River valley.

"Then you shouldn't be in the army at all," said Malloy. "Killing is what war is all about."

"Why *did* you enlist?" Stephen asked Jacobson.

"We had too many mouths to feed," he said. "And I was the third son with no prospect of inheritance. It was join the army, or work the rest of my life on my father's farm for room, board and pocket change. It was not a difficult choice."

"How can the army change all that?" Stephen continued.

"It means travel, seeing new places, the chance of better luck somewhere down the road."

"And there's also the chance of dying," said Malloy.

"Perhaps," Jacobson allowed, "but after all, not every soldier dies in a war."

"That's true, but every soldier thinks it's the other fellow who will die; and those who command us to fight depend on that thought, or they could not win a war," Malloy observed.

"You paint a very dark picture," Stephen said.

"War is a very dark undertaking," Malloy replied.

"I will take my chances," said Jacobson.

"Then you like the odds," said Richard Parier, as he deftly shuffled a deck of cards. "How about a game of poker? Your odds are even better at cards. Why not try your luck?"

"Watch out for him," Malloy cautioned with a smile. "Parier himself told me he was asked to leave a riverboat in St. Paul because of his expertise with those cards."

Such talk by men who had never experienced war went on for ten days, interrupted only by hours of drill and drudgery, until at last the regiment was ordered to march to the Navy yard where the men were loaded aboard steamboats for a short trip down river to Alexandria, Virginia. There the First Minnesota joined volunteer regiments from New York and Pennsylvania in bivouac amid rumors of impending battle. Even the prospect of fighting was welcome after camping amid angry secessionists in Alexandria. It therefore was with great pride that the Minnesotans were ordered to lead the march to Centreville beginning on Tuesday, July 16, a hot and sweltering day.

"The heat is different here," John said during the regiment's first break. "I'm soaked with sweat already; how will it be at noon?"

"Hotter," said Stephen. "At least the wool tunics cover our red shirts. We won't make such easy targets."

"What about that New York regiment with its red pantaloons!" exclaimed Malloy. "Talk about giving the rebs an easy target."

"I guess it depends on where you want to get shot," said Parier. "I'd say your odds of surviving are better in red pantaloons than in a red shirt."

"I heard we're going from Centreville to a place called Manassas Junction," said Malloy. "They say Johnny Reb is there."

"I wonder who decides where to fight. Do the generals get together and say, 'Let's fight here'?" Malloy asked.

"I heard it's the terrain, the lay of the land," Stephen replied. "A company clerk said there's a creek or a river there. Running water might be an obstacle for one side and protection for the other."

"And what's the steam called, General Shevley?" asked Parier.

"Rumor says it's called Bull Run," Stephen answered.

"I don't care what they call it," said Malloy. "I just wish they'd picked someplace closer."

In their exhaustion they welcomed nightfall, thinking it might bring some relief, but all it brought was mosquitoes and horse flies and more sweat. Another full day's march brought them to the Centreville where they were ordered to a position above the village, looking down on an encampment so huge that it filled the surrounding meadows nearly as far as the eye could see. This massive array of men and equipment gave Stephen his first real sense of the anonymity Charles Whitcomb had described, the feeling of being lost amid the crowd. He was one man among tens of thousands, and it made him feel safe, if not invincible. But fear lurked there, too, fear evidenced by the brave and boastful talk of his fellow frontiersmen. It was as if they needed to remind themselves who they were and where they came from before they vanished in the multitude – or in the ultimate anonymity of death.

The torpid movement of the army began late that night and continued into early morning. At one o'clock, after a short and sleepless night filled with the high-pitched song of crickets and the murmuring of men teetering on the sharp edge of anxiety, the First Minnesota was ordered to form up and move out. The men, nervous and wide-eyed, were too filled with the fear of the unknown even to notice their lack of sleep. In the darkness they moved in columns of four at route march to a hilltop above the village where they remained until after sunup. In the pre-dawn hours they were conscious of movement all around them as other units passed by in the shadows, grumbling companies of infantry goaded along by officers on horseback, clanking columns of artillery and teamsters harshly cursing their hapless horses. As first light dawned they could see the endless streams of men under arms. The whole panorama passed by them until at last they turned to one another and wondered aloud if in all the confusion they had been forgotten there on the hilltop. But soon their orders came, and down the hill they marched to join in the advance toward Manassas. In the distance they could see horse-drawn carriages, wagons, buggies, vehicles of every description, moving across the face of the hills overlooking their route of march. Civilians fleeing the impending battle, some said, or standing by to serve the needs of the wounded. It was mid-morning before it became clear that the civilians were spectators, jockeying for vantage points from which to watch the battle. Some, confident of an unobstructed view, had tethered their teams and spread blankets upon the grass and now sat laughing and chatting amid a clutter of parasols and picnic baskets, exclaiming at the loud reports of cannon in the distance and pointing excitedly at puffs of smoke that blossomed with growing frequency on the horizon and drifted skyward on a gentle breeze.

"My God," Stephen muttered. "We're to have an audience."

"Look at the fine ladies and gentlemen," said Malloy. "They must have driven all the way from Washington to see the show."

"Then we must give them our best," said John.

Stephen tried to think of other things – the devilishly hot sun, the clouds of dust that enveloped them, the sweat-soaked tunic of the man in front of him, the rattling of thousands of canteens and cartridge boxes as the columns snaked their way to Manassas Junction. He thought it useless to worry. Someone, somewhere must be guiding them with as much logic as could be expected under the circumstances. Yet the same landmarks seemed to reappear. Could it be that in the confusion of war some units were destined to march in circles? It would have seemed like a nightmare, if it weren't for the dust that choked him, the sun that baked his brain, pain of a budding blister on his heel. Then suddenly they came to a halt in a grove of trees behind a small hill where the order came to dress their formation and stand at ease. They were told to place their packs and blanket roles at their feet, and to check their muskets, cartridge boxes and bayonets. Then their company commander appeared on horseback, shouting above the booming of nearby cannon. The captain's instructions were simple: There was an artillery battery just over the crest of the hill; they were to defend it with their lives.

D Company was marched to the forward slope of the hill, passed behind the battery and then toward a wooded area some thirty yards from the left flank. The company was drawn up short by the sudden appearance of another unit that emerged from the thicket. Some wore red shirts much like their own. Others were dressed in gray uniforms much like those of a Massachusetts regiment they had seen in Centreville. The order was passed to hold fire while their officers conferred. So there they stood, gawking at their counterparts a mere stone's throw away, waiting some sign. It came in a moment in the form of a line of blue smoke at the tree line, followed by the crack of musket fire.

"Jesus! They're shooting at us!" Malloy shouted as bullets zinged overhead and kicked up dust at their feet.

"Rebels!" a sergeant shouted. "Return fire!"

Stephen dropped to one knee, lifted the heavy musket to his shoulder, and pulled the trigger. He did not look to see if he had hit anyone, but flung himself to the ground, rolled into a supine position and reloaded his weapon. In a moment he was up again and aiming at the line of men coming toward him, sunlight glinting from their bayonets, erratic blasts resounding from muskets, the pungent odor of black powder hanging in the haze of blue smoke that gave a surreal aura to the scene. Before he could fire a second shot, a barrage from distant Confederate cannon began to explode in their midst. One blast ripped the turf in front of him, showering him with dirt and stones, stunning him and sending his musket flying in one direction, himself in another. He lay motionless, momentarily deafened by the blast, feeling the sting of small wounds and wondering if he were about to die. A bead of sweat rolled from his brow to the bridge of his nose and into the corner of his eye. The brine stung and he squinted through the smoke and could see a figure approaching him through the haze.

"Are you all right?" John shouted, gripping his collar with one hand. "Come on, get up!"

Stephen staggered to his feet and stumbled over to pick up his musket, then followed John across the face of the hill along with other members of D Company. A salvo from the federal battery on the crest of the hill sent six-pound balls whistling over their heads in response to the rebel pounding. Twice they were forced to throw themselves headlong into the dirt and bury their faces to escape the explosions that churned the earth around them and filled the air with shrapnel. Between the blasts they could hear the cries of the wounded, and then the shout, "Here they come!"

Below them, charging uphill with muskets leveled, a line of Confederate infantry emerged from the clouds of dust and smoke not thirty yards distant. Their first volley whizzed overhead, drawing scattered fire from D Company, and then the cry, "Fire, fire, fire!"

Stephen rose to one knee, aimed at the advancing line and pulled the trigger. It was an impersonal act, with no distinct target, no sensation other than sheer panic. If his bullet struck anyone, he did not know it. But the company's scattered fire took a heavy toll of the rebel line, giving Stephen and his fellow Minnesotans time to reload and fire once again before the rebels fell upon them with the fearsome gleam of fixed bayonets. Stephen braced himself for the onslaught, his own bayonet thrust forward, glinting in the sun. His chance opponent, now only a few feet away, was a young man whose eyes were filled with fear and fury. His arms were upraised as he swung his musket like a bludgeon toward Stephen's head. Ducking the blow, Stephen summoned all his strength and lunged forward with his musket, driving his bayonet deep into the youth's rib cage. The force of the blow coupled with the youth's own momentum sent a jolt through Stephen's arms and into his shoulders that caused him to lose his grip on the musket. The impact of his thrust released a surge of blood like water expelled from a burst balloon. The splash covered both his hands and forearms with gore, leaving his fingers warm and sticky. His victim fell backward and collapsed at his feet, the dark stain of his gushing blood staining the earth around him. As Stephen stared in horror and fascination at the sight of death two hands grasped his leg and he looked down into the face of Ernest Drescher staring up at him wide-eyed in fright.

"Let go of me!" Stephen cried in fury. "Get away!"

Paralyzed by fear, Drescher clung to his leg like a drowning man. Unable to break the grip, Stephen reached down and grabbed Drescher's tunic with his bloodied hands and shook him ferociously.

"Let go, you damned fool, let go!"

Drescher's wild eyes fell on Stephen's blood-covered hands and his mouth gaped open. He loosened his grip on Stephen's leg and flung himself back in horror.

"What are you staring at?" Stephen cried.

Speechless, Drescher clambered to his feet and pointed at Stephen's gory hands. At that instant a bullet caught the frightened man along the side of his head, ripping open his skull and exposing the bloodied gray matter of his brains. The blow tilted his head to one side, but he remained erect for an instant, his glassy eyes still fixed on Stephen's bloodied hands. Then he slowly sank to his knees and pitched forward on his face. Repelled, Stephen grasped the musket and bayonet that was still wedged in his victim's body, placed his foot on the rebel's chest, and pulled the weapon free. The touch of hot metal and the heft of the musket seemed to calm him. He dropped to one knee, opened his cartridge case and withdrew a round. He put the paper-wrapped cartridge between his teeth and tore it open, poured the black powder into the barrel of his musket, placed the ball into the muzzle and pressed it down with his thumb. Next he drew his rammer, placed the end of it on the ball and pressed it home. Then he returned the rammer to its carrying groove, cocked the hammer, and removed the old percussion cap. Finally he drew a new cap from its pouch and pressed it into place under the hammer. This well-practiced procedure took only a matter of seconds while hand-to-hand combat raged all around him, yet it was performed with an eerie calm, as if no harm could possibly come to him until he was ready once again to join the fray. It didn't take long to begin.

"Here they come again!" shouted the sergeant. "Stand ready!"

Stephen rolled into a hollow in the earth left by an exploding shell and came up on his elbows, his musket pointed at a new wave of men in gray trudging up the hill toward them, bayonets leveled for a fight. He fixed his sights upon the nearest man to his front and held steady. His first frenzy had passed. A passiveness came over him as he waited patiently as his target drew nearer. A salvo from a battery of distant cannons exploded somewhere to his rear, while to his front the crack of simultaneous musket fire enveloped the advancing rebels in a cloud of blue smoke. In a moment his target emerged from the haze only a few feet from him. It was a young Confederate officer in a fancy dress uniform, a cockade decorating his hat and his sword held high. Stephen squeezed the trigger and the young officer flung his arms wide as if to embrace his enemy as his sword went flying. His eyes were cast heavenward and for a moment he appeared to be a macabre crucifix. Then he dropped his arms and went limp as if he were a puppet whose strings were let go, his limbs flopping crazily, his intestines oozing languidly from a gaping hole in his belly. Stephen was momentarily transfixed by the sight until John grabbed his sleeve and tugged at him.

"Let's go!" he cried. "We've moving back."

Good, dependable John, Stephen thought, always looking out for me. He was instantly filled with affection and concern.

"Are you all right, John?" he asked.

"Yes, dammit, now let's get moving."

They scrambled up the hill on the heels of the others from D Company, passing through the remnants of the artillery battery which lay scattered amid complete devastation. They ran carefully through the jumble of blue-coated bodies, past the ripped carcasses of horses and the tangled wood and steel of cannon and caisson. The company raced wildly down the back of the hill while the rebel force that had routed them sent desultory fire into their ranks with little effect. The victors were too busy celebrating the destruction of the Union battery to be concerned with the fleeing members of D Company. Soon safely out of range, the Minnesotans came upon their packs and blanket rolls all neatly aligned just as they had left them. Grabbing their gear and dumbly responding to shouted orders the remnants of D Company formed a column of fours and moved out at the double quick. Once sheltered by a wooded grove, they slowed to a route march, exhausted by the heat and the rigors of battle. Sergeant Wright, a non-commissioned officer from Winona, dropped back along the column, one arm hanging limply at his side, the sleeve of his tunic covered with blood. He paused and kept pace for a moment with Stephen, observing his bloodied arms and hands.

"Are you hurt bad?" he asked.

"I'm not hurt at all, Sergeant," Stephen said with a big smile that made his response sound very much like a boast.

"Good," said the sergeant with a quizzical look.

"You were hit," Stephen observed.

"It's not bad," said the sergeant.

"There were a lot of packs still back there," Stephen noted.

"I know. I'm trying to find out how many men we lost, how many might have bolted. Good luck." Then he fell back along the column, stopping now and then to urge the wounded to keep pace as best they could.

"I wasn't boasting," Stephen said to John who walked at his side. "I didn't mean to sound boastful."

"Of course you didn't," said John. "Forget it."

But Stephen could not forget. Far from feeling boastful, he was ashamed. His words now stuck in his throat and gagged him. He wanted to spit them out and grind them into the dirt, erase them from his memory. He could see the youth whose blood stained his soul. He could see Drescher, his face etched with fear, then his head exploding. He could see the rebel with his arms outstretched performing his graceful pirouette of death as his guts oozed out.

"Damn that Drescher!" he muttered.

"What? What about Drescher?" John asked.

"Nothing. He's dead."

"You saw him?"

"Yes."

"That's too bad."

"Yes," Stephen agreed. "It's a crime."

The magnitude of their defeat became obvious as they retraced their route to Centreville. The fields on either side of the road were littered with bodies of men and horses, shattered wagons and caissons, and the lesser debris of war. Across the scarred terrain straggled the disorganized survivors of the battle. The men of the First Minnesota, though near collapse, did their best to maintain a semblance of military formation, but were near collapse by the time they reached the village. Given their ease, they sought what little shade was to be found. Most sat in stunned silence. Others slept, some wept. Many simply stared off into space in shock. John, ever the practical one, pulled off his boots and began brushing the dust from them..

"You'd do better to clean your musket first," said Sergeant Wright.

"My musket won't take me home; these boots will," John replied. "They've brought me this far and I'm alive. They're good luck. They belonged to my father, you see. These boots, and a piece of paper good for a plot of land in Minnesota – that was his legacy to me. I'm grateful for both."

The boots were tall and black with shiny silver buckles on the straps across the instep. When they were clean he took a bit of oil from a tiny flask he carried and rubbed the leather until it glistened. Then he held them up to admire them.

"You're crazy," Stephen muttered wearily.

"You ought to be resting," the sergeant said. "We've a long walk ahead of us tonight.

"You're crazy, too," Stephen said to the sergeant. "We're too exhausted to walk another step."

"The captain said D Company performed well today," the sergeant said. "You held your ground and retired in good order."

"We were whipped and ran away," Stephen corrected him.

"No," he said. "Many units ran away, but not D Company."

"Then it really was as bad as it looked?" John asked.

"Yes," said the sergeant. "We had the hell kicked out of us."

*   *   *

The guns were quiet and night sounds emanated from the darkness along the road. The crickets' song, and the frogs, and the eerie ululation of owls serenaded their staggering steps. They were no longer merely exhausted, they were virtually numb with fatigue. Stephen's legs were rubbery, but somehow he maintained a metronomic pace, placing one foot ahead of the other until his eyes fell shut and he stumbled and fell, only to rise again to establish the painful pattern over again. Try as he might he found it difficult not to dwell upon the horrors of the day. After nightfall it became impossible. His mind became a void where the specter of death held sway. Drescher with but half a head conducted the music of the night while the officer in his cockaded hat danced a grisly minuet with the youth who had a bayonet protruding from his chest. The hypnotic rhythm of the scene played in counterpoint to the groans and moans of the wounded, the irregular clip-clop of horses' hooves and the creaking of passing ambulances, their lanterns swaying behind. In an effort to dispel the terrible images from his mind Stephen would fix his drooping eyes on each lantern and try to follow it until the next rig passed and demanded his attention. Each time his eyes fell shut the bloody apparitions would appear to resume their dance of death as if responding to the strings of some cosmic puppeteer.

Only the light of dawn could dispel his nagging nightmare. Then the birds sang and the sound of human voices floated on the air and men rejoiced at having survived to see another day.

"I don't remember any of this," said John as he looked about. "Are we really on the right road?"

"If we are lost, we are not alone," Stephen observed.

309

Far ahead of them a cheer arose, rippling down the road toward them, bringing the column to a halt. Every hundred yards or so a rescue wagon came to a stop and the retreating soldiers crowded around it for a share of bread and tepid coffee. He was surprised to see that their unexpected breakfast was being dispensed by women who wept as they handed out a roll and whose hands trembled as they tried to pour coffee into the empty canteens thrust toward them. Stephen's appearance caused the woman to turn her head away in disgust and the coffee she spilled washed the blood from one hand. As he sagged into the ditch beside the road to eat Stephen realized why she was so repelled. He still was covered with blood, his tunic stiff and black with gore.

"It couldn't have been me," he said absently.

"What are you talking about?" John asked.

"Yesterday. It couldn't have been me. I was born only an hour ago when the sun came up."

"Then welcome to the world. I'm sorry you were born so far from home."

They laughed insanely, sprawling in the dirt and holding their aching sides, tears flowing in rivulets down their cheeks.

"Oh, God, how I'd love to sleep right here, sleep and never wake up," said Stephen. He rolled over on his stomach and buried his head in his arms and wept inconsolably.

"There, there," said John, patting his back gently. "We can't be that far from camp. A few more miles at the most."

Stephen looked up red-eyed and laughed in his face.

"You lying Dutchman! You don't have any idea where we are. You said so yourself."

"Yes, that's true," John said with a laugh. "But I see it this way: If we're lost, we've got a lot of company, and maybe one of them knows where we are."

He nodded at the bedraggled masses of men and vehicles that stretched as far as the eye could see in both directions. Then they both became convulsed with laughter until they lay teary-eyed and gasping for breath. Soon the order came to rejoin the fleeing procession, and in the full light of day Stephen got a clearer look at the shadowy images of the night. Mingled throughout the wretched collection of defeated soldiers was a surprisingly diverse sampling of the war's victims – neatly attired officers from the rear echelon guiding their mounts disdainfully through the ranks battled-stained veterans, walking wounded hobbling along in a vain effort to keep up with the movement of the column while falling ever further toward the rear, ambulance wagons crowded with bodies of the maimed and dying. Stephen also noted a motley collection of civilians caught up in the frenzy of retreat – two gentlemen of apparent means, their fine clothes torn and soiled, their faces stained by sweat and dust, supporting between them a limp and horror-stunned young lady, her blond hair matted against her cheeks and hanging in disarray about her shoulders. And marching proudly amid the ranks of uniformed soldiers was a civilian well beyond middle age dressed in linen trousers, a gray cutaway and ruffled silk shirtfront and carrying a scavenged musket over his shoulder, an infantryman's cap on his head, and cartridge case at his waist, all apparently plucked from the debris of the battlefield. The sight of him made Stephen wonder whatever had driven a man of his age to respond to the drums of war.

In the heat of the afternoon the first glimpse of Alexandria sent a stir of hope through the ranks. As they drew near the officers of the First Minnesota ordered the regiment to form orderly ranks for a cadenced march into town. Overcoming their pain and exhaustion they paraded smartly through a jeering crowd of secessionists and into their bivouac area. There with a minimum of ceremony they were called to attention and formally dismissed. As they sank into the grassy field a bolt of heat lighting split the gathering clouds of a summer storm and a rumbling roll of thunder lulled them to sleep. Long after the summer squall had passed, they were awakened to assemble again for the march into Washington. The suck and pluck of their feet through the mud of the well-soaked road demanded the last of their energy and all of their spirit. Each step brought with it a twinge of pain as aching muscles protested the unreasonable demands put on them until at last they were halted in a field near a church where they were to spend the night. A meager ration of hardtack and tea was distributed, and after nightfall Stephen, John and other members of D Company found shelter in the church where Stephen stretched out in a pew muttering a heart-felt "Thank God!" to which John supplied a resounding "Amen!"

Chapter 19

Stephen slept dreamlessly and awoke in a flash of panic, his nose pressed against solid wood. His eyes flicked open and he shoved against the wood, his legs flailing to escape the terror of the coffin. Then it came back to him: He was lying in a church pew, not in a coffin. Above him was a beamed ceiling across which elongated shadows danced demonically in the lantern light as the denizens of this particular hell went about the grisly work of separating damaged limbs from writhing bodies on an altar that served as an operating table. The conscious victims of this bloody ritual uttered frantic wails between teeth clenched on a wooden dowel, while orderlies went back and forth along the center aisle of the church bearing stretchers to and from the sacrificial ceremony. A growing pile of severed limbs grew steadily beneath a cross whereon even the compassionate Christ cast His eyes heavenward as if unable to endure the carnage at His feet.

A stretcher bearing a body covered from head to foot with a blood-soaked blanket was carried by, and Stephen forced his aching body erect and followed the stretcher out into the night. A corporal stopped him as he left the church, holding a lantern high to look him up and down.

"Friend of yours?" he asked.

"I don't know!" Stephen exclaimed. "My God, maybe he is."

He ran after the stretcher and lifted the blanket and quickly covered the corpse again. He watched as the stretcher bearers went to a row of bodies, gently tipped their burden and allowed it to fall into place in the line. When they left to return to the church, Stephen went up and down the row, staring into the faces of the dead.

"Find who you're looking for?" asked the corporal who had followed him.

"No! I don't know any of them," he cried exultantly.

"Easy, lad," said the corporal, shrinking away from him. "Why don't you have a bite to eat? It'll calm you down. See over there beyond the trees? They're serving hot soup and bread. You'll feel better after a little hot food. You go along now, and leave the dead in peace. Everything will be all right."

The corporal gave a nod to two burly guards who took Stephen by the elbows and led him away.

"Everything's not all right," Stephen yelled back. "They're all dead! Every one of them. Don't you see? They're all dead!"

"What's the matter with him?" asked a familiar voice.

"You know him?" asked one of the guards. "Take him, and keep him away from the church."

"John!" Stephen cried. "Did you see? They're all dead!"

"Yes, I saw them," he said gently. "You just come along now and have a bowl of soup. Then we can talk about it." In the light of the commissary lanterns he could see that Stephen was shaking violently. He put his hand on his forehead. "You're burning with fever, Steve. Here, sit down by this tree and I'll bring you something to eat." Stephen was asleep when John returned.

Shortly after daybreak John helped him to his feet, led him to the road and helped him aboard an ambulance wagon that carried them to the field where the First Minnesota was setting up camp. There he spent the next two weeks in the infirmary tent, before he was well enough to rejoin D Company. John had saved him a place in a tent he shared with Sergeant Henry Wright and Private Jim Malloy. They were to spend the next several weeks there in relative tranquility while rumors of war swirled all around them. It was here that the first mail from home caught up with them, including a letter to Stephen from his father:

My dear son,

It has been weeks since we cheered you and your comrades on your way to war, but only now have we learned of your heroic achievements in the Battle of Bull Run. I must take pen in hand to convey to you and your fellow soldiers the deep pride your actions have brought to all of us here at home. Since your name did not appear in the tragic lists that came after the battle, we shall assume that you are well. We offer our thanks to God Almighty for your deliverance.

Little has changed here. New regiments are being raised and sent off regularly, with never a lack of volunteers. So many men are signing up that we are certain we shall defeat the rebels by sheer force of numbers. Word now is that you all will be home by Christmas, although no official word has been issued. We pray that the rumors are true.

We tend to your mother's grave daily, keeping it neatly trimmed and surrounded by the most colorful of the summer's flowers. Sarah went to that hallowed place as soon as we heard of your heroic victory and told my dear Eleanor all about it, just as if she were there to hear the tale. Perhaps her spirit lingered somewhere nearby. She may even be smiling down on you now with great pride in her heart.

Business has declined somewhat since the start of the war, but continues at a profitable pace. We are developing a large inventory of finished lumber that Roger assures me will leave us in a healthy competitive position once this damnable war is over. I hope his estimates are true, for I look upon this business as your legacy once the eagles of war have folded their wings.

We are all well. Sarah has become an avid reader of periodicals by which she keeps up with the events relating to the war, and also spends a good deal of time in the library. I have encouraged

"What is the news from home?" John asked.

"They are hailing our great victory at Bull Run."

"Well, we survived," he said with a touch of irony. "I guess that's a victory of sorts."

"The folks at home wouldn't think so, if they had marched with us from Centreville," said Stephen.

*   *   *

Several weeks of drill and boredom vanished in a moment when orders came for the division to move up the Potomac. Rumor had it that a campaign against rebel forces in the Shenandoah Valley in western Virginia was in the offing. But rumor or not the orders brought relief and boosted morale of the men in D Company. There was a quickness in their step now and a buoyancy in their spirit that remained even after they learned that the march upriver was not aimed at engaging the Confederate cavalry in the Shenandoah, but merely to stand guard against a rebel invasion from northern Virginia. The Second Corps was spread along several miles of the Potomac, with the First Regiment, Minnesota Volunteers, assigned to a three-mile stretch in the vicinity of Edwards Ferry. The regiment established an encampment in the rolling hills and called it Camp Stone in honor of the division commander, Gen. Charles P. Stone. The men labored through the latter weeks of that steamy summer to make their new home secure and as comfortable as possible. In groups of four they dug several feet into the earth, lined the walls with logs, and

316

erected a framework of poles upon which they stretched their tenting. Sergeant Wright again selected Stephen, John and Jim Malloy as his tent mates, and was quick to take advantage of their talents. While John applied his expertise to construction and maintenance of their new home, Stephen was given the chance to wield an axe again to keep them supplied with firewood. Jim, whose talents were more refined in nature, was assigned to the gathering of contraband – fresh vegetables from nearby farms, berries from the bushes that lined the river, and an occasional chicken when he could run one down. To show his initiative he also made contact with a purveyor of spirits, a commodity with which he kept them all well supplied. Although the three subordinates were thus kept busy, the sergeant, as befit his rank, exercised little more than his authority. But in so doing he managed to keep his tent mates free from less desirable details, and closed his innocent eyes to Jim's illicit activities.

If it weren't for a single combat operation that took place in the chill of October it would have been difficult to convince any of them that a threatening Confederate army lay hidden on the opposite bank of the Potomac. For that operation the First Minnesota was roused in the pre-dawn darkness, issued combat rations and ammunition, and marched to Edwards Ferry. Shortly before first light the regiment was transported across the river in cumbersome canal boats and deposited on the soil of Virginia where they were ordered to set up a defensive perimeter. They met no resistance during these maneuvers. Indeed, reconnaissance patrols sent forward beyond the perimeter returned to report no evidence of the enemy, although firing could be heard in the far distance. The day passed, night fell and the men slept fitfully, ever alert for an attack by the enemy. Outlying pickets reported probes by rebel patrols, but no shots were exchanged. During the second day it became apparent to the men in the ranks that the regiment was a reserve force. The action was taking place elsewhere. The men of the First Minnesota slept easier that second night, and next day were withdrawn and returned to Camp Stone. Later they learned that they had played an insignificant role in a major debacle at Ball's Bluff some four miles east and south of Edwards Ferry. Federal forces with the river at their backs attacked up a steep seventy-foot cliff against entrenched Confederate troops. Some compared the carnage that ensued to shooting fish in a barrel. Survivors agreed that the Potomac ran red with Union blood.

*   *   *

The cold, rainy winter reminded Stephen of his last season in the pineries of Minnesota. There was little snow, nothing to relieve the dull gray monotony of the landscape. He again was assigned to the firewood detail and took out his frustrations by swinging an axe. The Union Army might sit out the war there in the Maryland countryside, he didn't care. His axe would keep him company during the day, and at night there was the cozy camaraderie he shared with his tent mates. In off-duty hours he had an occasional drink of contraband liquor to warm his insides and to help ward off the ghosts that had haunted his memories since the bloody engagement at Bull Run. But one vision he could not dispel was that of his mother lying pale and helpless in her bed. He would awake at night with a start, reach out to her in the dark, and fall back muttering to himself that he was not alone in failing her. He was elated in the early spring when orders came to leave Camp Stone and move upriver. The regiment marched to Monocacy and camped for the night in a drizzling rain that had followed them all day along the muddy roads. There was a lot of grumbling, not the least of it from Jim Malloy, who took offense at Stephen's high spirits.

"What kind of madman are you?" he asked. "Look at him, he's a leering lunatic. I suppose you think this is a damned picnic!"

"I'm happy that we're on the move again; is there anything wrong with that?"

"It's inhuman to smile complacently while we sit in this freezing mud hole eating slop that any self-respecting pig would refuse."

"The coffee's not bad," said John, huddling under his cape.

"Not bad!" shouted Jim. "Why a dipper of mud out of my boot would taste as good or better."

"Well, it's warm," John responded lamely. "How's yours, Steve?"

"I pay it no mind."

"No, you'll pay for it with your innards; it'll rot them out," said Jim.

"Easy," Stephen cautioned. "Save your steam for the rebels. We'll be on them soon enough."

"How would you know that?" John asked.

"I don't know for sure, but it seems reasonable. The captain himself said we're the only division between Washington and Jackson's forces in the Shenandoah. Now if we'd been ordered down river toward the capital, it might be a defensive move. But since we're moving upriver, it must be that we're chasing after Jackson."

Chase him, they did, from Harper's Ferry to Winchester to Berryville and back to Harper's Ferry again, but the Confederate cavalry eluded them in the valley mists and left them sitting dejectedly in the spring's persistent downpours. Wet and cold, and with dysentery rampant in their ranks, their morale soon ran off like the rain in ever-widening rivulets that soon eroded any enthusiasm for battle. At last they moped back to Washington and sprawled in the muddy and familiar field east of the Capitol where they had first camped nearly a year earlier. Here they got their first mail to be delivered since the regiment left Camp Stone. For Stephen there was a letter from Sarah.

Shevley House, February 20th, 1862

Dear Stephen,

So much has happened since you left that I hardly know where to begin. First I must tell you that we all are well and miss you very much. Your father has been gone most of the winter, but we expect him home as soon as the spring drive begins. So many young men have gone off to war that he couldn't find dependable men for the logging crews, particularly foremen. So Mr. Vincent Shevley and Mr. Ben McAlpine have spent most of the winter in the pineries looking after things.

Mother and I have closed off the house and make do with the kitchen and our bedrooms, staying close to the wood stove on cold nights and worrying about everyone being away, especially you, what with the war and all. We will be very happy when you and your father are home again. This is a very big and lonely house with everyone away.

We take good care of your mother's grave, as best we can, what with all the snow, and pray for her soul every night. We keep a little path shoveled out to the knoll where she rests, because your father likes to go there when he is home. I am going to school this winter, because I know your mother would want me to. She always encouraged me to read, and that's what school is mostly, and I like that a lot.

The town is still growing although not as much as before the war. Young men, even some boys, are still leaving. I see them sometimes as they gather downtown and then march off to the fort to get uni-forms and things. Even Patrick Callaghan has gone and old Mr. Callaghan runs the blacksmith shop all by himself. Patrick left in December just before Christmas, so I suppose you've seen him by now. He said he was going to look you up as soon as he got to the war. Mother and I do what we can. We've knitted socks and once a week we go to the church to roll bandages. I do hope you don't get hurt, but if you do you may see some of the bandages we rolled.

*Don't worry about us being alone here in Shev-
ley House. Mr. Roger Frasier looks in on us every
now and then and tells us not to be shy about asking
if we need anything. We're going into town this
afternoon to shop and we'll give this letter to Mr.
Charles Whitcomb to post for us. He has told us
that he'll see that our letters get to you promptly. I
hope that it does for we send with it our fondest
regards and earnest prayers for your well-being
and your safe return.*

Your friend, Sarah Ann Carpenter

Stephen wept.

*   *   *

Not long after the regiment returned to Washington
Stephen was assigned to Headquarters Company for
temporary duty as a messenger. He did well carrying orders
to regiments in bivouac all around the capital, and soon was
entrusted with a more important assignment – carrying a
dispatch case to Headquarters, Army of the Potomac, located
in the Winder's Building on 17th Street opposite the small
brick building that housed the War Department. He found
the city's streets alive with activity. Carriages came and went
along the muddy thoroughfares, while crowds thronged the
board sidewalks – women in fancy dresses escorted by
officers in trim blue uniforms with polished brass buttons;
wounded soldiers limping along in bloodied bandages;
stragglers in small bunches, wide-eyed and looking more for
mischief than for their regiments; businessmen, prosperous
and happy, and street vendors hawking their wares. He
overheard extraordinary conversations in soft southern
accents about the impending fall of the capital, and wondered why treason ran so rampant in the very shadow of the
Capitol. Politicians in chin whiskers and cutaways could be
seen in urgent conversation in hansom cabs that plied the
avenue. Looming over all was the uncompleted dome of the

321

Capitol itself, looking for all the world like the symbol of a devastated, defeated nation. With worry in his heart he reported to the guard at the headquarters building, who directed him to an orderly in the foyer who in turn accepted the dispatch case and ordered him to return to his post.

"And private," the sergeant called after him. "See if your regiment hasn't a more presentable soldier to send here next time."

Stephen surveyed his wrinkled and muddied uniform and rubbed his bearded chin, comparing his appearance to that of the orderly in his neat blouse and trimmed whiskers. He could only smile. There was no use trying to explain. He ambled back into the street in no hurry to return to the cold, wet tent, day-dreaming as he went of a hot bath, a shave, and a fresh, clean uniform. On his way he passed the Soldiers Rest, and on impulse pushed his way through the crowd at the door. A large old home had been converted into a combination boarding house and relocation center with several tables set up to provide information on the where-abouts of military units. Lost troopers scanned the lists posted in the entryway while others took places at a trestle table where beef soup and fresh bread were being served. Stephen took a chair at the table and savored the aroma of the steaming bowl of broth that a smiling matron set before him. A basket of warm bread was passed his way and he ate hungrily.

"What's your outfit?" asked a grizzled corporal across from him.

"First Minnesota," he said proudly.

"Don't know it. When were you last with it?"

"About two hours ago."

"Two hours! You didn't waste any time getting lost."

"I'm not lost, I'm hungry."

"Well, I've known others to desert for a hot meal."

"I'm not a deserter," Stephen said angrily. "I'm here on business."

At that moment he caught sight of a woman carrying a pot of steaming soup to a nearby table. He arose slowly, following her with his eyes. She placed the pot on a table and as she looked up their eyes met. She studied him curiously as he came toward her.

"I beg your pardon, m'am, but aren't you Mrs. Jonathan Wells? I'm Stephen Shevley of Minneapolis."

"Stephen!" she cried, throwing her head back in happy laughter. "I thought you looked familiar – here, and in uniform! My, how you have changed."

"I guess I have," he said modestly. "You look just the same. I'm very pleased to see you again."

"And how is your family, how are things in Minneapolis?"

Her voice was unchanged. It had the same musical quality that had haunted his adolescent dreams. She was the same Grace Fairchild who had set his young blood to stirring so many years ago. She was still petite, still beautiful, still alluring.

"Everything's fine at home," he said. "My father is well, but I'm sorry to say that my mother passed away more than a year ago."

"I'm terribly sorry, Stephen. I'm sure Jon will be, too. He greatly admired Mrs. Shevley. He's here in Washington, of course. He's a member of General McClellan's staff. I work here while he's attending to his duties."

"That's very generous of you."

"Oh, it's the very least I could do. Now then, have you eaten? Can I get you anything?"

"Yes, I've eaten. I was on my way back to my regiment and thought I'd stop in for a hot meal. We've been in the field so long I'd forgotten how good hot food tasted. I suppose I shouldn't have, since I know it's meant for others. But the smell of fresh bread..."

"On the contrary, Stephen. The food here is meant for soldiers of the Union Army, whatever their circumstances. You are more than welcome here. But you must have dinner with Jon and me. He'll be thrilled to know an old acquaintance is nearby. He's a colonel now, and quite happy in his work. We've rented a small house and would be pleased if you'd be our guest. What a pleasure it will be to talk of old times. I'll make all the arrangements and Jon with get an invitation to you just as soon as possible."

"I'm sure the colonel has more important things to do, Mrs. Wells. But I must admit that the prospect of a home-cooked meal is mighty appealing."

"Then it's settled – Saturday night. I know Jon can make arrangements with your commanding officer." She smiled fondly, extending both her hands to him. He took them gently.

"Seeing you today has made all these months of madness tolerable somehow," he said. "I can't thank you enough."

"No need for that, Stephen. You are a link to a happy past. We shall look forward to the pleasure of your company."

"Until Saturday, then. Goodbye."

He strode back to camp with a broad grin on his face, ecstatic at his prospects. He could savor the meal already: a richly larded roast of beef; thick, dark gravy over a mound of creamy mashed potatoes; serving dishes heaped with vegetables; crusty bread hot from the oven, and a pie oozing with sliced apples in a glistening syrup and a crust so light it dissolves on the tongue. Once vicariously gorged, his imagination turned to the beautiful face across the dinner table. He heard again the melodious voice and saw the twinkling eyes that had awakened longings that transcended conventional morality. But there was no time for gluttony, let alone adultery. Instead of an dinner invitation, he got orders to prepare for a march. The First Minnesota, after only three days of rest, was headed again for Alexandria. It was rumored to be the beginning of the long-awaited march on Richmond.

*   *   *

The leaden skies that had shrouded the army throughout a dismal winter failed to change with the seasons. A good day was a day without rain, and there were few good days. The soldiers soon forgot when last they had been warm and dry. Boots mildewed on their feet; uniforms rotted on their backs, and weapons rusted in their hands. Chills and fever were epidemic. When whiskey was to be had, those in authority looked the other way; there would be no enforcement of anti-drinking regulations, so long as a sip of liquor could ward off a chill, make a man forget his misery, or keep him alive when death seemed a happy alternative. All the whiskey in the world could not impede the Army of the Potomac half so effectively as the cold, the rain and the mud that plagued that ill-fated offensive.

The Minnesota volunteers were but a small, insignificant element in the master plan that Maj. Gen. George B. McClellan devised to take Richmond, the capital of the Confederacy. It was a plan thwarted at every turn by the elements, by the elusive enemy, and by the general's own indecisiveness. Although the campaign on the peninsula was marked by great misery and suffering it was not so much at the hands of the rebels as by the will of the fickle gods of war. Along with thousands of others Stephen suffered from fatigue, discomfort and debilitating disease. But his only confrontation with death came as the army arrayed itself upon Malvern Hill on the James River outside Richmond. McClellan commanded the high ground, extending his flanks into the steaming marshes, his cannon dominating the low-lying approaches to the city. When the rebels attacked, Union shot and shell wreaked havoc upon them and the carnage was great. The First Minnesota, low on the right flank, was spared the brunt of the onslaught. All day long the battle raged until the field was piled with Confederate dead. In the rainy night when the guns fell silent the dank air was filled with the moans and cries of the wounded. In the morning mists when the federal troops marched away the bloody slopes were alive with squirming wounded. It was a hell well rid of, a horror best forgotten, and yet not the worst of war by far. That was to come days later when the seemingly senseless impulses that inspire the architects of battle moved the army again to that same Malvern Hill en route to God knows where. The Union forces camped for a night looking out over that gory field; the vistas of hell could not have been more shocking. The constant rains had washed open shallow graves, exposing the bones of the dead festooned with green and moldering flesh. Eyeless sockets stared accusingly and the stench of death was inescapable. Stephen, fighting a losing battle with the swamp fever that riddled the regiment, was brought low by the sight of it. He gave up, surrendering to the fever, longing for it to end his misery. Weak and delirious, his brow afire, he was loaded aboard a wagon amid a host of suffering soldiers for a jolting ride over miles of rutted roads. Death struck all around him, not with the blinding flash of battle, not with the swiftness of a bullet or slash of a saber, but in its meanest, most miserable manner. The fever suffocated the will to live. Men died slowly in agonizing pain. Though Stephen longed for a quick release, it did not come. When his burning body cooled at last, he was summarily banned from the ambulance wagons and forced to join the walking wounded. Upon rejoining his regiment at Newport News, he discovered that it was not just the sick and injured who were retreating down the peninsula. The entire Army of the Potomac was retreating toward Washington. The vaunted march on Richmond, they learned, had ended in failure.

*   *   *

"So it was all for nothing – all that death and destruction," Stephen said as he shaved. There was time for such self-indulgence aboard the steamboat as it churned upriver toward Alexandria.

"All useless," John lamented, waiting his turn at the mirror.

Stephen felt the power of the engines under his feet, and it reminded him of the Galena and his voyage up the

Mississippi when he was a boy of fourteen. The face that looked back at him from the mirror was a much older face. There were heavy lines at the corners of his eyes and with four months of beard scraped away he saw that his cheeks were red and ragged with fever blisters. D Company was jammed into the river boat's salon, and he recalled with an ironic smile how his mother had enjoyed dinner with Jonathan Wells in a similar salon aboard the Galena. He wondered if Colonel Wells had tried to deliver a dinner invitation to him, or if he, too, had been called to duty. As he gazed into the mirror he saw the reflection there slowly transform into the battlefield at Malvern Hill with the skeletons of the dead seeming to rise from the mud. He shivered. "What's the matter, can't you stand to look at yourself?" John asked irritably. "I'd like my turn at the mirror."

"Yes...ur, no. I was just thinking that there's more to it than we bargained for, isn't there, John."

"I didn't expect it to be a picnic."

"But we survived, right? We did our duty."

"You talk as if it's all over," John said with a touch of melancholy.

"I thought it would be different somehow, and I can't seem to get over it," Stephen said. "We all had the same experiences, yet all of us reacted differently, each in his own way."

"Yes," said John. "Some of us died while others lived."

"I wonder how it's decided – who lives, and who dies? And I wonder what it's all about. Why didn't we make an end of it at Richmond? Why did so many men die for nothing?"

"I don't know," John said. "I only know I'm tired of it and I want to go home."

"It's nearly harvest time, isn't it?"

"It is," said John looking forlornly into the distance. "I should be in the fields. I want to walk off this steamer as soon as it docks and keep right on walking until I'm home."

John had taken his place at the mirror and Stephen saw a tear fall from his eye and cut a lazy furrow through the lather on his cheek. He gripped John's shoulder to comfort him.

*   *   *

If McClellan's Army of the Potomac had struggled in vain on the peninsula, at least it had retired relatively intact. Not so the newly formed Army of Virginia under the command of Maj. Gen. John Pope. The news at Alexandria was that the Second Corps, including the First Regiment, Minnesota Volunteers, was to march to Centreville to cover Pope's retreat from the second Union disaster at Bull Run. Except for the absence of civilians, the fleeing remnants of Pope's command reminded the Minnesotans of their own retreat more than a year before. With the pride and aplomb of veterans they aligned their ranks and marched smartly past the disorganized, defeated army.

"Watch out for Jackson!" the fleeing troops warned. "He's gored our flanks and he's waitin' for you."

As the whimpering legions limped back to Washington, and the fields all around lay silent and deserted, the Second Corps took up positions to confront the advancing rebels led by Gen. Thomas J. Jackson. The enemy soon closed the gap, and its harassing musket fire nipped at the heels of the Union rear guard. But then a line of cavalry could be seen on the horizon and Confederate artillery batteries behind it unleashed a barrage. The men of D Company hugged the ground and took what cover they could find at the edge of a wheat field and waited for the rebel attack. The September sun hung low in the sky and turned the field of waving grain into a carpet of gold. John positioned himself carefully, trying to avoid crushing the ripening crop.

"There's nothing you can do about it," Stephen shouted impatiently. "Get your head down or they'll blow it off."

"It's a damn shame," John responded, "tearing up a fine crop like this."

"Maybe so, but maybe it'll give us a crack at Johnny Reb. Why don't they come?" Stephen asked through clenched teeth. His eyes flicked anxiously over the field, searching for a target, listening for the chilling cries and thundering hoof beats that accompanied a cavalry charge. But the artillery barrage intensified to the point where nothing could be heard but the incessant explosions that turned the wheat field into a churning mass of dust and smoke. Stephen clung to his musket and buried his face in the dirt as the air around him came alive with flying shrapnel. The cannon fire ripped through their lines and then suddenly fell silent, and all he could hear were the moans and screams of the wounded. Then he thought he heard the distant rumble of pounding hooves, and he rose up to confront the enemy.

"Get down, Craft, get down!" shouted Sergeant Wright.

"They're coming!" Stephen shouted. "I can hear them!"

"That's cannon firing again," John cried. "Get down!"

Stephen was standing erect, scanning the wheat field, searching in vain for some sign of the rebel cavalry. But there was nothing. Then shells from the renewed barrage began bursting all around him, showering him with dirt. Something punched him in the chest, and he dropped his musket and fell to his knees.

"Get your head down, Steve," John shouted.

Still on his knees, Stephen looked down and saw that his tunic had been ripped open and that blood was oozing from a gash across his chest. He clasped his arms about himself and collapsed in pain, screaming: "God help me! I'm hit."

Chapter 20

Stephen awoke in the chill of the night. A heavy mist obscured the moon and stars and settled in upon him, dampening his face and diffusing the light from nearby lanterns. There was a powerful odor of whiskey in the air and his head throbbed as if he had had too much of it. The blanket over him carried the stench of death mingled with the fetid odor of human waste. A bedlam of moans and groans, cries and curses filled the atmosphere. His arms and legs were numb and his extremities tingled. Movement of his right arm brought on excruciating pain across his chest that was tightly bound. He gingerly raised his left hand and felt a thick bandage that swathed his torso. It was difficult to take a deep breath; each gasp hurt, and he was hungry. A squat figure of a man came and leaned on the wheel of a wagon next to where he lay.

"How ya' feeling'?" he asked.

"I'm hungry," Stephen replied.

"I'll be god-damned," the man exclaimed.

He was a nightmare character in a beaver hat, rimless glasses and a blood-soaked apron. He had a bulbous nose and his face was puffy. His shirtsleeves were rolled up and his thick, hairy forearms were covered with gore.

"There ain't nothin' to eat right now," he drawled, reaching under his apron and withdrawing a plug of tobacco. "How about a chaw?"

"No thanks. Are you a doctor?"

The man threw back his head and laughed.

"I pass for it," he said finally. "Don't know how in hell I got into this. I'm a barber, for Christ's sake! I got volunteered a couple of weeks ago and haven't stopped sawin' and choppin' since. So I guess I'm a god-damned doctor now, I tell ya', and I got the corpses to prove it!" He guffawed again and chomped down on the tobacco plug and put it back in his pocket. He shook his head wearily, and said, "I ain't slept for four days, I swear."

"Where are we?"

"Damned if I know; somewhere in Virginia. Mule-skinners say we'll be back in Washington sometime before dark tomorrow – no, today. Must be past midnight by now. How d'ya feel?"

"I feel like I got kicked in the chest."

"Ain't much wrong with ya'. I remember working on you last evenin'. Got ripped up a bit, but no broken bones as far as I could tell. Shrapnel," he said sagely. "Must have come up this way." He drew a finger diagonally across his own paunch and made a sound he likened to ripping flesh. "Another inch either way and it would have taken your head right off, or spilled your guts. Can't say if you're better off or not."

"I'll heal," Stephen said confidently.

"That's just what I mean. You'll heal and they'll send you right back into the line. Have a swig?" He reached into his back pocket, brought forth a pint of whiskey, and stooped down to put it at Stephen's lips.

"Wait...wait a minute," he said, raising himself painfully on his left elbow. The erstwhile doctor put the bottle to his lips again and he took a big gulp. The liquor burned his throat and brought tears to his eyes.

"There, that ought to fix you up," he said, spitting tobacco juice.

While his benefactor slipped the bottle back into his pocket, Stephen looked around him. A line of ambulance wagons stretched off into the darkness. Laid out on the ground beside them were other wounded like himself, waiting to be loaded aboard the wagons for the last leg of their journey. Some were still as death; others squirmed fitfully, crying softly in pain. Occasionally there came a call for God's mercy, or a mother's touch. Among them moved the less seriously injured, looking for friends, offering solace. In a nearby grove several lanterns faintly illuminated tables surrounded by shadowy forms working over the wounded.

"Army surgeons over there in the trees," the night-mare man said. "Been learnin' me the trade. Got so's I can take off a limb clean as a whistle. Taught me where to slice and saw. I use my own razors; they lent me a saw with little teeth that cut right through the bone and gristle. Sharp as hell. Took off arms and legs by the dozen that first night after Manassas. Got pretty good at it, or so the major says. Got pretty fast, too, after a couple of 'em bled to death. Got to do it quick and tie it off, ya' know."

"Can I get up?" Stephen asked.

"You can dance a jig, if you've a mind to. But if I were you I'd stick around these wagons. You'll want a ride in the mornin', and you won't be moving too fast."

He bent down, slipped a sturdy arm under Stephen's shoulder and raised him slowly to his feet.

"Hang on to the wheel," he advised as Stephen swayed with dizziness. "Don't try to move around much 'til you get your bearings. You're likely to fall on your ass."

"Thanks. I'll be all right."

"Hope so," said the man as he picked up Stephen's blanket and adjusted it around his shoulders. "This'll keep the chill off. Take care. I gotta get back to work."

He winked broadly and left Stephen to fend for himself.

As he moved among the wounded he was overcome by a sense of guilt at the sight of the most devastated. One image in particular was to linger in his memory. The youth's face was pale and drawn, the skin so taut in his agony that his teeth were bared and his eyes seemed to protrude from his skull in disembodied terror. His stubbled jaw moved almost imperceptibly in an inaudible supplication. His left hand rested upright on his chest in prayer, the fingertips pressed against their missing counterparts. His right arm was gone, probably still lying in the grotesque heap of severed limbs that was accumulating near the makeshift surgical center. The youth seemed not to notice the loss, so dulled was his brain by pain.

Beyond that miserable infirmary lay a neat row of stretchers whose occupants were officers in various states of distress. He was about to turn away from the officers' area when an orderly passed by bearing a lantern whose light fell upon a familiar face. Stephen went to the wounded officer and knelt down.

"Colonel Wells?"

The officer's head rolled wearily toward him. A spark of recognition lit his rheumy eyes and the glimmer of a smile twitched at the corners of his mouth.

"I know you," he muttered. "You're Stephen Shevley. I had hoped to see you under quite different circumstances."

"I'm sorry it couldn't be that way, sir."

"Have you been hurt?"

"Yes, but not seriously."

"So many young men," he said. "I'm glad it's over for me."

"Surely you'll be going back..."

"No," he said sadly. "Not with one leg."

Covered as he was with a blanket, Stephen had not noticed.

"I'm terribly sorry," he said.

"A ball shattered my knee and killed my horse. Damned rotten luck."

He said he'd been ordered by General McClellan to coordinate the movement of the Second Corps with the retreat of General Pope's command, but stumbled into a Confederate patrol and was caught in a hail of gunfire. For many hours he lay unnoticed by the fleeing Union forces, and as darkness fell he crawled to the road where he was found next morning by elements of the 19th Massachusetts.

"That was yesterday, I think. I've lost all track of time. By last evening we'd caught up with this travelling butcher shop. I only hope that I live long enough to see Grace again. They say we'll be back in Washington tomorrow. I've got to make it."

"Of course you will," said Stephen.

"I'm not so sure. Death comes at such inconvenient times." He studied Stephen's face in the dim light. "One thing you can do for me, if you will. Take a message to your mother. There's so much that had to go unsaid. You must tell her – tell her I'm sorry."

"An apology?" Stephen asked, wondering why his wife hadn't told him that Eleanor was dead.

"Yes, she must be told how remorseful I am. Tell her I carried my love for her – and my sorrow – to the grave."

As he spoke, Jonathan seemed transformed. The lines that pain had etched in his face disappeared. He relaxed and his eyes became soft and luminous in the dim lantern light. They took on a faraway look as he peered into the past. Stephen hung on his every word, comparing his own recollection of events with Wells' rambling account. There was a measured urgency in his voice that marked not hysteria, but determination. Stephen's appearance seemed to have broken the dam that held back memories he'd repressed for years, and now they all came pouring out in a torrent of reminiscence and regret.

"I was very much in love with Eleanor. We were lost souls who came together in our loneliness and we dreamed a hopeless dream. I rejected the temptation at first, but when I suspected that she might share my feelings I pursued her shamelessly, recklessly. The weaker she grew the more relentless my pursuit. It was unforgivable of me; I tried to take her away from her husband and family. And I would have succeeded had she not been the very essence of virtue. She admitted to no more than a fondness for me, but I was convinced that we could have made a good and beautiful life together. Her devotion was to you, Stephen, and to her husband and the vows she had made. She would never forsake them, despite the emptiness she felt. She once confided to me that her husband had become a stranger to her, and that she hated the frontier and how it had changed him. She even felt that he had won you away from her in some sort of contest I never could understand. She was destitute, but her inner strength was remarkable. When she felt most alone and helpless she struck out on her own, seeking new challenges to divert herself from an empty life. I misread those signals, flattering myself that I had a chance to win her over. It was not to be, of course. She would never leave her family, no matter how it hurt her. As it turned out it was I who hurt her most by my persistence and for that I apologize most sincerely. You must tell her that, Stephen. She must be told how I have suffered from the guilt I bear to my last day. Even now it is the greatest pain I bear. She had turned to me in confidence as a dear friend, and I answered her trust with deceit. I wanted to carry her away; I insisted upon it, pleaded with her. And at last she collapsed, literally collapsed in my arms. I carried her to her room that day, more frightened than I have ever been in my life. And to think that I had done this to her! I deserved the wrath your father wreaked on me that day. I fell back in anger and self-pity. I've not been the master of my own soul since that troubled time. Help me unburden myself, please. Tell her how remorseful I am. Beg her forgiveness on my behalf. Tell her – tell her that I still love her and that I will to my dying day."

He had grasped Stephen's hand as he spoke, and now he relaxed his grip. His chest sank and his eyes closed in peaceful sleep. Stephen gently laid his head on the officer's heart and heard a rapid, erratic beat slowly subside into faint regularity. Satisfied that all now was well, he brought the blanket close around Jonathan's neck and laid a hand on his shoulder as if in forgiveness. His eyes lingered a moment on his placid features, then lifted to the sky where clouds drifted across the face of the moon.

Perhaps she had heard him, he thought.

He returned to the darkness at the edge of the road and lay down again next to the wagon. Fatigue nearly overwhelmed him, but he resisted sleep. He knew that the dampness and the cold would stiffen his muscles and bring more pain come the dawn. He bundled himself in the blanket and thought about what Jonathan Wells had told him about his mother. He could see her again in all her fragile beauty, and felt a deep regret for words he'd left unspoken, of love he'd withheld. More profoundly than ever he felt the guilt that weighed heavily on his conscience. He had failed her in the time of her most desperate need. His youth was no excuse; he had been blinded by his own hurt, and had left her alone in a maze of loneliness. A selfless commitment might have saved then both, but he had been unwilling to make that sacrifice. He had deserted her, leaving her to fall prey to the blandishments of a stranger whose offer of love had torn at her conscience. He knew now that he had condemned her weaknesses at the very time that she was displaying her greatest strength. He had shied from petty hurts, while she was suffering from unbearable wounds. Worst of all, he had left her to die alone. He wept bitterly, his heaving chest clawing at his ragged wound. He longed for release, but found only a troubled sleep.

The aroma of hot coffee awakened him before daylight. His right arm was immobilized by his bandages, the fingers numb and tingling as he opened and shut his fist to give them life again. Awkwardly he rolled onto his left side and with his one good arm pushed himself up and staggered to his feet. The walking wounded already were lining up at the cook fire to receive a ration of rancid hardtack and a cup of coffee. He joined them, got his share, and turned to leave.

"Hey, where you going with that cup," said the corporal in charge.

"My colonel needs this coffee," he said. "He can't walk."

"Colonel, huh? Well, see that you return the cup. There's others waiting."

He found Wells where he had left him the night before, lying upon a pallet, staring into the brightening sky. He rolled his head slowly in Stephen's direction as he approached.

"I've brought you some coffee, sir."

"Good lad," he said, trying to lift his head. He placed one hand on Stephen's and guided the cup to his mouth, but the pain was too much and only a swallow found its way between his parched lips. He sank back, shaking his head.

"Too much," he said. "Thank you, but it's just too much."

It was nearly daylight. Wells' face was pale as death, his skin sallow and taut. He reached up and grasped Stephen's hand, his eyes filled with fear.

"I'll stay with you, sir," Stephen said. "Don't worry."

The wounded were beginning to be loaded into the wagons. Stephen struggled to his feet and hovered about as two orderlies picked up Wells' pallet and slid it into the wagon bed.

"Give me a hand up," said Stephen. "I promised I'd stay with him."

"No," said one orderly. "You can walk."

"But I promised!"

"Orders are that those who can walk, must walk. Stand back out of the way."

"But I may not be able to keep up," he protested.

"Too bad, but you can't ride, 'cuz you're able to walk."

As the stretcher-bearers went back for another load Stephen reached in and grasped Wells' hand.

"They won't let me aboard," he said. "I'll try to keep up."

Wells smiled weakly and nodded as if it didn't make any difference now. He smiled faintly and his eyes turned heavenward. He flexed his fingers to let Stephen know that he understood. When the wagon lurched off down the road, Stephen hung on to the tailgate with his good arm, but soon lost his grip and fell painfully into the road. Dragging himself out of the way he watched as a parade of horse-drawn vehicles with their grisly loads passed him by. In the field where they had passed the night a burial detail began gathering up the dead. Slowly, painfully Stephen got to his feet and began trying to keep up. The last thing he remembered was looking into the rising sun. He awoke in a tent, a man's head upon his chest.

"Ah, just so," said the fellow. "A strong heartbeat."

"Who are you?"

"I am a doctor, young man. You were unloaded here late today and placed under our care."

"Is this a hospital?"

"It passes for one under current circumstances."

"What do you plan to do with me?"

"I plan to remove that filthy bandage and see what lies beneath it," he said, snipping gingerly at the rags with a pair of scissors. "Ah, ha! Look at this. Some devil out there knows his business."

"What's that!" Stephen gasped as the doctor held up what looked like a dead rodent.

"Sphagnum. It's a form of moss, an ancient remedy that frequently works wonders. It has healing properties. Now, let's see," he said, poking his finger at the wound across Stephen's chest. "Yes, the skin is knitting well. We'll just have to wash you up a bit and put on a clean bandage. You'll be fine a week or two. Any broken ribs?" he asked, punching Stephen with a stumpy finger.

"Ouch, that hurts!" said his reluctant patient.

"Take a deep breath."

He sucked in air and to his surprise felt no pain.

"Orderly, get this wound cleaned up and bandaged. And see that this soldier gets breakfast. If he's like all the rest, he's starved."

Stephen lingered for a week in the Sanitary Commission tent, sleeping much of the time and gradually regaining his strength. By the beginning of the second week he took to ambling about the ward, seeking a familiar face and comparing experiences with other patients. But when officers came through seeking veterans who were fit to return to their units, he quietly slipped away from the comforts of the hospital and went in search of Col. and Mrs. Jonathan Wells.

"Mrs. Wells is not here today," said the matron in charge of the Soldier's Rest. "Can I help you?"

"I'm a friend of the family. I was with Colonel Wells shortly after he was wounded. We spoke at length and I..."

"Then I am sure Grace will want to see you. Here, I'll write down her address. May God pity her."

"Is she taking it very hard?"

The matron sadly nodded in the affirmative, handing him a scrap of paper with an address on G Street. Carefully dodging his way past patrols looking for deserters, he came at last to the Wells' small frame house. It was on a quiet lane devoid of the bustle and traffic that surrounded the Capitol area. It could have been in any town, so unaffected did it seem by the turbulence of war. He went quickly to the door where he hesitated before rapping. He recalled standing like this before at the door of Grace Fairchild in a past now almost forgotten. Like then, he was concerned about his appearance. He was unshaven and dressed in an ill-fitting tunic, his boots were dusty and scuffed, one sole splitting away from the top. He knew that he looked the part of a deserter, but was sure the colonel would understand. He looked up and down the street, then knocked softly on the door. The curtain in the parlor fluttered and in a moment the door opened. Grace Wells let him in quickly.

"Stephen Shevley!" she exclaimed. "How did you know I needed a man's strength just now? Please come in. Your timing couldn't be better. I've been trying to get a trunk downstairs, and I just can't budge it." She looked harried, her face flushed and her hair mussed. She avoided his eyes as if ashamed of her appearance.

"I'll help, of course," he said. "But I must ask how the colonel is faring. I saw him several weeks ago at a field hospital. He had been badly wounded."

"My husband is dead, Stephen, dead and buried."

"I'm so sorry! I don't know what to say. Is there anything I can do?"

"You can help me move my trunk," she said calmly. "But not this instant. Please come into the parlor and let me get you something to eat. Would you like a cup of tea? I should dearly like to hear of his last days, if you don't mind." She led him into the ghostly room where all the furniture was covered by sheets, the curtains closed against the afternoon sun. She pulled back the covers from two facing chairs and a small table that stood between them. "Please make yourself comfortable. I'll just put water on to boil. Everything is in turmoil. I'm preparing to move, you see. I've been packing all week. It's such a chore. Isn't it amazing how much one can accumulate in just a few years?"

"But where are you going? What will you do?"

"I really have no idea. All these things – Jon's things, my things. I was going to seek a drayage company to pick up my trunk, but I wouldn't know where to send it – not yet."

"Is there family?"

"No. Neither of us had family. We were alone. The army was Jon's home, and now the army wants this house back. We were just a couple of strays," she said helplessly.

"But surely you'll be taken care of – the army, a pension?"

"A widow's mite? Perhaps, when I can take time to look into it. I'm not of a mind to right now. The army has done its part," she said bitterly. "They brought me the news, and they gave me a sword and told me it was his. I knew very well that it wasn't for I had polished his sword many times. That put an end to it, as far as I was concerned. I'm not inclined to ask the army for anything. I don't mean to sound bitter, but the fact is that I am. I'm all cried out. No more tears. I've been alone before, alone and destitute. We did have a little money put aside. I can fend for myself."

"These are difficult times," Stephen observed. "It won't be easy to start anew."

"I've been alone most of my life. I'll get along. I must get along. I must get away from here. But here I am talking about myself, when I want to hear about Jon. You saw him recently?"

"Only briefly. We met by chance in a field hospital."

"You were hurt?"

"Not seriously. I'm on the mend. The colonel told me a bullet had shattered his knee and killed his horse. He said he had lain in a field for many hours before he crawled to a road where a patrol found him and carried him to a field hospital. They had to remove his damaged leg."

She swayed slightly at this reference and he feared she might faint. However, after closing her eyes tightly as if to dispel the vision of her wounded husband, she opened them again and they were clear, alert and inquiring.

"And he was alive when you saw him?" she asked.

"Yes. We had a long talk. If only I had known, I would have engraved his words in my memory. I remember kind and affectionate concern for you," he said.

"It's comforting to know he spoke of me. Was he in pain?"

Stephen avoided her question.

"He was alive next morning. I helped put him aboard an ambulance wagon, but they wouldn't let me stay with him. I held his hand briefly, but couldn't keep up with the wagon. That was the last I saw of him."

Impulsively she reached forward and took his hand in hers, caressing it as if it still held some essence of her lost husband, something of him she could absorb by touching a hand he'd held.

"They sent an orderly to tell me he was dead," she said vacantly. "He told me where and when the burial would be. After the ceremony they gave me the sword that wasn't his."

Stephen jerked his hand free in anger and frustration.

"The damnable unfairness of it all," he exclaimed. "The awful stupidity of war..."

"You mustn't feel that way on Jon's account," she said. "He loved the army, and he died doing his job. He was a dedicated man, but not an emotional one. He was not one for a cause. He could have fought for either side. He made me understand that much, and it's made all the difference to me these past few days. I can accept his death on those terms. It was his way of preparing me, just in case."

"You're very brave."

"No, not brave. I've cried myself to sleep each night since then. But now there are no tears left, so it's time to move on. All that was yesterday; this is today."

"And tomorrow?"

"I'm not concerned about tomorrow. I can fend for myself."

"I remember a sign on your porch long ago, a sign about music lessons."

"I could do that again. And I've done some tutoring. I'm not a helpless female. I can make my own way. But it's growing late, and I haven't even put the water on to boil. You must stay and have supper with me. There's not much, but we can manage. First let me get you a glass of sherry. This won't be what I had in mind when I asked you to dinner, but it will have to do."

She brought out a decanter and two sherry glasses and poured forth a dram of wine.

"Well, now," she said as she settled back in her chair, "we've talked quite enough about me. I want to hear about you. How long will it be before you have to report back to your regiment?"

"I'm not really sure. I'm on the hospital rolls now and free to roam about within limits."

She sat upright and asked, "Are you badly hurt?"

"A slight wound, and I'm on the mend. It's a small price to pay for my freedom, however temporary."

He raised his glass to her and their eyes met in a smile. She was much like he remembered her, older, of course, more matronly. But her beauty remained – the pale skin and lovely hair that she had brushed after she left the room. It was pulled back neatly and gathered in back with a comb so that curls danced at her shoulders when she moved. There was color in her cheeks, a youthful glow that offset the fatigue and weariness in her eyes. Her ample bosom and tiny waist that had fired his passion as a boy were still provocative. He could well remember the softness of her as she stood behind him at the piano, leaning against his back as she moved his hands over the keyboard. They spoke of those days and shared a laugh in happy recollection. They dined on leftover pot roast, bread and wine, and it was a repast he would long remember. Like actors on a stage, they ignored whatever demons lurked in the darkness beyond the footlights and improvised a bright future, full of laughter and happiness, a fantasy world far from the realities of war with its fear, pain, death, and its fearsome uncertainties. They seized the moment, holding it in their grasp as if it were a glass of fine wine, savoring its rich fullness until it warmed them to the depths of their being.

*   *   *

"I didn't tell him she was dead. I was afraid to. I knew he still loved her. A woman can tell, you know. There was always something he held back, a restraint that couldn't be explained any other way. If I had told him, it might have meant the beginning of a real marriage for us, or it might have meant the end of what little we had together. We were good friends, and we were lovers. But we were not husband and wife in the traditional sense. We never spoke of having children, of settling down in a home of our own, not once. It was as if we were sharing an adventure together. It was fun at times, worrisome at others. It didn't get off to a good start. We rushed into it while running away from other things. I was running away from the merciless demands of making my own living, the loneliness of a young woman alone in a frontier town. He was running away from the misery of his lost love. He loved your mother very much, you know, even though he never said so. The rules of our game were that unpleasant things were never mentioned. The object was to escape our past. And why not? Our relationship might have developed into something good and permanent. I prayed that it would, and I believe that he did, too. I never lost hope. That's why I was so afraid to tell him that Eleanor was dead, afraid that I might lose him. That seems shameful, doesn't it? But it's true."

He drew her closer to him to comfort her, saying nothing.

"Now the war has shattered all our hopes," she continued. "And strangely enough I'm not afraid anymore. There's nothing to be afraid of now. My hopes may be gone, but so are my fears. I have nothing else to lose now. I used to worry about tomorrow, but the war destroyed all my tomorrows. It's left me with the here and now, and that gives me a great sense of freedom. It's a form of bondage to live for tomorrow, and I've spent all my life in that kind of bondage. Now I'm free, Stephen, free!"

She pressed her naked body close to his and ran a finger gently along the ugly scar across his chest. He brushed the hair from her forehead and kissed her. Her eyes were bright in the first light of day, and there was no trace of tears.

"I'm a scavenger of war," she said. "I'm stealing each moment and treasuring it as if it were my last. And when I've squeezed all the happiness I can from the moment, I'll cast it aside and take up the next wherever it finds me. In a world gone mad it's all right to make up your own rules. I'm going to spoil myself. I haven't had time to indulge in self-pity. But now I'll revel in it, if it suits me. The war will be my excuse for everything. Who would deny a bereaved widow a little self-pity, or a few hours of happiness? I've scavenged that much from the battlefield of life, and now it's mine. It's all right to live just for the moment, isn't it?"

He pulled the quilt snuggly about her, drawing her to him. She shivered, then grew relaxed and warm and pliant.

"Yes," he said.

*　　*　　*

"I don't want to go back. There's someone out there somewhere who's going to try to kill me. I don't want to die. It's not my war. I want to live and celebrate the simple fact of being alive. War means pain and death. It's foul and disgusting. I know because I've seen it. It hasn't taken my life yet, and I'm not inclined give it another chance. I'm

344

afraid, Grace, and I don't mind admitting it. Like you, I'm free now – we are free. Let the whole world roll on without us. We don't need it, so long as we have each other."

He was sitting on the parlor floor, his long legs stretched out toward the fire, his head resting against her knees while she reclined on the divan, idly toying with his hair. He reached up, took her fingers and kissed them. The winds of late October rattled the shutters. The joints of the house creaked. She nestled deeper into the cushions, pulling her shawl close around her, and leaned down to bring her face close to his. Her eyes were bright in the firelight. Her weariness was gone. She studied him intently.

"We are content here, aren't we?" she asked.

"Reasonably," he said looking away to the fire.

"I'm content here," she said, "and reason has nothing to do with it."

He turned quickly toward her again.

"I love being with you," he insisted, "but reason does intrude every now and then. I have nothing, and you know your money is running short. You even face eviction. If only I could trade the smallest bit of my joy for a basket of groceries. I can't have you pawning your jewelry to feed me."

"You think I've compromised you," she said to tease him.

"No, but I do wish I could do more. I like making our own rules, but occasionally I wonder what we'll do when the sugar bowl is empty."

"Then we'll know just how sweet our lives can be," she said, smiling coquettishly. He kissed her and all reason flew like a wisp of smoke up the chimney.

Chapter 21

"I went by the Soldier's Rest today. It was good to see all the ladies again. There's still so much work to do there. The Sanitary Commission wants me to come back. They look upon me as a helpless soul in need of work to help me forget my loss. They're really all very kind; it makes me feel guilty about our self-indulgent arrangement. But I made no promises. I said I'd do what I could and brought home some cast off clothing to mend. We could outfit you rather nicely, if you don't object to hand-me-downs. It's all quite proper, as I see it. The donated clothing was intended for destitute veterans, and you *are* that, are you not? I could find you a shirt here, a pair of trousers there. I'd slip in some of Jon's things to make up for it. That's fair."

"What do you hear about the war?"

"All the talk is about McClellan. Lincoln's not happy with him, but he remains popular with the people. There's a rumor he may try to take over the government, so unpopular has the president become."

"What does Lincoln expect?"

"He expects him to go after Lee, but McClellan refuses."

"Maybe the war will end in a stalemate."

"Not likely, given the temperament of the southerners. Now here's a fine wool shirt. Let me hold it up to your shoulders. It's a good fit, but needs a button or two. I could fix that."

"What else do they say? Damn, I wish I could get out for a day. Hiding away like a criminal is not to my liking. I peek out the curtains like a fugitive, afraid I'll be seen. I go to the privy after dark, for fear the neighbors will see me. What other news is there? Is the Soldier's Rest crowded? Are there many wounded?"

"It's always crowded. Some are wounded and recovering. I doubt that many are inspired to return to their regiments, but the patrols come through almost daily and send back those who are fit."

"I can't blame the reluctant ones. They can't all be as happy as I am."

"Are you really, Stephen?"

"Sometimes I think about my friends, about John Koenig for example. I often wonder about him, how he's faring, if he's well. He's like an older brother to me. If anything should happen to him, while I'm..."

"While you're safe here making love to me?"

"Deserters are usually shot," he reminded her.

"You could always go back," she said hesitantly. "Or you could change your name, go to work in the hospital as a volunteer. It would ease your conscience."

"I might find out where my regiment is."

"The hospital can always use volunteers."

"It would mean risking discovery."

"Who would recognize you in civilian clothes?"

"If only I had a pass from the doctors."

"Here," she said holding up the woolen shirt with a new button. "Take off your tunic and let's see if it fits."

He stood naked to the waist, his ugly black scar exposed.

"If they doubt your patriotism, show them this," she said, running a finger over the length of it. "You'll carry this forever."

"It will remind me of many things, not all of them unpleasant," he said, taking her into his arms.

"You must promise me you'll never go back. I couldn't bear to lose you."

"I have no desire to."

"You're cold," she said, sliding her hands under the shirt and rubbing his back to warm him. "The fire needs another log."

"I've banked it," he said. "There are other ways to keep warm."

*   *   *

"I went to the Sanitary Commission today seeking work, and I found it."

She turned to him with a smile.

"I knew you would," she said happily.

"They gave me a pass so that I could come and go without being arrested, and a small wage."

She came to him and put her arms around him. "Your greatest compensation will be from the men themselves. You'll see it in their eyes."

"No, I'm afraid I won't. They assigned me to a graves detail. The only men I'll serve are dead and laid out in rows."

She shrank back in horror.

"Death repels you," he observed. "I guess I've grown used to it. It's the same with the citizens of the town who pass by, preoccupied with Christmas shopping and petty gossip. The women look away and whisper behind their hands, while the men turn up their noses and shake their heads. It's unbelievable. They seem to resent the presence of death in their city. These were the men who held the enemy at bay, the men who saved the lives and property of these citizens. But their presence is offensive now. I wanted to cry out to them to look at the carnage, this unholy waste of human life. There were nearly twenty bodies in the row, young and old. A sergeant in charge held a handful of cards, each bearing a name, rank and regiment. He handed them to me and told me to put one card on each coffin. I asked how to tell them apart, and he said it didn't matter; they're dead anyway. Then we wrapped each body in a discarded sheet from the hospital, lifted them into wooden boxes made of green planking and tacked a card onto each coffin. It was a nightmare, and I earned few pennies for taking part in it. I'd sooner work in hell. Here, take the money; I want nothing to do with it."

He cast the rumpled five and ten-cent notes onto the table and looked away to the fire as she gathered them up.

"I have to shop tomorrow," she said quietly.

"I'd rather steal my bread!" he raged. "I won't go back to it. I'd rather starve."

"We'll manage somehow. Stay home tomorrow. Don't go back."

"All that horror, and I learned nothing except that the dead were from a battle at Fredericksburg; a bloodbath, some called it. I don't know if the First Minnesota was engaged or not."

"Let me see the pass they gave you," she said. "Who is Craft?"

"It's my mother's maiden name, the name I used when I enlisted."

"The pass should work for a time, until you look fit enough to return to duty. And all it says is that you're on limited duty with the Sanitary Commission. That means you could try another hospital tomorrow and ask to help with the wounded."

"I could do that," he conceded. "At least I'd hear the rumors, maybe find out about my regiment. The wounded might be able to tell me something; the dead can tell me nothing."

He sank into a chair, his elbows on the table.

"Tomorrow," she said, laying her hands tenderly on his shoulders. "Tomorrow may be different."

*　　*　　*

"It's nice to see you come home with a smile on your face," she greeted him at the door.

"I saw true goodness today," he said. "I'd begun to think it didn't exist anymore. I saw goodness in the form of a truly sweet and gentle man. I thought he was a preacher at first, so Christ-like he seemed. I was carrying in stretchers when I saw him moving among the cots, stopping here and there to chat in a kindly way. He took time to talk to each man, handing out foolish little things – a bit of hard candy, a small packet with needle and thread. But mainly he gave of himself – his time and an attentive ear, a few words of comfort. He sat for nearly an hour with one boy, jotting down notes, perhaps a letter to a loved one, and when the fear of death gleamed in the boy's eyes he caused it to disappear with a few soft words, a touch of his hand to the fevered brow. The boy seemed to glow with a serenity one would not think possible at such a terrifying time. He died with a smile on his face, one hand gripping the hand of the man so tightly he had to pry the fingers loose. The man placed those young hands on the boy's heart, leaned over and closed his eyes with kisses. Yes, he kissed those eyes shut and I saw his tears fall on those young cheeks. It was the most touching sight I've ever seen."

"But who was he?" she asked.

"I don't know. I was moved to speak to him, but when I approached he had moved on to the next patient. I was surprised to find that he was not as elderly as I first imagined. He had long gray hair and beard, but his eyes were youthful, though weary, and his skin was pink, almost womanly. He was dressed in a rumpled white suit that looked as if he'd slept in it. But his expression was truly beatific. He passed by me later and asked if there was anything he could do for me! I could only shake my head in shame. Then one of the wounded called to him and asked him to read. The man took a sheaf of papers from his coat pocket and began to read softly. I couldn't hear the words, but his cadence was poetical. Then another wagonload of wounded arrived, and I had to get back to work. But I couldn't help think what a very different world it would be, if poets ruled the fate of mankind, instead of warriors and politicians."

"It touches me that you were so moved," she said. "Was there any word of your friends?"

"Yes. An ambulance driver said the regiment was engaged at Fredericksburg, but emerged relatively intact. He said the Second Corps was later moved to Falmouth. I wonder how far it is to Falmouth."

*   *   *

"Our lives are what we make of them. We've proved that, you and I, these past few months. Even here in the eye of the storm we've been happy, haven't we?" she asked.

"Yes, my dear. We have been very happy."

"It would be easier somewhere else, somewhere away from all this. It's so difficult to find happiness when we're surrounded by war. We could go west, open up a shop somewhere, a shop with an apartment behind."

"You're breaking your vow!" he laughed. "You're not only looking to the future, you're trying to plan it. Where is my fatalistic companion of yesterday? Where is the woman who lives for the moment with no thought of tomorrow?"

She blushed and tugged him toward a shop window, noting the diversity of music boxes on display.

"Aren't they beautiful?" she gushed.

"An apartment with a music box!" he teased.

"It's the Christmas season. I always get sentimental at Christmas, sentimental and moody. I cry at the simplest of things."

Indeed, he noticed, there were tears in her eyes.

"Don't cry," he said softly. "I want to make you happy, not sad. You've known enough sadness."

"I'm sorry. This is ridiculous. I'm carrying on like a schoolgirl. And I'm not a schoolgirl, am I? I'm much older, if not wiser. I'm older than you are, after all, and I should be wiser. I promise I won't cry anymore."

But she did on Christmas day. She wept violently, the sobs robbing her lungs of air, leaving her gasping.

"It's the most beautiful present I've ever received," she wailed. There was a touch of hysteria in her voice, a despair that startled him.

"You mustn't cry, please. I'd hoped to please you, not upset you."

"You have pleased me, you have," she cried. "But you shouldn't have done it. We'd agreed it was to be a day like any other, a very ordinary day, because we couldn't afford anything special. And now this."

"I thought it would bring a smile, a touch of happiness."

The music box tinkled merrily in the cold parlor. The chill winds of winter knifed in at the window edges around the frosted panes. She was on her knees in front of the fireplace where few meager coals glowed. She pressed her hands to her face, the tears squeezing out between her fingers. He knelt beside her and put his arms around her to comfort her.

"You told me the season made you melancholy. I shouldn't have provoked you this way."

"Oh, Stephen, I'm sorry I spoiled the day for you. Will you ever forgive me?"

"Of course, my darling. It was my fault. I had hoped to make you happy. No more tears, please."

He took her in his arms and kissed her tears away.

"Let's go on as we planned," she whispered. "We'll have an early supper, and then we'll build up the fire and just sit and talk. No more looking forward, ever again. I promise."

The evening went as they had planned, quietly and happily. She was her old self again, and it made him wonder at her odd swings of mood, her passions, the suddenness of their coming and going. In the morning he awoke slowly, feeling the warm emptiness in the bed beside him. He could hear her bustling about in the kitchen, and drifted off to sleep again. When he next awakened, the house was uncommonly quiet.

He spent the day searching for her. She had not been to the Soldier's Rest. The railway station was crowded, but there was no sign of her. In growing desperation he returned to the little house on G Street and found that the trunk she had packed months ago was still locked. He looked through closets and drawers, and found that a few things were gone, others left behind in disarray. He sat alone with a single lamp at nightfall when the cold made the rafters creak and the wind moaned in the chimney. Suddenly he remembered the music box, and his searching began all over again. It was nowhere to be found. He cried aloud and called her name into the emptiness of the house and cursed himself for upsetting her. The house creaked in reply and he cried himself to sleep.

*   *   *

Washington, January 4, 1863

Dear Father,

It has been many weeks since I last wrote, and I regret any concern this lapse may have caused you. I am presently in our capital city recovering from a wound suffered during the Virginia Campaign. It is nothing serious and is healing nicely. Since the First Minnesota, and the Second Corps, of which it is a part, has been in the field this winter, I thought it best to tell you that I have not been under fire with them. I thought it prudent to remain in a hospital here until I had achieved a full recovery. I have spent my time doing what I can to assist in the care of the wounded, of which there seems to be no end. I am now considered fully recovered and eagerly await orders to rejoin my comrades.

Shortly after the second battle at Bull Run I had occasion to be in a field hospital where I resumed acquaintance with Colonel Jonathan Wells, formerly of Ft. Snelling. He served here on the staff of our commander, General George B. McClellan, and was severely wounded while helping to coordinate the movement of General Pope and his forces from Bull Run to Washington. He asked me to tell you that he was sincerely sorry for any injustice he may have committed in the past. I had no idea what he meant, but I promised faithfully that I would so do.

We were separated soon thereafter, and upon reaching Washington I had occasion to ask about him and was advised that he had not survived the journey. This dreadful news, to my chagrin, was

353

conveyed to me by his brave and faithful widow, the former Grace Fairchild of our city. She said he now rests with those legions of heroes of whom this war has produced far too many. I did my best to ease the poor woman's grief, but alas I am not well equipped emotionally for such a sad task. However, that courageous soul was doing quite well without my feeble consolations and now has left Washington to seek a new life.

I have not seen John Koenig for these many weeks, but we had been close companions until I was wounded and evacuated. I hope to find him well when I return to duty. John is a good and brave soldier who greatly misses his home and family and looks forward to the day when he can return to the beloved soil of Minnesota. He is not much for writing letters, so please, if the occasion presents itself, convey his love and best wishes to his mother and siblings on his behalf.

This letter is being written as I wait for a ride with a supply train leaving later today with provisions for the Second Corps where I will rejoin the First Regiment, Minnesota Volunteers.

Please greet Sarah and Mrs. Carpenter for me, and also Ben McAlpine and Mr. Whitcomb. And my special regards to Roger Frasier. And to you, sir, my love and affection. I miss you all and live for the day when I can be with you all once again.

Your dutiful son,
Stephen

After a final, futile series of inquiries about Grace Wells Stephen left the Soldier's Rest and climbed aboard a wagon in a military caravan headed for Falmouth. He harbored no illusions about his return. It was as inevitable as the silver-gray sunset, as bitter as the January cold. He was certain that the fates were not through testing him, that there was no place on earth he would be safe from their fury. The painful lesson of Grace's desertion was clear: There was no escaping yesterday, there was no denying tomorrow. Their lives moved forward inexorably. They had tried to stop the clock and failed. They had shaken their fists at eternity, defied the devil, and now the debt had come due. Like children hiding in a hayloft, they had let the world roll by for a time, but they could not sever the chains that bound them to their separate destinies. Grace knew it all the while. As sure as the tears that dampened her cheeks, she knew it. She had gone off alone to meet her fate, and now he must do the same. Their experience illuminated a gap in Roger Frasier's philosophy through which logic was lost. A man would be a fool to think he could set his cap for whatever he wanted from life. On the contrary, man was fated to snatch whatever happiness he could find, for he was doomed to pay dearly for it at any rate. The whirlwinds of the past blew men inevitably into the future. Merely to exist was to live in the devil's debt, and death was the price Old Nick demanded of all men. For every moment of human warmth there would be hours of cold loneliness; for every fleeting joy, the long agony of despair; for every day of glorious freedom, years of bondage; for every noble gesture, the thankless reward of the grave.

*   *   *

Stephen found the First Minnesota bivouacked on a rise above the Rappahannock, looking across the river to rebel-held Fredricksburg and beyond to the already infamous Marye's Heights. He reported to regimental headquarters, was hustled to the quartermaster's tent for a fresh uniform, boots and a musket, and shown the way to D Company. The neat rows of tents reminded him of the bivouac at Camp Stone on the Potomac, with canvas tenting supported by lashed poles and snugged into log bunkers near ground level for protection against the cold. The rustic shelters had a homey familiarity about them, giving him an immediate sense of belonging. At the company commander's tent he reported to the duty officer. Record books were searched and verified and Stephen Craft was returned to the active duty rolls. He signed the pay roster and went to search for his comrades. He soon found John Koenig, bearded and bundled against the cold, hunched over a cook fire at the entrance to his shelter. He was stirring a thin stew and turning his head avoid the smoke. He caught sight of Stephen's shiny boots first, then scanned upward over the new uniform.

"For God's sake!" he cried. "It's you, Steve." He stood up and clasped Stephen's hand in a hearty greeting. "We'd about given up hope of seeing you again. Not many of our wounded come back."

"I guess I'm just a glutton for punishment. You're looking fit, John."

"Fit as can be. I had a touch of the grippe a week or so ago, but I shook it off same as I shake off rebel bullets. Come on in, you're just in time for dinner."

"Hurry with that pot," Sergeant Wright called out, "before the rats get the hardtack. Well. I'll be damned! Look who's here. We thought you'd be in Minnesota by now. Here, spread that clean blanket of yours next to mine, it might lure some of my lice away."

"It's good to see you, sergeant. Where's Malloy?"

"He's on picket duty, but ought to be back pretty soon. He's stopping by his whiskey cache, but he'll be here in time to complain about the food."

They shared a stew of salt port, turnips and onions, and at Stephen's urging told about their adventures over the past weeks at bloody Antietam Creek and Fredericksburg, which Sergeant Wright call a turkey shoot.

"Our lads were the turkeys. The dead were stacked three feet deep on a hillside, with the rebels pickin' us off from behind a rock wall at the top of the slope. General Burnside sent line after line of troops up that hill into a hail of fire, but Colonel Sully managed to keep us out of that fray. The artillery did knock us about a little. Ever since then we've been sittin' here trying to keep warm and dry, and not doing a very good job of it."

At that moment Jim Malloy climbed down into the shelter and dropped an armload of firewood. He looked in surprise when he saw Stephen.

"I'll be a son-of-a-bitch!" he exclaimed. "Last time I saw you you were running around in a wheat field trying to catch rebel cannon balls. I told 'em then you'd gone crazy, and now I see I was right. Why'd you come back here, for God's sake?"

"I came back for a good home-cooked meal and a drink of whiskey."

"See? He's crazy, just like I said. But I'm glad to see you, Steve. Takes four bodies to keep this hut warm at night, and we missed ya'."

Malloy ate his share of the stew, then hauled out a pint of whiskey and passed it around. The liquor, the small fire at the entrance, and the camaraderie kept them warm, even after the wind picked up, rattling the cold, stiff canvas over their heads and driving them under their blankets. John and Stephen talked in whispers long after the other two had gone to sleep.

"You sure surprised us, Steve. You had a free ticket home, as we saw it."

"Many of the wounded did take a hike, I figure. But roving squads are picking them up and sending them back to their regiments. Some were shot as deserters, I heard."

"Is that why you came back?"

"I don't think I really know why I came back," Stephen said, thinking for the moment about Grace. "I guess I could have walked. I had a hospital pass that allowed me out on the street. I admit I did think about skedaddling. I figured my luck had run out, that I wouldn't be so lucky next time. But you get this strange feeling. It happened to me when the wounded from Fredericksburg started coming in by the hundreds. I found myself searching for familiar faces, looking for names on the lists, all the while hoping I wouldn't find anyone I knew. I guess it was then that I realized that I couldn't get away from it. I knew my place was here with you fellows. I knew I was just as scared of dying as you were, and you didn't run. So why should I?"

"Oh, I'd run, if I had the chance," John said. "I've thought about it a lot since Fredericksburg. I saw hundreds of young men get chewed up in that grinder, and I thought, 'I'm not going to do that.' It was just luck that we didn't get sent up that hill."

"You wouldn't have run, John. I know you wouldn't."

"I'm not so sure. I don't care if a man owns slaves or not. It's none of my business. And I don't hate the rebels. They're not a bad lot, really. We talk to them across the river. They seem like nice sorts. And I don't care if this country is going to be one nation or two. I only care about my own acreage and a chance to farm it in peace. I want to get back to it so bad that I can almost feel the soil in my hands. I can smell meadow grass newly cut and hear my brothers and sisters playing in the yard. When I think on it, I just can't believe the rebels want to take my farm away from me. They probably don't even know where Minnesota is, and wouldn't want to go there if they did. But I guess we've got to lick 'em before I can go home again. I guess that's what war's all about."

*   *   *

The Army of the Potomac survived the ineptitude of its next commander, Maj. Gen. Ambrose E. Burnside, who was responsible for the debacle at Fredricksburg, and in the spring of 1863 yet a new leader took charge. He was Fightin' Joe Hooker, who grabbed the defeated army by its sagging spirits and raised it up in his own image – handsome, shining and ambitious. He improved the troops' rations, dressed them in new uniforms, and put them to work in camp and in the field. Morale soared. In June when word came that Lee's army was on the move Hooker took off after him. The Union forces followed the Confederates through the Virginia countryside and across Maryland like the tail of a meandering dog all the way to the Pennsylvania border. The First Minnesota, serving as Hooker's rear guard, finally halted at the Monocacy River where they found a valley filled with tens of thousands of Union troops with their artillery and cavalry and endless trains of supply wagons. There the Minnesotans rejoined the main body of the Second Corps and moved with it through Maryland to Uniontown at the Pennsylvania border.

On Wednesday, July 1, Stephen was awakened by the rumble of distant thunder. It immediately brought to mind the sudden storms of a Minnesota summer, when hot and heavy skies blackened on the wings of a hot wind and the rains came suddenly to drench the earth. The skies above him were clear, but still the thunder rumbled. Sadly he let his vision of a Minnesota summer storm fade and accepted the din for what it was – an artillery duel. Lethargic after a full day's rest he reluctantly dragged himself into formation as the Second Corps moved quickly toward the sound of battle. En route the men shared bits of news picked up from other units.

"Joe Hooker's out, I hear," said Sergeant Wright. "Bet that means McClellan's back in command for the big one."

"I heard there's a General Meade in charge," said Malloy.

"Don't know Meade," said the sergeant. "But if this is the big one, I hope McClellan's back in the saddle."

"I hear we're near the Pennsylvania border," said Stephen. "How could Lee have gotten this far? I thought we were dogging him."

"Maybe Hooker stopped to sniff too many trees," said the sergeant. "Maybe that's why he's out, cuz ol' Lee threw him off the scent."

Late in the afternoon they met the first of a long stream of routed Federal troops, most wearing the white crescent insignia of the Eleventh Corps. The men bore the telltale signs of deserters: two able-bodied soldiers assisting a single wounded comrade, while a fourth carried their collective belongings.

"Look at them," John said disdainfully. "They bolted again, just like they did at Chancellorsville. Where you running to, boys? Johnny Reb shout 'boo' from behind a tree?"

"Johnny Reb hell!" they hollered back. "It's the whole damn Confederate army. You'll run, too, when you see 'em. It's bloody up there, mark my words."

"We're out-gunned and out-numbered," said another. "It's awful, a slaughter house. Lee can have Pennsylvania, as far as I'm concerned, and Washington, too. I'm getting out while my hide's still whole."

"Damn your hide," Stephen yelled. "Where's the fight?"

"You'll be there soon enough, if you don't turn back while the turning's good. It can't be but a mile or two up the road, place called Gettysburg."

Chapter 22

The air was alive with shot and shrapnel. Stephen followed John into the tall grass at the base of the hill, rolled over and buried his face in the dewy weeds. Jim Malloy suddenly plunged between them as the earth shuddered with the impact of the barrage.

"That's the trouble with a reputation like ours," he said. "It always precedes us."

"Where's the sergeant," Stephen shouted. "Where do we go from here?"

"Not up this hill, I hope," said Jim as another load of miscellaneous iron peppered the ground around them. "If those gunners don't get the range soon, we're finished."

"Just a few stray shells," said Sergeant Wright as he crawled down the line. "Keep your heads down."

"I'd have to dig a hole to get any lower," said Malloy, "and I hear it's bad luck to dig yourself a hole before you're dead."

"We're to stay put," Wright said. "The rest of the corps is moving up to the line. We're to stay here."

"I'd like to know what's going on up there," Stephen said. "Sounds as if the rebel artillery may be chewing up our line."

"They're not doing so bad with us either," said John as another shell struck nearby, showering them with dirt.

They lay there in the grass all morning as the sun climbed higher and the hard-packed earth grew hot to the touch. Over and over they counted the sixty bullets in their cartridge boxes, while couriers cheated death racing back and forth through their position.

"I've never heard a barrage like this one," Stephen said. "Both sides must be firing every cannon they've got."

"I heard it once before at Antietam," said John. "I was wearing my lucky boots that day, or I'd likely not be here now."

"You'd better get them on again. If we ever needed luck, it'll be today," said Stephen.

John curled into a fetal position and pulled off his badly battered army boots and removed from his pack the shiny, well-oiled boots with the silver buckles, the boots he'd inherited from his father.

"Johnny Reb will be gunning for you, if he gets a look at those beauties," Stephen said with a smile. "I'd be obliged if you'd keep a distance between us."

The order to move forward didn't come until late that afternoon at the peak of sweltering temperatures. After lying idle all day in the hot sun with iron fragments knifing the air all around them, the First Minnesota responded eagerly to the command, clambering rapidly to the top of the ridge. An awesome spectacle lay before them. To the west a parallel ridge was clouded in the smoke of hundreds of cannon, while the valley between was alive with a fascinating panorama of war. An orchard and wheat field to the left front was a hotbed of combat as Federal troops battled furiously against an advancing line of Confederate infantry. A glance to the right revealed that the entire valley as far as the eye could see was astir with other clashes of men and steel. Above it all boomed the constant, thunderous blasts of artillery as each side exchanged salvo after salvo. Through it all could be seen the spasmodic movement of men and horses, the pageantry of flapping regimental flags and guidons, the glint of sunlight on saber and bayonet. But the most compelling and fearsome clash seemed to be taking place directly to their front, mesmerizing them even as they responded instinctively to the order to shift left to protect a battery of the 4th U.S. Artillery. The sanguine serge of battle captivated them; the moving specter of death held them spellbound. The awful din deafened them and dulled their minds. Colonel Covill, their regimental commander, rode the line behind them warily watching the carnage below. The blue line wavered now and again, then sagged at last under the weight of the gray onslaught. At length the Union line broke and the Federal troops began to fall back. The fracture was gradual at first, like the bending and cracking of a dry branch. But when the stress at last reached the breaking point, the men in blue flew like so many splinters, racing up the slope toward the First Minnesota.

"They're going to run right over us," John shouted. "Their officers must be gone. They're in a panic."

"Here they come," yelled Malloy. "Turn and fight, you bastards, before those rebels wind up in our laps."

"Steady men, steady," cautioned Sergeant Wright.

A general officer suddenly galloped amidst the retreating troops, swinging his saber and trying futilely to rally the routed infantrymen. But in their panic the fleeing Federals raced through the regiment's line in a mad scramble to reach the top of the ridge. The general, dust-covered and flushed with anger, found himself alone to face the Confederate charge as it moved unopposed across a road in the valley below and began advancing toward the artillery battery on the ridge top. Desperate, the general wheeled about and galloped up the hill to Colonel Covill.

"What regiment is this?" he demanded.

"The First Minnesota, sir!" shouted the colonel.

"Charge that line!" the general roared.

Stephen's muscles tensed. John straightened his shoulders and glanced at him.

"My God," he exclaimed. "There must be a thousand of them, and we can't be more than two hundred or so."

"Right shoulder, shift!" came the command. "Forward!"

The depleted regiment set off down the slope, bayonets leveled and banner flying. Stephen's feet pounded the hardened turf, jarring away the fear that threatened to paralyze him. In its place he felt a grand exhilaration, an excitement that brought a broad grin to his face, a thrill that even the bullets whizzing over his head could not diminish. To his left and right he was dimly aware of his own lines. He could see men dropping as the rebels came into range. He fixed his eyes first on the amorphous mass of gray that advanced inexorably despite a rain of shells exploding in its midst. As the Confederate infantrymen scrambled up the slope the men of the First Minnesota broke into a quickstep, rapidly shrinking the distance to the foe. Here and there screams arose as shot and canister raked the line and more bodies fell away. Then he saw the colonel's saber rise into the air and heard him shout the command to "CHARGE!"

They accelerated to a dead run, leveling their bayonets as they galloped toward the enemy. Stephen felt alone now, oblivious to everything but the gleaming point of his bayonet and the first gray coat that loomed before it. A bullet burned his cheek just as he closed with a beardless, barefoot youth, filthy and ragged. Stephen parried the rebel's thrust and plunged his bayonet into his belly. The youth doubled over and fell without a cry, his hands gripping the barrel of Stephen's musket. With a mighty tug Stephen withdrew the bloody blade and sought a new target. All around him arose the cries of hand-to-hand combat – the curses, the screams, the groans. An old man in a floppy hat appeared suddenly before him, then flew backward into eternity as Stephen discharged his musket into the man's chest. Instantly another attacker was upon him, bayonet aimed at his midsection. Stephen dodged aside and took a swipe at him, his bayonet nearly decapitating the man. The force of the blow snapped the catch and the bayonet went flying just as two men in gray converged on him. He grasped his musket by the barrel and flung himself upon them in a fury, swinging the weapon as he might an axe. The butt of the musket caught one rebel on the side of the head and it split open in a burst of blood. The second rebel turned quickly away and bumped headlong into one of his comrades, sending them both to the ground. They hastily scrambled to their feet, turned and ran for their lives. Up and down the thin line the Confederate troopers broke and fell back upon their onrushing second line, until it, too, collapsed. A general rout ensued as Stephen and the remnants of his regiment flung themselves into a dry creek bed at the base of the hill and took cover.

"Load and fire, load and fire!" the command was shouted down the line.

"Where's your musket, for Christ's sake!" cried Malloy who had hit the ground next to Stephen.

"I don't know."

"Find it, for God's sake. They're likely to turn back on us any minute."

Malloy rammed home a shot, rolled around into the prone position and fired at the retreating rebels, then rolled back to reload.

"I think the stock broke," Stephen muttered. "I dropped it." He turned over on his back and looked out over the field through which they had just passed. Bathed in the red glow of the setting sun that filtered through the smoke and haze of battle, the field presented a vivid picture of hell itself. Not since the slaughter at Malvern Hill had he seen so many bodies. The hillside was carpeted with heaps of blue and gray, many still as death, some exhibiting terrifying spasms as they frantically gasped for life. Child-like cries and muffled moans mingled in the dusk.

"Oh, Jesus!" Stephen sighed.

A blue-coated survivor inched his way toward him. His arm raised up for a helping hand then slowly folded. Stephen reached out for his collar and pulled him into the ditch.

"Sergeant Wright!"

"He's bleeding bad," said Malloy. "Get his musket – no, never mind. Johnny Reb's out of range. Here, let's have a look at him."

They huddled under cover of the parched scar in the earth, picking at the sergeant's bloody tunic.

"Jesus, Henry, I thought you had better sense," Malloy scolded him. "Here, take a nip of this." He tipped his canteen to the sergeant's lips. He swallowed a few drops, licked his lips and coughed. A trickle of blood oozed from the corner of his mouth. He smiled benignly, closed his eyes and died.

"Whiskey helps," Malloy explained, capping his canteen and brushing the tears from his eyes.

"Look there, back on the ridge," said Stephen. "Here come reinforcements. Where in hell were they when we needed them? Damn your hides!" he shouted.

Then the command came down the line, "First Minnesota, fall back!"

Slowly the exhausted remnants of the regiment got up from the dry streambed, giving up their places to the relief unit. As they fell back they picked their way through the carnage, stopping to aid wounded comrades, studying the faces of the dead searching for friends.

"John's out here somewhere," Stephen said. "Help me find him, Jim. He was running beside me. I didn't see him fall."

They located him at last, sitting with his back against a berm. His musket lay on the ground beside him, the ramrod lying loose next to it. His chin rested on his chest, his dead eyes fixed on his cupped hands that held a quantity of soil now soaked with his blood. Stephen picked up his musket and ramrod and moved on.

*   *   *

Of the more than two-hundred and sixty men who charged down Cemetery Ridge that day, only a third of them answered roll call that night as the survivors camped behind the ridge. Stephen lay on his side staring into the flame of a small cook fire as Jim boiled a tin of coffee. Crushed by the loss of his best friend, his mind floated aimlessly from one memory to the next. He saw John again as the hardy young farmer building his home on the banks of the Rum River, tilling the soil for his first crop, guiding a wagonload of fresh produce through the busy streets of Minneapolis, steering his sleigh through the pineries with supplies for the logging camp, sitting ruddy-faced and ill at ease at the Shevleys' dinner table, huddled in the frigid hovel at Camp Stone rubbing oil into the treasured boots that were his link to a father long dead. As a burial detail passed by carrying a stretcher and shovels, Stephen snatched up his bayonet and followed them over the rise to the battleground. The valley was an inverted heaven with dozens of lanterns flickering star-like in the darkness. He could hear the scraping of shovels and the soft voices of the living as they tended to the dead. He hurried to the spot where he had found John's body and was relieved to find it still there. He knelt down and gently closed John's eyelids.

"Sorry, my beloved friend, my dear Dutch uncle. I know you'd have something to say, if you only could. But you've given all you could give, and there's nothing left now. I've come to do what little I can to repay you."

He took hold of the silver buckles, lifted them, and with his bayonet cut the straps that held them to the boots. He wrapped them carefully in his handkerchief and slipped them into his pocket.

"These will go to your mother," he said. "I promise you."

*   *   *

At sunrise the survivors of the First Minnesota were roused, fed, and marched again to the top of the ridge. Stephen looked down the slope to the rock where John had lain. His body was gone now, resting in some unmarked grave, returned to the soil that he loved. The column moved into hastily built fortifications below an artillery battery where Stephen and Jim lay elbow to elbow behind shallow breastworks. They talked at length about the arbitrary nature of war. Why had they survived when John and the sergeant and hundreds, maybe thousands, of others had died? What did it mean? They concluded that their survival really had no meaning, but was completely arbitrary. Perhaps later they would understand, but for the moment they must deal with the soldier's primary objectives – kill the enemy, and try to stay alive. Satisfied with the simplicity of it, Malloy shrugged, rolled over on his back and fell fast asleep. Stephen smiled indulgently, and promptly followed suit.

He had barely drifted off when he heard the barrage begin, and by the time he was fully awake shells were falling all around them. He burrowed deeper into his nook as the battery above them unleashed a deafening barrage of its own. For two hours the artillery duel went on, and then suddenly a hush fell over the valley between the ridgelines. They peered cautiously over the parapet and were enthralled at the spectacle that lay before them. On the western ridge tens of thousands of Confederate infantrymen came into view with banners billowing. Their lines extended for hundreds of yards as they moved slowly down the slope in neat array. When they came within range the Federal batteries opened fire. As the attackers neared the valley floor the first salvos fell within their ranks, shrouding the lines with smoke and dust. When it cleared, gaping holes were visible in the lines while the infantrymen sidestepped to close the gaps. Still they came with stubborn deliberation, slowing to climb a fence, scrambling across the dry creek bed, and reforming their line to resume the assault. At the call of bugles the rebels broke into a quick step, their officers in the lead with sabers raised. Stephen rested his musket on the breastworks and took aim.

"Hold your fire!" came the order. "Fire on command!"

Closer came the Confederate thousands, and at a distance of fifty yards the Federal officers shouted, "Fire at will!"

Up and down the valley tens of thousands of muskets spoke in a single fusillade. The rebel lines swayed and faltered as hundreds fell dead or wounded, but in moments the infantrymen closed ranks again and resumed their charge at the double quick. Suddenly the line split, and a brigade-sized unit wheeled to its right. The maneuver exposed the rebel flank to the men of the First Minnesota who poured a rapid and deadly fire into the attackers. But the sudden shift succeeded in driving back a critical number of the Union defenders, and in moments the rebels overran a Federal battery. The First Minnesota was immediately ordered to charge laterally across the hillside to retake the cannons. Their assault met with furious return fire, and Stephen saw the Minnesotans' regimental flag topple, only to be snatched up again to continue the attack. The raising of the flag sent a wave of enthusiasm through the Federal ranks as the two sides clashed in hand-to-hand combat. Stephen would long remember those final moments: the sweaty, red-faced Confederate soldier who caught the blast of his musket; the panicky youth who tried to parry the thrust of his bayonet with his bare hand, and lost it in the bargain; the mustachioed officer who disdainfully fired his revolver into Stephen's belly an instant before Jim Malloy thrust his bayonet into the officer's breast. In minutes it was all over. The attackers who had overrun the battery threw up their hands in surrender, while a rousing cheer arose from the Federal ranks. Stephen, bleeding profusely, grasped the wheel of a caisson and tried to pull himself erect, but collapsed again into the dust.

*   *   *

"Have a drink, Yankee. I want to see if you leak."

Stephen, sitting against the wheel of the caisson where he had fallen, eagerly gulped the tepid water from a canteen held to his lips, only dimly aware that his ministering angel was a barefoot youth wearing ragged gray trousers.

"Thanks," he said hoarsely. "I've got a terrible pain. Is there anything anybody can do?"

"They're getting' the wounded back as fast as they can. I 'spect the surgeons will patch you up."

"Am I a prisoner?"

"Lordy no, Yankee; I'm the prisoner."

"Then we won?"

"All up and down the line," said the young rebel as he glanced wistfully out over the valley. "Our boys are headed back now, what's left of them."

"I'll be damned," Stephen exclaimed softly.

"Not yet, you won't be. That ball went clean through you and out the back, and you're not even coughin' blood. Must'a missed your vitals."

"Maybe," Stephen gasped. "But it hurts something awful."

"'Spect it does, but I hope you can walk. Litters are mighty scarce up here right now."

"I don't know. I feel pretty weak."

The young rebel looked about, then reached under a cannon and picked up a blackened swab. He wadded it up and handed it to Stephen.

"Stuff this under your jacket and press it tight. You're losing a lot of blood. Now get hold o' my shoulder and let's see if you can get up and take a step or two."

The pain was searing. Tears came to Stephen's eyes and rolled down his cheeks. His impulse was to scream, but he could only manage a low moan that turned into a breath-catching gasp.

"Easy, yank. Put your weight on me."

The two staggered down the back of the ridge to the road, where the young rebel eased him to the ground.

"Thanks," Stephen said. "An hour ago I might have killed you. Now I owe you my thanks."

"I could use a bite to eat," said the rebel. "Ain't had nothin' since yesterday, maybe the day before. You got any biscuits in your kit"

"Help yourself. Oh, Jesus, I'm burning up inside."

"Just rest a bit," said the rebel, rummaging through Stephen's pack and finding a piece of hardtack. "I'll just see if I can find you a litter."

He sat down to munch on the biscuit, softening it with a swig of water from his canteen, all the while watching the road. Suddenly he called out to two fellow prisoners as they approached carrying an empty stretcher.

"Hey! Twenty-eighth Virginia! I got a passenger here who needs a lift to the field hospital. I got a biscuit here for anyone who'll accommodate him."

Delighted at the prospect of not having to climb the ridge again, the two came forward, took the biscuit and gently loaded Stephen onto the litter. After some banter with the young rebel, the two prisoners lifted the stretcher and started off down the road.

"Good luck, yank," the young rebel called after them.

But Stephen had lapsed into unconsciousness.

*   *   *

He awakened to the drumbeat of rain on the canvas over his head. Around him lay dozens of wounded, and through the tent flap he could see the downpour. He was lying on his side, and even in his dreamlike state he could feel the pressure of a tight bandage around his midsection. He could plainly hear the conversation above him.

"This one seems to be coming around."

"Watch him. I doubt if he'll make it through the day."

"Yes, doctor."

"Keep him near the door so you can get him out without disturbing the others."

"Yes, sir."

"And if he's in pain, give him more laudanum."

"Yes, sir."

He had been dosed with laudanum before. It was the drug that gave him the feeling that he had escaped his battered body and seemed to be floating above it. It didn't hurt now unless he tried to move. If he was going to die, he thought, he was already on his way to the next station in his worldly sojourn. He wondered idly where death would finally take him.

"Might know you'd find a dry spot in this downpour. I've been looking all over for you. And here you are curled up high and dry while I slosh around in boots full of mud."

Stephen smiled. Things would be better now that Jim Malloy was here.

"Can you get me out of here?" Stephen asked.

371

"I don't know. Can you swim? It's awful wet out there."

"I've got to get out of here."

"What does the doctor say?"

"He says I'm going to die."

"Hell, we're all going to die. So what?"

"So get me out of here. I don't want to die here."

"I know what you need," said Jim, reaching inside his cape.

"Keep it, Jim. No whiskey. Not now."

"At least the devil would know you didn't waste your last hour on this miserable earth. Do you remember what happened?"

"I got shot in the belly."

"Ya, I know, I saw it. I got the bastard that did it."

"Good for you, Jim. I want you to do something else for me. Find me a piece of string."

"What in hell do you want with string?"

"Never mind. Get it."

Jim stepped away and in moments returned with a bootlace.

"Where'd you find that?"

"I took it from the lieutenant's boot. He won't be needing it."

"Now take these..."

"Jesus, Koenig's boot buckles!"

"String them on that boot lace and tie them around your neck. See that they get to John's mother. I promised him."

"You're balmy on that laudanum. Of all the crazy..."

"Now put 'em around your neck and try to stay alive until the war's over. Help me keep my promise."

"I'll help you, all right," said Jim, kneeling down and putting the lace around Stephen's neck. "You wear 'em. If you think they're so damned important, maybe they'll keep you alive."

The surgeon bustled by just then and confronted Malloy.

"What the hell are you doing in here?"

"I came to check on my brother," said Malloy with a hangdog expression on his face.

"Well, he'll do a lot better without you bothering him. Now go on about your business and leave him alone."

"Yes, sir, I'll do that, sir," said Malloy, giving Stephen a broad wink as the doctor went on his way.

"Malloy, you rascal..."

"Now, Steve, m'boy, you heard the doctor. Save your strength for the trip home. I sure wish I could ride out of here in an ambulance wagon."

"We'll have a drink together in Minneapolis, Jim."

"That's the spirit. Hold tight to those buckles. Remember your promise."

"I will. Goodbye, my friend."

Staying alive would not prove an easy task. There were times as the ambulance jolted over the muddy, rutted roads that Stephen prayed fervently for death, so agonizing was his pain. The orderly administered liberal doses of laudanum to ease the hurt, but couldn't ward off the fever that soon came over him. Even in his delirium he was aware that the man lying next to him was dead, and he envied him. He lapsed in and out of consciousness, and finally awoke in a proper hospital building surrounded by the dead and the dying. Such surroundings brought down upon him a terrible depression. To shut out the misery he retreated into the past, skulking behind a wall of guilt and regret over a lifetime of promises unfulfilled. In his darkest hours, fever-ridden and physically debilitated, he clutched the silver buckles that hung about his neck and concentrated on the final promise he now might never keep. Strangers came and went. He lay silent and unresponsive as they looked down on him impassively, shook their heads, and walked away. Each cry of pain brought an orderly with another dose of laudanum, that tincture of opium that sent him into eerie dreamlike reveries. Even when his fever subsided and his once festering wound began to heal, he lurked behind his wall of silence. The words of those who came to him fell on deaf ears, and he looked upon them with eyes that did not see. He had turned in upon himself so completely that now he held only dark and dreadful communion with the ghosts that haunted his troubled mind – ghosts of loved ones he had failed, ghosts of friends he had seen die, ghosts of strangers he had slain. When at last his wounds were declared healed he was certified unfit for further military service and sent home, his body little more than a coffin for his youth, a dungeon for his soul.

*　　*　　*

Charles Whitcomb, notepad in hand, entered the infirmary with his usual sense of dread. His Sunday visits to Fort Snelling had become a matter of routine, but he had been unable to steel himself against the pathetic scenes and situations he found there. These visits, during which he gathered information for weekly articles in The Frontiersman, had evolved as his single most painful contribution to the war. The articles spread the fame of his small newspaper to the far-flung villages of the state, for they told the stories of heroism and personal accomplishment and sacrifice of the sons of Minnesota in the battles to preserve the Union. But more importantly, by focusing on the returning veterans, his stories served to bring together wounded soldiers and their anxious families. The government bulletins that were hung in the post offices were merely lists naming the dead and the wounded, the battles and the regiments involved. Whitcomb's writings, on the other hand, captured the drama behind those lists, and they were eagerly read throughout the state, at least as far as fragile newsprint could travel while being passed from hand to hand. But it was a demanding task for the editor and he paid dearly for it in heartache each week in order to produce a few inches of prose.

"There are some new arrivals," said the adjutant. "One in particular you might help us with. They've come back to us in all sorts of conditions, but this one is unique. He's a living dead man. His wounds are healed, but they took so much out of him that he's become oblivious to the world around him. When they brought him up here from the landing, he had only a torn fragment of his discharge papers. All we know about him is that he's from the First Regiment. No name, no medical records. The doctors say his wounds are healed, but that he suffers from soldier's disease – too much laudanum has dulled his brain and left him speechless. He will not – or cannot – tell us about himself. We thought if you brought his plight to the attention of your readers we might locate his family."

"I don't know how I could help, if he can't speak," said Whitcomb. "I suppose I could describe him, list his personal effects."

"He had nothing but a cord around his neck with two silver buckles hanging from it. He's quite protective of them, so be careful. Could they be of help?"

"Most unusual. Indeed they might help. Where is this man?"

The captain led him to a cot in the far corner of the ward.

"We try to keep him separated from the others, for fear of what he might do."

The gaunt figure that lay upon the cot seemed not to notice the two men who stood at the end of his bed. Rather he stared out a nearby window where a bright sun filtered down from a crystal-clear winter's sky. His hair was long and shaggy, as was his beard. His skin pale, his cheeks sunken.

Whitcomb moved in for a closer look, tentatively reaching for the silver buckles that lay upon the man's chest. Instantly the patient's bony right hand flashed from beneath his blanket and grasped the buckles in a tight fist.

"Be careful," cautioned the captain. "That's his usual response, and he'll become violent if you persist."

Whitcomb studied the pallid face with its deep-set eyes, its furrowed brow, its translucent skin pulled tight over his cheekbones. There was something about that face that held his gaze. Then he was struck by the shock of recognition.

"Your mystery is solved, Captain," he said. "I know this man."

"Well, thank God for that!" the officer exclaimed. "I hope you can reach his family. We can't care for him here indefinitely."

"I get hold of them. But I must have time to break the news to his father. It will be difficult, as you might imagine. I'll be back tomorrow to take him off your hands."

Whitcomb lingered a moment at the bedside after the officer departed, still stunned by the appearance of the young veteran.

"I'm no doctor, Stephen, but I can see the fires of hell in your eyes, and I wonder if they can ever be put out."

*   *   *

"Oh, my God!" Vincent moaned. "Look what they have done to him."

They had stripped away the coarse army blankets to dress Stephen and wrap him in quilts for the journey, exposing his ugly scars and emaciated body. His once-powerful muscles now hung slack on bones sharply outlined under his yellowed skin. His eyes, dull and lusterless, stared blankly at Vincent, showing no sign of recognition. His right hand grasped the silver buckles so tightly his knuckles turned white.

"I'll get an orderly to help," Whitcomb said, turning away.

"Yes, we must get him home," Vincent said. There were tears in his eyes.

At Shevley House they laid him in his own bed in his own room overlooking the back garden and beyond to the grove of oaks that stood naked and black in the frozen earth. Mrs. Carpenter scurried about teary-eyed and muttering exclamations until Vincent, exasperated, shouted, "Damn it, Mathilda, get the broth!" The poor woman nearly ran headlong into Sarah who entered at just that moment with a steaming bowl of beef and vegetable soup.

"Get along now, both of you," Sarah said. "This confusion can't possibly help him. Let me feed him in peace and quiet."

As she spooned the warm broth between his lips she heard her master's self control slowly dissolve into a ranting, profane soliloquy that ended in a rising cry that echoed through the house:

"My God, his mind is gone!"

She put that idea immediately out of her thoughts and began a patter of encouraging words designed to penetrate the veil of Stephen's withdrawal, all the while probing patiently into his dark world, seeking to set off some spark of light. When he would take no more broth, she fluffed his pillows and adjusted his quilts, discovering for the first time the silver buckles around his neck. As she reached for them his hand came up and touched hers and she held it gently, searching his empty eyes.

"These are precious to you, aren't they, Stephen," she said quietly. "It's a good sign that they mean so much to you. It gives me hope that someday you'll tell me about them. Not now, but when you're ready to tell me. I want to know all about them. I know you will tell me when you can."

She chattered on in soft, soothing tones until his eyes closed in sleep. Then she quietly fed the fireplace in the corner, turned down the lamp and settled into a chair near his bed. Her mother tiptoed in later, tucked a blanket about her and left her there asleep.

Chapter 23

Sarah was nearly seventeen and mature beyond her years. She had been blessed with common sense and an aura of self-assurance that made her a woman despite her age. In childhood she had displayed wisdom and understanding seldom associated with adolescence, and as she grew older she developed strength of character that many fail to achieve in a lifetime. Though plain-featured and not in the least interested in personal ornamentation, she nevertheless was attractive in a spiritual sense, her inner beauty seeming to glow from every facet of her being. She could be assertive, yet unfailingly humble, incapable of a mean or petty thought. The love and kindness she dispensed so freely and innocently came back to her a thousand-fold. Everyone in town knew Sarah Carpenter and adored her. But for all that she had no suitors as she neared marriageable age. The war, of course, was partly to blame, because it had taken away so many fine young men. But what of the others? Perhaps it was her very goodness that intimidated prospective beaux, for it did set a lofty example. She also was known for a formidable sense of purpose, a single-minded determination that might discourage a shy young swain. Or perhaps others saw what was obvious to her mother: Sarah was in love with Stephen Shevley, and had been since she was a little girl in pigtails, despite her mother's efforts to discourage her. If confronted with such an idea, Sarah would have scoffed for she paid little attention to the workings of her own heart. Her eye, as usual, was on the practical. Stephen had come home sick, and it was her duty to help him get well.

In the town they said he was mad. He had come home wounded and mute, exhibiting strange behavior that kept him confined to Shevley House, and no one – not his usually voluble father, nor his talkative housekeeper, nor the housekeeper's personable daughter – would say a word about him. So the gossips said the war had driven Stephen mad. The old-timers weren't surprised. They remembered him as a strange, solitary lad who wandered the woodlands alone, shunning the companionship of other boys. A sudden-tempered lad, others recalled, who was known to have fought a bloody fight on the school grounds years before in a fit of anger. And no one could forget the incident on Nicollet Island when he had attacked and nearly drowned a terrified young girl in full view of holiday celebrants. If additional proof were necessary, all agreed that he was an undisciplined young man who had run off to war to escape the scandal of public drunkenness. All reason enough, they whispered, to stay away from the mansion in the oak grove, for a madman stalked the shadowy halls of Shevley House.

Far from stalking the halls, however, Stephen could usually be found being propelled through his home in a wheelchair guided by Sarah. Her plan was to expose him to familiar areas and tell him stories about each place until he showed some response. Each morning Vincent helped her ease Stephen and his chair down the back stairway and into the kitchen for breakfast. Then, after they had eaten, she began a regular circuit, first to the parlor where she might peck out a tune on the piano, and then encourage him to strike the piano keys himself. Next she would wheel him into the library where she would take one of his favorite books and place it in his hands, or she might select a passage and read it aloud. In the dining room she would point out familiar objects on the sideboard, and the candlesticks on the mahogany table. And finally she would take him back down the center hall to the kitchen where her mother would serve them lunch and speak amiably to him about events of the past, always searching his face for some glimmer of recollection.

At first nothing elicited a response from him. But as he grew stronger Sarah noticed several things that encouraged her. He would smile faintly at the sound of the piano or the sight of a familiar book. In the dining room he would frown at the mention of familiar names – Dr. and Mrs. Ames, Jonathan Wells, Grace Fairchild. And when John

Koenig's name was uttered he would grasp the silver buckles that hung around neck and tears would fill his eyes.

"It's plain to me," Sarah told his father, "those buckles remind him of Mr. Koenig. I think they belonged to him. Why else would he treat them so? Why else would his very name bring tears to Stephen's eyes?"

"You may have something there," Vincent agreed. "I must remember to look in on the Koenig family next time I go up the river road."

Most heartening were those moments when he sat nearby while she dusted the furniture, or chopped vegetables, or played the piano. Occasionally she would look up and find him staring at her, and as she went about the room his eyes would follow her, and the emptiness that dwelled in them would vanish for a time. Then she would whisper his name, hoping against hope that he would answer her. She would tread carefully at moments like these, and speak slowly and quietly so as not to alarm him. Her movements would become slow and graceful and she would touch his hand softly, being careful not to startle him.

Doctor Ames came by once a week to look in on him, turning to Sarah for a report on his progress. She would eagerly relate the small successes her patient had made, but she did not stint in describing his bad moments.

"They usually come after lunch, when we've taken him up to his room to rest. We can hear him stir, and when I go in to check on him I find him covered with sweat, his face distorted, his teeth clenched tight and his eyes wild as fire. And he shakes – he shakes something awful. And when this fit passes he falls into a deep sleep and looks for all the world as if he were dead."

"It's the laudanum the army gave him to kill his pain," the doctor explained. "It's highly addictive, a derivative of opium. His body has come to crave it, and reacts violently when it's deprived of it. I've seen many such cases since the wounded began coming home. There's nothing anyone can do but withhold the drug – and be patient."

"Oh, yes, there is something we can do," said Sarah with grim determination.

She conspired with Vincent to accelerate Stephen's recuperation in order to get him to speak, but begged him not to interfere. After dinner as Stephen dozed in his wheelchair she approached him stealthily and removed the buckles from around his neck. As she backed away he stirred and looked up to see her dangling the two silver buckles in front of him. He reached for them, but she stepped away, still holding the buckles just out of his reach. He grimaced in frustration for a moment, and then his hands found the wheels of his chair and with great effort he turned the wheels and moved toward her. She continued toward the piano bench, her eyes fixed on his, the buckles glinting in the lamplight. She continued her slow retreat, and he followed until he had closed the gap between them. When he reached the piano he lunged for the buckles, rising from his chair and falling heavily against the piano bench. His hands landed on the keys sending a dissonant chord into the far corners of the house. Now erect, his hands splayed across the keyboard, he uttered a low, mournful cry.

"Oh-h-h-h-h-h, God!" It was the first word he had uttered since his arrival home.

Sarah came to him, placed the cord around his neck, and eased him back into his chair. Then she hugged him while tears of happiness rolled down her cheeks. Vincent went across the hall and into his office to be alone.

The impact of Sarah's experiment ripped a small hole in the shroud that divided Stephen from the world, letting in a light to guide him on his journey toward recovery. Soon the terrifying emptiness of his eyes began to give way to a lively interest in everything around him. With her persistent coaching he soon was uttering the names of things around him – piano, book, candle, plate – Sarah. There was nothing miraculous about his progress. It was a slow, painstaking process, but it provided huge rewards – the gladness that shown from Sarah's face when he spoke her name, Mrs. Carpenter's tears of joy when he thanked her for breakfast,

Vincent's spontaneous bear hug when he first met him at the door with the greeting, "Hello, Father."

But still the sights and sounds of the past haunted him:

The whistle of the westbound train that carried his father away. Old Williams stretched out on his table, gray in death. His mother's rambling soliloquies that sapped his youth. Her weeping late at night that filled him with fear. His father and the harsh frontier that brought all those fears to reality. His mother in the arms of another man. The green glass vase that cast a ray of light across the bed where death had found her. The horror in a comrade's eyes as the gore of war dripped from his hands. The strangers he had slain for reasons he would never understand. His fingers slipping from the dying colonel's hand as the wagon trundled into eternity. The piano teacher's bosom soft and warm against his shoulders as his fingers bumbled over the keys. Her metronome that clicked away the precious moments of youth – tick tock, tick tock – until the music box picked up the beat and they danced while time stood still. The futile search for her through empty streets, and the mad dash down a dusty hill where bayonets burst the fragile balloon of life and bathed the world in blood. The good farmer who died holding a sanguine sample of the soil he loved, leaving Stephen only two silver buckles as a legacy, and a burden of guilt.

Sarah came to him as he knelt at his mother's grave, his hands resting on the wrought iron fence, his forehead pressed tightly against them, the silver buckles dangling from the cord around his neck. She felt his fevered brow as he looked up at her with deep sadness in his eyes and she helped him to his feet.

"I worried about you," she said gently as they walked slowly to the house. "You might have fallen."

He settled into a kitchen chair and turned the silver buckles over and over between his fingers as Mrs. Carpenter put the kettle on for tea.

"What do they mean?" Sarah asked.

"They're John's," he said.

"He was your good friend, wasn't he. I'm so sorry. Do you want to tell me about it?"

"Yes," he muttered.

"Let him rest," said Mrs. Carpenter, placing a steaming cup of tea in front of him. "Can't you see that he's exhausted?"

"He wants to talk about it," Sarah asked.

After a long silence he said, "They're for his family."

"That's very kind of you," she said. "You want to tell his family about him."

He nodded, closing his eyes.

"Then you must get your strength back; you must find the Koenig family and give them the buckles, but you must grow stronger so you can do that."

Later, when Vincent came home from work, he asked about his son.

"He's upstairs asleep. He had a difficult afternoon."

"Is he better, is he well?" he asked impatiently.

"Yes, he's very much better. He went out to Mrs. Shevley's grave by himself today. It was the first time he's walked that far alone, and I was very worried."

"He once worked from dawn to dark in the woods," Vincent said dejectedly.

"And he may well do so again," Sarah said. "It will take time. We must be patient and help all we can."

"How can I help, when I can't even talk to him?"

"He will, eventually. He told me about the buckles today."

"What about them?"

"They belonged to John Koenig, just as we thought. He wants to give them to John's mother."

"That was very decent of him. I was told she's sold the farm. Can't blame her, after losing both the older boys. Not much she could do alone."

"Where did she go?"

"I have no idea. Not even sure that she's gone yet.

"We should ask around," Sarah said. "Stephen will want to find her. He'll want to talk to her."

Vincent gave her a doubtful smile.

"He did talk today," Sarah said defensively. "I didn't coax him – much. He had something to say, and he said it. They were his own words, expressing his own thoughts. You must encourage him. You must show your faith in him."

Vincent nodded. She had a gentle way of scolding, he thought, but it was unmistakably a scolding.

*　　*　　*

By April Stephen had abandoned his wheelchair and begun taking walks about the property. He moved as rapidly as possible over the spring-softened earth, leaning gently on his cane when he became tired, but keeping up a rigorous pace to condition his body. As he walked he carefully reconstructed events of the past in order to properly adjust to the present. The war was by far the most influential of all his experiences, and he was certain that someday he would to be able to look upon it objectively. To refresh his memories of it he recreated conversations, calling out the names of his colleagues – John Koenig, Jim Malloy, Henry Wright, Colonel Wells, even Grace who had vanished from his life as certainly and completely as if she had died. Upon such bedrock memories he built a bridge from yesterday toward a better awareness of today. So absorbed would he become during these sessions that a sudden intrusion could come as a shock. It so happened one day as he approached the pond below the oak grove, speaking loudly to companions long dead – and startling a deer that had paused for a drink of water.

"Easy, my friend," said a familiar voice. "It was only a doe, nothing more."

"A deer," Stephen said.

"Yes, so you must not be alarmed," the man said softly, as if he meant to calm him.

"I'm not alarmed," said Stephen.

384

"But you cried out," said the man. He had dismounted and was leading his horse as he approached. "You called out a name."

As the horseman drew nearer Stephen could see that he was a dapper figure, if somewhat ill at ease, judging by the apprehensive look on his face.

"Roger!" Stephen exclaimed. "It is you, isn't it?"

"So you do recognize me. I had assumed you might not, but having been forbidden to call on you, I didn't know for sure. Now that we have met by chance, I don't see any reason for your father's concern. You appear quite well to me."

"My father kept you away?" Stephen asked as he shook Roger's hand. "I don't know why he would do that."

"He told me you were sickly and unable to receive visitors. Yet you seem hearty enough to me. I can imagine what the townsfolk would say if they had come upon you today, stumbling about alone and muttering like a madman. But to me it was just Stephen Shevley, his own peculiar self again. Welcome home."

Stephen threw his head back and laughed. "That's what I needed, a cynic like you to prod me. I dare say I'd have been up and around much sooner if you'd been allowed to call."

"I notice you do have a catch in your gait, and another in your voice. Is that that the sum total of your disability?"

"That's a fair summation."

"Then you'll soon be coming to lay the rumors to rest?"

"What rumors?"

"The rumors that you're insane, sequestered in your house here on the fringes of civilization. Oh, there are all sorts of rumors going around. But you always had a knack for stirring wild tales."

"I'm not mad, as you can plainly see," Stephen said, drawing himself erect and speaking slowly and evenly, obviously indignant at the suggestion of insanity. Roger eyed him steadily as if to make up his own mind about the rumors. "I've been ill, of course, and the illness took its toll. But as you can see I'm nearing full recovery and quite myself again."

"So it would seem, and just in time."

"What do you mean?"

"Your old regiment has returned from the war. A final review is scheduled tomorrow at the fort. Surely you plan to attend."

"I would like that very much..."

"Your father didn't mention it, did he? I guess I'm not surprised."

"He's gone off to the pineries. He probably forgot."

"I'm sorry if I've spoken out of turn."

"Nonsense. Of course I'll attend the review."

"You look tired, Stephen. Let me give you a ride home."

"I'm not tired. I can manage quite well, thank you."

"Then I'll bid you good day, with the hope that I'll see you again soon."

As he rode off he looked back over his shoulder to see Stephen standing erect, his head held high, his cane behind his back. When the horse and rider disappeared from view, Stephen began the slow trek back to Shevley House, a troubled look on his face. He thought he was nearly finished wrestling with the demons of the past, but there was still a major challenge to face.

*   *   *

They had been reduced to be a tiny band, these soldiers who had stood a thousand strong upon that field only three short years before. But the crowds they drew that day attested to the pride they had engendered in their fellow Minnesotans. With their ranks thinned to but a quarter of their original number they stood smartly at parade rest while dignitaries including the governor of the state paid them homage. From their place amid the spectators at the edge of the field Stephen and Sarah watched the ceremonies. A lump came to Stephen's throat and tears to his eyes as he scanned the ranks to find the tattered guidon of D Company, now marking only a handful of men. Sarah took his hand and squeezed it gently.

"You should be out there with your companions," she said. "You've certainly earned the praise they're dispensing here today."

"No, no...I have no uniform. I'm not part of it now. It's all in the past and best forgotten."

"Sh-h-h-h-h. Listen."

"Hundreds of your associates have fallen...they sleep their last sleep and never will awaken to glory again until God's last reveille shall summon them to the soldier's eternal rest...Your banners are torn and tattered, but have never been dishonored...Your deeds have earned world-wide renown...the battle-scented breezes from Bull Run, Edwards Ferry, Yorktown, Fair Oaks, Savage Station, Malvern Hill, Antietam, Fredericksburg, and the immortal field of Gettysburg have wafted your acclaim to the most distant climes...the seal of your blood was stamped upon twenty-odd battlefields...the blood of more than seven hundred of your companions has hallowed those fields, and more than two hundred and fifty of those heroes have passed from the smoke and clangor of battle to their eternal bivouac in the skies...may merciful Providence direct you and crown you here with earth's brightest honors...but however brilliant may be your future, your proudest boast will ever be, 'I belonged to the First Minnesota!'"

The speeches were all too much for Stephen. As the remnants of the regiment broke ranks with a mighty cheer, he sank to his knees and buried his face in his hands, bawling like a child, uninhibited in the raw emotion of the moment. He wept hysterically, the sobs crushing his lungs, forcing him to gasp for breath. Those who stood around him stepped back to give him room, while Sarah knelt beside him, trying to comfort him, speaking to him quietly, fighting back her own tears.

"Can I help, m'am?" asked a gentleman in the crowd.

"No, thank you. It was to be expected. This was his regiment, but we should not have come. There's nothing anyone can do for him, thank you."

The glory, the guilt and the ghosts had all come together and overwhelmed him, and when at last they were swallowed up in the joyous tumult around him he stretched out in the grass exhausted. Sarah wiped his face with her handkerchief, smiling confidently at him, offering her calm, her serenity, and her strength to lift his spirits. He could see the crowd now mingling with the honored heroes amidst a jubilant din. A profound sense of relief came over him as if the great burden he had carried for so long finally had been lifted.

"Are you feeling better?" Sarah asked.

"Yes," he said, sitting up.

"Shall we go?"

"Yes," he said, rising on one knee. "Let's go home."

They walked slowly to their carriage, him leaning heavily on his cane, she with a supporting arm around his waist. She helped him into the carriage and climbed into the driver's seat. As they rode along he said to her, "It's almost over, Sarah. It's almost over."

*   *   *

Stephen gave a lot of thought to his feelings about Sarah as his recuperation progressed. He thought about her as he exercised in the early morning by chopping firewood. He thought about her during his long afternoon walks. He thought about her at night as he lay in bed unable to sleep. There really had been no change in their relationship. She had always been kind to him, attentive to his needs, sympathetic to his situation no matter how distressed he might be. She was capable of sharing his joys and his successes as well as his grief and his disappointments. She was masterful at raising his spirits, a considerable talent given his many moods. Yet hers was not a puppy-dog devotion that thrived on occasional acts of kindness. On the contrary, he realized that she was a keenly independent young woman of no small stature in the community. She recently had been graduated with honors from the new Union School where she was acclaimed for her mastery of classical literature. She was extremely presentable with her rosy-cheeked freshness, her sparkling blue eyes and her soft brown hair. Though she had been somewhat awkward as a child, she had grown into a graceful and lovely young woman who carried herself with dignity and pride. He realized that he had developed a great admiration and a deep respect for her. They were feelings that he had not experienced with any other woman in his life. It could not be compared to his infatuation with Gaily Gladstone. And it was absolutely unlike his uninhibited passion for Grace Wells. It was unlike any emotion he'd ever felt toward a woman, and it exhilarated him. The more he thought about her, the harder he swung his axe.

"I see you're beginning to get some muscle into that swing."

He let the axe fall with a thud, the blade wedging into the oak chopping block. He left it there and went to greet his father, hand outstretched. Vincent took his hand, but instead of shaking it he turned it over and inspected it.

"Still have some toughening up to do," he said.

"It's just a blister. How are things in the camps?"

"No better than we anticipated, what with this dry weather. Most of the cut will never get to market, not this season anyway. The drought is the best argument yet for punching a rail line into the woods. With a rail line we could bring timber to the mill year 'round."

"When will that day come?"

"It's closer than you might imagine," Vincent said, wiping the dust from his sweaty face.

"You came down the river road, I see. Did you go by the Koenig place?"

"No sign of them. The house was empty. Looks like they've been gone awhile. I ran into one fellow who said they'd gone down to the city."

"I'd sure like to find them. They might need some help."

"If they came to town they might stop by the mill. Hard to tell. We'll put another notice in Whitcomb's paper. Most likely they're somewhere nearby."

*   *   *

Vincent parked the surrey in front of a new, three-story stone building on Bridge Square and proudly escorted Stephen into the lobby and onto a lift.

"Hang on," he said. "Up we go!"

With a great clanging of gears and the creaking of cables the elevator rose to the third floor where they got out.

"This is quite a contraption," Stephen marveled.

"Saves a lot of climbing," Vincent said modestly. "I like it up on the top floor. We rent out the first two floors."

Up and down the hallway each door bore the Shevley Company name. They went to the end of the hall and entered a door marked "Executive Offices." It opened into a suite of rooms and there behind a huge oak desk sat Roger Frasier.

"Well, the scion returns!" he said, rising and extending his hand. "Welcome back, Stephen. We saved a desk for you. Are you ready to go to work?"

"Slow down a bit," Vincent cautioned him. "Let him catch his breath."

"The elevator was supposed to save our breath," Roger said.

"It's the opulence of this place that took mine away," Stephen said. "This is quite a change from the mill office."

"It's quieter, too," Vincent explained. "Got so noisy at the mill we couldn't hear ourselves think."

"And it's more comfortable," said Roger. "That's a good thing, since I seem to spend the better part of my life here."

390

"That's his way of complaining about being over-worked," Vincent said. "But it's his own damned fault. He's taken it on himself, not at my bidding."

"Your father still spends a lot of time in the woods," Roger explained. "I believe he thinks the trees won't grow without his personal blessing."

"They grew all right this past winter, despite the dry weather. But most of the cut won't make it to town. Rivers are too low. Now, if we could push a rail line into the pineries..."

"That's another of his preoccupations," said Roger. "He got himself named to the board of directors of a railroad to see if he can convince them to lay a rail line to suit his personal convenience."

"For everyone's convenience," Vincent insisted. "We all stand to benefit from the railroads. A main line north to Duluth with spur lines into the harvest areas – why, we'd have year 'round operations independent of the weather. It'd be good for farmers, too, to get their crops to town. And the millers. It would revolutionize industry. It would revolutionize Minneapolis. We'd no longer have to depend totally on the river for transporting goods. The big railroaders are working on a line that'll stretch from coast to coast. A Minnesota line could run south to connect with the transcontinental line and carry our goods throughout the nation. The day will come, mark my words."

Stephen went to the window and looked out over the city, marveling at the growth that had occurred since his departure. Below him a covered farm wagon with a young boy at the reins made its way through the crowded street, but he did not see it.

"It's a sight to behold, isn't it!" Vincent exclaimed. "It's not just a mud-rut village anymore."

"No, indeed," Stephen agreed. "I was just thinking how it looked ten years ago when I first saw it – even before the mud ruts. I wonder where it all will end."

"It won't end! That's the beauty of it. Growth, pro-gress – it never ends. We'll see a mighty city here in our lifetime, a great metropolis to rival Chicago, Boston, New York. And even that won't be the end of it. It'll continue to grow. Our lumber will build it. Our money will finance it. Our spirit will drive it forward."

"You've never lost the dream, have you?" Stephen observed.

"No one loses a dream like that," said Vincent. "That's why I'm so glad to have you home again. It's a dream that needs sharing. It's too much for one man, too much for a hundred men. Every man can share in it, and a big piece of it is rightly yours – your right and your responsibility."

"Perhaps," Stephen said with a smile. "But first I'd like to see that railroad of yours."

"Let's drive over to St. Anthony station and watch the William Crooks pull in from St. Paul. Come on, or we'll miss it."

"Be careful, Stephen," Roger warned, "or he'll put you to work laying track – and I need you here in the office."

*   *   *

The boy at the reins of the farm wagon was happy to leave the congestion of the city. The air was fresh with the greening of spring and along the way the tilled soil lay open and waiting. Frau Koenig stole a glance at her last remaining son. How much like his father he was, and like his oldest brother, too, tall and handsome like them both, God rest their souls. Martin had grown up so fast, all too late. At fourteen he was strong and willing to work, but there were no older brothers now to train him. He had not learned the hard lessons of the land and she knew she could not teach him. He needed a man to teach him those things. She sighed and turned quickly away as Martin looked at her with a smile.

"You should smile," she thought. "I got a good price for the farm and the animals, enough to last until we can get settled again. First we'll find a small village. I can sew and the girls can keep house. And you, my last son, can hire out, learn to farm. Then we'll find a piece of land to homestead and start anew. We'll begin with a vegetable garden and a few chickens. You can hunt – at least August showed you how to hunt."

Though these were her thoughts, she did not share them with her children. They preferred the new language, and she spoke no English. She could not think in English, let alone express her thoughts. She turned away when they jabbered to one another in the new language. She refused to learn. It had been very lonely for her since John went away to war. He spoke German to her and was polite and respectful. If only he had come back to teach the younger children. But they told her he was dead, and so was brave little August, and there was no one to turn to, no one to run a farm or to teach the younger children. So they would move on, looking for some of their own people to talk to, to learn from. She had heard there were Germans in the river valley to the south. Martin could hire out; Anna and Lotte could find nice German boys from the old country. In the meantime they could do housework to earn a bit of money. But poor Hildy – at thirteen she was still too childish even to think of working or of meeting nice German boys. She had changed very little since the fever struck her. She had lost all of her hair and nearly gone blind. And now it was as if she would never grow older. But she was a good girl, a little child-like, but a good girl. She could stay at home and take care of her mother in her old age. Everything would be just fine once they were among their own kind.

The horses dipped their heads low and drank from the waters of the marsh. From the top of the hill it had looked like a meadow they could cross to reach the river. But now, standing up in the wagon Martin could see there was nothing but swampland between them and the river. He shook his head.

"We'll have to go back to the foot of the hill and follow the trail," he said. "If we take the wagon in there, we'll get stuck."

The setting sun had turned the surrounding hilltops to gold and a brisk breeze chilled the valley lowlands. The wind carried with it the aroma of new-cut hay. Somewhere upwind was a farm. He could smell it. As he pulled the horses away from the water he was startled by the sudden appearance of a horseman. He was dressed in black and wore a white shirt with a waxed collar. His broad-brimmed hat shadowed his features, and he was close upon them before Martin could see his kindly eyes and friendly smile. He looked him over, noting that the horseman's hands were smooth, his nails clean. He was not a farmer, Martin concluded.

"Good day, friends," the horseman said. "I see you're turning back. That's good. You can't get across the river this way. But upriver there's a ferry that will take you to Jordan."

"Thank you," said Martin. "How far is it to the next farm? It's getting late and my mother and sisters are tired."

"Not far," said the horseman. "Are you the man of the family?"

"I am," said Martin, drawing himself up to his full height.

"And where are you heading?"

"We heard there was a German settlement in this valley. My mother is anxious to find it. She misses the old country."

"You won't have any trouble finding German families in this valley," said the horseman. "There are many German families here."

Martin looked to his mother who beckoned him close and whispered to him.

"She wants to know if they're Lutherans or Catholics," he said.

"Both!" said the horseman with a laugh. "Just what kind of Germans were you looking for?"

"Lutherans," said Martin, smiling sheepishly. "But I don't think it makes much difference."

"You will find what you're looking on both sides of the river. Keep to the trail. You'll find a farm before dark.

Tell them Judge Chatfield sent you 'round. They'll welcome you."

"Thank you, sir," said Martin.

"Good luck, son."

The horseman went his way down river, and Martin guided his team upriver along the trail. Just before dark he saw a farmhouse and stopped the wagon.

"Hand me my boots," he said.

The girls stood up and stretched their stiffened muscles while Martin pulled on his boots.

"I hope they've got a loft full of hay," said Lotte. "I am so tired."

"I'm hungry," said Hildy.

"Be quick, Marty," said Anna. "It's growing dark, and we can't knock on a stranger's door after dark."

There was a different scent on the breeze now. Frau Koenig sniffed the air and smiled. Somewhere nearby cabbage was boiling. The familiar odor was a comfort to her. It would be good to be among their own kind again.

Chapter 24

There were good omens on the winds of autumn in 1864. Lincoln had found a general to lead the Union armies, and the forces under Robert E. Lee were being pressed on all fronts. Grant was hounding the rebels through Virginia and laying siege to Richmond. Sherman had cut a devastating swath through Georgia, and put Atlanta to the torch. The war seemed to be grinding to an end.

It was a bright season for Stephen, too, a time of renewed vigor and enthusiasm, a period of gain and accomplishment. If the war had left its mark on him it was indiscernible to the casual observer. Only infrequently did the horrors of battle intrude upon his dreams, disrupting his peace of mind and leaving him trembling, stammering, and in a sweat. But he was no longer alone; he had Sarah to confide in. Her love and understanding helped him come to grips with his mental scars. There were happy thoughts now to brighten the shadowy corners of his mind, pleasant dreams to replace the nightmares that had haunted his darkest hours.

As he regained his health and more importantly his self-confidence – thanks to the tutelage of Roger Frasier with whom he worked elbow to elbow – he developed a very different outlook toward his father's world of lumbering, railroads, business enterprises and all such manifestations of progress. Not only did he feel ready to assume his duties and responsibilities as heir to Shevley Lumber Company, he began to feel it was time to settle down.

"What do you mean, settle down?" Roger asked.

"You know, a place of my own, a wife, children."

"Doesn't that usually require a partner of the fairer sex?"

"I suppose it does," he said as if realizing it for the first time.

"Ah, ha! You've been keeping something from me. Who is the lucky young lady?"

"I – I haven't given it much thought yet."

"Well, I suggest that you do. I can't help but feel you're a bit naïve when it comes to women. Does your father know?"

"No, and don't you breathe a word of this. I've still got a few details to work out."

"My lips are sealed," Roger promised with a wry smile. "Just take your time and think things through. It's a decision that shouldn't be made in haste."

The only certainty, in Stephen's way of thinking, was that the time was right. The prospect of being master of Shevley House with a fond wife at his side to offer love and companionship and children was quite attractive to him. He was not getting any younger. He was nearly twenty-six years old and wrinkles were forming about his eyes, and an occasional gray hair was to be found in his brush. Sarah had been the first to notice these small changes, and had teased him about aging. Dear Sarah, he had been fond of her ever since she was a little girl. He could still see her perched atop a pile of luggage on the day she and her mother arrived at Shevley House. The events of the intervening years had brought them ever closer together until at last they were now as close as two young people could be without tumbling headlong into some romantic entanglement. She had been everything to him: loving sister, tender nurse, understanding confidante, spiritual guide. She had snatched him from a state of living death and led him into the sunshine of life. She was more than a sister and a friend, she...

"Sarah," he said somberly, "it's time we thought of marriage."

"I beg your pardon?"

"I think we ought to get married."

"Stephen!" she exclaimed. "What in the world are you saying?"

"I'm saying that we ought to be married."

"To one another?"

"Of course."

"You're taking a great deal for granted, aren't you?"

"I'm sorry if I offended you. You seem angry."

"Who said I was angry? I didn't say I was angry," she said, growing angry.

"Yes, you are."

"I *will* be angry, if you persist in telling me how I feel."

"Somehow I didn't expect it to be this way," he said, obviously disappointed.

"That's precisely my thought," she said with a frown.

"Then I've gone about this badly."

"On that we can agree. You don't ask a girl to marry without any warning, any preparation. We have been inseparable for months on end, and you've never once given me cause to believe we were anything but friends."

"But it just came to me."

"You see?" she asked, kicking angrily at the dried leaves as they walked. "You just take me for granted, and a girl does not want to be taken for granted." She stormed away along the edge of the pond, then knelt down and looked at her reflection in the smooth surface of the water. Suddenly his face appeared above hers, and she ran her hand through the water to erase the image.

"I'm sorry, Stephen. This is not what I expected either. It's all so sudden. I think we should take time to think about it. We're such good friends, as you say, but what you propose is quite beyond friendship. Marriage would mean great adjustments. It will require a lot of thought. I couldn't possibly give you an answer right away."

"But you will think it over?" he asked.

"Yes, of course I will."

She took him by the hand and they strolled around the pond and through the oak grove toward home. He could not fathom her mood. Did she mean yes, she would marry him, but not now? Or did she mean no, not under any circumstance? At last it came to him: He *indeed* had taken her for granted and had injured her pride. He stopped and forced her to look at him.

"I've been thick-headed and insensitive, Sarah, and I'm sorry."

"Don't be," she said sincerely. "You said what you had to say. I suppose that's better than mooning over someone and never saying anything. You're direct and to the point, and I suppose that's a man's way. But I dreamed of something quite different. I guess all girls do. I can't deny that I'm flattered by your proposal, but we both must consider it carefully, discuss it at length. We must tell our parents, naturally. Have you thought about what they might say? Have you thought about how it might affect them? Have you thought about how it will change things in Shevley House?"

He knew she was right. He had run roughshod over her emotions in his selfishness. He had been a fool – but she had not rejected him. He must remain steadfast and be patient. First he would discuss it with his father. Surely his advice would be helpful.

"You what!" Vincent exploded.

"I've asked Sarah Carpenter to marry me," he repeated.

"Little Sarah?"

"Sarah is eighteen years old, and she's no longer little."

"Undoubtedly she turned you down."

"No. She's agreed to think about it."

"Ah, a girl of good sense. Too bad you didn't think about it before you asked her. Can you imagine what it would mean, marrying a servant?"

"I don't think Sarah planned to be a servant all her life."

"But a servant in your own home? And her mother a servant here, too. Can't you imagine the problems it would create?"

"I imagine all young people face certain problems when they marry."

Vincent, his elbows on his desk, buried his face in his hands.

"Things will never be the same," he said. "You've disrupted the peace of this household."

"I fail to see..."

"Then you must be blind. Consider the possibilities: If she rejects you, then you're both left in untenable positions. How could either of you live in this house after such an embarrassment? Or if she accepts your proposal, what then? She could no longer be treated as a servant. And if she remains under this roof after your engagement, how could decorum be maintained? My presence here, and her mother's, only makes the situation more bizarre. How could your prospective mother-in-law remain as housekeeper? Where would she go? What would she do? What would *I* do?"

"There are problems I hadn't foreseen," Stephen said, rising from his chair and going to the window to look out over the oak grove. "But no problem is insurmountable."

"Well, don't come up with some romantic solution involving me. I have no intention of getting married again, and certainly not to Mrs. Carpenter."

"No, of course not." As he spoke he watched the autumn winds tug at the last leaves of summer. Across the brilliant blue sky small fluffs of clouds raced about like children at play. It would be a good afternoon for a walk with Sarah, a time to sort things out.

*   *   *

Sarah spoke softly, hoping to set the tone of her mother's response. They were alone in the house, enclosed in the kitchen along with the rich, spicy aroma of pumpkin pies baking in the oven. The pots and pans and mixing bowls had been washed and put away and the counters cleared and scrubbed. Dinner chores were an hour or more away and there was time to relax over a cup of tea.

"Stephen is so proud of his accomplishments," she said. "He really seems to enjoy his work."

"He's grown up now. The army did it. The army and the war did it. It changed him. It made a man of him."

"Or it could have been the years, the passage of time. He's twenty-five years old, you know."

"And high time he was getting married and settling down," said her mother, who knew instantly that she had said the wrong thing. A frown of apprehension clouded her face, and Sarah was delighted with the opportunity the slip provided.

"His thoughts exactly," she said. "He's indicated his desire for a wife and a family." She let the words flow slowly, softly, watching her mother's expression. When she saw that she was growing tense, she reached for her hand. As their fingers touched she got quietly to the point. "He has suggested that we – he and I – might make a happy marriage together, because we have been such good friends for so many years."

As she stroked her mother's hand she saw her face grow somber. She was nodding her head as if reluctantly accepting the inevitable.

"I told him it was an idea worth exploring," Sarah continued. "But I did nothing to encourage him, mother, nothing. We realize there are many obstacles to overcome, many things that need careful consideration. I promised only that I would think about his proposal. I told him I'd discuss it with you and that we could talk more about it later. Of course I want to hear your views, or I couldn't possibly reach a decision."

"Oh, God," her mother cried, tears brimming in her eyes. "Tell him yes. No, tell him no, it's impossible. Oh, Sarah, I was afraid this would happen. I don't know what you should tell him. I just don't know. Don't listen to me. Listen to your heart."

"Not now, mother. This isn't the time to listen to my heart. It's time to carefully consider everything that's involved in such a decision."

"But I know how you feel..."

"Naturally I'm fond of him. He's been like an older brother to me for so many years. We are truly good friends. But I fear that our closeness may work to our disadvantage. Because of it I was shocked by his proposal, shocked and afraid. I feared that he only asked me to marry him out of a sense of duty. I did nurse him back to health, but I don't want him to think he owes me anything. You don't marry someone out of gratitude. As for me, I could be reacting to the same influence. It would be safe and quite convenient for me to accept his offer. There are obvious advantages to marrying a wealthy young man."

"Sarah, you wouldn't," her mother exclaimed.

"No, I wouldn't marry any man for his money, but the fact is that's what people would say. We'd have to deal with that. Poor servant girl marries her master for his money. It would be practical, wouldn't it, and I've always been practical. But in this case I want to be more than practical. I also want to be emotional, romantic. I want to be courted like a princess, wooed with promises of everlasting love. I want what every other girl wants. And ours has never been that sort of relationship. I want him to marry me because he's madly in love with me, and I don't know that he is."

"Then it's time to find out, child, time for a proper courtship. And how can a proper courtship take place when you both live under the same roof?"

"My thoughts exactly. That's why I've decided to move out."

"You can't! Where would you go? What would you do?"

"I've had long experience as a live-in maid. I'll seek a position in a respectable home, asking only my room and board and a small stipend so I might put away something for my dowry. I'll do nothing rash. I'll take my time. I won't be rushed into marriage. I shall have the love and the romance I've dreamed about. And if Stephen wants to share that dream, he'll have to court me as any other man might."

"Oh, Sarah, you're a brave one, you are, talkin' like that. It's easy to say such things while you're sittin' here in a cozy kitchen with a pantry full of food behind you and a warm bed just down the hall. But when you leave Shevley House, you'll leave the only home you've ever known."

"That's true, mother. And then we shall see who's ready for marriage and the duties of family life. It will be a test both for Stephen and for me."

*   *   *

As Dr. George Ames' practice grew, so did his wealth and his influence in the community. In keeping with his soaring fortunes he built a fine home on Second Street that quickly became the meeting place for men of destiny – political aspirants, financial leaders, would-be king-makers and social trend-setters. Over dinner in his home took place the intrigues and the strategy sessions that were to shape the future of the city and the state. It was George Ames who set the bones, delivered the babies, and cured the fevers of the families responsible for the railroads, the university, the art galleries, the theaters, the hospitals, the water mains, the streets, the parks and the schools. His was the role Vincent Shevley once had dreamed of playing until his domestic problems made it all but impossible. But there was no jealousy between them. Vincent focused on business matters, the doctor on his practice and his social status. Their friendship remained firm. Thus the Ameses were shocked when Sarah came to them looking for work.

"Good heavens!" Amanda Ames exclaimed. "Vincent would never hear of it."

"Oh, I'm sure he'd be agreeable. With the top floor closed off now, and as little entertaining as he does, I know I'll not be missed."

"For shame, Sarah. You must know how fond he is of both you and your mother. He'd be lost without you."

"I will appeal to his business sense," said Sarah resolutely. "The fact is that I am an employee with very little to do. I barely earn my keep."

"That's nonsense. He credits you with saving Stephen's life."

"That's far-fetched. In his condition he needed help and I provided it. It was as simple as that. Now that he's

403

well, I long to exert my independence. Mr. Vincent Shevley will vouch for me. I am a conscientious worker and a good cook. And I eat modestly. My mother has been a serving woman all her life, and she has taught me well."

"My dear girl, you needn't go on like that. We're well aware of your capabilities. It's Vincent we would be concerned about. If he agrees that this would be a good thing, then we can come to some arrangement. We have a cook, of course, a housekeeper and a coachman. But I could use a personal maid and we could become good friends – all contingent on Vincent's approval, of course."

"I would be forever grateful," Sarah said excitedly. "I'll speak to him tonight and ask his blessing. And thank you, thank you so much." Impulsively, she gave Amanda Ames a hug just as Doctor Ames' carriage pulled up in front. He was accosted as soon as he came into the parlor.

"George, I have wonderful news for you. Sarah may be coming to work for us."

"Yes, I know. How very nice that will be."

"What do you mean, you know?" she asked.

"Oh, I had lunch with Vincent today. He told me Sarah might be stopping by. Welcome, Sarah. We look forward to your becoming a part of this household."

*　　*　　*

For the first time since Stephen's return from the war the four occupants of Shevley House sat down for dinner at the kitchen table. Informal dinners in the kitchen had become routine after Eleanor's death to spare Vincent the loneliness of dining alone, although he frequently preferred having his dinner with friends at the Nicollet House downtown. As usual, his presence at the table unsettled Mrs. Carpenter, who considered it improper to break bread with the master of the house. She was constantly leaping up to fetch this or that and between times nibbled self-consciously at her supper as if it really didn't belong to her and she feared getting caught sampling even the tiniest morsel. At last Sarah demanded that

404

her mother cease her fluttering about and sit quietly to listen to what she had to say.

"First of all," she began, "let us all understand that Stephen has asked me to marry him and that I have not as yet given him my answer."

"Sarah..."

"Hush, Stephen. Let me finish. One of the reasons I can't give him an immediate answer is that we're all too close here. It was fine when we were servant and master, but now it's as if we're in limbo. Our closeness has become oppressive for all of us. I can't think clearly under such circumstances, and therefore I've decided to leave."

"But you can't!" Stephen interrupted. "Where would you go?"

"Be quiet and let her finish," said Vincent, pleased that the topic at last was open to discussion.

"Thank you, sir. I knew I could count on your support. I shall, with your permission, leave on Monday to take up my duties as personal maid in the home of Dr. and Mrs. George Ames on Second Street."

"Good old George," Vincent beamed.

"That's ridiculous," Stephen exclaimed. "We can work this out without..."

"We could have worked out nothing under the present circumstances," Sarah said. "We both need time to think this through and the privacy to think it through clearly."

"You didn't have to hire out as a maid," said Stephen.

"And why not? That's what I am. I see nothing wrong with serving in a respectable home employed by kind and generous people."

"It would be much simpler if I moved out. I'll take a room at the Nicollet House. It's close to the office and you wouldn't have to demean yourself merely to get away from me."

"I'm not demeaning myself," she said sharply. "I resent the implication."

"That's just a man's wounded pride you hear," said Vincent. "Don't make a fool of yourself, Stephen. There's no need for you to move; this is your home."

"Exactly," Sarah said triumphantly. "I'm glad we agree that my solution is best for everyone."

Unable to restrain herself any longer, Mrs. Carpenter stood stiffly erect, her eyes looking straight ahead, and announced in a quavering voice, "I'm going, too. I'm going home to Chicago to visit my sisters. I just can't stand this any more. I'm going home!"

She then dissolved into tears and raced down the back hall to her room and slammed the door. The others sat stunned for a moment. Then Vincent pounded his fist on the table hard enough to make the flatware jump.

"See what you've done?" he said to Stephen. "You've driven poor Mrs. Carpenter to tears. I warned you this would happen."

"It's entirely unnecessary," Stephen stormed back at him. "I don't know why this can't be settled without all this..."

"Without all this shouting," Sarah interjected quietly but firmly. "It never helps to shout. If my mother has been driven to taking a well-deserved vacation, I say it's about time. She's talked about such a trip for years, but I never thought she'd really do it." She got up then, smiling smugly at the two men. "When you get over those long faces you might offer mother some encouragement, unless you feel she doesn't deserve a vacation."

"Of course she does," Vincent blustered. "I'll insist upon it. I had no idea the dear woman wanted to see her sisters, or I'd have seen to it long ago. I'll get train tickets for her tomorrow. That ought to be encouragement enough for anyone."

"Mrs. Carpenter doesn't need encouragement, I do," muttered Stephen. "How did this all begin anyway?"

"Don't tell me you've forgotten already," Sarah teased. "Men are such fickle creatures."

*   *   *

The third floor had been closed since Eleanor's death, and now the dining room was also sealed to cut the winter drafts. The two men ate in the kitchen, although this meant only breakfast and an occasional supper. Both father and son ate out a lot, since neither excelled at cooking nor relished the chore. Simply as a matter of self-preservation Stephen took it upon himself to prepare their meals. Vincent would have been content to work half a day on a cup of rancid coffee, but Stephen's morning appetite was strong. His father was indifferent to food so early in the day, but always ate whatever Stephen put in front of him and was properly grateful that he wasn't required to do any more than that. However, after several weeks the kitchen began to overflow with unwashed pots, pans and dishes, and the table had become a collection place for all sorts of items, including old newspapers and even a hand axe that had been used to split kindling for the cook stove.

"We ought to hire someone to clean up this mess," Vincent said one morning when he found Stephen standing helplessly in front of a pile of dirty dishes.

"We'll have to do something," Stephen said. "There's nothing left, unless we get out the fine china."

"Maybe we could ask Sarah to drop in once a week to look after things."

"No. We'd never hear the end of it. We'll find someone else, maybe put a notice in the paper."

"I'll talk to Whitcomb today at lunch," said Vincent. "Let's get the horse hitched up. We'll drop off the laundry on the way downtown, then get breakfast at Louie's on Washington Avenue."

*　　*　　*

Martin's shoulders ached and his fingers were numb with fatigue. He shook them as he walked from the barn to their small cabin, too tired to look where he was going, following the well-worn path in a daze of exhaustion. Since dawn he'd been swinging the Armstrong reaper, cutting and cradling an acre or more of wheat. Now he wanted only to take a few bites of food and go to sleep. Halfway to the cabin he was brought up short by the rich aroma of fresh baked bread. Over the hill he could see the top of the main house with smoke billowing from both of its chimneys. He cursed and spat and continued on his way. The women would be coming home late from the main house where they had spent the day cooking and baking for the wedding on Sunday. No one would be home to cook for him. He'd have to fend for himself. Inside the cabin Lotte's wedding dress hung from a hook in the ceiling and the floor below it was cluttered with pins and snippets of material. His mother's shears lay across the footstool along with her measuring tape and a piece of chalk. He stepped carefully around the dress and opened the cupboard and took out a loaf of bread. From the cooler he took some bacon left over from breakfast and made a sandwich, washing it down with water that he dipped from the pail. Then he lit the wick in the lard dish and stretched out on his bed to watch the wedding dress twist slowly on the hook, first one way, then the other. Lotte would be the first to marry, he mused, while Anna would mope around for weeks complaining that she was destined for spinsterhood. He smiled fondly. Anna would get over it. She was the prettier of the two, but Lotte – well, Lotte had a twinkle in her eye that a man finds intriguing. Anna was too serious, too stern and forbidding around men. Lotte was more open and friendly, even out-spoken at times. She was a match for any man, a good companion. It did not surprise him that she was the first to find a husband. And young Adolph Hespen-dorff was a good catch, the last of old Herman Hespendorff's eight children to marry. He was twenty-three years old and not bad looking at all for the hard-working farmer that he was. He was red-faced and bright-eyed, with a shock of black hair and a big stomach that testified to his love of good beer and rich food. Anna had been old Frau Hespendorff's favorite, but Adolph did his own choosing, and he chose Lotte. She could make him happy. She could drink a mug of beer with him and laugh at his jokes and carry on at times just like the men, and Adolph liked that in a woman. He had a lust for living and he wanted a wife to share it. After all, any woman could share hard work and sorrow and drudgery. It took a special kind of woman to do all that and share the joys of life, too. On the minister's visit three months ago Adolph had made all the arrangements and only then did he propose to Lotte almost as an afterthought, it seemed. And now the last Hespendorff son was to marry a daughter of the hired family, a perky young girl he'd first seen only a year ago as she swung on a rope in the hayloft.

It had been a good year, he thought as he dozed in the darkening room. The shadows of evening had filled the corners of the cabin and crept close around the flickering wick of the lard lamp. There'd be more room soon, he thought, with only Anna and his mother to share the cabin. Lotte and Adolph were building their own place a mile or so down the road, and Little Hildy had long since moved into the main house to help kindly old Frau Hespendorff with the cleaning and the cooking. Maybe he'd even build on a room for himself come winter, Martin thought. Things would be better for them all, once they were part of the first family of the valley. There might even be a piece of land in it for him someday. He liked farming and old man Hespendorff was getting on in years.

As he dozed he could hear laughter and loud voices echoing down from the main house. More of the womenfolk had gathered to help with the wedding preparations. Tomorrow there would be others and on Sunday all the family and their friends would be here, and the crowd would spill out into the yard and the tables would be laden with food and kegs of beer and there would be music in the air. But tomorrow would be just another workday for him, swinging the reaper and stacking the grain, and he needed his rest. He did not hear the women come home or feel his mother's hand upon his brow as she covered him with a warm quilt. Nor did he hear Lotte's excited giggling and chatter. He was exhausted and he slept soundly.

Chapter 25

The snows returned with a vengeance that winter of 1864-65, accompanied by high winds and bitter cold temperatures. Snowdrifts blocked the entrances to store fronts around Bridge Square and brought travel to a near standstill in downtown Minneapolis and throughout the state. The railroad tracks that linked the city with the state Capitol in St. Paul were closed. Horse drawn sleighs and snowshoes were the only practical means of transportation for many days. The weather influenced every facet of existence, including Stephen's courtship of Sarah Carpenter. She was free on Wednesday evenings and on Sunday afternoons, and Stephen was promptly at her side on those occasions. On Sundays they rode through the white wonderland along the river, with sleigh bells jingling and the crisp fresh air clouded only by the vapors of the trotting horses. They were bundled to their noses in furs and woolens and with caps pulled snugly down over their ears so that only their eyes showed through to marvel at the beauty of the snow-encrusted countryside. On Wednesday evenings they sat in the Ames' kitchen while Sarah served tea and they spoke of how they were faring in their new circumstances.

"My father and I are surviving," Stephen said. "We hired a cleaning woman to come in on Saturdays, but it's not the same. It's not like it was when we were all together."

"It's not supposed to be the same. Those were unusual circumstances that are gone forever. You do understand that, don't you?"

"I do, but it's difficult, Sarah. How we miss you and your dear mother. What have you heard from her?"

"She's very happy. Her sister is retired and has her own flat, thanks to a generous bequest from her long-time employer. She had everything but companionship, and with mother there her joy is complete. Mother feels very guilty, leaving me alone here. She wants me join her in Chicago."

"Surely you're not going, are you?"

"I couldn't, not now. I'm saving every penny so I'll have some sort of dowry when I marry. A girl must have a dowry if she expects to attract a suitor," she said mischievously.

"You're only saying that to entice me. Why can't we get married now? This is such a waste of precious time, sitting here in someone else's kitchen, when we should have our own."

"You'd be happy to have me in your kitchen, wouldn't you – washing dishes, cooking meals, a slave to domesticity."

"You know very well what I mean."

"I do, but I still think it's much too soon. I've never enjoyed more than a fleeting conversation with any young man other than you. I want to be sure in my own heart, as you must be in yours."

"What chance do you have, closeted here with the Ameses?"

"I do get out, after all. I shop several times a week. The butcher boy is quite taken with me, and just yesterday I met a former classmate of mine at the dry goods store where he's a clerk. His name is Joshua Wheelock, and he asked me to go for a sleigh ride with him on Sunday."

"But you're riding with me on Sunday!"

"I am not," Sarah countered. "Since you hadn't asked me, I felt free to accept Joshua's invitation."

"You'd go riding with a clerk?"

"Why not? Don't be such a snob, Stephen. If it would make you any happier, his father is a partner in the store."

"I don't really care about young Wheelock's position in life. The important point is that I always go riding with you on Sundays, and I think it was reasonable to expect to do so again this Sunday."

"And it was equally reasonable to expect you to ask me – which you failed to do. You do not own me, Stephen."

"I don't presume to own you."

"You presumed too much nevertheless."

"Well, by George!"

"Stephen, let's not argue, please. I'll tell you frankly that I'm thrilled at the prospect of enjoying some time with a friend from school. I look forward to seeing him on Sunday, just as I looked forward to seeing you tonight. There's nothing wrong with that, and nothing you can say will make me feel guilty about it. I'm flattered that someone else has shown an interest in me. If it would make you feel any better, why don't you invite another young lady to go riding? There must be dozens around town who'd be delighted to go for a ride with you."

"I don't know any other young ladies! I can't just go up and down the streets extending invitations to perfect strangers."

"Temper, temper. You're beginning to sound very much like your father."

"Well, we can't have that, can we? I'll have to take my bad temper home and hope that I haven't spoiled your evening."

Sarah shook her head helplessly and smiled.

"You're not spoiling my evening, Stephen, but you are spoiling your own. Please don't go away angry."

"Why shouldn't I be angry?"

"Because no one has asked me to go riding a week from Sunday."

"Oh, for God's sake, Sarah!"

"No one has – yet."

"All right, will you do me the honor of riding with me one week from Sunday?"

"I would be thrilled to accept your kind invitation, Mr. Shevley. Thank you so much for asking me."

"Sarah, you're such a tease. How could I go away angry when you're wearing that impish smile?"

She got his overcoat from the front hall closet and helped him on with it. He donned his fur hat and his heavy mittens and brushed his lips gently against her cheek.

"I love you, Sarah," he whispered.

Her eyes were shining, her face radiant with happiness, but all she said was, "Good night, Stephen."

"You're getting the romantic courtship you wanted, aren't you," he said, squeezing her hand, "complete with a lover's quarrel. Good night, my dear Sarah, good night."

*　　*　　*

Ben McAlpine had gone to Mille Lac to winter with his wife and her tribe, but by January he was back in town with his daughter, Marie. It was Vincent's first thought that the woodsman's wife had died, or that the winter had become too severe for life in a home of branches, bark and deerskin. Neither was the case, however. Ben sat uncomfortably in Vincent's well-heated office, sweat pouring down his brow.

"I've come to find a place for the girl," he said.

"Too cold for her in the woods?" Vincent asked.

"No."

Vincent stuffed his pipe and lit it slowly to allow Ben time in his Indian fashion to come to the point of his visit.

"A lot of snow this season," he said, exhaling a cloud of sweet-smelling smoke.

"A lot of snow," Ben agreed.

"You came a long way on snowshoes."

"We did."

"It must be important to you. Where is the girl?"

"Out in the hall. She's good on the trail, strong like her mother."

"Is her mother well?"

"She is well."

"And you look well."

"I am."

"And the girl, is she well?"

"She is. But she is no longer a girl. She has become a woman," Ben said self-consciously.

Vincent nodded in understanding. "The years pass quickly," he said.

"The young bucks know," Ben explained. "They know she is a woman now, and they hang around like

413

wolves. They prize her for her blue eyes. They want to buy her from me."

"So you brought her to town."

"I want more for her than Indian babies. Marie is different."

"She is your daughter, Ben. That alone sets her apart."

Ben's steel-blue eyes seemed to look right through Vincent, as if to read his thoughts.

"She speaks her mother's tongue as well as mine. She can fish and cook in the Indian ways. She is quiet and obedient. She is strong, and her mind is quick. She could be taught to read and write. I would like that. It would please me to know that she could read and write. I would be willing to pay."

"There are the church schools," Vincent suggested.

"No," he said simply. "I came to you."

Vincent considered the possibilities. She could keep house for him. She could learn to cook on a wood stove. He could have a tutor in to educate her. It would cost very little. He presented his thoughts to Ben.

"I have plenty of money," Ben said. "I'd pay."

Vincent nodded his head in agreement. Ben had plenty in the bank. Like all the early settlers he had claimed land and then sold it. If the truth were known, this grimy and odiferous old woodsman was a very wealthy man. Ben's gaze was steady; he saw that his request was being favorably considered.

"If you let me take her into my home, she could work and pay her own way. She could keep house, and I would see that she was properly fed, clothed and educated."

"Your women are gone?"

"Yes."

"Then I will accept your offer."

"Are you sure you want her to be like a white woman, and not like a squaw?"

"Yes. Her people won't like it, but that's what I want."

"Then that's the way it will be. Tell her to come in and we'll get acquainted."

Marie stepped silently into the room and stood with her head bowed shyly. She was a handsome girl, unusually attractive for one with Indian blood. Her hair was jet black and her skin was light, unlike the pureblooded Ojibway. Her eyes were blue, large and sensual, a white woman's eyes. They were deep-set above her high cheekbones, giving them a natural shadow, dark and mysterious. Her nose was like her father's, straight, not flat like her mother's. She was of medium height, her clothes layered and wrapped around her against the cold so it was impossible to see if she were thin or fat. She was shod in fur-trimmed moccasins and leather leggings. Over her shoulders she clutched a buffalo robe, which she allowed to hang loosely about her shoulders. Despite her shyness, there was an eagerness about her as if she might at any moment burst into happy chatter. Her eyes flicked from Vincent to her father as she waited for them to speak.

"One thing," Ben said at last. "She speaks too well at times. She has to be reminded to keep silent. I have told her that she will learn through her eyes and ears, not through her mouth. But she is a good girl, and will be a good woman once she is educated. Someday when I come here to the falls to live, I'll take her off your hands and she can look after me in my old age."

Vincent looked him over carefully, thinking it would not be long before that day came. Ben's copper-colored hair was turning gray, and the joints of his fingers were swollen.

"Where will you go now," he asked.

"Back to Mille Lac."

"Back to your squaw."

"Yes, she is growing old, too. In the winter it takes two to keep a hut warm. I have to get back."

"The day will come when Marie will want a man."

"Yes. But after she lives in town for a few years, she won't want an Indian, and no white man will want her because of her Indian blood."

"When that day comes she'll need a father's guidance."

"I won't be far away. I'll visit her. I will leave money for her food and clothes. I want her to have the right clothes. I want to be proud of her, just as if she were a son."

"I'm sure she'll make you proud, Ben. We'll do everything we can for her, you can depend on it."

*	*	*

Stephen was surprised by this sudden turn of events, but quick to see its possibilities. Marie's appearance on the scene would solve the domestic problems at Shevley House, and her education would bring Sarah back to serve as Marie's tutor.

"The poor, dear girl," she exclaimed when Stephen dropped by to tell her the news. "She'll need looking after. Where is she now?"

"At the house. Father took her there as soon as Ben left. She's in your old room."

"She's all alone in Shevley House? In my room that's been closed all these weeks? Why, she'll be frightened to death! I'll see if I can get away for an hour or so to help settle her in and make her feel welcome."

"There's a lot more you can do, if you're willing. Ben wants her educated, and my father wants you to be her tutor. He says she's a bright girl and speaks some English."

"I would love to. But first I'll ask Mrs. Ames if I can get away for an hour or so this afternoon."

They found Marie huddled in a corner of Sarah's former room with her buffalo robe wrapped around her against the cold. There was tinder and kindling under the pot-bellied stove, and sulfur matches on the table next to the oil lamp.

"Let's get a fire going. It's chilly in here," said Stephen. Sarah went directly to the girl, raised her up gently and led her to a chair. She sat down tentatively, staring at Stephen.

416

"You remember me, don't you, Marie?" he asked as he lit the fire. "I visited you and your family a few years ago."

The girl nodded, giving him a shy smile.

"Since you two know each other, perhaps you'd introduce me," said Sarah.

"Marie, this is Sarah. She's come to help you get settled. This was once her room."

The girl said nothing, but her expression revealed her fear.

"Don't be frightened, Marie," Sarah said. "It's your room now. We only want to make you comfortable. But first we must warm the room. It has been closed off for quite a while."

Stephen got the fire going, then gathered up Marie's buffalo robe from the floor, while Sarah admired the elaborate beadwork on her buckskin dress. In no time at all the two young women were engaged in a lively conversation. Sarah called out to Stephen as he headed for the back porch with the buffalo robe.

"Put some water on to heat, please, and get the copper tub from the porch. We're going to have a lesson in bathing, and then we're going to find a proper dress for Marie to wear for dinner."

He built up the fire in the kitchen stove and put several kettles of water on to heat, then carried in the copper bathtub before going into the parlor to wait. When he returned an hour later he found them chatting like old friends, picking through a collection of Sarah's out-grown dresses. They paid no attention to him, so he returned to the parlor to reflect on the wondrous way in which Sarah took people into her heart.

She also was eager to take charge of Marie's education. She got permission from Amanda Ames to spend two hours each afternoon at Shevley House to begin Marie's lessons and to help her begin the evening meal for Stephen and his father. She was back on Second Street by five to help Mrs. Ames dress for dinner. Stephen saw even less of her during this period, since she had insisted on giving up her Wednesday evenings off to compensate for her sessions with Marie.

"I'm not sure I approve of the new and independent Sarah Carpenter," he complained. "We seem to be seeing even less of each other than before."

"I should think you'd prefer an independent woman to a docile housemaid. Or perhaps the latter is more appealing to you."

"Ah ha! That's a thought. I could wait until Marie comes of age. She would do my bidding with never a complaint."

"You're a wretched man, Stephen Shevley," Sarah laughed. "Don't let Marie hear you talking that way even in jest. She's as fond of you as I was at her age, and she's completely guileless and trusting. You could very easily break her heart."

"I'd never take advantage of her; you know that."

"I'm sure you wouldn't, but I don't think you realize that she has quite a crush on you."

"If only you felt the same way. You know that I love you, Sarah. I've been diligent in my courtship, constant in my devotion – what else can I do to win you over?"

"You could kiss me," she said.

He took her hands and looked longingly into her eyes, then drew her close to him and kissed her passionately. He was certain that she shared that moment of pleasure, but when he looked into her eyes he saw only an enigmatic smile.

"I will wait a lifetime, if I must," he said resolutely.

"It won't be that long, Stephen. When I can profess my love for you with the same certainty, without any reservations, without the shadow of a doubt – then I'll accept your proposal."

"I hope it will be soon," he said.

*　　*　　*

Sarah encouraged Marie to use copies of The Frontiersman to practice her reading skills, which were greatly improved by the time spring arrived. She was reading the paper at the table one evening when Stephen came into the kitchen.

"I don't understand this word," she said, pointing to a large black headline across the top of the page. "Let's me see," he said, looking over her shoulder. "Assassination – it means a killing"

"It must have been an important killing," she said innocently, awed by the size of the letters that spelled out the word.

"Very important, Marie. It's the story of the assassination of Abraham Lincoln, the president of the United States."

"I see his name here," she said, pointing. "I saw it before when I read about General Lee surrendering to General Grant. Does the killing of Mister Lincoln mean the war will start all over again?"

"We should pray that it does not," he said.

"I don't understand. The warriors of the south surrendered, but they killed their enemy's chief anyway. That's not fair."

"Indeed it's not."

"Then why don't you make war again and kill General Lee?"

"Because war is a terrible thing, Marie."

"Then it's good that it's over?"

"Yes, it was a long and costly war."

"Sarah said you were a brave soldier."

"No braver than anyone else."

"Does your enemy's land belong to you now?"

"No. We weren't fighting over land."

"Then I don't understand why you fought in the war."

"Many of us who fought don't understand either," he said. "But I knew one man who did, a man who died to protect his land, a small farm."

"Then his spirit must be happy."

"Yes, I suppose his spirit is happy, even though his family left the farm and moved away."

"Where did they go?" she asked.

"I don't know," Stephen said, reaching inside his shirt and pulling out the silver buckles from John Koenig's boots. "These buckles belonged to that man. I promised to give them to his mother, if I can find her."

"You will find her," she said, taking a thong from around her own neck and revealing a flat stone she wore concealed next to her heart. He recognized it immediately.

"It's the gift I gave you many years ago," he said with surprise.

"And it led me here where I found you," she said intently.

"No, it was only chance that brought you here," he said.

"Maybe, but it was the stone that led the way. If you hold these," she said seriously, pointing to the silver buckles, "they'll lead you to your friend's mother."

"I hope so," he said, smiling indulgently at the child's faith. He told Roger the story several months later as they dined at the Nicollet House.

"So the stone you gave her has become her talisman. She believes it has magical powers. If I were you, I'd watch my step."

"She's only a child. It's simply innocent nonsense."

"Not to her. She's obviously a mystic. I repeat, be careful."

"There's nothing to fear. She knows that Sarah and I hope to marry soon. She'd never do anything to hurt Sarah."

"I know nothing about Indian culture," Roger said, "but I've heard that they sometimes share their wives with visitors as a matter of courtesy. If that's true, she might see nothing wrong in a dalliance with you despite her regard for Sarah. Perhaps she even believes in polygamy. By the way, have you and Sarah set a date?"

"No, but I haven't given up hope. Her mother's due home soon, you know. I think Sarah's been waiting for her to return before making up her mind. I'll stop by on the way home to see her. Never say die, as the saying goes."

*   *   *

It was a sultry July night, the air stagnant and heavy with moisture. The sky had been filled with swirling black clouds all day, but no rain had fallen. Crickets chirped loudly in the darkness and in the distance a barn owl hooted eerily. As he walked down the street he could hear the hushed voices of people on their front porches seeking relief from the heat. He could hear the creak of rocking chairs and porch swings. He could see a shadowy figure on the Ameses's porch as he approached the house. He paused on the walkway, not wishing to startle the person standing there.

"Is that you, Stephen?" Sarah whispered.

"Yes. Why are all the lanterns out?"

"Because it's too hot to light them, and they would only attract mosquitoes."

He climbed the steps and felt his way along the railing until he reached her side.

"It's after ten o'clock, and people are still up."

"It's too hot to sleep," she said. "Where have you been?"

"I had dinner with Roger. I'm on my way home."

"It's a beautiful night despite the heat. Look how the clouds float so gracefully over the face of the moon."

As she leaned forward to watch the clouds her hair brushed his cheek and the scent of her was sweet and inviting. It sent a thrill of anticipation through him. He took her hand and she squeezed his fingers gently. In a moment she was in his arms and he kissed her. As she looked up into his face he could see that her eyes glittered in the moonlight. They were filled with innocence and wonder and he felt suddenly ashamed.

"I have no right to make love to you this way," he whispered, holding her close. "You should send me away."

"I don't want to send you away. I'm lonely and I want you here."

"I would stay by your side forever, if you'd give me the chance. Marry me, Sarah, and we'll never be lonely again."

"I will Stephen, I will marry you. I love you."

Her sudden acceptance stunned him momentarily.

"Sarah," he exclaimed, "I'm delighted! When shall the wedding be?"

"In the fall when it's cool at last and the leaves are brilliant and colorful, the air crisp and clean. Fall is my favorite season of the year. It's a rich, comfortable, happy season, a time of fulfillment, the perfect time for a wedding."

He kissed her gently, restraining his excitement. Then he held her away from him and looked into her eyes. They were moist with tears of joy and she wore a broad smile.

"The fall will be our season of fulfillment, indeed, my dear. But why...how...?"

"I know it took me a long time to make up my mind, but it just had to happen. It was nothing you did, or maybe it was everything you did. I don't know. But I do know that I love you, though I can't tell you why. I think love just needs time to grow. It has grown, and I am sure now that I want to be married you."

"I'll never question your love, Sarah. You've explained it very well, and I think it's wonderful."

He kissed her again, long and longingly, and in the distance the barn owl's call wafted through the night air, and the crickets sang, and in his heart Stephen knew the greatest happiness he had ever known.

*   *   *

Anna Koenig burst into the cabin muttering to herself. Martin looked up from his supper, admonishing her with a frown.

"I don't care," she insisted in a loud whisper. "I'm sick of it all. I'm sick to death of being the poor relation, bowing and scraping to that Hespendorff family. I am treated like a servant in my own sister's home."

"How is Lotte? Has she had her baby yet?"

"Of course not. I would have told you if she had."

"Sh-h-h-h-h-h! Mother's sleeping."

"Look at her, poor soul. She's so pale and weak. After a lifetime of hardship she has nothing but a rope bed in this hovel that she can't even call her own. Oh, Martin, what's to become of us? Will we all go to a pauper's grave?"

"Hush. Sit down and eat some supper. Put your cares behind you. There's work to be done, and complaining will not turn the soil or harvest the crops. It will only make those tasks more difficult. Eat now, and go to bed."

Anna nibbled half-heartedly at the cornbread and sausage, and cabbage with stewed tomatoes. She was a pretty woman, but lines of stress were beginning to form around her eyes. She brushed some loose strands of hair from her face, and her eyes glossed over with tears.

"Stop that," her brother whispered. "Save your tears. You'll need them soon. You know mother is dying."

"If only it weren't in this drafty old cabin," Anna cried. "It's not fair. Why should she have to suffer like this?"

"Maybe when she's gone we should move on," Martin said. "There's no future for us here."

"Where would we go, what would we do?" Anna asked plaintively. "If only our brothers were here. How different it would be if they hadn't gone off to war. We could have kept the farm. We could be prosperous and happy now."

"I've done the best I could," Martin said softly, his pride wounded. "Mother knew I wasn't ready yet, but she was right to move on. I've learned a lot here. I'm ready now to make my own way, if only..."

"I didn't mean to fault you, Martin. There was nothing you could have done. Our luck is bound to change."

Their mother's moan interrupted them. Her eyes were open, but they saw only into the past. Her words came haltingly.

"I can feel the baby. It's time, Johannes, it's time. Come to me, Johannes. Bring little John with you. It's time. I pray it's another son for you. The pain, Johannes, the pain. Oh, it's a boy! Thank the good Lord it's a boy!"

Anna, weeping, knelt beside her and grasped her hand.

"Mother, oh, Mother!" she cried.

Martin laid his hand on her shoulder and spoke softly.

"She's gone, Anna. She's at peace."

Chapter 26

A mutual dependency developed between Sarah and Marie, a dependency that led to a strong friendship. Marie needed a patient and understanding guide as she learned the ways of a strange new society. Sarah needed another young woman to share her excitement over her impending marriage and the changes it would bring about in Shevley House. In no time they became as close as sisters.

"Some things will remain the same," Sarah told Marie. "Your room will be as it is now, as will Mr. Shevley's bedroom on the second floor. We'll not do anything with Stephen's room until we know what my mother decides to do. On the third floor, Stephen and I will use the large bedroom, with one of the guest rooms becoming the nursery in the event we have children."

"The third floor bedroom has been closed for a long time," Marie noted.

"Yes, it has. But I don't think that will pose a problem."

"It was *her* room," Marie said ominously. "It is never opened."

"Poor Mrs. Shevley – I doubt she would have approved. It's as if a ghost were enclosed inside. What a shame. It's a beautiful room with a wonderful view of the gardens. For too long now it has served only to keep her things collected, things that no one ever sees. It's like a shrine that's never visited. I'm sure she wouldn't want it that way. I believe she would want us to pull back the drapes, fling open the windows and let in the sunshine and fresh air."

"We'd better ask Mr. Shevley first," Marie advised solemnly.

"Dear Marie, you are so loyal. I know how he cautioned you to stay away from that room, but things are different now. He wants Stephen and I to live here, and there's no other way but to open Eleanor's room."

Their conversation was interrupted by the sound of the front door closing.

"Stephen, is that you? You're home so early. Is your father with you?"

"He'll be along soon. Ben's in town to discuss plans for the winter harvest. Where are you?"

"Up here on the third floor. Marie and I are discussing a few changes I have in mind."

"Ah, here you are," he said, panting from his run up the stairway two steps at a time. He caught a glimpse of Marie as she disappeared down the back stairs at the end of the hall. "I was going to tell Marie that her father will be with us for dinner."

"She'll be delighted. Unless I miss my guess, she's probably run downstairs to change into a prettier dress."

"Now what changes do you have in mind?"

"I think the third floor should be for us, but Marie fears your father might disapprove."

"Nonsense, unless he wants to give us his room, and I'm sure he wouldn't do that." He tried the door to his mother's bedroom, but it was locked. "We'll have to get the key from him."

"You don't think he'll mind?"

"Of course not! This old pile of stones is going to be a home again at last. A real home with love and sunshine – and children. The rear guestroom will make a perfect nursery. And the guest rooms across the hall will be for our children to share as they grow older." In his enthusiasm he grasped her around the waist, lifted her high in the air and twirled around as if on a dance floor.

"Stephen, put me down! This is a serious matter."

"What is?"

"Your mother's old room. It doesn't disturb you?"

"At one time it would have," he said soberly. "But I've learned to live with my past. There are no ghosts lingering in my yesterdays, not now. A wonderful woman brought sunshine into my life and all the dark memories vanished in her glow. And that's just what we'll do with mother's room. Let the sunshine in to chase the shadows away. It will be our room, filled with our love and happiness."

"My sentiments exactly. But I'm still concerned about your father."

"He won't object," Stephen said with certainty.

"There's one sure way to find out. We'll ask him. But right now I should get down to the kitchen to help Marie prepare for dinner. She'll want it to be special with her father here."

*   *   *

Ben McAlpine stood before them in his newfound sartorial elegance. He wore a new wool suit of yellow and green plaid set off by a bright blue satin vest. His shirt and collar were stiffly starched and adorned with a startling orange cravat held in place with a diamond stickpin. His flowing locks had been trimmed and brushed until what little remained of their original copper tones glistened like rare metal in a bed of gray ore. Though his hands had become twisted by disease, he stood proudly erect, his piercing blue eyes lively and youthful. The hint of a smile came to his face as he allowed them to admire his new clothes.

"Ben's thinking about retiring," Vincent said, "and figured it was time to get some store-bought clothes."

"I wanted to look good for my daughter," Ben explained shyly.

"Marie!" Vincent bellowed. "Come in here. Your dad has something to show you."

She came into the room slowly, but with an unmistakable eagerness shining in her eyes. She gasped and held her hand to her mouth when she saw her father in his new finery. Then she spoke to him in her native language.

"What did she say, Ben?" Stephen asked.

"She likes my city clothes, but warns me that her mother won't."

427

They all laughed, and Ben gave a nod to Marie and she quickly returned to the kitchen.

"Where will you live once you leave Mille Lac," Stephen asked.

"Near the mill," he said simply.

"He could live just about any place he chooses," said Vincent. "He holds title to property going 'way back to the squatter days. He's a rich man, no matter how you slice it."

Ben took this as a cue. He reached inside his coat pocket and withdrew an official looking paper.

"This is for you and your woman," he said, handing the paper to Stephen.

"Thanks, Ben. What's this...say, this is a deed."

"In honor of your wedding," Ben explained simply.

Stephen adjusted the paper carefully and studied the map that accompanied it. "Say, this looks like the Benson property. You remember it Sarah; it's where the Callaghan family used to live."

"The land's adjacent to ours," Vincent explained. "Ben's owned it for years. Rented it out to the Bensons, and then to the Callaghans. It's empty now, and Ben wants you two to have it."

"But what about the Callaghans?" Stephen asked his father.

"They moved on not long after their boy died in the war."

"I'm sorry to hear that. But thank you, Ben. We're very grateful. It's such a generous gift."

"It'll be worth something some day," Ben acknowledged. "The city's moving this way. You'll be able to get your price for it."

"Thank you so much, Mr. McAlpine," Sarah said. "Such a thoughtful gift. We are very grateful."

"It's a small gift. Your gift of schooling for Marie is much greater," said the old woodsman.

"I suppose we could even fix up the old house on the property and live in it," Stephen mused.

"No you won't," said Vincent. "This is your home. This is where you should live. That's why I built this place, to pass it on to you. I'll move into that old house, if you don't want me here."

"Of course we want you here," Sarah interjected. "We've been talking about that very thing. I was thinking that Stephen and I could use the big bedroom on the third floor."

"Great idea!" Vincent exclaimed. "I'll have Marie clean it up tomorrow. Your mother would be happy to know it's being used again, Stephen. And you just tell me what you need to make it comfortable, and I'll get it for you. Yes, yes," he exulted, "it's high time that room saw the light of day again."

*   *   *

Somewhere in the dim past Mathilda Carpenter recalled being raised as a Catholic. But over the years she had drifted away from the church and developed a new faith based on hard work, loyalty, and a trust that God would care for the honest toiler no matter what path they followed to heaven. Sarah had shared her mother's faith until she went to live with Doctor and Mrs. Ames. They had taken her to Sunday services at Gethsemane parish where she was baptized and eventually confirmed her faith through the auspices of the Protestant Episcopal Church. The rector, the Rev. David B. Knickerbacker, was a personable man who warmly welcomed Sarah into the mysteries of the faith. She attended services regularly in the church at Fifth Street and Seventh Avenue in the midst of a prosperous and quite pleasant neighborhood. She approached her religion with characteristic enthusiasm, and lured Stephen to services on occasion by suggesting it might make her more available later in the day for a buggy ride or a picnic. Stephen, however, did not take readily to religion. He had seen too much of the world's evils to easily accept the concept of a benevolent God. He found it impossible to accept the idea that man, in all his wretchedness, could ever have been created in God's image. He had no problem accepting God as creator of the world – how else, after all, could the world be explained? But he felt it exceedingly presumptuous to believe in a personal deity to whom one spoke when in need of a good harvest, a passing grade in school, or a lucrative business deal. He also was filled with a mistrust of orthodoxy, for hadn't it led to various disasters throughout history as Protestants fought Catholics, and Christians fought Muslims, while Buddha sat passively on the sidelines as if to condone such carnage.

Therefore Stephen was always vaguely uncomfortable in church, and at no time more uncomfortable than the present moment as he stood at the foot of the altar looking out over the congregation assembled to witness his marriage vows. It helped, naturally, to search the pews for friendly faces. Ben McAlpine was there in his outlandishly colorful suit, seated next to his exotically beautiful daughter. And his father was there, lending a fresh handkerchief to Mathilda Carpenter to dab away her tears. Charles Whitcomb was there in his dual role as guest and reporter, seated next to Amanda Ames whose husband stood poised in the narthex with Sarah on his arm, awaiting the musical cue that would propel them down the aisle. His only comfort came in the presence of Roger Frasier, who stood stalwartly at his side as best man, ring at the ready.

Suddenly the music, long redolent with quiet religiosity, burst forth with the strains of the bridal chorus from Richard Wagner's Lohengrin. The assemblage arose and turned to watch the beaming bride float gracefully down the aisle in a gown of white satin while clinging to the arm of a rather frightened looking George Ames. The proxy father guided his charge to within inches of the groom and gently turned her over to him. As their fingers touched Stephen could hear a loud sob in the front row where Mrs. Carpenter sat. Sarah's delicate hand was warm and moist in his as they turned to face the priest.

"Dearly beloved..."

Stephen's recalled little of the ceremony, feeling in retrospect that he was merely a confused bystander. Not that he didn't respond loudly and clearly to the simple questions the priest put to him, but they were given by rote and seemed to him hollow and monotonous. He remembered clearly that Roger stood calmly at his side throughout the service. And he would never forget the piercing eyes of the Most Rev. David E. Knickerbacker – not the whole priest, just two hypnotic, disembodied eyes that held him fast in a spell while the rhythm of the service enveloped him like morning mist from a meadow as it gave up its dew to the first rays of the sun. When the priest's eyes finally released him and he pronounced them man and wife, Stephen lifted Sarah's veil and discovered that this young woman, whom he had known since childhood, had been transformed into a radiant beauty. It was as if the goodness of her soul had suddenly manifested itself in every facet of her physical being and now shown forth brilliantly, dazzling him. As their lips brushed lightly together a thrill passed through him such as he had never before experienced. He stood transfixed until the exultant opening chord of Felix Mendelssohn's wedding march filled the church. They strode rapidly up the aisle to the tempo of the music oblivious to the clamor of good wishes and good cheer that lined their way. In the vestibule they stopped and in an instant she was in his arms and he kissed her fervently. When he drew back to look into her face he saw that her miraculous beauty was still there.

"Let's go home," he said.

*   *   *

"I don't mean to belabor the point," said Roger, "but this is an excellent beginning. You are the man of the hour, and I am proud to call you my friend."

"If I've earned your favor, then all must truly be well. Where is my wife? How I love the sound of that word."

"Stability," Roger went on. "It was all you lacked, and now you have it at last. You've proven yourself over and

431

over again in every phase of your life, and now you have achieved the force that binds it all together – stability, your crowning achievement."

"If that means you'll keep me on the payroll, then I'm pleased beyond measure. But really I must find Sarah. Who can be monopolizing her time this way?"

Then he saw her across the room, veil thrown back with abandon, smiling as the sun smiles on an adoring world, surrounded by a bevy of admiring ladies, young and old, chattering happily. He could not interrupt her joy. For a moment, just a moment, he had time to catch his breath, to accept a fresh glass of champagne. Then he, too, was surrounded by well wishers. When one group dissolved, another formed until the crisp October afternoon eased into dusk. Mrs. Carpenter, composed at last, had assumed her duties as hostess in the familiar surroundings of Shevley House, taking charge just like in the old days. Stephen finally caught up with her in the kitchen where he found her elbow-deep in dishwater.

"What are you doing?" he asked.

"Just cleanin' up a bit."

"But your hostess duties – you're neglecting your guests."

"They're not my guests, they're yours and Sarah's, and I think it's just wonderful. I still can't believe this has happened. I have to pinch myself to see that I'm not dreamin'. I've never seen Sarah so happy."

"If she is only half as happy as I am, she must be in heaven."

"I pray your happiness lasts forever," she said, drying her hands on her apron. Stephen gently embraced her as her tears began to flow. He kissed her lightly on the forehead and thought how sad it was that his own mother could not be there to enjoy his happiness – and then he began to get teary too. They were both daubing at their eyes when Vincent stomped into the kitchen roaring.

"What's this? Mathilda Carpenter in tears? Crying has no place in this house, only tears of joy, d'ya hear?

There's music in the parlor and they're dancing in the front hall. Take my arm, my lady, and let us show the young folks how it's done. Come along and leave that apron behind. Revelry awaits us!"

As he ushered her toward the door he turned to his son with an anxious frown.

"Get on upstairs and get your clothes changed," he said. "Roger's loaded your luggage aboard the surrey, and the horse is ready and waiting. Get along now. Sarah's about to toss her bouquet, and then she'll go up to change. You're not spending your wedding night at this party – this party is for us!"

With that they waltzed down the hallway as music filled Shevley House.

*   *   *

They changed their clothes shyly in their bedroom, he in elegant black, she in rich blue satin. When they were ready he offered her his arm and together they descended the staircase to the cheers of the happy throng. The ladies showered them with rice, and the gentlemen shouted "God speed" and they left the party and raced through the night to the Nicollet House where a bridal suite awaited them. They dined by candlelight alone in the crowded dining room, discovering each other at last, finding everything new, fresh, wondrous and enthralling. When their lips fell silent their eyes continued to commune, their fingers touching and their hearts beating in unison. When they arose to leave the table, the room grew silent and dozens of heads turned to follow them out the door. They left behind them happy diners who found it impossible not to share their love.

*   *   *

Lotte Hespendorff rejected the cup of coffee disdainfully.

433

"It does awful things to your innards, you know, or so Adolf tells me. But he never drinks anything but beer, so how would he know?"

Her lusty laughter filled the small cabin and she struck her knee with a resounding slap. She was ruddy and well fed and her eyes sparkled with the happiness of a good and comfortable life. Her brother smiled nervously, watching his infant nephews clambering over the rude furniture, threatening to tip over everything their pudgy little bodies came near. He wondered at his sister's fertility, for it was obvious that she was carrying another child. Her first two, just a year apart, seemed to be growing up without discipline of any sort. Martin ruminated on the prospect of a river valley filled with rich, incorrigible Hespendorffs, and he cringed.

"Henry, get away from that table. You're going to spill everything onto the floor," Lotte admonished her oldest child. The baby was seated on the earth floor, suspiciously picking at a cold potato, his knees black from crawling about. His attention was fixed for the moment on the edible treasure his Aunt Anna had given him in a desperate attempt to save her rustic home from destruction. Anna held her breath as her sister spoke.

"I've convinced Adolph that you should have the land and the cabin to do with as you like. Forty acres of good soil, plus a little timber. Take it or leave it, he says."

She winked broadly to ease the blow that the threat represented to her brother. He did not smile.

"A quarter of a section is enough to feed us, but a man can't prosper on it," he said. "Our prospects would be limited."

"At the moment you have no prospects, Martin. Don't look a gift horse in the mouth. Be grateful that old man Hespendorff has taken an interest in you. He worries that you will not find a wife down here by the river. He thinks you ought to marry. There are people in town who think you and Anna are husband and wife. That doesn't do much for your prospects, nor Anna's."

Anna blushed, furious at the implications of her sister's comment. Martin gently but firmly removed a piece of kindling wood from young Henry Hespendorff's hand. The toddler was using it to pound on the iron stove with deafening effect.

"We are pleased that your husband and his father are concerned about us," he said. "Only last spring old Herman himself told me how wonderful the farmland was in the Dakota Territory, almost inviting me to leave the land. Now he wants to give me forty acres and a cabin. Is it because we have become an embarrassment to him – or to your Adolf? Are we thought of as poor relations?"

"Don't speak that way, Martin," said Anna.

"Hush," said Martin. "Ask instead what they propose for you. Maybe they've found a husband for you."

"I will not listen..."

"Nothing of the kind," said Lotte. "A job is being offered to you, Anna, an honest job. The Hespendorff's want you to run the hotel in town. You could live there and manage the place and take thirty percent of the profits, if there are any!" She laughed again, her loud, piercing shriek that irritated them so and widened the gap between them. "It's like my Adolf says, we take care of our own. You'll still be free to marry, Anna, and you'll find your chances much better in Fair Prairie. No man even knows you exist out here, hidden away like this. You may meet some nice drummer coming through town. At least you'll be doing something useful."

Anna could not stand the embarrassment any longer. She arose angrily and snatched the dipper away from the ubiquitous Henry Hespendorff who was pouring water on his baby brother's head.

"I resent the implication that I do not lead a useful life," she said evenly. "I make a good home for my brother, as comfortable a home as our circumstances permit. And if I do not have a husband yet, it may be because I choose not to throw myself at every man I meet. I will accept the offer of your husband's father to run his hotel, but only that I might not stand in my brother's way. Once I am gone, he will be free to move west, out of reach of these people. But be sure that I will not consider myself on display in the hotel like a pastry in the bakery shop. I am not chattel to be bought and sold. I merely have the misfortune to be a poor woman with no dowry. The Hespendorff's may own Fair Prairie and most of the farmland around it, but they do not own me. I want you to make that clear to them all, do you understand?"

Lotte, stunned by the outburst and unfamiliar with the reciprocal anger that stirred within her turned as usual to bawdy good humor to fend off the attack.

"It seems to me that at twenty-four you'll soon be running out of years, and if you're inclined to land a man, a hotel is as good a place as any to be so inclined."

Her shriek of laughter caused both her siblings to shudder. When it had subsided she picked up her infant child in one arm, grabbed the toddler by the other, and made for the door.

"Borrow whatever you need from the big barn, Martin. This is your farm now, so make something of it. And next time you're out mending fences pay some mind to neighbor Nyquist's place. He has a daughter, you know. I saw her in town the other day and she's a brassy young thing who might put some spark into your life. Not bad looking, either, for a Norwegian. Don't get up. I can turn a wagon around. Bye, bye!"

*   *   *

"It's a pretty poor piece of land, all right," said the Nyquist girl.

Although Martin took pride in the grubby plot, he took no offense at her remark. She had an accent strange to him, a lilting cadence to her speech that matched her broad smile, her chubby cheeks and her devilish eyes. It would be difficult to be angry with this happy cherub.

"I'm going to move to a better place some day," he said. "I'll get a bigger spread somewhere out west."

She leaned back, her hands grasping the fence rail, and tilted her face skyward, taking a deep breath of the crisp fall air. She was very young but full-breasted and pretty in a Nordic sort of way with her blond hair and ruddy cheeks.

"I like the smell of it here," she said. "It's clean and fresh, not like the city."

"You lived in the city?" he asked in disbelief.

"Do you think I grew up here with the hollyhocks?"

"Why, your old man's been a farmer all his life!" Martin exclaimed gleefully, thinking he had her in a trap.

"You think old man Nyquist's my pa, don't you."

"Isn't he?"

"He ain't. He ain't even my uncle."

"Then how does he come by you?"

"The Nyquists took me in after the Sioux killed my folks. The soldiers brought me to his place and they just took me in, him and his wife, because they could understand me. They had no kids of their own, you see, so they took me in. I've been with them ever since."

"I'll be damned."

"It's true. The Indians killed my folks, they really did."

"I'm sorry."

"I guess I am, too. They had a nice farm down by Birch Coulee. It's all gone, I hear – burned to the ground."

There was no bitterness in her voice. It had all been so long ago when she was a toddler.

"We had our own place, too," Martin said. "It was up north on the Rum River. We sold it and paid off the mortgage after my older brothers got themselves killed in the war. I was too young then to farm it alone with just my sisters and my mother – she died, you know."

"I heard the Nyquists say so. Are the Hespendorffs your kin?"

"Sort of. My sister married one of 'em."

"I don't hear much good about them around my house."

"I 'spose not. But I can't complain. They set me up on this," he said, gesturing to the slopes that ran down the hill to the river bottoms.

"Pretty poor piece of land if you ain't a goat," she said.

"My sister runs the hotel in town," he said, trying to recover from the insult.

"The married one?"

"No, the other one."

"We wondered about her," she said, her voice heavy with suggestion.

"She's really my sister," he said defensively. "Used to keep house for me and my mother. She lives at the hotel now."

"And you live here all alone."

"Yes."

"Well, if that cabin looks as bad inside as it does outside, it must be a mess, with no woman around to keep it."

She leaned back again to sniff the air and thrust out her chest. She was very pleased with her breasts and wanted him to notice them. He did.

"I guess you never saw a cabin look so bad," he said, trying not to stare at her voluptuous figure. "I wouldn't want you to look in there until I'd cleaned it up a bit."

"Say, what do you mean by that? I wasn't invitin' myself in, if that's what you think. What kind of girl do you think I am, anyway?"

Martin blushed purple and wanted to turn and run, but there was no way he could move; his feet were rooted to the spot. He wanted to die, just to shrivel up and die. She saw that she had embarrassed him half to death and moved in for the kill.

"Now if you'd come around and ask to see me, why old man Nyquist just might let you in. He's a reasonable sort."

"Maybe I'll do just that."

"So, you plan to come courtin' then?"

He chuckled nervously, uncertain whether she was teasing him or was just as guileless as she seemed. In either case she was a formidable young woman and she fascinated him with her sparkling laughter, her outrageous statements, and her robust figure.

"I guess I do," he said.

"Does that mean you're lookin' for a wife?"

"I guess I am," he said, determined not to let her audacity rattle him. "I just might come courtin' one of these days."

She laughed with delight and the valley rang with her unbridled joy. It reminded him of Lotte's laughter when she was a little girl, and it lifted his spirits. It was good to hear happy laughter again, for it had been a long, long time.

Chapter 27

They had intended to get up in time for services at Gethsemane, but they didn't. Stephen carefully lifted his watch from the nightstand so as not to awaken Sarah. It was nine o'clock. He was groggy from a deep, untroubled sleep, the sleep of the innocent. It was another miracle of their love, the way Sarah's innocence enveloped them both. It was as if he had never known a woman before. Shyly, eagerly they had come together in the darkness to experience the wonder of love for the first time. What they shared then was new and good, and nothing that had gone before mattered. She had never asked, and he had never told her. As she lay next to him in the bridal bed he studied the beauty of her face and he knew that nothing he might have done would have made any difference. Their love was a beginning. In its goodness it erased the past. He was reborn in the glory of her love, and in her trust he became absolved of any transgressions. Sarah stirred and as her arm touched his she sprang immediately awake.

"Good morning," he whispered.

She nestled her head on his shoulder and said, "I'm glad it was as it was."

"What in the world does that mean?" he laughed.

"It means that everything was perfect, just as it should be. I feel much better now about the past few years. I've often felt guilty about things, you know – about making you wait so long."

"You had no reason to feel guilty. Events have proved you right. And I agree, everything was perfect."

He turned slightly toward her, a shift that exposed the long gray scar across his chest. Her finger traced the length of that numb, lifeless mass of hardened flesh.

"I haven't seen this for a long time," she said. "I'd forgotten it."

"When did you ever see it?" he asked in surprise.

"When you first came home from the war. It was I who bathed and dressed you after all."

"I'd forgotten – if I ever was aware of it."

"Why Stephen, you're blushing. You were so strange then, so far away and lost. There were times when we despaired of ever reaching you."

"It was your love that reached me, Sarah. Your love and your caring heart. That's how I knew that I wanted to be with you the rest of my life."

He kissed her and held her close.

"That's so sweet, Stephen. You make me gloriously happy."

"I want to make you happy every day of your life. Our lives will be happy, I just know it. Even though there may be bumps along the road, our love will get us over those rough spots."

He held her even closer as if to keep the thrill of love from ever escaping his grasp. It was nearly noon when he awakened and looked at his watch again.

*   *   *

Sarah had always wanted to understand Stephen's love of the woodlands, so when they planned their wedding trip she had rejected more exotic excursions and asked instead that they go into the pineries, roughing it wherever necessary. No inconvenience or outright hardship could dissuade her. They traveled by train and by wagon, on horseback and by canoe. At times they went on foot in order to experience the cathedral-like calm of the woods. They slept on the ground and endured the bone-chilling cold of autumn that warned that winter was just around the corner. Then, with their food running low, they headed back to the Rum River to their canoe, and downstream to their wagon. As they trundled down the tote road toward the rail line they passed by the site of the Koenig farm, where Stephen paused to silently reminisce.

"You have a promise to keep," she reminded him.

"I know," he said. "I haven't forgotten." He could feel the chill of the silver buckles against his chest.

On the train back to Minneapolis they recounted their adventures and vowed to return each fall to recapture the peace and solitude they had known in the pineries. But by summer Sarah was uncertain whether she could undertake such a journey in the fall.

"We're going to have a baby," she said.

Stephen was elated and profoundly moved by the news. Sarah's announcement was delivered almost apologetically, noting that it undoubtedly would mean changing their anniversary plans. But Stephen didn't care. He was awed by the significance of their pregnancy. It seemed to tie them both into the master plan of the Universe, knitting them firmly into the human fabric that stretched from the very beginnings of time to the present day. It gave them hope for man's only real grasp of immortality. Strange, he thought, how an event of such animal simplicity could give rise to an almost religious experience. It made them kin to all who had gone before, from peasants to princes, from sages to simpletons, from kin to kings. They now could claim their place in the vast panorama of history. The blood of centuries that ran in their veins had given life now to a new generation. Humanity was assured of one more leaf in the genealogical book of history – their leaf. He wondered if his own father had felt this same glimmering of immortality when he learned of his son's impending birth.

"Well, I don't know about that," Vincent said after listening to Stephen's exuberant profundities. "But I know I'm mighty happy for you two. I'll tell you it's a great satisfaction to know that another generation is coming along to carry on our name and the work you've started. What'll you name him?"

"We haven't gotten quite that far yet," Sarah said.

"Well, it doesn't make any difference. Marie!" Vincent shouted. "Fetch a bottle of brandy from the sideboard. We've got some celebrating to do."

Later in the privacy of their bedroom Sarah could not help but laugh.

"Have either of you even considered that our baby might be a girl? It is possible, you know. Not all babies are boys."

"I guess that's true," Stephen acknowledged with a smile. "And how glad I am of that. Men are really so helpless and insignificant at a time like this, and so vain. As one of the stronger gender, one who'll bear the pain and the glory, you'll have to forgive us our conceit."

"I will, my dear husband, if you will give me the option of presenting you with a daughter."

"You could will it to happen, I do believe. I have that much faith in your powers. I've seen the miracles you have worked."

It would have taken more than a miracle to save the child. In the fourth month of her pregnancy Sarah took to her bed in great pain and in a few hours began to hemorrhage. Marie and Mrs. Carpenter did their best to care for her while Stephen raced across town to summon Doctor Ames. He arrived in time to save Sarah, but it was too late to save the fetus. Stephen was heart-broken and hid his face as Marie brushed by him with the grisly burden.

"Why? Why?" he cried, falling on his knees at Sarah's bedside.

"Easy, lad," said the doctor. "Don't try to speak to her, not now. She's very weak and needs her rest. She's lost a lot of blood, and it will take time for her to recover."

Stephen took her hand in his and pressed it to his lips. It was warm and limp, but she gave his hand a little squeeze to let him know she understood his pain. When he looked up her eyes were closed and tears ran down her pallid cheeks.

"Oh God, Sarah, don't cry," he said softly, and for a time they wept together, saying nothing as their sorrow spent itself and she slept at last. He arose and went to the burial plot where his mother lay and prepared a tiny grave. Then he rode slowly into town to find the Rev. Mr. Knickerbacker.

Sarah lay abed for nearly a month under her mother's care, gradually growing stronger. Her ordeal had left her skin colorless and her eyes had lost their sparkle, ringed as they were with dark circles. Her first steps were cautious, halting. She made her way to the gabled windows and looked down on the gardens and to the knoll above where a small mound of earth could be seen next to Eleanor Shevley's resting place. She closed her eyes and silently prayed for the soul of the unborn child. Opening the window she took a deep breath of fresh air. It carried with it the first faint scent of the coming spring with its promise of new life. She inhaled deeply and felt the stirrings of renewed vigor. Marie was coming up the drive from a shopping trip and Sarah waved to her. In a moment the front door was flung open and Marie raced up the stairs to her.

"Are you all right!" she asked breathlessly.

"I'm fine, Marie, just fine. Isn't it a beautiful day?"

The next day she had Marie remove the cot from the bedroom, the cot where Stephen had slept each night since the miscarriage. The windows were opened and fresh linens were put on the bed, while all evidence of Sarah's recuperation were removed from the room. She was seated comfortably in the parlor when Stephen came home from work.

"Sarah! What are you doing here? You should be in bed."

"I'll never get my strength back lying in bed," she said. "I had hoped you'd be pleased to see me up."

"Oh, I am, my darling. But it takes time to build up strength. I'm only afraid you might do yourself harm by moving about too soon. You should consult Doctor Ames in such matters."

"His last advice was to do whatever I feel I can do, that only I truly know my limits. And the fact is that I felt just fine today, and I was so anxious to be up and around again. I feel so useless. The world is moving on without me, and I want to be a part of it again."

With this she arose carefully from her chair and stood proudly erect. Her courage and determination touched him and he came to her and took her gently in his arms.

"You're a brave and wonderful woman, Sarah." He kissed her and then looked into her eyes. "The truth is that I've looked forward to this moment for weeks. I just don't want you to suffer a setback by trying to do too much. It's painful to see you suffer."

"Nonsense, Stephen. My suffering was no more than many women endure. Doctor Ames told me that many women are unsuccessful with their first child. It's not their fault; it's just nature's way of testing them to be sure they're fit to bear a child, he said. So it's all for the best. I'm stronger now, and gaining strength every day. It's time for me to begin my life again."

*   *   *

Vincent had gone into the pineries to get the spring drive underway. The mill saws were idle in quiet anticipation, but over them hung an air of expectancy as mechanics readied the machinery to receive the winter's cut. Stephen took time off from his own duties to spend every possible moment with Sarah. They strolled together in the oak grove and rode to Lake of the Isles to picnic on a carpet of spring flowers. They seldom visited the family plot where the small mound of earth marked the resting place of their lost child. Sarah had rejected the idea of a headstone, as if the life that had never come into the world had never really existed. It was not a callous decision; she accepted it as God's will. If the Creator had meant for that new life to become a fully viable human being, an infant that could respond to their love, then surely He would have willed it so. Since He had not, she would not question His wisdom. Stephen concurred, not out of religious conviction, but in deference to Sarah's wishes. He did, however, consult with Doctor Ames.

"Women have a sense about these things," the doctor told him. "If she feels ready to conceive again, then we have to take her word for it. Have no fear, Stephen. She knows better than either of us. She's growing stronger, and if she wants to try again, so be it."

By July Sarah knew she was pregnant again, and the doctor confirmed it. But by fall she was suffering wretchedly from morning sickness. Doctor Ames insisted that the her pregnancy was going well, despite her misery, and there was no reason to expect anything but a normal delivery. With those assurances Stephen ordered work to begin on converting a guest bedroom into a nursery. He stayed close by during the weeks of Sarah's indisposition, and when moving about the house became difficult for her he brought out the wheelchair he had used when he returned from the war. To her mother, who had moved into Shevley House to help her daughter, Sarah confided that her late term pains had become a cause for concern. Doctor Ames tried to put her fears at rest.

"You're not a field hand, Sarah," he told her. "You are a delicate woman – healthy, but delicate. You feel pain deeply, but there's no reason to suspect a problem. The important thing is to get all the rest you can and let nature take its course."

In the latter weeks, Stephen could see the fear in Sarah's eyes, though she tried her best to conceal it. Even Doctor Ames began showing some concern. Finally, after careful inspection, he confirmed that it might be "a difficult birth." The prognosis brought tears to her eyes and Stephen knelt by her bedside and did his best to comfort her, silently cursing his own helplessness.

*   *   *

Martin Koenig and Luri Jungblat planned to be married in the Fair Prairie Hotel, the only facility large enough to accommodate a wedding reception. Anna handled all the arrangements with efficiency, demanding and getting financial assistance from the notoriously tight-fisted Thor Nyquist who protested that he already had made major sacrifices to rear the foundling girl who was Martin's bride to be. But Anna's argument was a strong one: If Martin did not take that foundling off his hands, Nyquist faced several more years of financial liability for the sixteen-year-old. Some hasty calculations convinced the frugal Norwegian of the soundness of her argument, and he readily assented to everything Anna asked of him, including a fee of two dollars for rental of the hotel for the ceremony and reception, but not including rooms for overnight guests, should there be any. Her demands were in keeping with the reputation she had established as the hard working proprietor of the hotel. She began building that reputation during her first week on the job, cleaning every room from top to bottom, applying paint where necessary and maintaining the establishment in spotless condition. With her brother's help she erected a laundry shed, installed a large wood stove, and personally boiled the sheets and pillow slips before hanging them out to dry. The amount of steam that emanated each morning from the shed attested to the surge in business that resulted from her management. Her next step was to persuade old man Hespendorff of the wisdom of purchasing the saloon next door and turning it into a restaurant to serve hotel guests and those members of the community who could afford to dine out occasionally. There was only one dispute: Anna wanted to do away with the barroom altogether; old man Hespendorff wanted to keep it. So a compromise was reached. It would be relocated to the rear of the restaurant, walled off to preserve the family atmosphere of the dining room, and its primary entry would be from the alley by her laundry shed. The revelers and wastrels who were used to frequenting the former saloon rapidly diminished in number, due in no small part to the fact that the stern Anna herself usually served as barmaid. In time the barroom was closed altogether and its polished mahogany bar became a seldom-seen museum piece.

Although the drinking men of the town were forced to seek their pleasures elsewhere, Anna's innovations brought in a new clientele that boosted both the reputation of the hotel and its monthly balance sheet. Nothing was free under Anna's reign. Even the outhouses were locked, the key available free to registered hotel guests; bar patrons were to pay a penny. Most of the Hespendorff clan were invited to Martin and Luri's wedding, although only Anna's sister Lotte and Adolf and their children attended. The Hespendorffs did release her sister Hildy from her chores at the main house so she could attend her brother's nuptials, since she had been delegated to help serve refreshments at the reception. Lotte and Adolf presented the happy couple with the most important wedding gift they were to receive – a leather-bound Bible that Adolf traveled all the way to Minneapolis to purchase. It was a huge volume that Anna felt would bring the blessings of Providence upon the marriage, even though the ceremony would be performed by Judge Andrew G. Chatfield, who had established a law practice in Fair Prairie after retiring from the bench. The wedding ceremony was as austere and proper as the judge himself. In his serious judicial manner he instilled in all present the grave responsibilities entered into by the young couple, leaving no doubt in anyone's mind that Martin Koenig and Luri Jungblat were married as solidly and as irrevocably as if they had been united by a man of the cloth. On a lighter note the judge announced to all present that he was delighted to officiate since he had met the groom when the Koenig family first arrived in the valley. It was he who had warned Martin not the cross the swamp that separated him from the river, but to seek a safe crossing further upstream. The judge stayed only briefly after the reception began, but graciously consented not only to sign the new family Bible, but to help the bride and groom sign, too. Martin was relieved because his handwriting was poor, and his bride could not write at all. It was at this signing that Luri Jungblat's name came to be entered as Laura Youngblood, and so it was to remain forever thereafter. She herself soon learned to write it just that way under Anna's tutelage.

Then came the revelry. Norwegians made up the largest contingent of guests, the Nyquists having invited several families from their own enclave. They came mostly out of curiosity about the German community they had viewed with suspicion for years from their side of the river. They conducted themselves with great reserve, sitting stiffly in chairs around the edge of the restaurant, until Hildy, serving tea and cakes, insisted that the children present enjoy the refreshments, too. The ice thus broken, the Norwegians began to mingle. Finally Adolf suggested that the men might like to join him in a celebratory drink and led them through the connecting door to the barroom out back where he had earlier tapped a keg of good German brew. With the women now chatting amiably with one another in the restaurant, the men trading farming stories in the bar, and the children gorging themselves on sweets, the reception was deemed a great success.

After the last guest had left Anna prepared a light supper for the bride and groom and then disappeared into the kitchen with Hildy to begin the cleanup. Later, while the newlyweds held hands across the table and spoke in whispers, she went to the top floor suite and lit the candles on the nightstand so they cast a pale romantic glow over the bed. She turned down the covers, fluffed the pillows, and opened the windows a crack to let in the cool night air. Only then did she go down the hall to her own room where she lay happily awake until she heard their soft footfalls upon the stairs. She smiled in deep satisfaction. The sole surviving male Koenig had taken a robust young bride, and it was reasonably safe to assume that the family name would be preserved.

*   *   *

The little Swede got the sickness first. It came upon him in the early morning after a feverish, restless night. He was the cook's helper, and when he first heard the banging of pots and pans he was grateful that night was over. He crawled out of the bunk and into the frigid air with a sigh of relief. He sat down on the deacon's seat, bent over and

449

pulled on his boots. The effort made his head spin, making it difficult to focus. He slowly pulled on his outer clothes and went for the water buckets. Instead of going directly to the stream to fill them, he headed straight for the privy and made it just in time. He sat there awhile with his head in his hands, his elbows on his knees, his brain afire. Maybe it was the stew he ate last night, but he didn't dare suggest it to the cook. He could get himself beaten bloody just for thinking such a thought. But whatever was to blame, he knew there was something drastically wrong with him. His insides churned and he was racked with pain. He was sweating profusely, even though it must have been twenty below. He struggled to his feet, pulled up his pants and headed out the door, his boots splashing in the spillage from the latrine. The pit had not been deep enough to serve so many lumberjacks for such a long winter. It had filled to overflowing, and stained the snow outside and froze in an ugly mess all around the privy. The discoloration spread as the effluent found its way downhill toward the river. The Swede took a deep breath, picked up his pails, and staggered down the bank to fill them. With great effort he pulled a rusted old axe from the stump and broke up the sheet of ice that covered his water hole at the river's edge. He was still very hot and he worked in a stupor, dipping the buckets into the water to fill them, then with difficulty lifting them out of the hole and onto the bank. There was a dark line in the ice where he worked and he saw that it began at the outhouse and wended its way to the river. He shrugged and lifted his buckets and made his way laboriously up the bank and back to the shanty. Entering the kitchen without a word to the cook, he emptied his buckets into the water barrel and listened with an expert's ear to the splash it made inside the barrel. Two more trips, he calculated, and the barrel would be full. But after his second trip he collapsed at the shanty door, spilling the water from his buckets.

"What in hell is wrong with you?" yelled the cook who ran to see what the noise was all about.

"I'm sick," said the Swede. "I've got the fever."

"Damn lazy Swede."

"No, I'm sick. I'm burning up."

"Then get into the bunk and stay there. Sleep it off. You'd better feel all right when it's time to wash the dishes, or there'll be hell to pay."

Unable to rise, the Swede crawled in through the door and across the floor to the deacon's seat and from there pulled himself back into his bunk. He lay on his back staring at the ceiling with eyes that did not see. He didn't hear the others when they got up and dressed and filed by him to breakfast. He was breathing heavily and did not respond when someone asked him what was wrong. He heard only his mother calling to him to come in from his play so he could try a bite of the apple pie fresh from the oven. She was a broad, red-faced woman with a big smile and a jolly laugh. He was her youngest, her runt, she called him affectionately, and she was forever plying him with good things to eat to "make him big." Staring off into space the little Swede could smell the hot apple pie and see his mother's big smiling face. He smiled back at her with his eyes opened wide, and he died that way – eyes open, a smile on his face. They put him outside to keep while the smithy set a fire in the stumpage area to thaw the ground. Two more men came down with the fever before the day was over, and by the end of the week ten were dead. The air was filled with smoke as fires burned to thaw the ground. It was a large camp, one of the largest in the Shevley chain that stretched far into the pineries. They soon quit counting the dead and merged two depleted gangs to form one and sent word back down the tote road that more men were needed to keep up with the work.

"Tell those brass collars I need healthy men to fill out my crews," the straw boss told the teamster. "Tell 'em I got more men diggin' graves than I have cuttin' trees. Tell 'em that, damn it."

*   *   *

"What does Doc Ames advise?" Stephen asked.

451

"George says there's not much we can do. Keep 'em warm, try to feed 'em enough to keep them alive. But they get so weak they can't even eat. Then it's only a matter of time."

"What will you do?"

Vincent laid aside his paper and filled his pipe.

"We'll take up a load of food and blankets. Not much else we can do. But we've got to sign up some men to fill out the crews." He struck a match and sucked on his pipe. The flame bent down and fanned out over the tobacco, exploring the inside of the bowl. A cloud of blue smoke enveloped him.

"Where will we find loggers looking for work in January?"

"I'll leave that to you. Ben and I leave for the pineries tomorrow, and I can't be in two places at once. I'll order more supplies for you to bring along when you come up with the men."

"Why do you have to go? Let the regular teamsters do it."

"We've got a dozen camps to supply. I can't spare 'em. I have to go see for myself. It's hard to believe things are as bad as they say."

"It seems pretty risky – you and Ben."

"We're too old, you mean?" he asked with a smile. "You're talking about a couple of old war horses. We can manage. Besides, I've been cooped up all winter. It's time I stretched a leg. I want you to find workers. Check the mill, make the rounds of the taverns. Promise bonuses. Do what you have to do. There must be some around who want to earn an honest day's pay for a little hard work."

"I'll do my best, but I still wish you wouldn't go. Why don't I go?"

"You've got Sarah to worry about; don't worry about me."

"Worry about what?" Sarah asked, guiding her wheelchair into the parlor.

"There's a fever spreading through the camps," said Stephen.

"What kind of fever?"

"Doc Ames says it sounds like a gastric fever of some sort. Pretty miserable stuff. Some loggers have died, a lot more are sick."

"Ben and I are taking up beef and blankets. We want to see for ourselves how bad it really is. I've asked Stephen to see if he can find some men looking for work and bring them up before I have to close down camp number seven."

"Bring them up?" Sarah asked.

"It'll only take two, three days – less than a week, anyway," Stephen said. "I wouldn't want to be away any longer than that. I should be here with you."

Sarah's eyes fell at his reference to her condition. She was very large in the eighth month of her pregnancy and confined to the wheelchair. With the men gone, she'd be bedridden, and she knew it. So did Stephen; it would be too much for Marie and Mrs. Carpenter to carry her downstairs.

"You mustn't worry about me," she said. "I'll be in good hands. You do what you have to do."

They carried her upstairs for the last time that night, with her mother worrying along behind them. Mrs. Carpenter was glad to see her daughter confined to bed, comfortable and safe.

"You let me do the runnin'," she advised. "It's good for my stiff old joints. There's nothing you'll be needin' that I can't fetch. You'd just be under foot downstairs, what with Marie cookin' and cleanin'."

Vincent and Ben left the next day, loading the emergency supplies aboard the train to Little Falls, where they would off-load it to sleighs and then head into the woods. Stephen spent a week canvassing the taverns along Washington Avenue for able-bodied men. But rumors of the epidemic had preceded him, and it was difficult to find anyone interested in spending the rest of the winter in the camps. He found only seven men to make the commitment with the inducement of a five dollar bonus in advance, payable when they boarded the train at the St. Anthony depot.

"I'll be lucky if any show up," he told Sarah as he prepared to depart.

"You will be careful, won't you?"

"Of course. I'll be back within a week. Please don't worry about me." He brushed her hair aside and kissed her tenderly on the forehead. "Sweet Sarah, how I do love you." She took his hand and held it against their unborn child.

"Feel the movement?" she asked. "Sometimes he gives quite a kick."

"So, you've decided it will be a boy!"

"I can't be sure, but I hope it is, for your sake. I know how you want a son."

"A healthy child of either sex is what I want, and a healthy mother to care for it. Do be careful while I'm gone."

"I will, my dearest. I love you."

Chapter 28

To Stephen's great surprise the five drifters he recruited in various taverns and the two good hands from the mill all showed up on time at the St. Anthony depot. Not only that, but one of the mill hands brought along a friend, a big, grinning Irishman who grasped Stephen's hand in a hearty greeting.

"Damned if I ever expected to see you again, Steve!" said Jim Malloy. "How in hell have you been?"

"Jim! After all these years," he greeted his old friend from his army days. "When was it we last..."

"It was pouring rain, and we were under cover of a hospital tent. I remember I swiped the laces from the boots of a wounded officer for you before I got the bum's rush."

Stephen reached inside his jacket and pulled out the cord that held John Koenig's silver buckles.

"Still got the buckles," he said with a smile. "I think they kept me alive, just like you said they might – these buckles, and the love of my good wife."

"You still have the buckles? And you're married? My lad you've obviously missed my guidance over the years. We'll have to do something about that."

"If we didn't have to get aboard this train, we could celebrate with a drink," Stephen said.

"Ah, no, Stevie m'boy. I've had a bit of a problem with strong drink over the years. You see standing before you a reformed drunk who figures a few months in the woods might ease his cravings for the stuff. I decided I'd kick the booze for good, or freeze trying!"

Later as the train rumbled toward the pineries, Stephen settled in for a chat with Malloy.

"The men seem rather quiet," he said.

"They're afraid," said Malloy.

"Of the fever in the camp?"

"No, of you. They know you're a big boss, and they're afraid. Even after you gave them their bonus, they were suspicious."

"You'll have to tell them I don't bite."

"I'll do that," said Jim. "My, you've done well with the Shevley Company. How long you been with 'em?"

"All my life."

"Now what in hell do you mean by that?"

"I lied about my name when I enlisted, Jim. My real name's Shevley."

"By all that's holy, you come from money!"

"I guess that's true, but I earn my share. I've worked in the camps; I've worked in the mill. I know how to earn a dollar and how to break a sweat doing it. I didn't start at the top."

"Good lad, but you oughtn't be caught with the likes of me. It'll taint your reputation and lessen your clout."

"It'd be cold day in hell before I'd turn my back on an old friend, particularly one I fought beside in the war."

"Those were rough days, Steve. Can I call you Steve? I never learned how to talk to a boss."

"I know you're a man who speaks his mind, Jim, and I like a man who does that. They make good foremen. If you don't mind working with me, you can be just that. I know you're a man I can trust."

"That's not the way my work ticket reads, but I suppose you can change that."

"Indeed I can. It'll mean more money in your poke."

"It's settled then. But let me speak my mind, since you admire a man who does so. I'm disappointed that you never gave those buckles to John's kinfolk, like you said."

"I was sick for awhile after I mustered out, and when I was finally able to go look for them, I was told they'd pulled up stakes and moved on. Then one thing led to another. You know how it is. Now I wouldn't know where to begin looking. But I haven't given up. I'll find them someday."

"Koenig, wasn't that his name?"

"It was."

"Seems I know that name from somewhere – it brings to mind a back alley saloon somewhere down in the Minnesota River valley. I remember I was pretty drunk, and there was this beautiful barmaid – anyway, I wound up in the county jail. I'll think on it and let you know."

*   *   *

It was like old times, gliding over a tote road in winter. Stephen, at the reins of the lead sleigh, put Jim Malloy in charge of the second, urging him to keep within sight of him lest he get lost along way. It was overcast and cold, but the air was crisp and invigorating. The howling winds blew fiercely at times and quickly covered their tracks. At dusk Stephen slowed his team to a trot and struggled to keep sight of the road. More than once he stopped altogether to study the darkening landscape before proceeding cautiously again. He was relieved to catch his first glimpse of light from a logging camp. The base camp was headquarters for six other Shevley camps, the site where the operations superintendent made his office. In this person Stephen found a familiar face.

"Your lights are a welcome sight, Big Neil. There's nothing blacker than a snow country trail at new moon."

"I know your face," Big Neil said, trying to place him, "but I can't put a name on you. You're welcome here, whatever you call yourself. It's a hell of a night."

"That's a warmer greeting than I got the first time we met. Tell me, has Vince Shevley been by this way?"

"He has, and he had Ben McAlpine with him. Ben wasn't looking well, if you ask me. I think he's getting too old for the trail. They left early yesterday for the camp a few hours west of here. The crew there are dropping like flies. I don't know what they think they can do about it, but they were carrying food and blankets. I see you've brought some men. Now that's what we really need."

457

"I'll leave seven men with you to assign as you see fit. And we've got additional supplies. Can you see that they get where they're needed? We've got to get back to the city."

"Hell no. I haven't got a man or rig to spare. But I'll keep the seven new hands. I've been sending my own people to fill in where they can and we need the replacements here. This is a clean camp with no fever. You'll have to deliver the supplies yourself. It's only a few hours ride. Meanwhile, pull up to the table and have some supper."

"Thanks. We'll take care of our horses first."

Big Neil collared Stephen when he came in from the stables.

"I think I got you placed," he said. "Didn't I know you as a kid? A city kid as I recall, back on the Rum River in 'sixty-one."

"That's right," Stephen smiled.

"We've cut a lot of timber since then, fella'."

"We sure have," Stephen agreed.

Two more days, he thought, up and back. We'll still be home within the week. Sarah will understand.

*   *   *

They had breakfast with the loggers and were on the trail at first light. An overnight sleet storm left the snow covered with a thin crust of ice that crunched underfoot, and now a light snow was falling. The road was easy to follow at first, but as the morning drew on the wind came up and whipped the snow, making it difficult to see the trail. Stephen did his best to keep the runners squarely in the icy ruts of the road with Jim following close behind. Near noon they stopped to feed the horses.

"How far do we have to go?" Jim asked, munching on a piece of jerky.

"Not far, from what Big Neil said."

"I hope your team knows the way; I can't see a damned thing but the ruts in the road."

458

"Do you catch that smell?" Stephen asked, sniffing the air.

"Smoke," Jim said. "Maybe we're closer than you think."

"There's an oily smell to it. Hard to tell with the wind."

"It seems to be coming right at us."

"Wait – I know that smell; I remember it from the war. That's the smell of burning flesh."

"You're right, Steve. We'd better go have a look."

They gathered up the reins and led their teams forward toward the source of the smoke. In no more than a hundred yards they came upon a clearing and saw that a whole camp was ablaze, every log and thatch. The roof of the shanty had collapsed and thick clouds of smoke swirled up and into the winds. The stables and the blacksmith's shack were afire, and in the center of the camp a solitary figure sat upon a tree stump watching the conflagration. They tethered their teams and headed toward him, their cold-stiffened bodies warming now in the midst of the inferno.

"Hey there!" Stephen shouted. "Are you all right? What's happened here?"

The man turned toward him and Stephen recognized the wild, crazy eyes of Orville Potter, the blacksmith from his winter on the Rum River. The one-legged smith raised one of his crutches and waved to the fire all around him.

"It's the wrath of God!" he cried.

"Get hold of yourself, Potter, and tell us what's going on. Where has everyone gone?"

"They've fled before the sword of the Almighty, but there's no escaping His vengeance. His curse has fallen upon them all and they're all doomed to purgatory. The others are already in hell. See! There goes some of them now." He waved a crutch in the direction of the burning shanty where flames suddenly exploded through a pillar of black, oily smoke. The burst of flame filled the air with the stench of death.

"My God! There are bodies burning in there!" Jim exclaimed. "Let's get out of here."

"Wait," said Stephen. "They can't all be dead. Where are the others, Potter? Where have they gone?"

"Some lie yonder in the glen in the icy embrace of death," Potter answered. "Others ran away. The big boss came through and told 'em to head for the next camp, that it was their only hope. Then he and his half-breed friend set this place afire. They said it was the only way to fight the fever – a purge of fire. They had the living carry the dead into the shanty and set it ablaze. Then they sent them away."

"Why didn't you go with them?" asked Jim.

"On these crutches, in the storm?" he asked with a grim smile. "I knew I couldn't escape the fury of the Almighty. So I stayed to keep the fires burning." He nodded to a five-gallon tin of lamp oil that rested at his feet.

"We'll take you with us," said Stephen. "Which way is it to the next camp?"

"That way," said Potter, pointing with his crutch. "But in this storm you'd never make it. Better wait until morning."

They drew the sleighs together and fashioned a shelter between them with the blankets they carried and all three wrapped themselves against the cold and lay down to sleep. The last thing Stephen remembered was the snoring of Jim Malloy and the red glow of the dying fire dancing in the eyes of Orville Potter.

At daylight they found themselves amid a blackened smoldering ruin. The wind had subsided and no more snow fell. Instead the overcast skies rained down a dusting of ash that covered the ground and the surrounding trees. Stephen wandered among the ruins, wrinkling his nose to ameliorate the awful smell of burned bodies.

"Let's get out of here," said Jim as he joined him. "The old man is dead."

"We can't just leave him," said Stephen. "The wolves will get him."

They picked up Potter, blankets and all, and carried him to the remains of the blacksmith shop where several timbers still glowed. They laid him in the ashes and doused him with the lamp oil, then kicked some embers on him to set him afire.

"God rest his troubled soul," Stephen muttered.

They reached the next camp in early afternoon and found it nearly deserted.

"They're at work in the woods," said the cook, putting food on the table for them. "We lost a lot of time caring for the sick."

"Where are the sick?" Jim asked.

"The camp boss wouldn't let 'em in the shanty. There's a half dozen or so bedded down in the stable. The one's who hadn't picked up the fever are working with the crews."

"Who's your camp boss?" Stephen asked.

"Name's Shaw. You'll find him in his cabin across the way. He'll be happy as hell to get those blankets. And thanks for the beef; I've got a lot more mouths to feed."

Peter Shaw had changed little since Stephen had last seen him. He had the same commanding presence, an aura of authority that made him a natural leader.

"Come in out of the cold, Steve," he greeted them as they entered the small cabin. "What are you doing up here in the middle of nowhere?"

"We've brought you some goods," he said. "This is my friend Jim Malloy. We just left a side of beef with the bull cook, and we have a couple of dozen blankets here that might come in handy, along with some other supplies."

"I've been expecting someone. The loggers who straggled in here said Vince Shevley sent them and that he and Ben McAlpine were on their way here with supplies."

"Strange we didn't see them on the road," Stephen said.

"They stopped to burn down a camp," Jim said. "Guess they thought it would kill whatever was causing the fever there."

"There was only one man alive when we arrived," Stephen added, "and he died overnight. We saw no sign of Vince and Ben."

"Maybe they headed back down state. The men who escaped the fever said old Ben looked pretty sick," Shaw said.

"One way or the other, we should have crossed trails with them," said a worried Stephen.

"They might have taken a short cut," said Shaw. "Ben knows these woods pretty well. And they couldn't get lost following the rivers."

"We'll look for them on the way back," said Stephen. "There's nothing more we can do here."

"You can't go now," said Shaw. "There's only a couple of hours of daylight, and you'd never pick up their trail in the dark, not after the snow we had yesterday. Get a good night's rest and leave in the morning."

"All right, but it's going to be a long night," said Stephen.

*   *   *

Not three miles away, two men lay in the wreckage of a sleigh.

"Sorry, old friend," said one to the other. "We must have hit a stump under the snow. Next thing I know we're flying off the road and down the embankment. One of the horses is still alive. If I could reach that rifle, I'd put her out of her misery. Might even use it on myself, but I can't get at it with my leg pinned under the runner."

Ben stared at Vince with cold, dead eyes.

"Don't blame me, Ben. I just didn't see it. I was in hurry to get you to a doctor, but you were probably dead already. Doesn't make any difference. You're sure as hell dead now, and I won't be far behind you. I keep thinking that Stephen will be by soon. I'll call out if I hear him, but it better be soon."

He dozed then, weak from his injuries and shivering in the frigid temperatures. When he awakened Ben was still staring accusingly at him and he looked away. Shadows were gathering among the trees. In anger and frustration he shouted as loud as he could, but the only response was the wind whistling through the trees.

"Thank God it's getting dark. I can't stand you looking at me like that. I need some sleep. Can't hold my eyes open any longer. Oh, how I wish things could have been different." After a long pause he cried out, "Eleanor! Can you hear me? I'm sorry, Eleanor. I did everything I could...no, I guess I didn't. I had important things to do. Just had to do them, because that's the way I am. I worked in these woods for nearly twenty years to make this land mine, and I did it! This land *is* mine. It'll be for our son, Eleanor. It'll be Stephen's land now – Stephen and our grandson. Yes, our grandson! Can you believe it, Eleanor. We're going to be grandparents. Oh, God, I wish I could see him before I die. Help me, dear God, please help me!"

His cry was swallowed up in the dark woods and the futility of it set him to laughing until tears came to his eyes and froze on his grizzled cheeks. Then he cried hysterically, not because he was in pain, for the cold had numbed him, but because it was all over. His dream was ending all too soon, and there was so much left to do. As the darkness closed in around him he peered into the sky through a tangle of alder branches and saw a sliver of the new moon against the black heavens. He shouted again, defiant and angry:

"It's my land, God damn it! I could have made this the greatest state in the Union. I could have done it, I swear!"

Then he slept, and his dream died with him.

*   *   *

Long after Vincent's sleigh careened over the embankment and crashed on the rocks and ice below, Jim Malloy spotted the wreckage. In daylight it was the logical place to look. The road, merely a narrow trail through the scrub pine and often covered with drifted snow, veered close to the river's edge at that point, and there was nothing at the edge to stop the sleigh as it plunged down the steep decline. In poor light or in a blizzard a passerby could not have seen the evidence of tragedy. But in daylight Jim could see not only the sleigh but the stark evidence of blood against the pristine snow. A pack of timber wolves had come upon the scene and made a feast of one of the horses. It was the gore they left behind that caught Jim's eye. Stephen had driven by without noticing it. Only when he realized Jim was not following behind him did he halt his sleigh and double back on foot. Together they scrambled down the embankment and began pawing frantically at the snow that had buried the victims. Stephen came upon his father's hand first, stiff and lifeless. Then he knelt down and gently brushed away the snow that covered his father's face. Vincent's eyes were closed as if in sleep, and Stephen stroked it lovingly. It was the first time he could remember touching his father's face, and a wave of grief swept over him. He fought to maintain his composure, rocking back and forth, shaking his head, pounding his fists on his knees. Nothing could hold back the passion he felt, and he cried out, "My God, I'm too late!"

Malloy, who had come across Ben's body, looked away and let Stephen work out his grief. When it was over, he sized up the steep cliff. It was only thirty feet high, but too steep to carry up the bodies.

"We've got to get them out of here," he said. "The wolves will be back."

"If we can free them, we can carry them downstream and find an easier climb. We've got to get them home," Stephen said.

They continued digging out the bodies, and when Jim next looked up he saw Stephen was in tears.

"I guess you two were pretty close," he said quietly.

"Not really," said Stephen. "He was my father."

At that point grief returned like a lightning bolt, the shock bringing back memories of the past, the remorse over missed opportunities, the words left unspoken, the years lost never to return. As the day drew on he sank deeper into his sorrow and fell silent. When his team took a wrong turn, Jim thought he had fallen asleep and yelled out to awaken him.

"Do you want me to lead?" he asked.

"No, I'll be all right."

When they reached the base camp, Big Neil urged them to rest before heading out again, but Stephen insisted they would move on. During one rest stop, Jim found him sitting in the snow, leaning against a tree, fast asleep. He drifted off again in the warmth of the undertaker's parlor in Little Falls, and Jim had to help him to his feet and guide him into the office to sign the papers to transport the bodies. Aboard the train to Minneapolis he found Stephen staring off into space, his eyes wide open, seeing nothing, lost in his own thoughts. Suddenly from the rear of the car came a baby's piercing cry. Stephen came immediately to his senses.

"You know, Jim," he said quietly, "I've been preoccupied with death all this while, when I should have been thinking about life. Do you realize that I may have become a father since we've been gone?"

They chatted amiably for a short time. Then Stephen yawned, closed his eyes, and fell fast asleep. Jim had to awaken him when the train pulled into St. Anthony.

*   *   *

The blizzard turned the fields around Fair Prairie into an undulating sea of snow. The drifts reached nearly to the eaves of the cabin and the windows were covered by them. Martin built up the fire and stacked an armload of firewood next to the stove. Laura put away the last breakfast dish and sank exhausted into her chair. She was very large midway in her pregnancy and even the slightest exertion seemed to sap all of her strength. Martin came to her and placed his hands on her flushed cheeks.

"Rest today," he said. "Keep the fire high and just rest."

"I'm sorry I can't do more," she said. "I'll get used to it. It's hard the first time. Next time it will be easier. I hate myself; I'm weak and ugly."

He laughed and stroked her hair.

"You're not ugly to me. It's our child who makes you fat and takes away your energy. In the spring when the child comes you will be slim and strong again."

"What if the baby comes, and I'm still fat?"

"You'll be too busy to be fat. Don't worry about it. Keep warm and rest. I have work to do outside."

He had to dig his way out the front door. He found his snowshoes buried in the drift, strapped them on and headed out over the fields and down toward the river bottom. In the fall he had found rich loam there, silt that had piled up over the centuries by the meandering river. He had spent the winter cutting down the river trees and digging out stumps to prepare the land for the plow. Two large brush piles, now covered with drifted snow like miniature mountains, attested to his labors. He went to one of them, dug into it and pulled out a handful of dried twigs and leaves. He struck a sulfur match and set the tinder ablaze. When the pile was smoking and sizzling with melted snow, he took his axe and began to work on the nearby stumps.

"In the spring I'll plow this land and plant corn," he said. "And in the summer I'll buy pigs and feed them corn until they grow fat. Then I'll sell the fat pigs and use the money to build a proper house for my family."

Martin Koenig smiled as he worked; he was a happy man.

Chapter 29

Shevley House was outlined in a halo of gold, that soft golden glow peculiar to a cold day when there are no clouds to obstruct the rays of the lowering sun and the midwinter sky is a pale and frigid blue. The oak grove already was in shadow and inside the house lamps were lit against the approaching darkness. In their light Stephen could see shadows moving across the windows of the third floor bedroom. There were two sleighs in front of the house as he sped up the driveway and around to the back door near the stables. Leaping exultantly from the sleigh, he burst through the back door and galloped up the rear stairway. At the end of the hall a splash of light fell out of the bedroom and amid the confusion of muffled sounds he distinctly heard the cry of an infant. In a moment he was at the open door where he was assaulted by a scene that he would never forget. Doctor Ames, his face clouded by despair, halted him in his tracks with a firm but gentle grip on his arm. He was in his shirtsleeves and his brow was wet with perspiration. Beyond him Sarah lay in bed, pale and beautiful in the lantern light. She wore a smile of happiness and deep peace; her eyes were closed, the bedcovers tucked high under her chin. At her side her mother sat upon a chair, her head bowed, while beside her a young priest murmured a prayer. In the chair by the fireplace Marie rocked quietly, a small bundle in her arms. The meaning of the tableau was unmistakable. He instantly looked Doctor Ames in the eye, silently demanding an explanation.

"I tried to save her, Stephen. As God is my witness, I did everything I could. But it was an impossible delivery, a difficult breech birth. There was no way I could save them both. Sarah knew it – she insisted that the child be given life. She made the choice, Stephen; I did my best."

The accumulation of the past week – the hardships, the shocks, the sorrows – all struck him at once. His tears flowed in a torrent and he uttered a plaintive cry of grief.

Staggering to Sarah's bedside, he fell upon his knees as the others in the room stepped aside. The young priest, an assistant to the Rev. Charles B. Knickerbacker, came to him and placed his hand upon his shoulder. Stephen buried his face in the coverlet and wept uncontrollably. Then he brusquely shrugged off the consoling hand and looked into the serene face of his adored wife. She was indescribably beautiful, surrounded by an aura of profound contentment. The slight smile on her lips left no doubt in his mind that the doctor was right: it was her choice to die that their child might live. He saw at once the awful bond that tied him to his father, and to his father before him, just as old Williams had said many years before. It was indeed a prophecy come true. His grandmother had died in childbirth, his mother had died forsaken, and now his wife had been taken in childbirth. He had forsaken her when she needed him most. Burdened with guilt, realizing that she was gone forever, he kissed the lips that once were so warm and pliant. Then he stood erect and uttered a blood-curdling cry of agony, a demonic cry that summed up all his grief and pain, his guilt and sorrow. He fell to his knees and slumped against the bed as the others rushed to his side, lifted him up and led him to a chair. With tearful eyes he gazed at them from the depths of his personal hell, from that netherworld where once before he had found escape from suffering and pain, the dark and lonely place from which only she had been able to rescue him.

"A brutal blow," muttered the doctor. "If only there had been some way to intercept him, to prepare him."

"May God's mercy be upon him in his hour of grief," intoned the young priest.

"Pray for him, pray that he doesn't slip away from us again. He's been through so much already in his young life," said Ames.

"It is God's way of testing him," said the priest with pompous assurance. "The Creator is preparing him, strengthening him for some greater calling. In His wisdom He has laid these burdens upon him. Oh, God of Love, help thy servant Stephen to see the goodness and the love that lie in Your ways. Help him to be thankful for the days of joy he shared with his beloved soul mate. Help him to be grateful that she has now been called to Your peaceable kingdom to bask in the glory of Your righteousness forever. Amen."

There was a penetrating power in the priest's voice that reached to the depths of Stephen's despair. But it brought no relief to his aching heart. Rather it inspired him to such a fury that he suddenly threw off the shell into which he had retreated, leaped from his chair, and flung himself upon the startled clergyman, grabbing his throat with both hands. The priest let out a cry and struggled toward the door, terrified by the frenzied attack. The doctor, equally surprised, fell back, gained control of his fear, and then moved in to pull Stephen off the hapless clergyman.

"Control yourself, Stephen, for God's sake!" he shouted.

"You dare to speak to me of God's love, you damned hypocrite! Even to mention the goodness of God in the face of this monstrous injustice is unforgivable. Get out of here, both of you, and take your mawkish lies with you. Sell them to the poor, weak souls who need to believe such nonsense. I'll have none of it! God doesn't reign in this house; death and the devil rule here. Get out, and leave me alone."

With a powerful thrust he sent the priest reeling toward the head of the stairway where he caught hold of the railing and clung to it for dear life.

"Stephen!" shouted the doctor. "For the love of all that's holy, get a grip on yourself. Have you gone mad?"

"Don't speak to me of madness, you cringing coward. It was you who allowed her to die when you might have saved her. Get out, and damn your soul to hell!"

"Wait, wait," he whispered. "Be calm. Think of the infant – your child, Stephen. You must think of your daughter now. With her last breath Sarah pleaded with me to save the baby. She laid down her life for that child."

"No, take it away. I never want to see it. No life is worth the life of my Sarah. Take it away."

The doctor and the priest retreated down the stairway under Stephen's vicious glare and joined Mrs. Carpenter and Marie in the front hall. The front door was open and Charles Whitcomb stood in the opening aghast.

"What in God's name is going on?" he asked.

"Sarah's dead," said Ames, "but the child survived. Stephen's gone absolutely berserk."

"I'm not surprised," said the editor sadly. "He just brought his father's body back from the pineries. Vincent Shevley is dead, too. And to come home to this..."

"May the saints preserve us," cried Mrs. Carpenter, falling to her knees in tears.

Marie stood by impassively, gently cradling the bundled baby in her arms.

*   *   *

The night was bitter cold and the road a sheet of ice. Martin snapped the reins and the horse lurched and sent the sleigh slamming into the snowdrift at the side of the road. Anna uttered a cry muffled by the huge scarf around her head.

"Sorry," Martin said.

"Slow down or Laura will be delivering her baby by herself," Anna groused. She was cranky after being awakened in the middle of the night, but she had volunteered to help when the time came. And who else could Martin turn to? He might have asked Lotte, but he was afraid Adolf might forbid her to come at the last desperate moment. And Hildy was no help. She could never get away from old Frau Hespendorff. A senile mistress and her simple-minded maid. What in the world would Hildy do when the old lady died? He had no choice but to bang on Anna's door at two in the morning and plead with her to come and help. Laura's pains were becoming more frequent. So Anna dressed, grumbling all the while, wrapped herself against the cold, and came along to do what she could. He knew she would, because

470

despite her gruff manner her heart was full of love and secretly she looked forward to giving a bit of it away.

"What?" she asked as they approached the cabin. "You didn't leave a light on!"

"Sure I did. I left the lantern lit. But the windows are covered inside with blankets to keep out the cold. And I left firewood by the stove to keep her warm. Now don't nag me – save your strength for Laura. She'll need your help more than I need a scolding."

They burst through the door quickly and slammed it to keep out the cold. Laura greeted them with a faint smile. The room was warm and moist from a steaming tub of water on the cook stove.

"I see you haven't completely lost your wits," Anna remarked, testing the water with her fingertips.

"Laura told me to put the water on," Martin admitted sheepishly. "What else can I do to help?"

"You can keep out of the way for the time being. Put more wood on the fire and get the cradle ready to receive your child. And bring in more wood; this will never last the night." Then turning to Laura she asked, "How are you my dear? Did you think we'd never get here? Well, it was a miracle, believe me. Your husband drives like a maniac."

"Anna, oh, Anna – it's so close," gasped Laura, her face contorted with worry and pain.

"Just relax and take your own good time. I have a few things to do, and then we'll get down to business. Martin, find me the shears." Then she rolled up her sleeves and dipped out a basin of hot water from the big tub on the stove. As she scrubbed her hands she chatted nonchalantly about the day, how busy she had been and how many customers had come in for dinner, and how many guests were staying the night at the hotel, and what an inconvenient time it was to be a midwife, and how the baby might at least have had the courtesy to wait for a decent hour to make its appearance. Laura didn't hear a word she said, but writhed and rolled from side to side with each jolting pain. Anna dried her hands and got clean linen from the chest – and then Laura let out a scream.

"Go out and get the firewood," Anna said to Martin, "and don't be in a hurry. I'll call you when you're needed."

"But it's cold outside!"

"Martin, just go," she said with mounting exasperation.

He lit a lantern and went quickly into the cold, quiet night. He unhitched the horse and stomped through the snow to the barn, leading the animal to its stall. Then he sat down on a bale of hay and covered his ears so as not to hear whatever it was he was not supposed to hear. He was grateful to be out of the wind and to have the horse for company, but in an hour he grew curious and went out into the cold again. Pressing his ear to the cabin door he could hear Anna talking calmly, incessantly, and there were soft little replies from Laura in words he could not make out. There was no sound of panic or concern, so he knocked lightly on the door.

"Come in, Martin, come in!" Anna called out. "I'm sorry we forgot you were out there."

"How is she?" he asked, wiping his snowy boots on the door mat and slipping out of his heavy coat. "How are you, Laura. You look tired."

"Of course she's tired. It's past four o'clock in the morning and she hasn't had a wink of sleep all night. Besides that she's just given birth to a son – your son, Martin. Well, go and meet your son!"

He knelt down beside the bed and wondered at the tears in Laura's eyes. How pale she looked, and so tired. But her smile assured him she was fine.

"Laura, where is he?" he asked, for he could see no baby. Gently she pulled the quilts aside and he got a glimpse of a red, furry head. A little more and he could see a tiny ear, the tiniest ear he had ever seen. And then the nose, which was hardly a nose at all, it was so small. The baby seemed to be asleep.

"He is quite small," he said at last. "Was it so diffi-cult to bear such a small baby? He is all right, isn't he?"

"My God, is that all you can say?" Anna asked.

"He's fine," Laura said in a tiny voice. "And I am fine, too."

"Thank goodness for that," said Martin. "And thank you, Anna, for your help."

"I didn't have the baby, Laura did. Thank her. She did all the work. And now go fetch some more water – I've got laundry to do."

Laura and the baby slept for several hours while Anna worked and ordered Martin about unmercifully. He was very sleepy, but he really didn't mind. He forgot about being tired and sustained himself on the excitement and the wonder of being a father. When daylight came he offered to take Anna back to the hotel, but she wouldn't hear of it. She implied that he couldn't be trusted to tend to his own wife and newborn son and she really didn't care about going back to the hotel when she obviously was needed right where she was.

"I've already collected in advance for the rooms," she said, "and I really don't care about the guests. Let them go somewhere else for breakfast. I plan to stay right here today."

Martin had no doubt that she meant what she said.

*　　*　　*

His world was much changed when Stephen awoke. The emotional blows had left him stunned and he wandered through the mansion like a visitor to the past. He neither saw nor heard any sign of life – and in the bedchamber, no sign of death – no evidence of the cruel drama that had unfolded there so recently. The bedroom looked as it had many years ago after his mother's death, a dim sanctuary furnished with the trappings of another time, all distant and divorced from the day's reality. The sight of the room stirred melancholy remembrances of that other time, that other tragedy. The silk

473

coverlet on the bed hung smoothly to the floor, unwrinkled and unreal. The chairs, the writing table, the draperies on the windows spoke of a life only dimly recalled. On the table stood the green glass vase, giving substance to what otherwise would have been an unnerving, other-worldly experience, a slide into madness, a tumble into that dark world from which he might not escape this time – now that she was gone. The vase was real. It was his mother's vase. It was the past and the present. He picked it up and held it, examining it closely as the images of the then and now slowly sorted themselves out in his mind. As he struggled to maintain an emotional balance a shadow fell across the room. He turned abruptly, half expecting to see her. But no, it was Marie standing in the doorway.

"Where is she?" he asked.

"They took her away to prepare her for the funeral."

"When will that be?"

"Thursday afternoon at two o'clock at her church."

"What day is this?"

"Tuesday – late Tuesday. I was about to fix supper."

He walked to the window and looked out over the front gardens, all buried in snow. It had been ten days since he had bid her his last goodbye here in this very room, and nearly a full day since he had seen her in death. And now there was no sign of her. The time was confused, but irrelevant. Nothing was really important anymore, particularly time. Things would be done, but perfunctorily. He must eat, he must sleep. The routine of daily life must go on, if only to denote each day's passage. One day would lead inexorably into night, and then a new day would begin. It would be a plodding and painful progression that led nowhere. It might even prove unendurable. He would have to wait and see. He would try to survive, but survival didn't seem important. A descent into madness, even death, might be preferable. In the meantime, he was hungry.

"I will want to clean up before supper," he said.

"There's hot water on the stove."

He washed off more than a week's accumulation of filth, the foul odors of sweat and death, and dressed in clean clothes. Then he built a fire in the parlor fireplace and sat there sipping brandy until Marie quietly called him to supper. She had set a place for him in the dining room, a single place at the long mahogany table, a single candelabra that dimly lit the room. When he finished eating he sat staring into the shadows, remembering Sarah as she had been, savoring the bittersweet recollections of the love they shared. He wondered if he would be able to carry on, if he really wanted to carry on. What use would it be? What would he do about the child? Why was this new burden placed on him? He couldn't care for an infant. Sarah was dead. His one great love was gone and had taken his love with her to the other side. He had no love to offer a child. His very presence would be like a curse on it, as it had been on its mother, who would be alive today, if it were not for him. If he entered the child's life, it would only lead to its destruction. A light rapping on the door interrupted his thoughts. It was Roger Frasier.

"Sorry, I didn't know you were dining," Roger said.

"I didn't hear you arrive," said Stephen.

"Marie let me in and asked me to be quiet."

"Impertinent of her."

"No, it was thoughtful. She didn't want me to disturb you."

"Well, you have, so what do you want?"

"I came to see how you were faring. I am glad to see you up and about. I've been concerned about your health."

"I did not bring back the fever, if that's what you mean."

"No, I wondered how you were bearing up under the strain."

"You thought you'd find me a raving maniac, is that it? I assure you I am not. But at the moment it does seem an alternative to be greatly desired."

"You cannot will such a transformation."

"Perhaps not, but I can tell you that during the past day I have willingly explored the black borders of madness, and I am no stranger there. I feel a strong temptation to just slip away from all the suffering of this world into the oblivion of insanity. There are times when my grip on this world is a tenuous one indeed."

"But grip it you must, for better or for worse."

"You choose a poor time to lecture me on how to live my life. Despite your theories we do not create our own destinies. I should be living proof that your philosophy is bogus at best, dangerous at worst. Life is not what we make it, Roger, we are what life makes of us. At the moment I find life burdensome."

"I don't like to hear you talk that way. The pain of the moment has made you irrational. You must concede that until these most recent sorrows your life was going well. There is reason to believe it might do so again. You could devote yourself to your daughter, find a new life in guiding her through hers."

"So, it's a girl, is it. I pity her for the life she has been born into, and I regret my role in creating her. I have done her a huge disservice. I will do nothing to add to her suffering."

Roger shook his head and helped himself to a brandy.

"You punish yourself unreasonably," he said.

"I find my attitude honest and realistic. I don't want to interfere in her life. I will attend Sarah's funeral, and that will put an end to it."

"It will be a double funeral. Both she and your father will be honored at Gethsemane and laid to rest here in your family plot."

"Convenient – double the agony."

"And then what do you propose to do?"

"I propose to put my affairs in order, and then go away. I don't know where, but there is nothing here for me but pain and heartbreak, and I've had enough of both. I'll want to assure that my daughter is well taken care of, of course, but I do not want to see her. It would be unbearable.

If someday she fails to understand why, then I hope she'll forgive me. She must never be made to feel that she is in any way responsible for her mother's death. It is I who am to blame. She must be allowed to grow up without my curse on her."

He poured another brandy; Roger declined.

"You'd walk away from your own flesh and blood, from a great fortune, from a thriving business, a proud name?"

"We view life from different perspectives, Roger. Think of what those things, the material things, have meant to me. The family fortune destroyed my family. The frontier in the last analysis led to the death of both my parents. And the name, cursed as it surely must be, caused the death of the only woman I've ever truly loved. If she had wed a shop clerk or the butcher boy she'd be alive today. Instead she took my name, and she died as a result. Yes, I can walk away from all that – I can *run* away from it. Even so, I know very well that I can't escape my fate, but I can do my best to protect others from the cloud of evil that hangs over me."

"That's sheer nonsense. I can't allow you to think this way."

"Why not? You have everything to gain and nothing to lose. I'll renounce all claims to the Shevley Company. It will belong to you and my uncles. I will put it in writing, everything you've always wanted."

"That's entirely unnecessary. I am already authorized by the partnership to assume control in event of your father's incapacity or death. I am also obligated to maintain the interest's of his heirs – you and your daughter. Don't cloud the issue with ill-considered theatrics. If you choose to run away as you did when you went into the woods or when you enlisted in the army, so be it. It will change nothing."

"Then take control, and be damned. I'll have no more to do with you or the company."

"Consider it done. What about Shevley House?"

"I'll remain here at least until after the funerals. I suggest that you hire my good and reliable friend, Jim

Malloy, to be caretaker here until the child grows up. Beyond that, I don't know."

"Who will raise your daughter?"

"What has been done for her so far?"

"She is with her grandmother at the home of George and Amanda Ames. She is being well taken care of. I've asked Marie to look after you until you make up your mind what you'll do."

"Do I need looking after?"

"Until you do something foolish like running away."

"Marie may want to rejoin her mother, now that Ben is gone. Has anyone thought to tell her about Ben's death?"

"One of the supply drivers has taken a message to Mille Lac. Ben was buried today at Lakewood Cemetery at Marie's request."

"I'll ask her if she wants to return to the village. She's free to do whatever she likes. I suspect she'll inherit a good deal of property, now that Ben is dead. You might look into it."

He poured another brandy, and it was obvious he was getting drunk. Roger looked at him contemptuously.

"And that's it?"

"That's it," Stephen replied.

"Just like that," he said, snapping his fingers, "and everything is disposed of. You think you can walk away with a clear conscience."

"My conscience will never be clear."

"Don't run away, Stephen. In the past your stubbornness and self-pity made me angry. Now it only makes me sad. I pity you not for the pain you have suffered, but for your inability to bear it. I pity you because you are weak and self-centered."

Stephen sat silently contemplating his glass of brandy. Roger's words fell like blows and he held his head between his hands.

"Are you finished?" he asked.

"Yes. I have nothing more to say to you, except that I find your behavior despicable."

"Get out!" Stephen shouted, standing and flinging his brandy into Roger's face. "Get out of here while I can still restrain myself."

He awoke late in the morning still seated at the table, his aching head in his arms, a blanket around his shoulders. He pushed his chair back, got up and walked down the hall to the kitchen on unsteady legs. Marie was there.

"I'm surprised to find you here," he said.

"I have no other place to go."

"I'm sorry I couldn't be with you yesterday at the cemetery. You should have told me."

"You slept all day."

"You said nothing at dinner."

She did not reply, but went ahead preparing his breakfast.

"You should be with your mother," he said. "She will need you now that Ben's gone. If you are owed money, Mr. Frasier will settle the account with you. What's that noise outside?"

"They are digging the graves. They came early this morning and are nearly finished."

"Yes, tomorrow is the funeral," he said, remembering. "I would be pleased if you would attend. Sarah was very fond of you."

"I will."

"But when this is all over, you'll have to go to your mother. You can't stay here. I'm closing the house, closing it for good. You won't be needed here then."

She could not hide the pain his words caused her. She lowered her eyes and bit her lip, then looked up at him hopefully.

"There's water on the stove to wash yourself," she said.

Later, when he had bathed and shaved and dressed in clean clothes he came down to the kitchen again. She took his plate out of a warm oven and leaned close to him to set it down. He couldn't help but catch the sweet scent of cologne about her, and saw that she had grown into a beautiful young woman, well groomed and self-assured. It was Sarah's doing, he was certain. Nevertheless it angered him that she was so close to him, watching him in the most difficult time of his life, seeing his weakness. He wanted her to go away; he could learn to do without her.

"Go to your room," he said. "Lay out your clothes for tomorrow. I don't want you hovering over me. And pack your things so you can leave after the funeral."

She looked him in the eye unflinchingly, with anger showing in her face. When she spoke her words were hot with intensity.

"It would be easy to just send me away. I'm just a half-breed and deserve no better from you. But remember that I didn't ask to come here. I had no choice. I can't go back where I came from, not now. And you say I can't stay here. What am I to do? I'm just as alone as you are, and despite my Indian blood, my grief is as real as yours. But I'll go away, if that's what you want."

Stephen was stunned by her anger, and ashamed that he had brought tears to her eyes.

"I'm sorry," he said feebly. "You have been good to us, and I have treated you badly. Please forgive me. It was selfish of me to overlook your loss and your grief. We will go to the service together tomorrow, and then we'll help each other as best we can. Let's help one another to be strong. We don't have much left but our loss."

He held out his hand to her and she took it. She embraced him and they wept quietly together.

*   *   *

They kept the side curtains closed as their carriage entered the streets of town. They parked a block away and walked arm-in-arm to the church. The small crowd parted to allow them to pass. They went down the aisle the same way, arm in arm, looking neither to the left nor to the right. Stephen could almost feel the eyes that followed them, the curious, wondering eyes. He resolved to show no trace of emotion. He resented the conventions that surrounded the burial of the dead. It was barbaric, he felt, to expose the bereaved to such a display. But he knew Sarah would not have shared his view, so he did this for her. They found an aisle seat and he stood aside and allowed Marie to enter first. Throughout the service they remained as they had been, erect and looking straight ahead, suppressing any sign of emotion. When the ordeal was over they went out the same way. Roger Frasier met them in the vestibule.

"Will you follow behind the hearse?" he asked.

Stephen nodded without a word. Amanda Ames, supporting a weeping Mathilda Carpenter, came up next.

"Stephen, I..." His expression told her he did not want to hear her condolences. "You're welcome to come to our open house afterward," she said.

He nodded. It was neither a yes nor a no, just a nod. Then they went down the block to their rig, closed themselves in, and fell in behind the hearse. He kept himself rigidly erect at the family plot, where the snow was dirty from the gravediggers' work. While the Rev. Mr. Knickerbacker read the burial rites and the coffins of his wife and his father were lowered into the earth he remained stolid. Marie, holding tightly to his arm, was equally stoic. When it was over they stepped forward and each took a bit of earth and dropped some on each coffin. Then they walked to the front entrance of Shevley House and stood on the stairs to acknowledge the departing mourners. Only Roger came forward to speak to them.

"I hope you'll come to the open house," he said. "Your daughter is there in the care of a nurse."

Stephen thanked him, but made no commitment. He gave Marie his arm and guided her into the house. Then he returned and stood at a distance to watch the workmen shovel the frosty earth into the grave. When they had finished they walked past him, bidding him a quiet, respectful good-day. But he did not respond. He pulled his heavy coat tightly around him and went to her grave where he stood motionless for a long time. He didn't notice the sky grow dark, nor feel the cold wind that whined through the bare branches of the oaks.

All he saw was the summer sunlight sparkling in her hair. All he felt was the warmth of her nearness. All he heard was her laughter echoing across the years.

*   *   *

The newest Koenig was given Christian names that honored his grandfather and his uncle. His father was honored, too. He was called John Martin Koenig. He was the delight of his Aunt Hildy whom the Hespendorffs sent down from the big house to help Laura during the first weeks after her delivery. Little John was a chubby, pink bundle of life that thrilled her and filled her with unbounded joy. She spent hours with the infant in her arms, rocking back and forth in front of the fireplace, cradling him carefully in her arms, looking into his bright blue eyes and relishing his jolly smile.

"Just look at him, Laura! Have you ever seen such a happy smile? He is the most wonderful baby ever to be born. How in the world did you get him?"

Hildy's question set her aback. Sometimes it was easy to forget that she looked upon the world with childlike innocence.

"The angels brought him to us, Hildy. I guess they blessed us with him because we were good and worked hard. Little John is our reward."

"Then I will be good and work hard, too, and I will pray to the angels that they bring me just such a baby. Frau Hespendorff prays to the saints. We get down on our knees in the corner in front of a little box on a small table. It has a doll inside and we pray for all sorts of things. Next time I will pray for a baby just like little John."

"You would do well to pray for a husband first," Martin said.

"That would be nice, too," Hildy agreed. "But most of all I want a baby. See him grab my finger. He's very strong."

482

"I'm glad, Hildy. We'll pray that he grows up to be a strong young man who can help his father on the farm. Martin works very hard for us, and I am happy that I was able to give him a son."

"No, the angels brought him," Hildy corrected her.

"Yes, my dear sister, that's true. The angels brought him."

"Now if they'd just bring me another section of land," said Martin, winking at his wife.

Chapter 30

Although Stephen had witnessed death intimately, it remained forever a mystery to him, a deeply fascinating enigma. He had seen its awful aftermath, its devastating impartiality, from the corpse of old Williams stretched out on a table, to the overwhelming carnage of the battlefield. He had known death's victims and counted among them his dearest friends and beloved family members. He'd seen death march across an open field and explode in his face, he'd felt its sharp sting as a bullet seared his innards – yet he had not been taken into its confidence. He'd served as death's cruel instrument and destroyed the lives of others. He'd been held in death's cold grip for months on end. But from all this he had learned little. He had felt the terrible emptiness that death left to the living as he kissed the bloodless lips of his dear wife, and though he had longed for death himself, it remained a stranger to him. He realized at last there was only one way learn death's awful secret, and that way demanded everything of him while promising nothing.

*   *   *

Jim Malloy banged loudly on the kitchen door. After a long wait, Marie answered his knock. He introduced himself and told her he'd come to see Stephen.

"Come in, please," she said, groggy from a deep sleep. While he waited she went quickly up the back stairs, only to return moments later, her face flushed with anxiety.

"He's not here!" she exclaimed.

They searched the house and the barn, and at last they found him in the family plot sprawled across Sarah's grave. Marie gasped, certain he had killed himself. But Jim leaned closer and discovered a breath of life.

"Let's get him inside," he said, lifting the cold, gray body and hoisting it to his shoulder. She directed him to her bedroom where the pot-bellied stove was still warm. Jim laid him on her bed and set about building up the fire. Marie quickly opened Stephen's coat, looking for blood, but found none.

"What are you doing?" Jim asked.

"I was afraid he'd hurt himself, but it's just the cold."

"The cold could kill him. Good thing it wasn't a bitter night, or he would be dead." He put his ear to Stephen's chest again. "Let's get him out of those wet clothes and cover him well."

"Will you help me with him?" she asked.

"Sure. A gent called Frasier says I'm hired beginning today. Might as well earn my keep. Is there any whiskey around – for him, not for me?"

Marie nodded and went to Vincent's office off the front hall and brought back a bottle from the desk drawer.

"We'll thaw him from the inside with this," Jim said, tipping the bottle to Stephen's lips. Enough of the searing liquid went into his mouth to bring on a coughing spell. "Easy does it, lad. Look there, m'am, his eyes blinked. He'll come around once we've warmed him up a bit."

Only semi-conscious, Stephen began shivering violently, his teeth chattering.

"I'll make some broth," Marie said, stepping out into the hall and into the kitchen. Jim pulled up a chair next to the bed.

"Aye, lad," he said, "it reminds me of that winter at Camp Stone with the rain and mud and the chill. You're lucky we didn't get a freeze last night or you'd be joining the rest of the family up there on the rise."

Marie made breakfast for Jim and the two stayed at Stephen's side all through the day as his body fought off the numbing cold. Every time he showed a sign of awakening she spooned hot broth into his mouth, but his shivering and shaking continued. To amuse himself and keep Marie's spirits up Jim regaled her with stories of their army days, and to hear him tell it Stephen was the only soldier in the Union army who even came close to being as brave and heroic as good ol' Jim Malloy. After dinner Jim announced that he'd been told to sleep in the carriage house, so Marie got him a lantern from the back porch and gave him an armload of blankets. He made his way across the grounds to the stable, fed the horses and climbed up the stairs to sleep.

Marie sat by Stephen's side all evening, keeping his quilts tucked well under his chin. She put a kettle of broth on the stove to keep it warm, and toweled the sweat from his brow. After more than an hour he still hadn't stopped his shivering. In desperation, she stood up, slipped out of her clothes, and slid naked into bed beside him. She nestled her warm body next to his and held him tightly in her embrace. Within an hour his shivering stopped.

Few would understand their relationship; none would condone it. At first they lived in separate rooms, resuming their roles as master and maid. But gradually they were drawn together by the unavoidable hunger for human discourse, companionship and intimacy. In each other they found the will to carry on with their lives. They found strength in the realization that they were not alone, despite their self-enforced isolation from all but Jim Malloy. Sharing their grief and their loneliness seemed to lighten their burdens. If they had to mark the point where the agony and emotional turmoil ended and the comfort of an intimate relationship began, they would recall the first time Marie broke down in tears and Stephen took her in his arms to console her. Like lost children they clung to one another, experiencing for the first time the heartening flow of exchanged energy. Not a word passed between them. They had no qualms, no shame, and no regret. Stephen had known such a sensation before, the sweet exhaustion that left him empty and brimming simultaneously. For Marie it was a new and wondrous experience that stirred her youthful passions, stimulated her deepest instincts with an intensity that left her gasping for breath, her breast heaving and damp with perspiration. It left her with a deep satisfaction that glowed in her wild and beautiful eyes. The word love never passed their lips. Theirs was not a dewy-eyed romance. It was an instinctive, natural drive that required no special words to be understood or appreciated. It formed a bond of loyalty and devotion between them that was uniquely theirs.

*　　*　　*

Jim Malloy stood in Roger Frasier's office looking very apprehensive. Roger read the letter he had brought to him, and then he read it again.

"This is incredible," he said, casting it aside. "What am I supposed to make of it?"

"I don't know. Steve asked me to bring it to you. He said he was going away, and I was to bring you this letter."

"He's a damned fool. And just when I thought he might be getting his life straightened out."

"Sorry, but it wasn't my place to stop him."

"Of course it wasn't, Malloy. No one blames you. Was Marie with him when he left?"

"Oh, yes. They'd been getting' things ready for weeks – food, clothes, tools. My guess is they plan to homestead someplace."

"Someplace?"

"Never did say where. I figured they'd head west."

"Unbelievable. Was he acting strangely? Did he seem to make sense?"

"Seemed fine to me. He asked me to take care of the place. We cleaned it top to bottom, the three of us did, and this morning we locked it up. Here's the keys. I'm to take care of the horse, keep the grounds trimmed up and tend to the gardens and the graves. Things like that. He said it'll all be for his daughter some day, and he wanted everything just so. But he said to clear it with you, because you'd have the final say."

"So it says in his letter. Do you want such a job, Malloy?"

"I've got nothing else to do, not at the moment any-way. Hell, it's a place to hang my hat. We fixed up a nice set of rooms over the carriage house. And left a horse for me to get around. I'll have enough to keep busy."

"Understand that it might not last long. Stephen's run off like this before. He might be back in month, or a year."

"He'd still need help keeping the place up, and I'd still need a roof over my head. The man's been through a lot, Mr. Frasier. I think he wants to get away, to try something new. I don't worry about him. Marie will take care of him, if you know what I mean."

"Yes, I know only too well what you mean. Just one more thing: Did he drop any hints – where he intended to go, what he planned to do?"

"No, sir. Like I said, nothing for certain. Even when he took a little too much to drink he never talked about his plans. I don't think he really knows."

"Well, Malloy, it seems he's left you and me holding the bag. You've got Shevley House and I've got Shevley Lumber Company. We're partners, like it or not. And may God help us."

As they spoke a wagon trundled by in the street below. The long, flat bed was the type commonly used to haul lumber, but this one was fitted with a tarpaulin stretched across its side posts and lashed in place. The driver was a tall, muscular man in a heavy mackinaw and hobnailed boots. A broad-brimmed hat was pulled down over his long hair that was gathered in the back and held with a knotted thong. He guided the wagon down Nicollet Avenue with the flow of traffic, studying the buildings along the way and the people who crowded the street. At the bridge he waited to pay his toll and looked back over the city, marveling at the changes that had taken place over the past twenty years. When he had first seen this town it had been a mere collection of shacks scattered helter-skelter in a sea of mud. Now row upon row of substantial buildings rose along its thoroughfares. Only the mud remained to remind him of the past. Some things will never change, he thought, like the muddy streets and the river that roared over the falls and raced beneath them as they crossed the bridge. The sun struggled through the morning overcast and glinted on the roof of the Shevley mill. In old St. Anthony he looked down upon the island where he had suffered a terrible humiliation during an Independence Day picnic many years before. He was content to leave it all behind, leave it to the eager millers who now crowded the riverbank, leave it to the shopkeepers and the bankers and businessmen who sought their fortunes here. He would leave it to them, and to the thousands of ordinary people who had come to work in the mills, the shops, and the factories, people who built homes and labored to create the city of the future. He knew that ultimately they would realize the dream his father had nurtured from the very beginning. They would live that dream without ever knowing what had gone before, ignorant of the debt they owed to Vincent Shevley and his peers who had tamed the wild frontier and profited from it, laid the foundation for – for what? He could not say for sure, because the city was in a constant state of change. But he knew the cost, the pain, the grief and the sacrifice of the early settlers. He knew it all too well, and that knowledge robbed him of the ability to evaluate the future objectively. He only knew that it had not been his dream, he had not sought its fulfillment, and he had served it only with reluctance. Now he was putting it all behind him. He paused at the river road to look northward toward the pineries. The woman at his side looked at him with a puzzled expression.

"That way lies trouble," he explained. "Shevley land, Shevley timber, Shevley camps. I want no part of it."

So saying he turned their wagon to the east toward St. Paul and beyond until they reached the shores of a placid lake where they made camp for the night. The woman built a fire and as she cooked their evening meal the flames danced in her beautiful eyes. When they had eaten, the man sat quietly by the fire, honing the gleaming blade of his axe, a confident smile on his face.

*　　*　　*

489

A mild spring followed the bitter winter of 1872-73, and the soft, rich earth had turned easily under Martin's plow. The bottomland he cleared added more than ten acres to his plot of land, and for the first time since they arrived in the valley his prospects for making a small profit were bright. He planted his fields with a happy heart and by mid-July rows of green marched neatly over the rolling land. The sun's first rays fell across his fields and the healthy plants turned to embrace the warmth of the day. He had come to farming not by choice, but by necessity. Now as success literally sprang from the earth all around him, he felt the thrill, the satisfaction that must have inspired his father and his father before him. The years of struggle and hardship suddenly seemed worthwhile and for the first time in his life Martin did not dream of escaping his lot. He was a farmer, and he had no desire to be anything else. He caught the aroma of the fat little sausages frying on the kitchen stove and strolled contentedly back to the cabin.

"It will be a good year, Laura," he said. "It's another beautiful day."

"One beautiful day doesn't make a good year," she said, laying a platter of hotcakes and sausage on the table.

"True, but one after another, after another – I think it will be a good year."

She smiled indulgently. It pleased her to see him happy and full of hope. Little John gurgled as he attacked his bowl of oatmeal mush with awkward jabs of a spoon held tightly in his fist. Laura ate sparingly, still trying to trim the fat she'd gained during pregnancy. She hopped up frequently to fill her husband's coffee cup, get more butter, retrieve and wash the baby's dropped spoon. At the sink she looked through the window at a sudden darkness in the sky.

"Rainstorm coming," she remarked.

"How could that be? The sky was clear."

"Come see for yourself." She gathered up the child and together they went out to watch the cloud that loomed in the distance. It was black and dense, unlike any rain cloud they'd seen. As it moved closer a strange noise seemed to accompany it.

"Hear that?" Martin asked. Laura put the baby down in the grass and came to her husband's side, grasping his arm.

"Maybe we ought to go inside," she said. "It's a tornado."

"I don't think so," he said. "There's no funnel cloud. It's something else. It's coming at us, and that sound is getting louder."

As the cloud drew near it obscured the sun whose rays filtered through it to cast a pale green aura over the landscape. As the noise grew more intense it sounded more like the rattling of paper magnified a million-fold. Soon the leading edge of the cloud came clearly into view.

"My God, they're grasshoppers, a huge cloud of 'em!"

Laura, struck dumb by the sight, stood with her mouth agape as the sound of the massed insects became a roar that drowned out her husband's words. Suddenly he grabbed a shovel and charged toward his fields swinging wildly at the invading horde of voracious insects. Their sticky bodies struck Laura in the face and on her arms and she screamed and brushed frantically at them. The air about her was thick with them as she raced to save her child who was covered with bugs. She snatched him up and ran to the cabin. Slamming the door, she tried to brush off the grasshoppers, stomping them under foot until the plank flooring was a slippery mess. The baby was crying hysterically, his eyes covered with the insects that were hopping in and out of his mouth. In a panic Laura grabbed a towel and began beating them off the baby.

Outside Martin stood helplessly in his devastated fields as the stragglers foraged on the last bits of green, all that remained of his crops. Meanwhile the vanguard of the marauding horde was moving steadily across the countryside, devouring everything in its path. Martin's face and hands were covered with the insects' sticky brown secretions; his clothing riddled with holes where the ravenous locusts had fed upon the fibers. The din of their stridulation still echoed in his ears as he plucked off the creatures that still clung to him. Trudging back to the cabin he found not a single plant that had survived the onslaught. Corn that had been several feet high now were barren stalks only a few inches tall. Acres of wheat had been mowed to the ground as if by a mighty reaper. Even Laura's flower garden and small plot that provided their household vegetables had been wiped out. Scattered over the ground were the remains of hundreds of thousands of the dreadful insects that had failed to survive their own gluttony. A drying towel at the outside wash basin hung in tatters. Martin snatched it off its hook and wiped his face. Then he shook his fist at the heavens.

"What do you want from me?" he cried. "I have worked hard. I have asked little. Now I am ruined!"

*　　*　　*

The plague of locusts presaged a year of bitter defeats for Martin, defeats that stripped him of hope and optimism and left him as devastated as his fields. With little left to salvage of his own farm, he hired out again to the Hespendorffs so that harvest time at least would mean some small income to help put food on his table. But the fates were far from finished with him, and before they were through they would find him capable of many things, including manslaughter.

Old Frau Hespendorff died in August and was buried on a hot and sticky Sunday afternoon. The whole clan congregated at the main house where the men drank beer and talked of farming and the women served up large bowls of hot potato salad, plump bratwurst, loaves of black bread and baking pans filled with succulent rhubarb strudel. Old man Hespendorff, his eyes vacant, sat on the porch rocking back and forth while a dribble of tobacco juice ran from the corner of his mouth, staining his long, flowing beard. Behind the scenes his sons spoke in whispers of how they would share their father's domain.

The boys, as they were called, kept Hildy Koenig at the main house to care for the old man, but so bereft was he of reason that he lasted only until the first frost. They found him in a nearby pasture, torn by brambles and nibbled by field mice, and they blamed poor, simple-minded Hildy for letting him escape, though it was obvious he had wandered off in the dead of night and that no one really could have prevented it. Once the boys had buried their father the plans that had germinated for decades in the fertile fields of their greed blossomed forth. The eldest son took over the main house and the lion's share of his father's holdings. The others shared what was left in equal portions. Although Lotte and Adolf fared well enough under this division of spoils, no provision was made for Hildy. There was a lingering suspicion among the other Hespendorff wives that hapless Hildy not only was to blame for the old man's death, but also was much too pretty and conveniently addle-brained to be left as a temptation for their menfolk. Better that she be delegated to Anna's care at the hotel than to serve in any isolated farmhouse. Lotte could have used Hildy's help with the children, but she was well aware of the undercurrents of jealousy that swirled around Hildy, and agreed that her sister would be better off in town. After all, her Adolf was a man, and not immune to Hildy's inadvertent charms.

Since Anna had accepted Hespendorff generosity and made a resounding success of it, she was expected to take care of her less fortunate relatives. She purchased a lot on Meridian Avenue from Judge Chatfield and had a three bedroom, two story house built on it, not for Martin and his family, but for herself. Her brother was given her apartment on the ground floor of the hotel and Martin and Laura took over the day-to-day operation of the establishment and its related jobs – desk clerk, barkeeper and general handyman. Laura assumed responsibility for housekeeping and laundry, and the restaurant, all with assistance from Hildy, who also looked after little John and performed whatever other duties Laura found distasteful.

There was nothing Martin could do but accept Anna's hospitality, for he held no deed to the land he had worked so diligently, and the man who had given it to him now was dead. The boys expressed their appreciation of his work and his plight, but they also made it clear that he had failed in his stewardship of their land, and therefore must relinquish it to its rightful owners. Martin protested that the grasshoppers had not come at his bidding to destroy his dreams, but he took their two-hundred-dollar balm and moved his family into the hotel.

The townspeople felt more comfortable with a man behind the desk, for although Anna's conduct had been irreproachable she did spend many long hours on the job amid the comings and goings of strangers, and that of course gave rise to gossip. As incapable of indiscretion as she was of flying, Anna paid little attention to the local busybodies. She continued as the brains behind the Fair Prairie Hotel, now a major stopping place and watering hole for travelers between points to the south and the twin cities of Minneapolis and St. Paul to the north, and continued to thrive. In keeping with an ironclad contract she had made with old man Hespendorff years before, Anna – along with the Fair Prairie Bank – now owned the hotel.

*   *   *

It had been a particularly busy Saturday night. Nearly every table in the restaurant was filled, five of the rooms were let, and a crowd of six lingered at the bar to drink beer and talk into the night. Among them was a red-haired drummer who came into town on the afternoon coach from St. Paul. He was a fat, freckle-faced man who had struggled into the lobby with a huge traveling case, sweating profusely and cursing the hot, muggy weather. Martin signed him in and collected his money for a two-night stay. At the bar that evening the other patrons discovered that the drummer

494

carried "notions" in his traveling case, expecting to sell his pins and needles, ribbons and bows, threads and yarn – to shops in the town. He also carried inside his coat a collection of obscene picture cards for sale to any man with a lewd curiosity and a dime to satisfy it. The cards were the hit of the evening in the barroom, but before long the notions salesman turned his attention from selling pornographic pictures to the real life charms of the pretty barmaid who served him his beer. From his position behind the bar Martin noticed the drummer making advances to the unsuspecting Hildy and informed the rascal in no uncertain terms that he was insulting his sister and was to stop it immediately. His pronouncement cast a pall over the revelers and the drummer left to go to his room. He returned later to complain that the slop jar under his bed had not been emptied and demanded that something be done about it. Since Martin was out back at that moment taking out the garbage, Hildy innocently complied with the drummer's request. It was her screams echoing through the hotel that brought her brother racing up the stairs to the second floor where he found the frightened and hysterical young woman lying in the hallway, her clothing in disarray, her face flushed with fear. Though unable to speak of the atrocity that had befallen her, it was all too clear to Martin. He charged into the drummer's room and confronted him.

"You filthy beast!" he shouted, falling upon the man with fists flying. Drunk and exhausted from his struggle with Hildy, the travelling salesman collapsed under Martin's attack, stumbling back and striking his head on the brass bedstead as he fell to the floor. Blood began gushing from a nasty gash on his forehead, but Martin continued pummeling him until he realized the man was either unconscious or dead. By this time the entire hotel was aroused and coming down the hall to see what was the matter. Laura ran down the block to fetch Anna and in no time the whole neighborhood knew that poor Hildy Koenig had been raped and that her brother had wreaked a terrible vengeance on the stranger who had committed the crime. Despite a crowd of witnesses,

Anna took full responsibility for all that had happened, and sent Martin and his family fleeing into the night a long step ahead of the sheriff, who had to be summoned from the county seat some seven miles away.

At the inquest Anna swore that it was she who attacked the rapist, whose body now was stored in the town's icehouse. After hearing testimony describing the outrage inflicted upon Hildy, Judge Chatfield, who presided over the inquest, accepted Anna's confession. He ruled that the drummer's death was accidental, and that Anna's fury was justifiable and that she in no way had intended to kill the culprit. His verdict was readily accepted in the community, although everyone knew that Anna was not the assailant. But their attitude did little to alter the course of events the tragedy set in motion.

Hildy with her childlike naivete soon forgot the awful invasion of her person. In due course she realized her long-cherished dream of having a baby of her own – a red-haired cherub of normal intelligence who grew up to be a devoted and loving son who cared for his mother until her dying day. In the face of public outcry, Anna closed the barroom, remodeled it, and reopened it again as a soda fountain. It was the only one in Fair Prairie with a twenty-foot long mahogany bar and a huge mirror behind it where eager children could look at themselves as they sipped their sodas and malted milks. Anna, now with a reputation for courage, continued to run a respectable, no-nonsense establishment for many years. Always a handsome woman, even into her middle years, she never married. Instead she hired a new manager and his family and moved Hildy and her baby into her own home, an arrangement that seemed to satisfy her natural instincts and to bring her much happiness.

Martin Luther Koenig was never heard from again – under that name. Frightened and guilt-ridden, he changed his name to Luther M. King and began life anew in a community many miles away. He and Laura kept in touch with Anna by mail, and although she assured him that no guilt would ever attach itself to him as a result of the unfortunate event at the

Fair Prairie Hotel, he declined to return. He relished the opportunity to start afresh, and under his new name homesteaded a likely plot of land in northern Minnesota where he resumed his search for success that thus far had eluded him.

Part III

Denouement

1897 to 1910

Chapter 31

She entered the house through the back door and paused to look into the kitchen. The fresh spring air spilled in behind her to displace the musty air that had been trapped for nearly a quarter of a century. Dust lay thick on the floor, faintly scarred by the skittering of mice. She lifted her skirts and tiptoed in, marveling at the dishes still on the table, set on a cloth that disintegrated at her touch. The ceiling was festooned with cobwebs and the spider's silken strands barred the doorway that led to the dining room. She brushed them aside and stepped in to see the massive mahogany table in its coverlet of dust, a tarnished candelabra standing proudly under a burden of cobwebs. She ran her finger over the backs of the chairs as she glided through the room in wonderment. At the head of the table the chair stood away at an angle as if its occupant had just gotten up and hurried away. In the library the industrious spiders had woven a veritable curtain across an entire wall of books. In the parlor they had knit a soft blanket of gray over the piano wires. She gently pressed a yellowed key and the blanket fell to dust while a muffled note echoed into the front hall, drawing her after it. There sabers of light cut through the boarded windows, growing broad and bold as they slashed through the shadows and flayed the marbled floor into strips of black and white. The office door was ajar and upon the desk she saw a clutter of yellowed papers, their edges curled and brittle, their contents faded. She reached out to touch them, but the sound of footsteps startled her and she hastened into the entrance hall again and began to ascend the stairs. But a hand reached out and grasped her arm, causing her to shiver violently.

"I didn't mean to startled you," he said. "But perhaps you shouldn't go any further."

"Nonsense," she responded. "There's nothing to be afraid of here. I don't believe in ghosts."

"I mean the condition of the place. Why don't we have it cleaned first?"

"Later," she said with the glint of defiance in her eyes. He smiled indulgently and followed her to the topmost floor. She paused at the front bedroom door, then gently lifted the latch and let it fall. The door creaked open slowly, revealing in the sun-split shadows a long, narrow room dominated by a canopied bed, tall and stately and covered with a white silk spread that hung to the floor. In one of the gabled alcoves stood a marble-topped writing table with a brass lamp and a green glass vase that still held a dried bouquet of yesteryear. She took all this in without entering the room, reluctant to intrude on the scene. The man came up behind her and quietly spoke her name.

"Stephanie..."

"Look at it, Jeffry. That's the bed where I was born; the bed where my mother died."

Jim Malloy met them later as they came out the back door into the bright spring sunshine.

"If I'd known you were coming, I'd have aired out the place," he said.

"I didn't want it aired out; I wanted to see it just as it was," Stephanie said.

Roger Frasier sat grimly in the carriage, his white moustache twitching with disapproval.

"Well, are you satisfied?" he asked.

"Quite satisfied," she replied. "You'll be pleased to know I didn't run into a single ghost, just dust and cobwebs."

"Let me sell it," he said. "Be rid of it, once and for all. Bury the past and look to the future."

She did not answer him, but went directly up the rise to the burial plot and stood at the iron fence to read the gravestones.

"Look," she said to Jeffry who had followed her. "There's my grandfather's stone, next to my grandmother Eleanor. And this is where my mother rests."

"Sarah Shevley," Jeffry said aloud, reading the inscription. "Died in 1873."

"That little mound is where her firstborn lies," said Jim, who had labored up the hill under a heavy burden of age. "No marker; she didn't want one, or so I'm told."

Stephanie, at first only curious, now seemed deeply moved. Her eyes were glazed with tears and she dabbed at them with her handkerchief. Jeffry stood near her, ready in case she needed assistance. She squared her shoulders and looked up into the tall oaks as a light breeze ruffled the leaves. She closed her eyes in order to compose herself and stood silent for a moment. Then she turned abruptly and went to Jim, taking his gnarled hands into hers.

"Everything looks lovely, Jim," she said. "You've done a beautiful job. It's all very nice, and I'm grateful."

"Thank you, m'am."

The three of them walked back down to the driveway where Roger waited in the carriage. There she said goodbye to Jim, adding, "You'll be getting company soon."

"What do you mean by that?" Roger asked brusquely.

"I plan to reopen Shevley House. I want it cleaned and completely refurbished. I hope to move in by the end of summer."

"You're just as stubborn as your father," Roger said, bristling with annoyance.

Stephanie fixed him with a cool gaze, the tears gone now, her eyes clear and hard.

"My father is quite another matter," she said evenly. "A matter I plan to address very soon."

"You're making a serious mistake," Roger said. "But I'm not fool enough to try to stop you."

"You could help me, if you wanted to. I simply can't believe you don't know where he is."

"Since you won't accept my denials, I won't repeat them," he said. "Goodbye, Jim, and thank you. It looks as if you will indeed have company soon."

"Goodbye, goodbye," the old caretaker called to them as they went down the drive and pulled cautiously into the traffic along the busy street in front of Shevley House. He looked up at the sound of the breeze rustling the ivy that covered the front of the house, and he wondered where Stephen was and if he knew that Shevley House would be opened again.

*   *   *

Jeffry sat in Roger's ornate office, rolling a thin cigar between his fingers as he emitted a stream of blue smoke through his lips. He was a tall, handsome man in his early thirties, well dressed and well spoken, a man of charm and obvious intelligence. Roger had taken a liking to him immediately. He admired qualities in Jeffry that seemed to reflect his own. The young man also had sprung from humble beginnings, an only child of a widowed mother. She had labored for years to raise and educate him, and he in turn had worked hard to be worthy of her love and support. He was a college graduate, had read law in a prestigious office, and made a success of his profession. In the end he provided well for her, making her last years comfortable and happy. But if she had given unstintingly to him over the years, her greatest gift came at her death when with her last breath she encouraged him to leave his native Philadelphia to seek his fortune in the west. It was because of her that he now found himself in Minneapolis by the Falls of St. Anthony, where he knew she had lived briefly during her early years. He arrived at a most propitious moment, for at the time Roger Frasier was looking for a young and talented attorney to handle the legal affairs of the Shevley Lumber Company. In addition to making a good impression on the company's president, Jeffry also caught the eye of the heiress to the family fortune, the beautiful and ambitious Stephanie Shevley.

"Stephanie is a remarkably competent young woman," Roger was saying. "She's more than ready to assume control of the company, and I am more than ready to retire. There's only one problem." He opened his desk drawer and took out a letter, yellowed with age. He handed it to Jeffry, who read it carefully.

504

"It might stand up in court, if it could be authenticated," Jeffry said. "But it would be better if we could find Stephen Shevley. If we proceed on the basis of this letter, purportedly signed by him, he might step back into the picture at any moment and create all sorts of problems."

"Exactly my thoughts," Roger said. "Finding him might be possible, but it might also stir up a hornet's nest."

"In all probability it would," Jeffry agreed. "But I've discussed it with Stephanie, and she wants nothing to stand in her way – not even the father who deserted her. We've got to find him and drive away the shadow he has cast over this company for the last two decades."

"I knew Stephen well," said Roger. "He was a man of curious strengths, but nearly fatal flaws – mental flaws, as I saw it."

"I've seen the company's books, Roger. Any man who would turn his back on the Shevley fortune and desert his own child is undoubtedly flawed. If I had him on the witness stand I could expose his shortcomings, possibly even have him committed."

"If your plan is to have him declared insane, let me warn you – you may find yourself riding a tiger."

"We're ready for him. Stephanie and I feel it's the only way to proceed. She can't believe he's alive. But if he is, she wants him found. She's eager to face him in court, to publicly denounce him for deserting her, to humble him, and in so doing convince even a skeptical jury that he's unfit to assume responsibility for a company of this magnitude."

"I wonder," Roger mused. "I wonder how she would react if they should come face to face in court. For that matter, I wonder how he would react."

"You may have the opportunity to find out. I've already sent investigators to track him down."

Troubled, Roger looked away. He had long lived with the fear that someday Stephen would walk through the door and lay claim to all he had nurtured and developed over the years. Now it seemed as if that might be a real possibility. His instinctive reaction was to fight. After all, he had always followed his instincts, and he had flourished. Why shouldn't he now?

"We'll have to be ready to confront him with every legal weapon available to us," he said. "There must be no doubt about the outcome. I want his defeat assured before we even lay eyes on him."

"Stephanie's outlook exactly," Jeffry said.

"But we can't depend on that. If Stephanie knows her father is alive, it could change her outlook entirely. Will you be prepared to deal with that eventuality?"

"I must admit that it's my only uncertainty. But I'm depending on her remaining resolute. She's conditioned herself to detest her father. But she's determined to confront the past and to deal with it. That's why she's reopening Shevley House. It's to test herself. I for one hope that at the eleventh hour she doesn't find that blood is thicker than water."

*   *   *

She'd gone off to school in the east as a girl with her eye on a business career, and returned a polished and sophisticated young woman intent on one day controlling the spreading Shevley business empire. Her guardians, George and Amanda Ames, were pleased with their ward in her maturity, but were unable to reconcile themselves to her ambitions. Childless themselves, they had formed firm opinions about a woman's place in the modern world – and it was not in business. They accepted women in professional roles – George had a female doctor on the staff at his Midwestern Hospital, and a female attorney on its board of directors. But he felt that the business world was no place for a lady. His wife concurred.

"Look," Stephanie reasoned with them, "you have devoted more than twenty years of your lives to me. You have sacrificed so much to give me a loving home. Now it's time for me to reciprocate, to go off on my own and let you enjoy your lives free of concern about me. I love you both

506

very, very much. I'd like to see you travel, to do all the things you might have done had it not been for me. I do want to live in Shevley House, but you know that my heart will always be here with you. You are my parents, and our love for each other will never change."

"We built this home for you," George said as he stood at the huge living room window looking out over Lake of the Isles. "We built this place when you were only a small child, hoping that it would always be your home."

"It will always be home to me," she said. "But Shevley House is my heritage. It represents the past that I never knew. I feel I must live there to come to grips with that past. For too long it has been a shadow over my life, and that should not be. Maybe I won't like it there. Maybe it will always be a burden to me. But if it is, then at least I will have allowed the winds of change to blow through it, to freshen it for today's world. I couldn't even sell it, as Roger wants me to do, in its present condition. I want to modernize it, make it a showplace again, have lovely parties, make it the envy of the city. Then, if I choose to sell it, I'll get top dollar for it."

Amanda Ames cringed at the phrase. "Really, Stephanie," she exclaimed. "You're beginning to sound like Roger Frasier."

"Why not? He's my mentor. And he's anxious for me to take over the company so he can retire. When that day comes, maybe I will move back home."

George smiled ruefully. He had built their grand mansion when Stephanie was an infant, following an exodus of the city's most wealthy and influential citizens to the shores of the lake and the rolling hills around it. He had hoped one day to leave it to Stephanie, content in the belief that she would be surrounded by friends and neighbors who had known and loved her over the years.

"Times have changed," he said. "I can remember when Indians lived along this lakeshore – and when proper young ladies wouldn't think of leaving home before they married. And as for women going into business, why it was inconceivable. But yours is an unusual heritage, Stephanie. I can understand your feelings about the company, about Shevley House, about the past. And you will always be welcome here. We have never considered you a burden, and we never will. It's just that we love you so much that we can't bear the thought of losing you."

Stephanie fell into his arms as she had so often done as a child, and hugged him, calling him by the only name she'd ever used.

"Oh, Daddy, Daddy, how I do love you both," she said, reaching out to encompass her mother in her embrace. "There must never be any doubt of that. But my life seems haunted by a past I never knew, by people I never met. I've seen the dust and the cobwebs of another age, and I feel I must sweep them away to prove to myself that Shevley House is just like any other. I feel it is my birthright, and that in order to be free of the past I must take responsibility for its future as well as for the future of the Shevley Company. Please try to understand that I do these things because I must, not out of any lack of love or respect for you."

"But my dear, why do you have to live in that musty old pile? So much misery and suffering has taken place within those walls. I wonder if happiness can ever flourish there," Amanda said.

"We all make our own happiness, Mother. You've said that yourself. You've told me how my natural mother brought sunshine and happiness into that house before she died. Let me prove that I can do the same."

*   *   *

Jeffry found Shevley house crawling with workers — men high on ladders removing boards from shuttered windows and washing the panes; teams of laborers lugging huge rugs into the yard where another crew beat decades of dust from them. The air inside the house was heavy with the scent of soap as women on their hands and knees scrubbed the floors while others polished furniture to bring out a luster buried by decades of neglect. He found Stephanie in the office off the entry hall, seated at the large desk and going over a sheaf of papers.

"You look quite businesslike, Miss Shevley. What is the state of your empire today?"

"You'd know that better than I," she replied. "But look what I've found."

"It's a map."

"There are dozens of maps here, most marking off areas for logging over the years up to the time of my grandfather's death. And then there's this one." She held up a larger map with a heading in fancy script. Jeffry read it aloud.

"Pompantium? What in the world is Pompantium?"

"It apparently was a town at the junction of the Rum River and the Mississippi. It's about where Anoka now stands, if I'm reading this map correctly."

"There's never been a Pompantium there, so far as I know."

"According to these handbills and newspaper clippings it was something my grandfather created, a proposed community that apparently never was built."

"Let's see the date...hmm, 1857. That was the year of the great panic. I've read that there were dozens of such maps drawn up to lure immigrants to Minnesota, but that they all failed for lack of funding. I know that Vincent Shevley cut timber in that area more than forty years ago. I'll have to ask Roger about Pompantium. Speaking of Roger, I've just come from his office. He had reports from our agents in the field. It's about your father."

Stephanie sat rigidly upright, her eyes cold and hard. "What have they found out?" she asked.

"He's alive, my dear."

"Are you certain?"

"As certain as I can be without speaking to him directly. He's alive and living only a few hours train ride from here."

Stephanie's face turned red as a fury rose within her.

"Then go to him," she said as dispassionately as possible. "Go to him and make absolutely sure it's the same man and not some strange coincidence of names. I want proof."

"I think we have it, although of course I'll verify it. We located him as a result of a clue we found in going over old records. He worked a couple of winters in the woods back before the war under the name of Steve Craft. He simply dropped his last name to avoid problems with the other loggers. Craft, as you know, was the name of his maternal grandparents. He later enlisted in the Army under the same name. Roger confirmed all this. I gave the name to my agents in the field and they came up with a match. There's a Steve Craft who manages a small lumber mill in the Hinckley area. One of our own retired superintendents, a reliable man named Shaw, confirmed to Roger that he ran into him just last summer. He's living there with..."

"Never mind," she said. "I don't want to hear anymore. Go there and find him. If you can verify that he's my father, I want you to spare no cost to put him legally out of my life. He must have no claim to or financial interest in anything that bears the Shevley name."

"Even you?" he asked.

"Most particularly me," she said, rising from her chair with anger in her eyes. "I want him out of my life forever."

Jeffry came to her and took her in his arms.

"You frighten me when you're angry," he said. "Don't waste your passion on him; save it for happier, more positive things. Save it for me."

She smiled faintly, but her tension remained, even when he kissed her.

*   *   *

Sheriff's Deputy John King strode confidently toward the saloon, his badge glittering on his shirt pocket. He stopped at the edge of the sidewalk, uneasy about the strange silence from inside the bar. Then suddenly the swinging doors opened and a logger emerged backside first dragging another man.

"Havin' a little trouble here?" the deputy asked.

The logger dropped his burden and turned to see who spoke. His face was raw from a beating, one eye nearly closed.

"Who wants to know?" he asked.

"Deputy King. What happened to that fella?"

"He forgot to duck."

"Looks like you forgot to duck a couple of times yourself."

"That's true. But it was a fair fight."

"You the one causin' this ruckus?"

"Nope. It's Billy Craft who's smashing up the place. We just got in his way."

"What set him off?" the deputy asked.

"He said his old man was the best chopper who ever lived, and we called him on that."

"You called him a liar?"

"Something like that."

"So you started it."

"I wouldn't go so far as to say we started it, but we thought we'd hang around to help finish it."

"You were looking for trouble."

"Sure. Nothing else to do."

John King smiled. He knew very well that there wasn't much to do at that season of the year, except to work on the fire lines or stay in town to drink beer until the money ran out. It was hot and the air was heavy with the smell of smoke. It didn't surprise him that loggers preferred a good brawl over fighting fires. It was their way to raise a little innocent hell while waiting for the first snow to fly. They weren't a mean lot, just young men letting off steam. John King was one of them, working during the off season as a lawman, and they liked him. He was known for locking them up only when they posed a threat to themselves or others, and this wasn't a lock-up case.

"You fellas better get along now and sleep it off," King said. "I think I'll go in and have a talk..."

Billy Craft came out of the saloon at that point, stepped over the unconscious form of one logger, and smacked the other on the side of the head, sending him sprawling.

"Hey, that wasn't fair, Billy," the deputy said. "He was lookin' the other way."

"That's your fault," said Billy. "You took his mind off the fight."

Young Billy Craft was tall and long-legged like his father, and swarthy like his mother. He smiled happily at the deputy, then suddenly flew into the air toward him and wrestled him into the dust. John King was a big man, big enough to pick Billy up bodily, spin him around a couple of times and chuck him into a watering trough. Billy came up sputtering and laughing as a crowd of idle loggers ringed the combatants to cheer them on.

"Come along, Billy," said the deputy. "I'm gonna lock you up until you're sober. You're likely to get hurt, fightin' drunk."

*　　*　　*

The chopper carefully ran his thumb along his blade. The finely honed steel caught the sunlight and flashed it among the trees at the river's edge. Over the stagnant, sluggish stream translucent dragonflies hovered and darted about, while near the muddy bank a bullfrog casually flicked its long tongue at passing insects while wallowing up to its bulbous eyes in the tepid water. Along the riverbank a wall of scrub pine locked arms and fenced in the mill, the lumber yard and the manager's cottage. The woods were tinder dry and the sky was gray with smoke, the fetid odor of it permeating the air. The chopper scuffed the dirt with his boots, settling into position, testing the distance to the tree with his axe. One at a time he rubbed the palms of his hands on his hips before wrapping his fingers precisely around the hickory handle of his axe until the tool became a rigid extension of the muscles that rippled from his wrists to his forearms to his shoulders and across his chest. When he stretched out his arms the blade of the axe reached exactly to the desired spot on the tree. He nicked the bark to mark his target, then lifted the axe gracefully over his right shoulder and swung it with all his strength. Again and again the axe whacked the tree with a thud that rang through the woods and sent wood chips flying. In a matter of minutes the tree swayed and the chopper placed one hand on it to hurry its descent. The surrounding woods swallowed the tree's loud cracking noises and muffled the crash as it hit the ground in a cloud of dust. The chopper stood in the heat of the afternoon, his torso gleaming with sweat. A long, ugly scar ran diagonally across his chest and around his neck two small silver buckles dangled from a leather thong. Pausing only a moment to catch his breath, the chopper moved forward and began rapidly removing the branches from the fallen tree with clean swipes of his axe. Midway he stopped to greet a visitor who approached with a wide, friendly grin.

"Hi, Mr. Craft," he called out. "Doing a little clearing?"

"Just in case the fire comes our way, John."

"Seems to get worse every day, don't it? Mom and the kids are moving out today, and Dad's loading the wagon to follow after."

"We could sure use a little rain. It's been a bad year."

"Heat lightning, that's what sets it off, Dad says."

"How is your father, John?"

"Well as can be expected, what with the drought and the fires. He's talking about moving west, maybe run a herd of dairy cows in the Dakotas."

"A big step for a man of his years. Takes time to develop a good herd. Don't know that I'd have the spunk to try something new at his age."

"Why not? You did it, and you're older than he is."

"Managing the mill was my way of slowing down, John, and I knew something about it when I began. Winters in the woods were getting mighty long. This keeps me busy and puts food on the table."

"Be fine if you could keep Billy busy, too," John said.

"Has he been raising hell again?"

"There just ain't enough for the loggers to do all summer. They tend to get into mischief on these long, hot days. Billy got himself into a tussle in town and I took him in to sleep it off."

"Been drinking, had he?"

"Yes, sir, he'd had a few beers."

"Is the sheriff in town?"

"No, don't expect him back until tomorrow."

"Then it's all right to keep Billy overnight, as long as the sheriff's not around."

"I know what you mean, Mr. Craft. Those two don't get along very well. He seems to have it in for Billy."

"He's not particularly fond of me either."

"No, I guess he's not. It's because of your wife, I imagine. He's got some powerful feelings about..."

"I know, John. You're a good lad to look after Billy. I'll be by for him first thing in the morning."

"Okay, Mr. Craft. I'll see you then."

That evening Stephen sat by the river's edge, leaning against a tree. Marie snuggled in his arms, her head on his shoulder. The sky was filled with the peculiar orange haze that had hung over the area at sunset since the fires began.

"I wonder if it will reach the town," Marie said.

"It's hard to tell. It's not just one fire, but a lot of little fires that skip and jump about in the wind. If the wind turns the fire back on itself it'll burn out for lack of fuel."

"I'm worried about Billy," she said. "I don't like him locked up when there's a fire threatening."

"I could go and get him out, but I thought he'd be safe enough with John King looking out for him, and the sheriff out of town."

"He was fighting over me, wasn't he?"

"No, he was just feeling his oats and raising hell. Maybe a night in jail will make him think twice before he goes at it again."

"Someone probably said something to him. I know they call him 'half breed' to make him angry. Or maybe they said something about me. They do talk about me; I've heard them."

"They don't talk about you when I'm around. They know better."

"You've put up with a lot because of me."

"You are my wife. I love you. It doesn't matter what they say."

"They hate me for my Indian blood. I've spent most of my life living as a white woman, but all they see is the part of me that's Indian, and they hate me for it. I don't understand."

"Some people just have to hate someone; it takes their mind off their own shortcomings. Don't let them bother you. Think about how I love you, and you won't have time to think about their hate."

He kissed her and later that night as they lay naked in their bed with the scant breeze blowing over their bodies he marveled at the way they sustained one another. It was a magic they shared that kept them vigorous despite the passage of years. He studied her as she slept. Her body was firm and well shaped, her face smooth and unmarked by time. Only a few strands of gray showed in her hair. They had spent more than twenty years together, and it had been a good life. She had helped him forget his unhappiness and given him reason to live. She had helped him forget the past and to live for the future. She asked for nothing but his love and to share his life. Over the years their passion for one another had grown into a solid bond of love. He watched the gentle rise and fall of her breast and the smooth stone pendant that rode atop that swelling sea. He was content with the steadfastness of her love. It was as pure and clean as a spring rain, as comforting as a cool breeze on a hot summer's night, as bright and beautiful as a winter's morning when the sun sprinkles the crusty snow with a sparkle like diamonds. Carefully he enveloped her in his arms and held her close and together they found a restful sleep.

Chapter 32

The morning air was heavy with smoke as Stephen strode into town. At the railroad tracks he paused and looked up the line that curved north through a long green corridor and disappeared into the woods. A gust of hot wind stirred the stifling air and furrows of worry creased his brow. In town the streets were empty in the early morning calm. The grocer appeared in his doorway, stretched and yawned. Lifting his long white apron he rubbed his eyes with it, then went inside again. There was nowhere to go to escape the sting and the smell of smoke for it was everywhere. At the jail Stephen did not hesitate, but walked in the open door and was surprised to see the sheriff seated at his desk.

"Don't you know how to knock?" the sheriff asked. He was a heavy man, not muscular, but thick and beefy. His cruel eyes were filled with contempt at the sight of his unexpected visitor. Stephen had tangled with him more than once and knew him for his meanness. He wore a badge not out of respect for law and order, but for the power it gave him over other men's lives. He was a man who thrived on hate, and he had decided long ago that he hated Steve Craft because he was a logger, and loggers caused most of the trouble in town. He hated him even more after he was hired as manager of the lumber mill, because as manager he made more money than the sheriff. He also hated him because his half-breed son was a troublemaker. And above all he hated him because his wife was an Indian, and the sheriff hated Indians more than anything in the world.

"I've come to pick up my son," Stephen said. "I understand he's here."

"Might be," said the sheriff with a sneer. "What makes you think I'd let him go?"

"He was locked up to sleep off a drunk. He must be sober by now."

"Oh, he's sober, all right. I saw to that as soon as I laid eyes on him this morning. He must be the soberest half-breed in town."

Stephen looked beyond the sheriff to the cell in the rear of the jail and saw Billy lying on the bunk.

"Billy, are you all right?" he asked. The figure on the cot stirred and with some difficulty raised himself up on one elbow.

"Stand up, Billy boy. Show your pa you're all right."

Billy put both feet on the floor and balanced himself gingerly on the edge of the cot. His face was swollen and bleeding and his eyes were blackened.

"You son of a bitch," Stephen said with quiet intensity. "You did that to him."

"So what, squaw man? The kid's a..."

Before he could get the words out Stephen was on him like a wild animal. With one hand he grabbed him by the hair while with the other he punched him sharply in the nose. The blow stunned the lawman and his nose began to bleed profusely. As he sagged toward the floor, Stephen slammed his fist against the side of the man's head and sent him sprawling across the tiny office. Snatching his keys off the desk, he opened the cell and helped his son to his feet.

"Easy, Dad," the boy mumbled. "My ribs are all kicked in."

"That dirty bastard! Here, take it easy," he said, guiding him out of the cell and toward the door.

"You'd both better stop right where you are," said the sheriff. He was still lying in a heap on the floor, but he had drawn his pistol and was pointing it at them.

"Put that away before someone gets hurt," Stephen warned him. "You had no call to beat up the kid."

"I had plenty of call, and I'll whip you, too, if I don't blow your head off first. Now get away from that door, both of you."

Stephen suddenly shoved Billy out the door into the street and dove for cover behind the sheriff's desk. When he looked out the sheriff was on his feet with the pistol pointed at him.

"Dumb move, squaw man. Now I've got good reason to kill you – assaulting an officer of the law."

"No one's done anything to merit a killing," Stephen said, "except maybe you for beating up on a sleeping kid half your size."

"I'll take care of the kid in my own good time. It's your hide I want tacked to my wall, and now I can get it legally. Get into that cell," the sheriff said, prodding him with the muzzle of his pistol. He turned the key in the lock, and stepped outside to make sure the gathering crowd saw his bloodied face.

*　　*　　*

It was mid-afternoon when the sheriff returned to the jail. He brought no food or water for his prisoner, but he did bring a visitor. Stephen had stripped off his shirt in the heat of the day and lay on his back on the bunk sweating profusely. He raised his head slightly and saw a young man with neatly clipped hair and moustache. His hands were clean, the nails well manicured. He was impeccably dressed in white linen, though obviously hot and uncomfortable in his collar and tie. He placed a briefcase on the sheriff's desk and laid his hat on it. Turning to the jailer he said, "This is the man I'm looking for. I'd appreciate some time alone with him."

"Watch your step," the sheriff cautioned as he left the office, "he's a wild one."

Once they were alone the visitor drew up a chair by the barred door just out of Stephen's reach. He unbuttoned his vest and dabbed at his brow with his handkerchief.

"I've never encountered such miserably hot weather, nor such disagreeable conditions. But let's make ourselves comfortable, for our business will be brief. This is my card, Mr. Shevley."

Stephen sat swiftly upright at the sound of the name he had left behind so long ago. He took the visitor's card and glanced at it.

"This was just a small town brawl," he said. "I don't think I need an attorney."

"I'm not here to offer my services, Mr. Shevley. You are Stephen Craft Shevley, are you not?"

Stephen picked up his shirt and pulled it on, turning his back to his visitor and asking: "What's your business here that I should answer that question?"

"I represent the Shevley Lumber Company. Does that explain my presence?"

"It might, if I knew the nature of your business."

"First it is to establish your identity in order to prove that you still exist. There have been rumors to the contrary over the years. The scar that you're covering up does that very nicely. You undoubtedly are Stephen Shevley. Gettysburg, wasn't it?"

"No."

"Whatever. You would be surprised to know that finding you was a very difficult endeavor."

"Wasted endeavor, I should think. I have nothing to do with the Shevley Company."

"Ah, that touches on our second order of business, which is to see that you don't have anything to do with the company – ever."

"Anyone in Minneapolis could have told you that. Isn't Roger Frasier still running things? Or is he dead?"

"Mr. Frasier is quite alive. As a matter of fact I am here at his behest. He wants to continue running things, as you put it, until he turns it over to its rightful owner."

"I don't understand. I gave Roger a letter when I left. Knowing him as I do, I'm sure that letter is in his files. It could have saved you a trip."

"That letter's not sufficient. It could be challenged on the basis of your mental condition at the time you wrote it."

"Who in hell would challenge it?"

"You might, unless I ascertain that your mental condition has not improved over the years. Judging from present circumstances, it appears it hasn't. My clients..."

"Clients? Who's this 'rightful owner' you mentioned?" He paused, suddenly aware of what the lawyer was saying. The young man easily read his expression.

"Yes, Mr. Shevley. I also represent your daughter, the child you deserted more than twenty years ago. She can't feel safe until you're locked up for good – committed, if you will."

Stephen sank onto the bunk and held his head in his hands, unable to immediately cope with such news.

"Don't tell me that after all these remorseless years you find yourself overwhelmed by shame, Mr. Shevley. I believe your record shows you've always had trouble handling shock, and obviously you still do."

"What do you know about shock or remorse, you insolent – if I weren't locked in..."

"Threatening violence – another sign of mental instability. But believe me, Mr. Shevley, I do not sit here in judgment. I'll leave that to a court of law. I've come merely to prove three points, that you are Stephen Craft Shevley, that you are alive, and that you are mentally incompetent and thus should be committed to an institution for the insane. I'm confident now that I can prove all three."

"You must be the one who's mad, if you think I wouldn't fight such charges. Who put you up to this, was it Roger? Or the girl? And what's in it for you that you would go to such lengths?"

"I don't mind answering your question, since it involves a priceless irony. You see, originally my goal was to seek you out to be my patron, but instead you've become my prey."

He leaned back in his chair and removed a cigar and a small tool from his vest pocket. He snipped the end from the cigar and fished for a match that he struck on the floor. He expelled a thin stream of smoke and smiled, seeming quite pleased with himself.

"What do you mean, patron?" Stephen asked sullenly.

"My dear mother, God rest her soul, urged on her death bed that I seek you out. She told me that you could assure my future, and as it turned out she was right. But she never would have guessed how it came about. Since you were no longer with the Shevley Company, I found employment there on my own merits."

"And ever since then you've been tracking me like some sort of legal bloodhound?"

"No, actually that came later after I met your daughter. She's a charming young lady, Mr. Shevley, if you care. You'll discover that for yourself very soon. She's practical, too. She set out to establish through me that you were dead. She couldn't believe that you were still alive and yet never had come to see her, never expressed a whit of interest in her. It was quite a shock to her to learn that you were alive, and now she wants to make certain that you never do express an interest in her. She wants you to remain out of her life, but she's concerned that you might sometime..."

"Why couldn't you all just leave me alone? Why must you open old wounds, stir up memories best forgotten? Let the past remain buried."

"Sorry, but that isn't my decision to make, although I confess I do have a stake in all this. I'm merely following orders now, but once your daughter and I are married I shall be giving orders as well."

"You plan to marry my daughter?"

"I do."

"Strange how all this developed," Stephen said. "Somewhere out of the past I can hear laughter, as if this has all been a huge joke. I suppose in a way it is, and it's on me. My daughter seems to have inherited the worst qualities of my father, and none of the goodness of her mother. God pity her."

"Stephanie Shevley is a talented and educated woman. She doesn't need God's pity or anyone else's.

Shevley Company is rightfully hers, and she is determined to have it without any interference from you."

"She needn't worry. I'll sign whatever you require. I want nothing to do with her or the company."

"That, sir, is inadequate."

"Why?"

"Because you could come forward later and protest that you signed the document under duress, or while suffering some mental incapacity. That would pose serious legal problems for us."

"Mental incapacity?"

"The record is full of examples of your strange behavior. Even today there are some in the city who remember you as the Madman of Shevley Mansion. Others recall an incident decades ago when you threw a young woman into the Mississippi River when she rejected your advances."

"That's nonsense!"

"Your drinking was legendary."

"I still take a drink occasionally. It proves nothing."

"At least one veteran of your regiment tells how you not only had a taste for liquor, but that you openly courted death on the battlefield in defiance of all rationality."

"Jim Malloy would never testify against me."

"We'll see. I also have a deposition from a military doctor who cared for you at Fort Snelling. He says you were out of your mind. Do you want me to go on?"

"No..."

"Your own daughter will testify that you abandoned her when she was only hours old and never once in twenty-some years came to see her."

"There are many things I have lived to regret."

"Yes, like today, when you attempted to kill the sheriff."

"If I had tried to kill him, he would be dead."

"You would kill a man for performing his duty?"

"Yes, I have killed men in battle who were only performing their duty. Does that make me a menace to society?"

"Military heroics have little cachet in the modern world."

"Yes, how soon we forget."

"I hate to end this conversation, Mr. Shevley, but I must arrange for a hearing where we intend to offer a list of incidents to show that you are mentally unsound. On the basis of that evidence we will seek to have you committed. Remember that we have credible witnesses in case you should force this matter to trial. If you should try to preempt us by using that evidence in your own defense, you will fail. Once you are safely locked away, your protests will only help our case, for they will seem to be little more than the ravings of a madman."

"Sometimes I think it's the world that has gone mad," Stephen said, idly looking at the lawyer's business card. The name of the attorney finally registered with him. "Wells! Then your mother must be Grace Fairchild Wells."

"That's correct. And my father was Col. Jonathan Wells. I never knew him. He died in the war."

"My God!" Stephen exclaimed, his heart racing. "You said you and my daughter plan to marry?"

"My private life has nothing to do with this case," the lawyer said indignantly. And with that he walked out of the jail.

*   *   *

At a homestead some miles from town John King drew his horse to a halt and leaped to the ground. The air was filled with hot ash that drifted down and covered everything with a mantle of gray. He looked inside the farmhouse and called out, but no one answered.

"John, is that you?" came a voice from the barn.

"Yes, Dad. I'm glad to see you're leaving."

Martin led a team of horses from the barn and tethered them at the pump, where they drank greedily from the trough. He looked over his acreage, all wilted and covered with ash, and shook his head. The air was so hot it hurt to breathe and his eyes stung from the fine debris in the air.

"I dunno," said the farmer. "Wind's from the south and driving hard. But it could shift."

"Yah, a rainstorm could put out the fire, too, but it's not likely," said the young deputy. "I see Mom and the kids got away."

"I sent 'em down to Pine City. Everyone's gathering there."

"You should hurry there, too. Nothing you can do here."

"I could pray," said Martin.

"Then go pray in a safe place. Get along now."

"Soon as I get hitched up. Gotta get these things to Laura and the kids, things they might need."

"Nothing here is worth your life," said his oldest son.

"Everything here is my life," he countered. "Where are you heading?"

"Back to Hinckley. I'm bailiff tomorrow for a special hearing."

"Be careful."

"I'll do that. Now you get a move on."

Martin climbed into the wagon and took hold of the reins.

"John," he said.

"Yes, Dad?"

"If I don't make it, I want Koenig on my marker."

"We all know that," said John. "Don't worry. God will know who you are."

"I want men to know, too. I'm not ashamed of my name."

"I know, Dad. Now get along. I can hear the fire's roar."

Martin snapped the reins and the horses took off at a trot out toward the county road. John followed, then turned his horse back toward town. He was glad his father was getting out safely. He pitied the man; he had worked so hard for so long and had so little to show for it. And now what little he had was in danger of going up in smoke. But he could rescue his name, and it was touching to the young man how badly his father wanted it back again. Ironic, he thought, that he wanted to die as a Koenig after raising a generation of Kings.

*　　　*　　　*

The Saturday morning skies over Hinckley were blacker than usual with smoke and ash. Although conditions were undeniably worse than they had ever been, there was little alarm among the residents. Fires had surrounded them at various distances and in various degrees of severity for nearly three months. Some of the outbreaks were closer than others, but none had yet posed a serious threat and none so far had shaken their confidence that they could protect themselves. Fire equipment stood at the ready. The huge water tank at the town pump was kept filled to brimming. Fire volunteers were always on the alert. Townspeople went about their business as on any other day, although with greater discomfort owing to the heat and the polluted air.

At the jail Deputy King came in early carrying a hearty breakfast for the town's only prisoner. Stephen, unable to sleep, was sitting on the edge of his bunk, stripped to the waist and sweating profusely. "What's new on the fires?" he asked.

"Seems to be bypassing Pine City. A lot of folks are heading that way for safety."

"Did your family get away?"

"Mother and the kids left early yesterday; Dad was leaving yesterday afternoon with the wagon. It was pretty sad."

"Lost his crops, did he?"

"Oh, yeah. Took the spirit right out of him; he was talkin' about dyin' and all. He wanted to be sure we get his right name on the gravestone."

"What did he mean by that?" Stephen asked.

526

"Oh, he had a bit of trouble way back when I was just a baby, down in Fair Prairie on the Minnesota River. Ran away and changed his name so he wouldn't get caught. He's still got a couple of sisters down there runnin' a hotel, but he'll never go back."

"What did he do?"

"Killed a man – accidentally, of course, but he took off on the run. Changed his name from Koenig to King and never went back. Now he's afraid he'll die and he wants Koenig on his gravestone."

Stephen, stirred by the mention of the Koenig name, looked down at the silver buckles that dangled around his neck.

"I knew a family once named Koenig," he said. "Lived up on the Rum River. The oldest son, John, and I served together in the war."

"That could be Dad's family," the young deputy said. "I was named after an uncle who died at Gettysburg. Dad was just a young boy then. The family later moved down to the Fair Prairie area to farm. Big German community down there at that time."

"I'll be damned," Stephen exclaimed. "You see these buckles? They came from the boots of my friend, John Koenig. He treasured those boots. They belonged to his father who brought them over from the old country. I came across John's body after the fight at Gettysburg. I knew how he felt about those boots, so I clipped off the buckles to bring back to his family. I've had them ever since."

"I'll bet they're one in the same man," John exclaimed.

"Then lighten my load, John. Take these as a keepsake, and I'll figure I've kept a promise to an old friend."

"Do you really think they belonged to my uncle?" the deputy asked, accepting the buckles. "Wouldn't that be somethin', though! I can't wait to tell Dad."

Their talk was interrupted by the sound of footsteps in the jail office. John put the buckles in his pocket and went out to greet Jeffry Wells.

"What an awful day," Wells said. "I hope this will all be over soon so we can get back to the city. Craft's daughter is coming in on the St. Paul and Duluth, and the judge is coming in later on the Eastern Minnesota out of Duluth."

"It must be pretty important for a Saturday court session," John said.

"A simple proceeding, but important indeed. Meanwhile I have some personal business with your prisoner, if I may."

"Sure, I'll wait outside. Not much privacy in here."

"Better yet, I wonder if you'd mind meeting the St. Paul and Duluth. The young lady in question will be aboard and will need a ride to the hotel."

John nodded and left the office; Wells went back to the cell to confront Stephen.

"Just a few preliminary matters to straighten out," he said.

"They can wait, Wells. First I want to know about your father and your mother, and why she happened to send you to me."

"I don't see that it's any of your business, but it's a tale simply told. My mother was an old friend of your parents. They introduced her to Jonathan Wells and that led to their marriage. When the war came he was called to duty in Washington. They maintained a home there. Later he was sent into battle where he met his death. My widowed mother then moved to Philadelphia where I was born."

"When was that?" Stephen asked.

"I don't know what..."

"It's an easy question," Stephen interrupted him, "but critical. When were you born?"

"September 3, 1863," said the exasperated attorney.

Stephen leaned against the bars of his cell and studied the young man closely. He could see similarities – Grace's nose, the same slant of the brow. His coloration was hers, the ebony hair, the pale skin. He weighed each of these elements while silently counting the months before arriving at an inescapable conclusion.

"I was with Colonel Wells only hours before he died," he said. "He died in September of 1862 following the second battle of Bull Run."

"What is that supposed to mean?"

"If you were born in September of 1863, it means he could not possibly have been your father."

"You're an unmitigated cad for suggesting such a thing," said Wells, his eyes blazing with anger. "If I weren't a gentleman, I'd thrash you."

"I haven't suggested anything yet. I'm simply telling you that Jonathan Wells could not have been your father. We shared the miseries of a field hospital and I helped put him aboard an ambulance bound for Washington. I know from your mother's own account that he did not survive that journey. He died a year before you were born."

"That's an extraordinary story, but what proof do you have? You're trying to besmirch the memory of my dear mother – but to what end? Are you really so insane that you'd expect me to believe your story?"

"I tell you only because I fear for your future and that of my daughter."

"Your daughter! Now I know you're mad. You haven't had a care about your daughter in all of her life. Why now? Are you creating this mischief so she'll believe she's marrying a bastard?"

"No, Wells. I'm trying to keep her from marrying her own brother."

Wells was momentarily stunned. Then his temper exploded and he lunged at the bars, grabbed the unresisting prisoner and shook him violently.

"I should kill you for that, you filthy, conniving..."

"I'm telling you this for your own good. The last thing in the world I'd ever do is cast a shadow over the reputation of your mother. She was a good friend, a kind and wonderful woman. I went to her only to see if she had been reunited with her husband. She told me herself that her husband was dead. I stayed to lend moral support to the grieving widow, and things just went on from there. It was not intentional. We fell together by chance, and separated the same way – just two more victims of a cruel war. We enjoyed a few months of warm friendship, of human love in the midst of a world full of hate and death and destruction. It might have lasted until this very day, if it weren't for your mother's reluctance to become a burden on me. She left me as suddenly as we had met, and now I know why. She must have known she was carrying my child and she didn't want to complicate my life. She knew I had to return to my regiment. And so she fled. That's it, I'm certain of it."

"You're a liar!" Wells screamed.

"Check Jonathan Wells's military records. They'll tell you when he died."

"They could be wrong. You have no proof."

"None that I could show you. Wait, there might be one thing. I gave your mother a present for Christmas in 1862, a music box. It was a silly little thing that played a little ditty. It was one of the few things she took it with her when she left Washington. You may have seen it."

The young attorney blanched. His eyes blazed with anger and frustration. His face was red and dripping with sweat in the stuffy room. Stephen's mention of the music box had struck a chord.

"I should kill you here and now – kill you and be done with you once and for all. I could say you grabbed me through the bars and I shot you to defend myself. Under the circumstances, who would doubt me?"

"Kill me and spend a lifetime with the memory of killing your own father."

"It's a damnable lie!" Jeffry screamed. "I swear, Shevley, if you breathe a word of this to anyone I'll put a bullet in you before you've uttered the last syllable. Your story is the product of a mean, perverted mind. You're insane, and you deserve to be put away for the rest of your misspent life. You're a sick, deluded man."

Stephen slumped onto his bunk, shaking his head and muttering, "I'm sure of it, absolutely sure of it. Maybe I am mad, but why not? How else could one survive in this mad world? The gods must be playing tricks on me for their own amusement. There's no other way to explain it. All right, I'll confess to anything you want. Let's get it over with. But remember, if you marry my daughter, your children could well be..."

"Shut up, madman! I'll listen to no more of your ravings."

*   *   *

Martin guided his team down the woodland road, keeping one eye on the blackening sky. The heat was growing more intense and the balky horses let him know of their fear. As he fought to maintain control of the animals an eerie silence descended on the area. He halted the team and watched as particles of ash drifted earthward in the vacuum-like atmosphere. He found it difficult to get air into his lungs. The horses reared and cried in alarm. In the distance he heard a muffled roar and as it grew louder he felt a fierce blast whip across the treetops, sucking up what little air remained. As the wind grew stronger the trees bent and burst into flame. Martin, leaning into the gale to keep from being blown away, closed his eyes tightly against the searing heat, but he still could see a brilliant flash of light as the air surrounding him exploded. In an instant it incinerated everything in its path.

Chapter 33

The St. Paul and Duluth left two passengers, a man and a woman, at the railroad depot. John King approached the woman shyly.

"Miss Shevley?" he inquired.

"Yes," she responded. "Are you the sheriff?"

"No, m'am. I'm his deputy sent to pick you up."

The man who had also disembarked stepped forward.

"My name is Frasier, Miss Shevley's chaperone. Please take us to the hotel as quickly as you can. The air is foul here, son, are you sure it's safe?"

"Lots of folks think so," the deputy said. "We got fires all around us, but we're safe for the time being."

"Then let's get on with it so we can get out of here."

"Yes, sir. My rig's around on the side."

The nearly deserted streets did little to increase their confidence, and Jeffry Wells did even less. They found him in the hotel lobby pacing back and forth and wringing his hands.

"Thank God you're here," he exclaimed. "Stephanie, this has been a most extraordinary day. Roger, you're right about him – he's full of surprises, a formidable adversary. He's already put me on the defensive, and I thought I was ready for anything."

"You must have known it would be difficult. You can't expect a man to cooperate in his own incarceration."

"Tell me about him, Jeff. What's he like?" Stephanie asked.

"Nothing at all like I anticipated. He's intelligent, and he's cunning. He's concocted a vile story that only an evil mind could imagine. But he's locked up safely in the town jail. He can't do you any harm."

"Why is he in jail?" she asked incredulously.

"He conveniently involved himself in a brawl with the local sheriff, of all people. I'm sorry to be the one to tell you, Stephanie, but he is a most unsavory character."

"It doesn't surprise me in the least, knowing what I do of him. I want you to tell me everything you can about him, so I can be on my guard. What's this story he's told you?"

"I can't bring myself to repeat it. He's a desperate man, my dear, lashing out with a viciousness of a cornered animal. If he tries to tell that story at the hearing, it could jeopardize our case against him. His resourcefulness in uncanny."

"This is no time for such exaggerations," Roger said. "What he has to say may make our job more difficult, but certainly not impossible. He puts us in the absurd situation of trying to outwit a man we're trying to prove is insane. But outwit him we must. If you feel you're not ready to engage him, perhaps we ought to call the whole thing off until we come up with a course of action in which we can feel confident."

"No, we're here now, and we must not waver," Stephanie said. "How hard could it be to convince a judge that the man we know is insane is also an evil genius intent on blocking our efforts? We must turn his statements against him. We'll claim that his defenses are the product of a warped mind that threatens both me personally and the Shevley Company in particular."

"Sound advice," said Roger approvingly. "Let's proceed this way: I will talk to him first. I've known him for many years and I think I may be able to tone down his opposition. He can't be as formidable as you say, Jeffry, not the Stephen Shevley I remember. But first I must know what he told you."

"It's an abomination," Jeffry said, "a filthy, disgusting..."

"Nonsense!" Stephanie exclaimed. "Nothing can be that bad. Tell me what he said and I will go and confront him."

"Forgive me, my dear, but I cannot. I must consider your sensibilities. You should not face him alone, if at all."

"My sensibilities be damned!" she flared. "What more could he do..."

"Obviously it would be best for me to approach him first," Roger intervened. "Your father and I were close friends once. He knows he can't deceive me."

Despite his wariness, Roger was shocked and put off his guard at Stephen's warm, affectionate greeting.

"My God, Roger! It's good to see you again after all these years. If ever a man needed an old and trusted friend, I need you now."

Roger turned away from the cell and watched Deputy King leave the jail. When they were alone he turned a stern and critical eye on Stephen.

"You won't take me in with your deception, Stephen. First let me correct you: I am not your old friend, I am a former friend, a friend you cast aside just as you cast aside your daughter and your other responsibilities. Not only can't I share your elation at our reunion, but I warn you that I'm not here as an ally, but as an adversary."

"I know the purpose of your visit, but I thought there might be a spark of friendship remaining from times gone by, or at least a bit of humanity. Has greed so overtaken your life?"

"Do you really believe that I'm here for selfish purposes? I'm here only as the protector of your daughter's interests. Someone has to look out for her."

"I deserved that, I know, but not from you, Roger. You should know better. I told you years ago that any child of mine would be better off in life without me. I sent you a letter stating so and asking you to look after her interests. I renounced everything with the Shevley imprint. I know you must still have that letter."

Roger stood several feet away from the cell door, leaning heavily on his cane, studying Stephen and shaking his head.

"Why are you staring at me like that? Are you looking for some evidence of madness? Shall I rant and rave for you, slobber and lurch about like some animal in this cage?

What do you want of me? Why couldn't you all just leave me alone."

"I look at you now and can only think of what you might have been," Roger said sadly.

"You didn't have to come; none of you did. You had my letter. You could have prevented this. Why must you persecute me?"

"You're not being persecuted; you are being forced to pay old debts, debts of honor that you have chosen to ignore for too many years. Your daughter has seen your letter and rejected it. She suspects you could renounce that letter just as you renounced her. She understands all too well your callousness; she doesn't trust you."

"Is that why her prospective husband came armed? Does the bastard plan to kill me if I refuse to cooperate with you?"

"There's no need for disparaging remarks like that."

"Oh, but he is a bastard, Roger. I tried to prove to him that he was, but he refused to believe me. Don't let them marry, not if you truly have my daughter's best interests at heart. It could result in tragedy."

"So that's why Jeff's so upset. You've been meddling with his mind. I don't know what you told him, and I don't care to know. Anything you do now can only be seen as an act of desperation. You have spent your life running away, Stephen, but you can run no longer. There was a time when you posed a threat only to yourself. But now you are a threat to the lives of others, and they will not let you run another step. They refuse to live with your shadow looming over them. They're a new generation, Stephen, not like the gamblers who opened this frontier. They're not like your father and the others who created the world that Stephanie and Jeff live in today. This new generation may be just as crafty, just as cunning, but they're not gamblers; they want a sure thing. They want to be free of the past, and they want to see into the future. And every way they look they see you barring their path. They're determined to eliminate you."

Stephen sank onto the cot and held his head in his hands.

"I've made mistakes," he admitted, "but God knows I've suffered for them. I paid my debts over and over again through uncountable miseries. Now that I've found a little peace and happiness, I want to hold onto it. I'm not a threat to anybody. I'll sign anything they want. They'll have free access to the Shevley fortune. I've never touched it, nor do I want to. It's all theirs. Tell them that."

"That won't do," Roger said. "You've left one debt unpaid, a terrible and unforgivable debt. You abandoned your own daughter and ran off to find your own happiness. You haunt her past and you cloud her future – and she demands a reckoning."

"Retribution, you mean. But you, Roger, what do you demand."

"I demand no more than I ever demanded of you. I demand you accept your responsibilities. I warned you long ago that I would not tolerate incompetence or negligence. I told you I would fight to maintain the primacy of the company against any threat. You may have made it easy for me by withdrawing from the fight. You freed me to run the company as I saw fit, and I did. I made it grow and prosper. I wanted to believe that you were dead, because it made everything easy for me. But that wasn't enough for Stephanie. I was as shocked as anyone when Jeff found that you were still alive – shocked and frightened. I was afraid I might loose everything I'd worked so hard for over the years, lose it to you who doesn't deserve it. I want Shevley Company to go to Stephanie. She's more than competent to run it, and she deserves some recompense for the burdens you placed upon her."

"Can't you see that I'm no threat to any of you? I want no part of the company, no part in their lives." He stopped short, realizing now that as father to both of them he was inextricably a part of their lives, a damned, blighted part that could not be cut out and cast away. His blood flowed in both of them, and dead or alive, the curse of his blood would plague them forever.

"Tell me, Roger – is she strong?" he asked quietly.

"She's Vincent Shevley all over again. Yes, she's strong, intelligent, talented – and stubborn. She is everything he was, everything that you might have been."

"Thank God for that. Perhaps then she can survive even the worst that I can do to her – and trust me, for her the worst is yet to come. I've got to see her, Roger. I've got to warn her ask her forgiveness."

"You'll have that chance. She's in town now, waiting for the judge to arrive from Duluth. Once the hearing gets under way you'll find out just how tough she can be. As for me, I will be glad to get this sorry business over with."

*   *   *

Through the small barred window of his cell Stephen could get some sense of the anxiety in the street. Horse-drawn vehicles traveled more rapidly than usual. Those on foot moved at a half-run. Ox carts lumbered along at their usual plodding pace, despite the caterwauling of teamsters and the crack of their whips. Down the street he could see a merchant hurriedly loading a wagon with goods from his store, aided by a crew of somber children and a worried wife. If he could just get out, Stephen thought, he could easily lose himself in the growing confusion. If only Marie would come to him, but he knew her fear of the sheriff would keep her away. The heat was growing more intense when John King returned.

"I stopped by the restaurant to get you some lunch, Mr. Craft, but darned if they weren't closed. Folks are beginning to run scared, I guess."

"John, I want you to help me, if you will."

"I won't let you burn up," the deputy said with a smile. "I promised those folks I'd get you to the hotel on time."

"Look, John, I don't want to go to the hearing looking like this. Will you ride out and ask my wife to bring me
some clean clothes and a bar of soap?"

"Sure I can. I'll ask her to bring you something to eat,
too. You must be mighty hungry by now."

"I'd be very grateful, but hurry, will you?"

"Getting a little edgy about the fire?"

"It's not the fire, John. I guess I'd just as soon burn
here as hereafter."

He was back in a half-hour with Marie who had
brought food and blankets. John immediately set about
gathering up the sheriff's official papers and stuffing them in
a sack.

"He's got his hands full, with all the excitement out
there," John explained. "Everyone's trying to get to Pine
City at the same time, and the sheriff's trying to keep order."

"I did what I could at home," Marie said as she embraced her husband awkwardly through the barred cell door.
"I sent Billy ahead to Pine City."

"The fire's that close?" he asked.

"Very close. What will happen to you here?"

"Don't worry, I won't let him burn," John said with a
wink as he unlocked the cell door "I've got to get down to
the depot. I hear they're putting together an evacuation train,
and there's likely to be a need for me there. Good luck to
you folks."

When the deputy was gone, Stephen and Marie embraced.

"John told me about the young woman at the hotel,"
she said. "It's your daughter, isn't it?"

"Yes."

"What does she want of you?"

"She wants me locked up."

"Then we must run quickly."

"No, I have to see her."

"She's come to do you harm. Forget about her."

"I fear for her life."

"I fear for your life. Let's get out of here!" she said impatiently. "She can take care of herself. You can see her later when all this over."

As she hurried him toward the door, Jeffry Wells stepped in off the street with his pistol in his hand.

"I thought you might take advantage of this crisis. Get back into the cell you two. You're not going anywhere except to hell."

"Put the gun down, Wells. We're not running from you; we're running from the fire, and I suggest you do the same."

"Not until I'm sure you'll never tell Stephanie the lies you told me," Wells said, raising the weapon and aiming it at Stephen.

Marie suddenly lunged at his arm and knocked the gun out of his hand, while Stephen jumped on him and wrestled him to the floor.

"You're a fool, Wells," he shouted. "If we don't get out of here quickly, we're all doomed."

"All right, all right," Wells gasped, as Stephen loosened his grip. "I'll get back to you later."

"That's better. Now let's get to the depot before it's too late."

As Wells got up he sprang at Stephen, grabbed him by the throat, and slammed him against the cell door.

"I'm going to kill you, Shevley," he screamed. "I'm going to kill you with my bare..."

A shot rang out and Wells's eyes opened wide, staring at Stephen. Then he collapsed in a heap. Marie tossed the pistol aside and took Stephen's hand. "Now we must go," she said.

*   *   *

Stephanie stood at the depot in a daze, watching the doomed city go up in flames. In the haste of fleeing the hotel she had lost her hat. Her combs had come loose and her hair was streaming in the torrid wind. Her face was smudged with soot and glistened with perspiration. Surrounded by a terrified crowd clambering to get aboard the train, she looked anxiously for Jeffry. Roger, touched by her plight, spoke with unaccustomed gentleness.

"There's nothing you can do now," he said. "Let's get aboard while we can, and trust that he'll make it in time."

"Why did he insist on going back?" she cried.

"I don't know. Perhaps he wanted to be sure Stephen was set free. Here, give me your hand, we have to get aboard," he said, leading her toward the packed coaches. In a moment they were swallowed up by the crowd and Roger lost his grip on Stephanie's hand. She was unable to resist the flow of the crowd as panicked residents of the town pushed and shoved their way toward the rail cars. The surge of humanity lifted her up and squeezed her aboard the coach. Terrified, she wedged herself against the wall and clung there for dear life. In a moment she caught sight of a little girl trapped in the surging crowd and in danger of being trampled underfoot. She reached out and pulled the girl to her and held her close to protect her. The girl buried her face in Stephanie's skirts and cried, her body shuddering convulsively. Stephanie gently ran her hand over the child's hair and murmured soothingly until the child's crying stopped.

"Thank you, m'am," she said, looking up with her tear-streaked cheeks. "But I've got to find my mother."

Reluctantly Stephanie released her hold and the child edged into the flow of people again and was squeezed down the aisle with the others. Stephanie followed her yellow curls until they disappeared near the rear of the car. Suddenly the coach gave a jolt and the train began to move.

*   *   *

Judge Rufus Lehman boarded the Southbound Limited that afternoon with only mild trepidation. The people of Duluth knew of the fire raging in the woodlands to the south, but they were no strangers to forest fires. They had come to accept them as a natural accompaniment to drought and as impossible to halt as the erratic flashes of heat lightning that often sparked them. The judge, after a dozen years in the state, shared the old-time residents' aplomb and confessed to his seatmate, an itinerant salesman of kitchen gadgets, that although he was concerned about the black haze that darkened the skies, he felt secure enough traveling in the wide swath cut through the timberlands by the St. Paul and Duluth Railway.

"The fire can't burn our iron rails," he said with pride, although his uneasiness grew as the skies darkened.

His trip to Hinckley was to repay a political debt to a friend and fellow SP&D board member, Roger Frasier. It had occurred to him that any element of danger he might face that day would provide him with a vast reserve of political good will that he could use later to boost his own ambitions. But as the air in the railroad coach grew foul he began to think that perhaps the price might be too high, and he began to regret that he had agreed to an extraordinary court session to accommodate his friend. The full fury of the fire was apparent as the train slowed on its approach to Hinckley and came to a stop in a veritable storm of hot ash and searing heat at the bidding of a band of refugees fleeing on foot from the doomed town. Although a hill stood between the engineer and the city it was obvious the fire had engulfed Hinckley, for the demonic flames already had leaped the Grindstone River and every other obstacle to its irrepressible progress and were sweeping now through the brush at the edge of the right-of-way.

"Get aboard!" shouted the engineer. "We've got to keep rolling."

His brake handle already was too hot to touch with a bare hand and ahead he saw a sight so spectacular and fearsome that he knew he could proceed no further. Only a backward dash could save his train and its passengers now, and even that would be little more than a race against death itself. The sight that traumatized him momentarily and then spurred him to an act of heroism was the sudden bursting into flames of the railroad ties that secured the iron rails in the rocky roadbed. As the ties burned the tracks themselves began to twist and it was plain to engineer Jim Root that this was no ordinary forest fire.

"All aboard!" he shouted above the roar of the firestorm. As the train lurched to the rear, the couplings clanged and the engine, four coaches and the load of frightened passengers began a backward flight for life.

Judge Lehman, near surrendering to fear and panic, fought to maintain his composure. Inside the darkened cars, now crammed by the addition of the refugees, the heat was growing intolerable. As the coaches filled with smoke children began to cry, women screamed and from the parched throats of the righteous and the wicked alike could be heard pitiful prayers for salvation. The passengers grew hysterical as the occupants of the rear coach, now leading the retreat, came charging into their midst screaming that their car had suddenly burst into flame. As pandemonium seemed at its peak the glass windows of the coaches began to explode, showering the hapless victims with shards of hot glass. Crazed with fear, the drummer sitting next to the judge let out a shriek, clambered over him and dove headlong out the window to his death. He was not alone in his panic. Fear drove others to cry out in terror and leap off the train to meet the devil on his own fiery turf.

In the cab Engineer Root, his hands blistered by the hot metal levers of his engine despite his heavy leather gloves, was startled to see his clothing suddenly burst into flame. Jack McGowan, his fireman, experienced the same terrifying phenomenon and leaped into the manhole of the engine's water tank to douse the flames. Emerging moments later, he splashed water over the burning engineer, filling the cab with steam and the popping and sputtering as droplets hit the hot metal floor. In the midst of their own private hell the brave engineer and fireman held their posts, driving the blazing train through a veritable tunnel of fire until at last it reached the relative safety of a small marsh known to the locals as Skunk Lake. As the train ground to a halt the remaining passengers stumbled out of their burning coaches, tumbled down the embankment and plunged headlong into the muddy pond with flames licking at their heels.

The judge, one of the last to leave his coach, leaped to the roadbed and rolled downhill toward the sound of splashing water. He struggled through reeds and mud and made his way toward the center of the marsh where he sat submerged up to his neck, marveling at the scene around him. On the elevated roadbed the train was now only a blazing skeleton, while around the water's edge great walls of orange flame stretched into the black sky. As the awful roar of the fire eventually subsided he could hear the cries and the screams of the passengers, punctuated by the low murmuring of victims praying for their lives to the accompaniment of the muffled moans of the badly burned. To this din he soon added his own quiet weeping.

*   *   *

If the Southbound Limited had failed to make it to Hinckley, there still was hope for the beleaguered citizens at the town's depot. The freight and passenger cars of the Eastern Minnesota were joined to form a train consisting of three boxcars, five coaches, and a caboose, all filled to capacity with refugees who by late afternoon were pouring out of the blazing town. It was this train that Roger and Stephanie boarded reluctantly, still hoping that Jeffry would appear with Stephen in tow. The train's operators, engineers Ed Barry and William Best, delayed their departure until dangerously close to the moment of no escape, but there was no sign of the missing men. Then the bell clanged and the whistle blew, and the train groaned into motion. Stephanie stared in helpless horror into the faces of those who were left behind. She saw many things in those faces on the depot platform – fear and courage, panic and calm resolve, tears of uncertainty and wry smiles of fatal acceptance. In the horror of that moment she felt two hands upon her shoulders and heard a steady voice in her ear.

543

"Be strong, my dear. Have faith that they will survive."

She looked into Roger's tired eyes and studied his dirt-smudged, wrinkled face and realized she had never seen him like this before, calmly accepting his fate and offering her support and encouragement. She felt strangely at peace and she smiled, even as her tears began to flow.

*   *   *

Stephen and Marie snatched up their blankets and fled the jail, leaving behind the body of Jeffry Wells. They shielded themselves with the blankets and ran to the town pump where the metal blades of the windmill spun rapidly in the fire's gale. Climbing onto the cistern's platform they began splashing themselves with water and soaking the blankets. In the distance they could hear the whistle of the departing train, and knew they were on their own. As they began to wrap themselves in the wet blankets they were called up short by an angry shout.

"Hold it right there, Craft, or I'll blow you both to hell!"

Stephen whirled around and saw the sheriff with a shotgun leveled at them.

"There's no time for that," Stephen said. "Come and share these wet blankets, or surely we're all going to die."

"You will die, that's for damn sure," the sheriff said. "I went by the jail and I saw that lawyer shot in the back. You've done it now, Craft. I'm arresting you and your squaw for murder."

"Don't be a fool," Stephen said. "All our lives are in danger. Put down that shotgun and come with us."

"That won't work, Craft. You caught me off guard once, but you won't do it again. You're going to pay for the lawyer's murder. I'm going to see that you hang."

Suddenly the squeaking windmill ground to a halt as a deadly stillness came over the area. Then the very air around them, heavy with ash and unburned particles, exploded with a blast that blew Stephen and Marie off the platform and into the cistern's holding tank. The last sound they heard as they sank beneath water was the discharge of the sheriff's shotgun.

*   *   *

John King heard the whistle of the departing train and raced as fast as he could back to the depot. He found the area crowded with people who had been left behind. They milled about hopelessly, uncertain which way to turn. Some knelt in prayer while others wept in terror and teetered on the edge of panic. John leaped upon a packing crate and called out to them.

"We can't stay here," he shouted. "This place could go up in flames at any minute. Let's head for the gravel pit. We might find some protection there. Follow me!"

Leaping down, he took an elderly woman by the arm and helped her across the maze of track, all the while encouraging the others to follow. Beyond the rail yard lay the Eastern Minnesota line's gravel pit, where the railroad men extracted what they needed to keep the roadbed in repair. It was some three acres in extent and twenty feet deep in some places. In the center of the pit, fed by underground springs exposed in the digging, was a pond some two to three feet in depth. Several dozen people already had taken refuge there along with their wagons and stock, seeking relief from the heat and the powerful winds. John led the crowd down into the pit and found a spot at the edge of the pond for the old woman, who immediately began splashing water over herself.

"Go ahead, m'am," he urged her. "Get right into the water and cool off. You'll feel a lot better for it."

He then went to see that all found a protected area in the pit before the fire could get at them. He was standing at the upper edge of the hole when the big explosion came. He had seen it develop – the wall of fire blowing wildly from the south until the tips of the flames rose a hundred feet into the air were blown off in great balls of fire that hurtled through the air over the doomed town. The fireballs ignited the gaseous air in an explosion that incinerated every flammable thing in its path. The force of the blast blew him off the rim and into the pit where he landed at the feet of a sturdy railroad man.

"What in God's name was that?" asked the railroad man.

"I don't know," John said, "but whatever it was, it took Hinckley with it."

"Everything?"

"Nothing could have survived a blast like that."

"Then let's get down on our knees and thank God it didn't get us," said the railroad man.

"No time for that. Let's get into the water and soak ourselves, then we'll make the rounds to see that everyone does the same."

They worked their way through the crowd, helping the refugees wet down themselves and their possessions. They dunked little children into the pond in playful games intended to save their lives. And when exhaustion finally caught up with them, they found a place in which to rest.

"Is there a handcar in the yard?" John asked the railroad man.

"Two, maybe three, if they're not melted."

"Then we'll rest for an hour or so and then see if we can get one rolling. If we can get to Pine City we might find some help."

*   *   *

The Eastern Minnesota's evacuation train sped through the woodlands with flames licking at its sides. At trestles it slowed and the brakeman leaped down to inspect the burning spans before signaling the engineer to proceed with caution lest the fire-weakened structures collapse under their weight. When the last car had cleared each doomed bridge, it was full throttle again toward the next. At one point the passengers watched in horror as a blazing trestle crumbled in a shower of sparks only moments after they had passed over it. The train stopped briefly in Sandstone and again in Partridge where helpful citizens supplied the parched passengers with water, shrugging off the engineer's warning of approaching disaster. The further they traveled the more distance they put between themselves and the fire. Occasionally a breath of fresh air brought them brief relief from the heat. And when the train finally reached West Superior they were gulping deep draughts of the cold night air off the great lake. Safe at last from the fire the weary refugees debarked. On the siding Roger kept close by as Stephanie searched the milling crowd, but Jeff was nowhere to be found.

"It could be that we missed him in all the confusion," Roger said without much conviction. "He could be somewhere on this very platform looking for you. If we don't find him now, we'll go back and find him later. I'm certain he's all right. He's a strong and resourceful young man. He can look out for himself."

Stephanie's face was drawn with fatigue, her eyes red and watery from the heat and ash that had irritated them for hours. She would not be mollified by Roger's assurances.

"I'm equally certain he's dead," she said quietly. "I can see that he's not here, and nothing could have survived that fire. I'll not give up hope, but I have little faith I'll find him. He's dead, Roger, and it's all my fault."

"You mustn't blame yourself."

"They're both dead, my fiancé and the father I never knew. And I'm to blame. I insisted we come to hunt down my father as if he were an animal. I wanted to see him captured and caged forever. It was a spiteful, evil thing for me to do, and now I'm paying for it."

"It's not your fault," Roger insisted in a vain effort to console her. "Jeff went willingly into this venture. If it cost him his life, you are not to blame."

"Greed drove me here, greed and vengeance. They were my failings, my weakness. I should never have allowed him to become part of it. He's paid for it, and soon I'll have to pay, too," she said mysteriously. "But whatever the cost, I swear I won't make the same mistake again, Roger, never. I refuse to let my heart be my guide. I'm going to be strong and never again give in to my emotions. I'm going to claim what is rightfully mine, and no one is ever going to take it away from me. I no longer look on it as an inheritance; I've paid for it now, and it's mine."

*　　*　　*

John King found his family safe in the Knights of Pythias Hall in Pine City, where refugees from the surrounding countryside had found shelter. His father was not among them.

"I left him yesterday on the wagon road," he said. "He was coming here to join you."

"We watched for him all day," Laura King said sadly. "There was no sign of him."

"We can't give up hope," said her son. "A lot of folks are still looking for loved ones."

"Poor Martin," she exclaimed. "He wanted to save what he could to start over again. Why?" There was the sound of desperation in her voice that told of her cruel loss and the pain that it brought.

"I'll go look for him," John said resignedly.

"Yes, yes," agreed his mother, a trace of hope in her voice. "We'll go back and start again. It's what Martin would do."

John wondered at her courage, her stoicism, and wished he had her strength. He had seen the devastation the fire had wreaked upon the land. In the dark of night as he pumped the handcar along the twisted rails the land around him glowed red where the fire had passed. As dawn came up he saw pine trees more than one hundred feet tall stripped of their branches, standing black and naked like silent sentinels over the smoldering landscape. It was a vision of hell, and he knew that only a miracle could have saved his father in the midst of a firestorm that had wrought such waste.

"I'll go look for him," he said again. "The last thing he told me was that he wanted to be buried as Martin Koenig. He seemed to be in no hurry, as if he knew he couldn't make it. He wanted everyone to know who he was."

"God will know him as a good, hard-working man," Laura said, "no matter what name is on his stone."

"Why did he change it, Mother? Is that what made him so sad?"

"Oh, he knew some happy days," she said defensively.

"Yes, but he carried a heavy burden that even a child could see. Yet he never spoke of it."

"It was a long time ago," she said, looking back across more than two decades to the shadowy hotel room where the body of the stranger lay in the lantern light. John was but an infant then, and he stood before her now as a man. He had a right to know. "He was very angry. He hit a man who had harmed his sister, and the man died. God knows your father didn't mean to kill him. But he thought that no one would understand. He was afraid he might be sent to prison. So we ran away. He was not a violent man, John. He was a good and kindly man. God will forgive him, even though he never could forgive himself."

Chapter 34

Hinckley was a flattened, smoking ruin. In the gray haze of dawn the survivors picked their way through the ashes in stunned disbelief. Deputy King, after a few hours of rest at Pine City, joined the relief crew and returned to the destroyed city. He found that the only people alive were the seventy-odd souls who had sought refuge in the watery gravel pit. He helped to record their names, and then joined in a survey of the devastated town. Not a single building remained standing. At city hall only the wrought iron fence still stood; the fire bell lay amid a mound of ashes. The steel bars of the cell were all that remained of the jail. Amid its smoldering ashes lay one body, charred beyond recognition. Nearby lay a blackened pistol. He gingerly slipped his pencil through its trigger guard and placed the weapon into his evidence bag. Down the block he came upon the metal blades of the windmill and what was left of the town's water tank – the huge iron bands that had held the tank together like stays on a barrel. A large circle of baked gray mud was all that remained to mark the site of the town's main well. In that hardened mud he saw what looked like footprints, or possibly signs of a struggle. Nearby was another charred body, its limbs frozen in grotesque imitation of life. The legs were braced, the arms uplifted as if to aim the shotgun that lay where the victim's hands would have been. Only the barrel and firing mechanism remained, and he duly added them to his bag.

Search crews gathered up hundreds of bodies over the next few days, burying the unidentified in a common grave. Those who had fled the conflagration slowly drifted back to begin the job of rebuilding the town and their lives. No sign of the sheriff could be found, and for a time John accepted the responsibility of organizing the relief effort and attendant investigation. But the grisly task and the lingering smell of burned flesh soon became overwhelming, so he discarded his badge and left the official duties to the militia sent in by the state. Only then did he take the long walk out of town along the wagon road, searching all the way to the site of the King farm for some evidence of his father. All he found was the charred carcasses of two horses in tandem and the iron fittings of a wagon. He was sure it must be his father's wagon, but no body was visible. It could be, he thought, that it had been collected by others and taken away to the mass grave. Or perhaps, he thought, there was nothing left of Martin Luther Koenig except his ashes that were now blended with the soil to become forever a part of the rich land that he loved.

Later he returned with his mother and young siblings to the site of the Koenig farm so she could inspect the ruins and look out over the ash-gray fields to meditate for a time on the years she had spent there. He left her alone for a time with her memories, and returned to find her standing where their farmhouse had been, holding an iron pot now twisted into a bizarre shape by the intense heat. Tears were streaming down her cheeks, and he made up his mind that he must take her away from that scene of sadness and loss.

"Let's go back to Fair Prairie," he said. "We'll stay with Aunt Anna until I can find work and make a home for us. Maybe I'll try my hand at farming, or look for a lawman's job. We'll make out all right, Mother, don't you worry. We'll leave right after the inquiry."

John's testimony became an important part of the official record of the disaster. Not only was he one of the few who had lived through those awful hours, but he had helped maintain order during the evacuation, had witnessed the explosive firestorm, and had returned to the scene with the first relief crew to help with the initial survey. But of all the accounts that were placed on record, the total number of dead would never be known for certain. One hundred and twenty-six bodies had been found in a dried up marsh along the wagon road north of town. It was presumed that they stumbled there in hope of finding protection, but found that only the parched earth remained after a long season of drought. And there they died a fiery death – men, women and children.

Several passengers died aboard the Southbound Limited before it reached Skunk Lake. More died aboard the Eastern Minnesota's evacuation train before it found the cool safety of West Superior. Others died in the streets of Hinckley, and in scattered sites around the county. Bodies were found in cellars where victims had fled to seek shelter and ultimately were baked to death or suffocated. Four hundred and seventy-six bodies were accounted for, some identifiable, but most unnamed. Only God knew the real number of the deceased.

John tried his best to answer the questions of survivors who returned seeking missing family members. Their descriptions were pitiful: A little girl about four feet tall, she would have been somewhere near the hardware store; an old woman, last seen making her way toward the depot carrying a small bundle of cherished possessions; a tall youth, known to have boarded the evacuation train, but gone when it reached West Superior; a mother and her three children leading a pony cart along the wagon road. John could only shake his head. How could he know these things? What could he tell them? The seekers could only plead and cry and go on their way. One man, a brawny logger seeking his missing wife, stood in the middle of the street, looked helplessly into John's sad eyes, and bawled like a destitute child. John could only touch the man's shoulder and go on his way, defeated and exhausted.

"Mr. King," a soft voice called out to him as he left, "I wonder if I might ask you a question."

He looked up to see the young lady and her chaperone, the same two he had picked up at the depot what now seemed like a million years ago.

"I'm glad you're safe," he said. "Can I help you?"

"The young man, Jeffry Wells – you met him at the jail," said Roger.

"I remember him," said John wearily.

"And the prisoner in the jail," added Stephanie. "Can you tell us what happened to them? Do you know if they..."

"I don't know," said the deputy. "I found only one body at the jail. But I did find a piece of evidence."

"Anything," Stephanie pleaded, stifling a cry. "We would be so grateful for anything that might end this awful uncertainty."

John led them to a tent in the recovery area near the relief headquarters and rummaged through a large box until he found the blackened revolver that still bore the tag he had fixed to it.

"This was near the body at the jail," he said.

Stephanie gasped.

"It's Jeffry's gun," said Roger. "I'm sure of it."

"Could it have been Mr. Wells?" Stephanie asked.

"There was no way to tell," said John. "I'm sorry."

She broke into a torrent of tears and fell into Roger's arms. He nodded in gratitude to the deputy, and slowly led her away.

John practically ran from the tent, fleeing the nightmare that had entrapped him for days, fleeing the heartbreak and the sorrow that had become too much for him to bear. He went back to Pine City to rejoin his mother and his siblings, and never looked back.

*   *   *

They sat in the kitchen of Aunt Anna's big house on Meridian Avenue in Fair Prairie, sipping elderberry wine and watching the windows steam over as the ham hocks boiled on the stove. In the topmost corner of a window pane John could see the tip of an elm branch blowing in the evening breeze, a few of its yellowed leaves clinging vainly to life. He watched as one leaf flapped wildly, then broke loose and flew across the back yard out of sight. He spoke during a lull in the women's conversation.

"Saw a woolly caterpillar today. It's going to be a long, cold winter."

"There's a chill in the air," his Aunt Anna agreed.

"I wonder what there is for a man to do around here in the winter," he said. "I know farming, and I know the lawman's work, but you say there's no work hereabouts."

"None I know about," she said. "But an honest, hard-working man can always find something to do to keep body and soul together."

"I'll need something better than that," John said, "now that I've got my mother and the kids to support. I haven't a lot of time to waste."

"I swear, John, you're so much like your Uncle John," Anna exclaimed fondly. "You never knew him, Laura, but the two of them are so much alike. My brother John died in the war, you know, as did another of my brothers, little August."

"I met a fella' recently who knew a John Koenig in the war," said John King. "Said they fought the rebels at Gettysburg, and the Koenig fella' was killed."

"Our John died at Gettysburg," Anna said. "It said so in the lists at the post office. What was the name of the fellow who told you that?"

"Craft," said John, "Steve Craft. He was a logger up in the Hinckley area. An older fella'; he managed the lumber mill at the time of the fire."

"John went into the army with a man named Stephen. They both worked for the Shevley Lumber Company."

"By golly, I think we may be talkin' about the same fella', Aunt Anna!"

"So what's this all about?" asked Laura.

"It's about a pair of silver buckles," said John, digging the badly tarnished mementos from his pocket. "This Craft fella' told me that he and his friend John Koenig went into the army together and Koenig got himself killed at Gettysburg. These boot buckles were a keepsake that he brought back to give to the Koenig family, but they'd moved from their farm on the Rum River and he didn't know where to find them. Carried these with him wherever he went; wore 'em around his neck, he did. He wanted me to give 'em to Dad, since he was a Koenig."

"Let me see those buckles," said Anna, inspecting them carefully. "You know, these are just like the buckles on my father's boots. He wore those boots in the old country, and kept them for dress-up once he got over here. My brother John inherited them when dad died, and wore them when he went off to war."

"Then we could be talkin' about the same fella', all right," John exclaimed. "Now isn't that the limit?"

"I used to polish my father's boots when I was a little girl," said Anna. "I know one way to find out if they're the same buckles."

She reached across the table and took a pinch of salt from the saltcellar and made a neat little pile in front of her. She wet a fingertip, dipped it in the salt, and gently rubbed the blackened crossbar of the buckle until the silver began to shine. Then she sat back in her chair with a look of smug satisfaction, saying, "It's the very same."

John looked closely at the crossbar where Anna's polishing had exposed some tiny print. It said "Koenigsburg."

"What's Koenigsburg?" Laura asked.

"It's a city in Prussia," said Anna. "It's where my father and mother lived. It's where my brother John was born, the only one of us kids who was born in the old country. My father served in the Kaiser's guard there many years ago. He had a grand uniform and fine pair of boots that he wore to march in parades. He brought the boots to America, he was so proud of them. And he told John they'd be his one day."

"What happened to the boots?" asked Laura.

"My friend Steve couldn't very well take a dead man's boots," said John. "So he cut off the buckles and brought them home. Now here they are where they belong, with the Koenigs."

"I'd like to put them on display in the hotel lobby," said Anna, "along with a picture of John in his uniform. You know he sat down in a chair for that picture just so the boots would show. A little display would be a nice tribute...but wait. These are yours, John."

"No, no!" he said. "You take them. What would I do with them? My name is King, not Koenig."

Anna had a faraway look in her eyes. From across the years she could recall seeing two young men scrambling over the naked rafters of the cabin John had built on the Rum River, racing to get the roof on before the snow began to fall. She remembered the boys, too, as they worked side by side in the fields, and sitting before the fireplace, talking quietly into the night.

"What happened to your friend, Steve?" she asked. "I would like to thank him."

"Too late, I'm afraid," said John. "He and his wife were among the missing after the fire – probably dead, sad to say."

Strange, thought Anna, how her big brother seemed to be reaching out from some distant, unmarked grave to renew her faith in her family, reinforcing ties that were stronger than any adversity. Theirs was a proud heritage, and the events of this day served to bolster her pride. The Koenigs were together again, what was left of them, and there was no need to worry about the coming winter, no need to fear what the future might hold. They must go to visit Lotte tomorrow, and Hildy and her son, to tell them the tale of the buckles. That would make the reunion complete. She raised the hem of her apron and dabbed the tears from her eyes then reached out to squeeze John's hand. He smiled shyly, and she wondered if he could feel the surge of pride that she was trying to pass on to him through her touch.

"Be proud of your heritage, John," she said. "Call yourself whatever you like, but always remember that you were born a Koenig. This family will endure, be they Koenigs or Kings, for as long as courage and hard work account for something in this life. There's nothing stronger than the bond of blood."

*   *   *

Stephanie remained in Minneapolis for only six weeks. She assembled a domestic staff of four and instructed them that Shevley House was to be kept in perfect order whether she was in residence or not. Jim Malloy, ever more restricted by the infirmities of age, was given similar instructions and ordered to avoid vigorous exercise and confine himself to superintending the maintenance of the house and gardens with a small staff to be assembled with the advice and approval of Roger Frasier. Then with a determination that no one dared question she announced that she was taking the Grand Tour, ostensibly to help her forget the tragedy of the fire and loss of her fiancé. She said she wished to broaden her knowledge of the world and its people in the hope that she might bring an enhanced sophistication to the job of running the Shevley Company. Then she boarded a train and fled with the winds of winter nipping at her heels. That was the last that anyone heard of her until Christmas, when George and Amanda Ames received a long letter from Rome in which she extolled the beauty and charm of Italy and advised that she would be leaving shortly to take up lodgings in Milan to enjoy the opera season at the Teatro alla Scala. Her next letter said she had taken an apartment in Vienna where she would rest for several months while planning the next phase of her tour of the Continent. Her letters then began to come regularly once a month until in late summer she advised that she was under a doctor's care and might postpone a scheduled trip to Paris until she felt in perfect health again. It was a full year before a spark of vitality returned to her writing, and then her letters were filled with the joys of travel and the thrills of Paris, London, and Berlin. It was impossible to see it all, to absorb it all, to truly appreciate the glorious accomplishments of Western Civilization in an abbreviated fashion, she wrote. Therefore she had kept her apartment in Vienna and returned after each foray to rest and plan her next trip. In her letters she began to mention someone named Andrew, and the Ameses suspected that romance had entered her life.

Amanda Ames was gratified to learn that something other than museums, art galleries, cathedrals and opera houses were keeping her ward from hearth and home. And sure enough, Stephanie began to use the plural pronoun more frequently. But before she could reveal Andrew's identity, she received a cable from Roger Frasier advising her that Amanda had fallen gravely ill. Stephanie responded with a brief note to advise him that she was returning immediately to Minneapolis. She arrived in April, 1897 by train with thirty pieces of luggage, a French maid, an English governess and a two-year-old son named Andrew Shevley-Wells. He was a fragile, beautiful child, but given to frequent tantrums that inevitably led to seizures that left him gasping for the breath of life. Amanda was spared the shock of this revelation, having slipped into a coma nearly a week before Stephanie's return and died within the month. Her husband, however, was shaken by the realization that his beloved foster child had given birth out of wedlock. The overriding sorrow occasioned by Amanda's death, however, mellowed him considerably and he soon came to accept the situation for what it was – a great personal tragedy that required love and understanding. After all, he rationalized, she and Jeffry Wells were intending to get married at the time the young attorney died. He was confident that no one would dare confront Dr. George Ames on the issue. After all, he was a man of importance, and no idle gossip could ever detract from his reputation in the community. This did not stop speculation, however, which often did get back to him, mostly in the form of glamorous rumors about the beautiful and mysterious Stephanie Shevley. One tale was that she had secretly wed a dashing young prince, had given birth to his son, and then had to whisk the child away to America to save him from certain death at the hands of unscrupulous palace plotters. George was particularly fond of that rumor with its air of danger and romance, but for very practical reasons: It served to explain not only Andrew's existence, but also his infrequent appearances in public where his life might be threatened by agents of some unnamed royal family of Europe.

Stephanie remained true to her vow to take full control of all Shevley Enterprises, and she proved to be all that Roger could have hoped for as his successor. She had a sharp mind, a penetrating intelligence, an appetite for the give and take of the marketplace and an instinct that told her just when to give and when to take. Business flourished under her management. Socially, she remained an oddity, constantly surrounded by male admirers but never the object of a formal courtship. Even the strongest of her business associates were intimidated by her talents, her power and her wealth. By the time she was thirty she was a legend in the city, involved in a constant whirl of activities that touched on every phase of community life. She never wanted for an active social life, but spent many lonely nights in the forbidding confines of Shevley House. In rare moments of deep melancholy she often thought of the dreadful fire that had taken her fiancé away. She wondered how it might have been if Jeff had lived, if they had married, and he had been at her side through all the passing years. He had been the only man she had known who was strong and commanding in her presence, who could help her without taking away her pride or diminishing his manhood. They might even have learned to love one another in time. But as it was he had burdened her with a son who would never be the man his father was, the man she wanted him to be. In her most bitter and disconsolate moments she pitied the afflicted child and herself, and wished fervently that both had perished in that great holocaust that still plagued her dreams.

*   *   *

Stephanie's wish for death was not uncommon among survivors of the fire. Many readily confessed they would have preferred death to life without their loved ones. The young farmer, for instance, who carried his pregnant wife to the safety of the gravel pit, only to find that she was dead. Or the shopkeeper who had run to the stable to release his horses and returned moments later to find his wife and children trapped in their burning home. Or the aged woman who wandered the streets for years chattering to herself, gazing toward the sound of sympathetic voices with vacant eyes, unable to comprehend what had happened to her family.

No one remained to see the scalded couple who emerged from the town's destroyed water tank. They had crawled through the rapidly drying mud, and escaped through the burning streets only moments after the firestorm moved through the town. Stonily silent in their agony, their heads shorn by the blaze, their exposed skin blistered so badly as to defy recognition, Stephen and Marie made their way out of town and into the woodlands toward the river. Collapsing on the riverbank, they rested until Marie felt strong enough to go to the water's edge where she soaked her blanket and returned to wrap it around Stephen who had fallen into unconsciousness. As darkness neared they immersed themselves in the flowing water to ease their pain, and in the morning resumed their trek along the river seeking an unburned area of the forest where they might find wild berry bushes. The woman saw that her husband could not open his blistered lips far enough to eat, so she chewed the berries and gently pressed her lips to his to feed him as a mother bird might feed her young. When evening came she made a net of her skirt and anchored it in the water to catch a trout, which she fed to him in the same manner. At night she wrapped him in wet blanket, but the pain still caused him to weep and the tears caught in his burned flesh and his eyes stung so badly he cried out that they were melting and running down his cheeks. He prayed aloud for death, and she lay beside him in a futile effort to comfort him.

"Let me die, please let me die," he cried through his swollen lips.

"No," she answered. "We need each other. We must live."

"I can't stand the pain," he insisted, "and I am blind."

"I can see for you," she said. "And I, too, am in pain."

They wandered for another day to the north and west and eventually found their way out of the fire-ravaged forests. In time they came upon a Chippewa hunting party from the big lake. The Indians fed them and looked after them. In another day they reached the village where Marie had been born, and the elders came out to meet them. The hunters regaled the leaders of the tribe with tales of the fire and how they had come upon the two pitiful creatures. They said the woman spoke their language, but that her lungs were seared so that when she spoke it made her cough. Certain women of the village who were practiced in the care of the sick and injured took it upon themselves to feed the wanderers, but their best judgment was that neither would survive their terrible burns.

But survive they did through the winter and into a wet and greening spring. By then both were well enough to move into an abandoned claim shack a few miles from the village where they took up a lonely but independent existence. Marie healed quickly and it was she who planted a garden and made the shack a livable home. Stephen healed more slowly, taking more than a year to regain limited vision, but the pain in his lungs never went away and his scarred face was so disfigured that he shunned his reflection in a pond and avoided all contract with anyone other than Marie. From the Chippewa they secured the tools they needed to exist, including an axe that Stephen used to keep themselves supplied with firewood. He spent long hours in the surrounding woods, assailing the puny second growth pine and mumbling incessantly to himself until Marie called him in for dinner.

Marie kept her head covered with a scarf for many months while her hair grew back again, and when she removed the scarf at last Stephen saw that her hair was pure white. By that time her burns had healed and he saw that she was still very beautiful and the sight of her brought tears to his eyes. He knew his face was scarred and ugly and it made him feel unworthy of her. In his frequent fits of depression he threatened to go away in order to relieve her of the burden that he had become. But she refused to let him go, and instead became more vigilant and caring for fear he would go into the woods someday and never come back. His thoughts seemed to come and go, crossing back and forth between the reality of their lives and the dark world into which he retreated more and more often as the years passed. When he was lucid their lives were as they had been before the fire, but in his darker moods she feared he would slip across the shadowy borders of his mind and be lost to her forever and perhaps even do himself harm. It was not unusual for her to find him off in the woods raving at the trees and shouting at invisible tormentors, or walking quietly in deep conversation with the ghosts who peopled his dreams, trying earnestly to explain to each why he had failed them and begging their forgiveness.

"I'm sorry!" he would cry, and one by one their names would fill the emptiness of the forest: Mother, Father, John, Grace, Sarah, Stephanie. In these desperate times Marie would approach him quietly, touch him ever so gently so as not to further agitate him, and lead him quietly back to their rustic home.

One night many years after the great fire he was awakened by a recurrent nightmare, screaming aloud that they must flee the fires that surrounded them. Marie took his hand and caressed it, murmuring quietly into his ear as a mother might whisper to a frightened child. When he was calm again she held him close and he clutched her with tears flowing and repeated over and over, "Sarah, oh my God, Sarah! I'm so sorry. Please forgive me."

Then he fell into a deep sleep until the first light of dawn when at last he stirred and looked at her as if from across the decades. "Marie," he said, "I'm very cold. Please hold me close, my love."

She took him into her arms, and there he died.

*　　*　　*

Stephanie was trying on dresses in her bedroom while her domestic staff prepared Shevley House for a New Year's Eve dinner party planned for Saturday night. As she stood before her full length mirror she adjusted the shoulders of a dress, then turned around to view the gown from the back. As she did so she caught a glimpse of an ancient dray as it trundled off the busy boulevard and wound its way up her driveway. She had been anticipating delivery of several cases of fine wine, but knew it wouldn't come in such an old wagon, and certainly not a wagon driven by what appeared to be an Indian. The driver guided the vehicle around to the back. Curious, she went to the window and saw on closer inspection that the driver was a woman and that her wagon carried only a large bundle that appeared to be a roll of blankets wrapped around two poles. To her surprise the rig went past the house and up the knoll to the family plot where the driver drew to a halt and climbed down. The woman carefully lowered the bundle one end at a time onto the snowy ground, then dragged it through the iron gate and positioned it next to the grave of Sarah Shevley.

At that moment Jim Malloy came out of the carriage house and trudged up the path toward the woman who stood watching him as he approached. When he reached her they spoke briefly and embraced. Then he led her back to her wagon and watched as she guided it down the driveway to the boulevard where it vanished in the traffic. Turning back to the burial plot, Jim stood for a moment with his head bowed before returning slowly down the path to the carriage house.

From the closet her maid interrupted Stephanie's reverie by calling out, "This is lovely, m'am, this red velvet with white lace."

But her mistress did not answer. The setting sun was shining through the bare oak branches, casting shadows like tentacles across the snow as if to embrace the abandoned bundle. Suddenly through the quiet of the great house came the spine-chilling cry of her son in the grip of a seizure. The maid dropped the red velvet gown and stared fearfully at her mistress, awaiting her reaction. But even as the youth's anguished cry echoed into silence, Stephanie's gaze remained transfixed.

"What is it, m'am?" gasped the frightened maid.

"It's my father," she muttered in stunned disbelief. "He's come home at last."